Oracle Database 12c Release 2 Testing Tools and Techniques for Performance and Scalability

Nicole,
Test. To. Destruction! :)

ORACLE® *Oracle Press*™

Oracle Database 12c Release 2 Testing Tools and Techniques for Performance and Scalability

Jim Czuprynski
Deiby Gómez
Bert Scalzo

McGraw Hill Education

New York   Chicago   San Francisco
Athens   London   Madrid   Mexico City
Milan   New Delhi   Singapore   Sydney   Toronto

Cataloging-in-Publication Data is on file with the Library of Congress

McGraw-Hill Education books are available at special quantity discounts to use as premiums and sales promotions, or for use in corporate training programs. To contact a representative, please visit the Contact Us pages at www.mhprofessional.com.

Oracle Database 12c Release 2 Testing Tools and Techniques for Performance and Scalability

1 2 3 4 5 6 7 8 9 LCR 21 20 19 18 17

ISBN   978-1-260-02596-5
MHID   1-260-02596-9

Sponsoring Editor	**Technical Editor**	**Production Supervisor**
Lisa McClain	Mauro Pagano	Lynn M. Messina
Editorial Supervisor	**Copy Editor**	**Composition**
Janet Walden	Lisa Theobald	Cenveo Publisher Services
Project Manager	**Proofreader**	**Illustration**
Surbhi Mittal,	Rick Camp	Cenveo Publisher Services
Cenveo® Publisher Services	**Indexer**	**Art Director, Cover**
Acquisitions Coordinator	Claire Splan	Jeff Weeks
Claire Yee		

About the Authors

Jim Czuprynski is an Oracle ACE Director with more than 35 years of experience in information technology, serving in diverse roles at several Fortune 1000 companies, including mainframe programmer, applications developer, business analyst, and project manager, before becoming an Oracle DBA in 2001. He holds Oracle Certified Professional (OCP) certification for Oracle Database releases 9*i*, 10*g*, 11*g*, and 12*c*. Since 2008, Jim has presented topics at Oracle OpenWorld, IOUG COLLABORATE, Hotsos Symposium, Oracle Technology Network ACE Tours, and Oracle User Group conferences around the world on Oracle Database technology features. He continues to write a steady stream of articles that focus on the myriad facets of Oracle database administration, with more than 100 articles to his credit since 2003, at databasejournal.com and the IOUG *SELECT Journal*. Jim's blog, *Generally … It Depends* (http://jimczuprynski .wordpress.com), contains his regular observations on all things Oracle.

Deiby Gómez was both the youngest Oracle ACE (23 years old) and Oracle ACE Director (25 years old) in the world and the first in his home country of Guatemala. He is also the youngest Oracle Certified Master 11*g* (OCM 11*g*, 24 years old) and Oracle Certified Master 12*c* (OCM 12*c*, 26 years old) in Latin America and the first in Central America. He is the winner of *SELECT Journal* Editor's Choice Award 2016 (Las Vegas) and a frequent speaker at Oracle events around the world, including Oracle Technology Network Latin American Tour every year since 2013, COLLABORATE (United States), and Oracle OpenWorld (Brazil and United States). The first Guatemalan accepted as a beta tester by Oracle Database (version 12cR2), Deiby has published several articles in English, Spanish, and Portuguese on Oracle's web site and Toad World, as well as hundreds more on his blog. Deiby was featured in *Oracle Magazine* (November/December 2014), as an outstanding expert, and he currently serves as the president of Oracle Users Group of Guatemala (GOUG), the Director of Support Quality in Latin American Oracle Users Group Community (LAOUC), and the co-founder of the OraWorld Team. He also currently provides Oracle services in Latin America with Nuvola Consulting Group (nuvolacg.com).

Dr. Bert Scalzo is an Oracle ACE, blogger, author, speaker, consultant, and Senior Product Manager for DBArtisan and Rapid SQL at IDERA. Bert also spent 15 years as chief architect for the popular Toad family of products at Quest Software. He has three decades of Oracle database experience and previously worked for both Oracle Education and Oracle Consulting.

Bert holds several Oracle Masters certifications, and his academic credentials include a BS, MS, and PhD in computer science, as well as an MBA. He has presented at numerous Oracle conferences and user groups, including OOW, ODTUG, IOUG, OAUG, RMOUG, and many others. Bert's areas of interest include data modeling, database benchmarking, database tuning and optimization, "star schema" data warehouses, Linux, and VMware. He has written for Oracle Technology Network (OTN), *Oracle Magazine*, Oracle Informant, *PC Week* (eWeek), *Dell Power Solutions* magazine, *LINUX Journal*, LINUX.com, Oracle FAQ, and Toad World.

About the Technical Editor

Mauro Pagano is a database performance engineer with special interest in SQL tuning and wrong results. He is an active member of the Oracle community, always willing to help or mentor his peers, and he enjoys giving back by developing tools and presenting at Oracle User Groups conferences. He is the author of the SQLd360 and TUNAs360 tools and the previous maintainer of other legacy tools such as SQLTXPLAIN and SQLHC. Mauro has more than a decade of experience in the Oracle world, from database tuning to applications development.

Contents at a Glance

Contents

PART II

Digging Deeper: SQL Performance Management Tools

PART III
It's Running Slow: Database Performance Evaluation

PART IV
Testing to Destruction: Real Application Testing

PART V

A Brave New World: Database In-Memory

Acknowledgments

The authors wish to thank McGraw-Hill and Oracle Press for the opportunity to assemble this book. As we began to realize the tremendous scope of topics that our book was undertaking to explain, Lisa McClain and Claire Yee at McGraw-Hill reminded us to take a deep breath frequently, contemplate alternatives when difficulties arose, and stay on target so we could meet our tight deadlines. And thanks to Surbhi Mittal and her team at Cenveo, we have been able to produce a professionally edited volume formatted to the highest publication standards.

We also wish to thank our technical editor, Mauro Pagano, for his tireless devotion to improving this book's contents. Without his deep expertise, significant knowledge, and alternative viewpoints on so many topics related to Oracle Database 12c—especially the nitty-gritty details of SQL performance tuning—our book would have contained numerous errors and less-than-clear explanations.

Introduction

Whether you are a newly minted Oracle DBA or an experienced veteran who can recite from memory exactly which Oracle Database release incorporated each new feature, this book is aimed at assisting you in your daily database administration tasks. We believe you will find it especially helpful in navigating the latest feature sets of Oracle Database 12c Release 2 (12cR2) as your IT organization begins its transition to that long-awaited version of the database.

Our book is all about discovering exactly what Oracle-provided tools are available to any Oracle DBA, when to reach for which tool, and how to use that tool properly once it's firmly in hand.

Our book's primary goal is to enable any Oracle DBA, regardless of current experience or skill level, to obtain immediate and maximum benefits from the in-depth exploration of each Oracle-supplied toolset for application workload performance tuning, including the often-neglected topic of regression testing (also known as testing to destruction). We've laid it out so that you can jump to whatever toolset you need right away to solve your particular issues, but if you're simply interested in obtaining a roadmap that lays out how these toolsets are intimately related and designed to work together with an elegant synergy, you're probably best served by just starting at the beginning and then soldiering on diligently through the individual chapters.

Should you be searching for a particular toolset, here's a brief list of Oracle-supplied toolsets that we explore in our book, many of which are brand new in Oracle Database 12c:

- SQL Tuning Advisor, including SQL Tuning Sets

- SQL Access Advisor

- SQL Plan Management (SPM)

- SQL Monitor, including SQL Operations

- Real-Time Database Operations Monitoring

- Real-Time ADDM and Emergency Monitoring

- Real-Time ASH Analytics

- SQL Performance Analyzer

- Database Workload Capture and Workload Intelligence

- Database Workload Replay

- In-Memory Advisor and In-Memory Central

We've taken an ambidextrous approach to mastering these toolsets: We'll show you how to leverage the considerable sophistication of Oracle Enterprise Manager (OEM) Cloud Control to gain immediate insights into your database's performance issues when reacting to a problem, as well as proactive usage of OEM's GUI-based tools, but we've also included volumes of example code and their resulting output so that if you decide to rely on a scripted approach instead of leveraging OEM, you'll be able to tackle your performance issues head-on with minimal development effort.

Online Code

We've captured all the SQL and PL/SQL code examples in our book into a set of code files that will allow you to leverage them immediately. A ZIP file containing these examples is available from the McGraw-Hill Professional web site at www.mhprofessional.com; simply enter this book's title or ISBN in the search box and then click the Downloads & Resources tab on the book's home page.

PART

I

Tools and Test Rigs

CHAPTER

1

Presenting Tools
for Tuning

The profession of Oracle database administrator (DBA) has been compared to that of a cardiac surgeon or airline pilot, because when any of these professionals does the wrong thing at the wrong time, something catastrophic is almost certain to occur. But in many ways, an Oracle DBA is also like a master machinist, because he or she must detect whether a complex machine is malfunctioning or is performing at less than optimal levels, determine the root cause for that suboptimal performance, and then—most importantly—employ exactly the right tool to correct the problem. And that's what this book is all about: learning what Oracle-provided tools are available to any Oracle DBA, when to reach for which tool, and how to use that tool properly once it's firmly in hand.

Whether you are a newly minted Oracle DBA or an experienced veteran who can recite from memory exactly which Oracle Database release incorporated each new feature, this book is aimed at assisting you in your daily database administration tasks. We believe you will find it especially helpful in navigating the latest feature sets of Oracle Database 12c Release 2 (12cR2) as your IT organization begins its transition to that long-awaited version of the database.

An Oracle DBA's Tool Belt: Tools for Tuning

The role of Oracle DBA has evolved significantly over the past two decades, corresponding to increasingly complex applications, sophisticated database architectures, and powerful enterprise-grade hardware and storage technologies. The relatively recent onslaught of the latest cloud-based strategies for deploying both application workloads and Oracle databases means that a modern Oracle DBA faces a dizzying array of complex technology to traverse when attempting to solve even a minor application performance issue.

But there is good news as well: Regardless of these dramatic shifts in underlying technology, any Oracle DBA can access some sophisticated tools to identify, investigate, and resolve performance issues, because, fortunately, these tools have maintained pace with that technology.

Figure 1-1 illustrates the cornucopia of tools that an Oracle DBA can use to solve just about any database application performance problem, whether it's dealing with an intermittent spike in unexpected application resource demands, planning for the next application or database upgrade, or even determining whether a particular hardware platform configuration is sufficient for significantly increased application workloads.

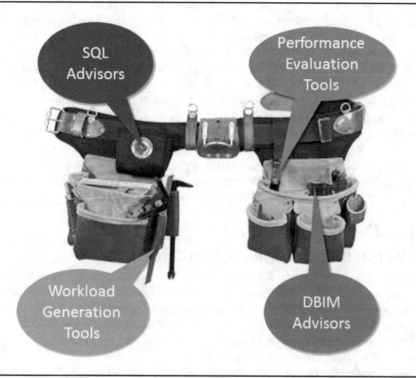

FIGURE 1-1. *Tools for tuning*

Chapter Roadmap

A primary goal of this book is to enable any Oracle DBA, regardless of current experience or skill level, to obtain immediate and maximum benefits from the in-depth exploration of each Oracle-supplied toolset. If you are looking to expand your knowledge about how a particular set of tools works and how it integrates with all other toolsets, the authors recommend following the roadmap laid out next for maximum effect; however, if you are looking to investigate and hopefully solve a specific performance problem, simply proceed ahead to the chapter that focuses on that issue.

Part I—Tools and Test Rigs

Chapter 1 describes examples of several common application performance conundrums, the types of Oracle-supplied tools you can use to delve into each situation, and how best to take advantage of those toolsets described within each chapter to analyze and solve those particular issues.

Chapter 2 details the configurations used—including the hardware, software, platforms, and database versions—for all tests performed within this book. We will also delve more deeply into the Transaction Processing Performance Council Decision Support (TPC-DS) model that we leveraged to generate and load enough sample data to create a robustly sized Oracle database. The TPC-DS schema we created—modified slightly to permit partitioning of its fact tables—enabled us to generate sufficient application workloads for detection of poor application performance via the Oracle toolsets we demonstrate in each section.

We will also illustrate how we leveraged the latest version of Dominic Giles's Swingbench workload generation tool to generate large-volume bulk transaction processing workloads as well as robust and complex query workloads with sufficiently diffuse bind variable values for the SQL statements that make up a full TPC-DS query application workload.

Part II—Digging Deeper:
SQL Performance Management Tools

Ultimately, of course, an Oracle database does work by executing SQL statements. Determining which SQL statements are candidates for performance improvement— at both an individual statement level and as a collection of statements that make up a complex application workload—is often at the heart of an Oracle DBA's job. Fortunately, Oracle provides several excellent diagnostic and tuning tools that help you make short work of these responsibilities.

In Chapter 3 we discuss the SQL Tuning Advisor, a powerful tool that accepts one or more SQL statements as input, resulting in recommendations for improvement along with the rationale for that advice and potential benefits. First introduced in Oracle 10gR1 Enterprise Edition with the Tuning pack, the SQL Tuning Advisor causes the optimizer to run in a tuning mode such that it collects the necessary extra information required to make recommendations. Although using the SQL Tuning Advisor can take longer, the results are often more than worth the wait.

In Chapter 4, we discuss SQL Access Advisor, a tool that was also introduced in Oracle 10gR1 and complements the work of SQL Tuning Advisor, SQL Performance Analyzer, and the other tools described in this book. After determining the impact of a change with SQL Performance Analyzer, you likely will want to know what to do to improve or fix the performance of a set of SQL statements, and this is where SQL Access Advisor can help. It recommends the creation of indexes and, even better, the most appropriate type of index such as bitmap, function-based, or B-Tree. It can also recommend creation of materialized views and materialized view logs and even recommend partitioning a nonpartitioned table to obtain better overall performance. SQL Access Advisor can advise whether to drop or retain indexes, materialized views, and materialized view logs—a very useful feature; because these objects use space, the database has to maintain them, and of course these maintenance operations also use valuable database resources. With this advice, an Oracle DBA therefore knows when to create, delete, or retain these objects, thus taking you closer to the performance levels necessary for your databases.

In Chapter 5 we discuss SQL Plan Management, the preferred method for preserving SQL performance over time while the database grows and evolves. SQL execution plans can be affected by naturally occurring items such as increasing row counts, changing partition counts, and changing data skew. Moreover, DBA activities such as installing patches, new versions, new objects, changes to statistics-gathering criteria, and database configuration changes can also wreak havoc on execution plans. SQL Plan Management helps DBAs to manage and control the regression behavior of their applications' SQL statements over time.

Part III—It's Running Slow: Database Performance Evaluation

Every Oracle DBA has encountered this scenario at least once during her first six months: It's a perfectly normal workday, with no particularly extraordinary or exceptional demand planned or expected for a crucial production database, and then a trusted user approaches the DBA's desk and utters the following words: "Is there something wrong with the database?"

Once the DBA's heartbeat returns to normal—perhaps squeaking out the word "Why?" in a panicky voice—it becomes apparent that something has gone terribly wrong with the performance of one or more applications running against this database, and the search is on for the root cause of that anomaly. In this situation, it is vitally important to select exactly the right tool for the job to narrow down the culprit behind the anomaly so that performance can be restored rapidly without any further disruption to the boundaries of the application workload's service level agreement (SLA).

In Chapter 6 we discuss SQL Monitor, a fantastic tool for dissecting real-time execution statistics or runtime profiles of long running, resource expensive, and parallel explain plans. First introduced in Oracle 11gR1 Enterprise Edition with the Diagnostic and Tuning packs, SQL Monitor radically simplifies the process of effective and efficient SQL tuning. We highlight several examples from the TPC-DS query application workload using Oracle Enterprise Manager, SQL Developer, and SQL scripts.

Oracle DBAs often inherit "plain vanilla" code that has not been particularly optimized for batch processing against Oracle databases. For example, data warehousing application environments often accept input data from numerous disparate sources at different times of the day, week, and month, and it's not unusual to encounter batch processing that occasionally underperforms when least expected. It's also not uncommon for dozens or even hundreds of disparate reports to be executed simultaneously within a batch window on a regularly scheduled basis. So if you are responsible for monitoring these types of processes, or if you suddenly encounter a database maintenance process that comprises a series of similar operations—for example, bulk insertion and update statements—Chapter 7 takes a look at one of the coolest features of Oracle 12c, Real-Time Database Operations Monitoring, and how it makes it easier to collapse and monitor formerly disparate operations into a single, monitorable packet.

What should an Oracle DBA do when a database system appears to suddenly hang or become nearly unresponsive? Prior to Oracle 12c, a DBA might have no other option than simply to terminate the database instance ungracefully and restart it, thus simultaneously terminating every ongoing transaction as well as thousands of user sessions that probably were not the root cause of the performance issue. Chapter 8 illustrates how to use two brand-new 12c tools, Real-Time ADDM and Emergency Monitoring, that enable an Oracle DBA to delve deeply into the true root causes of the database's lack of responsiveness and terminate only the process(es) causing the apparent hang before reaching for the proverbial "kill switch" of an instance bounce.

In Chapter 9 we discuss ASH Analytics, an Oracle Enterprise Manager Cloud Control 12c feature that nicely visualizes Active Session History (ASH) data and thus exposes the cause of database activity spikes. Combining ASH Analytics examination with ASH and AWR reports can often result in far quicker diagnosis and resolution of a performance problem. We highlight using such a combination to analyze the TPC-DS workload to find the worst bottlenecks.

Part IV—Testing to Destruction

One of the most overlooked responsibilities of the modern Oracle DBA is to provide guidance whenever a significant shift in technology appears on the horizon. For example, upgrading a complex application and its underlying database environment to a completely new Oracle Database release—say, from 11.2.0.4 to 12.2.0.1—is a decidedly nontrivial exercise that's fraught with peril. Other examples of significant risks that DBAs must assess and mitigate include shifting to a completely new hardware environment, moving database files to a different storage technology, and migrating from a big-Endian to a little-Endian operating system. And it would be foolhardy to ignore the ongoing and relentless transformation of IT organizations, as cloud-based environments are considered viable targets for existing on-premises databases and their workloads; the consequences of choosing an insufficiently powerful and manageable cloud strategy could have a devastating impact on application performance and SLAs.

Fortunately, the Oracle Real Application Testing (RAT) Suite provides some excellent methods to mitigate the risk of the aforementioned technological shifts. Introduced in Oracle 11gR1, RAT has been significantly enhanced in the 12cR1 release and it offers an Oracle DBA a powerful set of tools to ascertain and mitigate these risks for application workloads. RAT actually comprises two distinct feature sets.

Chapter 10 answers the question, "What is the performance impact of a change?" We discuss SQL Performance Analyzer (SPA), a tool that was introduced in Oracle 11gR1 that makes easy to test how a change would impact the performance of a SQL statement or a set of SQL statements in a production database. We explain every phase involved in this process, beginning with capturing the set of SQL statements of interest for analyzing, transporting that set of SQL statements to a test environment, executing them against that test environment, and then performing all the changes to analyze how they would impact a production database. We compare several performance metrics between the before-change execution plans and the post-change execution plans to determine the performance impact of those changes. Finally, we show how the initial question, "What is the performance impact of a change?" is answered by SQL Performance Analyzer: Based on the findings, we make decisions and apply fixes if they are required to reach the required performance level. We also discuss and demonstrate new SPA task parameters that were introduced in Oracle 12cR2.

Several third-party tools can easily simulate a CPU-intensive or I/O-intensive workload against an Oracle database. It is often difficult, however, to replicate an identical application workload that an existing production database experienced during a specific timeframe on another Oracle database to evaluate what changes might be beneficial at an overall system level—for example, shifting the database to a completely different hardware platform, operating system, or storage system. Since it's important to identify exactly how an application workload will perform in a new environment, Chapter 11 dives deeply into the features of Database Workload Capture and Replay. To illustrate the power of this tool, we first demonstrate how to capture an application workload from a pre-12c Oracle Database environment with no disruption to that workload's execution using the features of Database Workload Capture. We then investigate the features of Workload Intelligence, a new feature set of the Real Application Testing suite that was added in Oracle 12cR1. Workload Intelligence makes it possible to analyze application workloads obtained through a Real Application Testing Database Capture operation for specific code paths to the database's data objects. This is extremely valuable for Oracle DBAs who have little control over the application code that is being generated and executed, yet need to visualize the data access patterns adequately to associate them with actual workload execution statistics and provide performance tuning opportunities.

Chapter 12 concludes the investigation of Real Application Testing features as we then replay the workload previously captured in Chapter 11 against an Oracle 12cR2 database. We also show how to ramp up that workload significantly during its replay so that we can perform a test to destruction—literally exhausting the new environment to the point of extremely poor performance—so that we can reliably determine the maximum outer boundaries of its new platform's capabilities.

Part V—A Brave New World: Database In-Memory

First introduced in Oracle Database 12cR1, the myriad features of Database In-Memory (DBIM) had the potential to increase the efficiency of analytic queries dramatically, especially when huge numbers of rows from multiple tables needed to be retrieved, filtered, possibly discarded, and then aggregated. The initial release of DBIM included the new In-Memory Column Store (IMCS), In-Memory Aggregation (IMA), and In-Memory Joins (IMJ), but it still left many Oracle DBAs in a quandary on how best to use these features. Determining which tables and table partitions would be the best candidates for population within the IMCS, calculating the optimal initial size of the IMCS, and—perhaps most importantly—deciding when to remove an object that no longer benefitted from remaining within the IMCS became difficult decisions because of insufficient instrumentation.

Fortunately, there are several excellent tools that any Oracle DBA can easily leverage to provide the necessary guidance to deal with these issues. Chapter 13 discusses the basic concepts of DBIM, illustrates how it can dramatically increase the performance of complex queries, and then demonstrates how the In-Memory Advisor helps an Oracle DBA to determine which objects should be populated intelligently into the IMCS.

DBIM has been dramatically enhanced in Oracle 12cR2, so in Chapter 14 we first highlight those changes and then move on to demonstrate how the new In-Memory Central feature set provides the instrumentation that was initially lacking in the first release of DBIM, including the ability to visualize in real time which objects populated within the IMCS are growing "hotter" or "colder" depending on how they are being used during query execution.

Part VI— Appendixes, with Other Tuning Tools, Code Examples, and References

We complete our exploration of Oracle Database 12c's toolsets with some final guidance and added value. Appendix A lists some others tools that are not available directly through Oracle but that are extremely useful when the Oracle Diagnostic and Tuning Pack hasn't been licensed but we still need to have a way to predict a performance impact of a change, to diagnose an ongoing or past performance issue, to perform forecasts, and so forth. We also provide significant code examples in Appendix B that any Oracle DBA—regardless of current experience level or exposure to Oracle Database12c concepts—can leverage to immediate advantage in real-world, on-the-job situations. Finally, Appendix C provides information on several valuable reference documents that the authors found useful when researching this book's contents and examples.

Summary

Oracle provides extremely powerful diagnostic and tuning tools that supply viewpoints, analyses, and recommendations from the microscopic level (an individual SQL statement), through the macroscopic level (an entire application workload), and up to the universal level (the entire database). A major reason to leverage these tuning tools is that they are tightly integrated with existing nongraphical interfaces such as SQL*Plus and SQLcl as well as graphical interfaces such as Oracle Enterprise Manager 13c Cloud Control.

This chapter explained this book's scope for using myriad Oracle toolsets effectively; it also provided a roadmap for the best ways to leverage the following chapters so that any Oracle DBA can immediately search out and apply the appropriate solution for the problem at hand.

CHAPTER
2

Testing Methodology

If the authors' nearly 100 years of cumulative Oracle DBA experience has taught us anything, it is that no matter what our customers, clients, and user community may claim, one thing is certain: no single application workload is alike. That profound realization has driven us toward a neutral approach when selecting the best way to demonstrate the power and flexibility of the various Oracle Database toolsets and features we explore in this book.

In this chapter, we discuss the reasons for our choice of the TPC-DS benchmark and its corresponding database schema that focuses on answering realistic business questions via complex analytical queries. We also discuss our choice of Swingbench for generating a repeatable application workload against the TPC-DS schema and briefly illustrate some of that tool's features and capabilities.

TPC-DS: An Appropriate Benchmark for Testing

The Transaction Processing Performance Council (TPC) has produced several de facto standard benchmarks that accurately reproduce several distinct application workload types. Numerous hardware and software vendors have used these TPC benchmarks over the past several decades to measure the efficiency of various databases on an almost dizzying array of hardware configurations. The main purpose of these methods is to ensure that database application performance can be reliably reproduced within tightly controlled environments and carefully designed rules for data structures, database loading methods, query execution, and data refresh processes.

TPC published the latest version of its Decision Support (DS) benchmark, TPC-DS 2.3.0, on August 5, 2016, and we have adopted that version of this benchmark as the basis of all experiments within this book. We selected this benchmark because it accurately represents a scalable application workload that focuses on providing answers to complex, real-world business questions through analytic queries across multiple data dimensions. As the workloads generated in the upcoming chapters will indeed demonstrate, these queries often consume high amounts of CPU and generate considerable physical and/or logical I/O because they may query either very small or enormous data volumes that require intensive filtering, joins, and aggregation. Finally, the latest version of this benchmark is designed to accommodate both relational databases (RDBMS) and nontraditional Big Data/NoSQL databases and solutions (for example, Hadoop or Spark).

Disclaimer: There's No One Perfect Environment

The authors wish to make it extremely clear that although we have adopted TPC-DS 2.3.0 as the basis for our investigations, the results we have obtained are not intended to suggest that any one hardware platform, database, database version, or configuration is necessarily superior, nor should our results indicate that any particular Oracle Database feature or pack is superior or inferior to another. Our main purpose is to supply a standard, common starting point for our investigations and provide any reader an identical starting point when experimenting with Oracle Database features.

TPC-DS Database Schema

The TPC-DS schema is designed specifically to simulate a complex data warehouse application workload for a retail product supplier that is providing its customers the ability to generate merchandise orders through its three main sales channels: mail-order catalog, brick-and-mortar stores, and web site. The schema comprises seven fact tables and 17 dimensions that include handling returns from any one of the three sales channels as well as an inventory tracking function.

TPC-DS: Fact and Dimension Entities

The entities that make up the TPC-DS dimensions are listed in Table 2-1; those that make up the TPC-DS facts are listed in Table 2-2.

Entity Name	Description
CALL_CENTER	The call center that facilitated a customer's catalog sale or return request
CATALOG_PAGE	The catalog page from which a customer selected a product for sale
CUSTOMER	A customer who has purchased or returned an item through one of the company's three sales channels
CUSTOMER_ADDRESS	The corresponding address(es) for a customer
CUSTOMER_DEMOGRAPHICS	The corresponding demographic information for a customer
DATE_DIM	The date on which a customer transaction occurred

TABLE 2-1. *TPC-DS Dimension Entities*

Entity Name	Description
HOUSEHOLD_DEMOGRAPHICS	The corresponding household demographic information for a customer
INCOME_BAND	The corresponding income levels for a customer
ITEM	The product items that the company sells to its customers
PROMOTIONS	The special sales promotion channels the company has used to increase sales of a particular product
REASON	The reason for the return of a product
SHIP_MODE	The methods that the company uses to ship products to customers
STORE	The company's brick-and-mortar sales outlets
TIME_DIM	The time at which a customer transaction occurred
WAREHOUSE	The company's warehouses that hold its inventory
WEB_PAGE	The web page from the web site on which a customer selected a product for sale
WEB_SITE	The company's various customer-facing web sites

TABLE 2-1. *TPC-DS Dimension Entities (continued)*

Entity Name	Description
INVENTORY	The company's current product inventory, on hand at one of its numerous warehouses
CATALOG_SALES	Sales made through one of the company's mail-order catalogs
CATALOG_RETURNS	Products returned after being sold through one of the company's mail-order catalogs
STORE_SALES	Sales that have occurred at one of the company's stores
STORE_RETURNS	Products returned after being sold through one of the company's stores
WEB_SALES	Sales through one of the company's customer-facing web sites
WEB_RETURNS	Products returned after being sold through one of the company's customer-facing web sites

TABLE 2-2. *TPC-DS Fact Entities*

TPC-DS Entity Relationships

Figure 2-1 illustrates the relationships between the CATALOG_SALES fact entity and its corresponding dimensions; Figure 2-2 shows the relationships between the CATALOG_RETURNS fact entity and its corresponding dimensions.

Likewise, Figure 2-3 shows the relationships between the STORE_SALES fact entity and its corresponding dimensions; Figure 2-4 shows the relationships between the STORE_RETURNS fact entity and its corresponding dimensions.

Similarly, Figure 2-5 explains the relationships between the WEB_SALES fact entity and its corresponding dimensions; Figure 2-6 shows the relationships between the WEB_RETURNS fact entity and its corresponding dimensions.

Finally, Figure 2-7 illustrates the relationships between the INVENTORY entity and its corresponding dimensions.

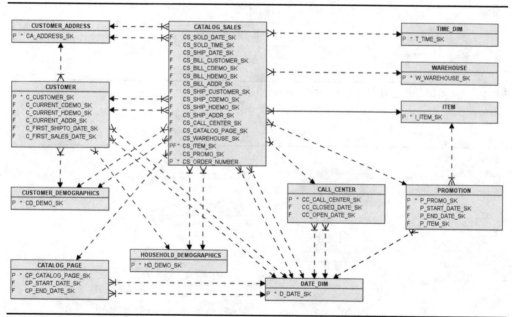

FIGURE 2-1. *CATALOG_SALES entity relationship model*

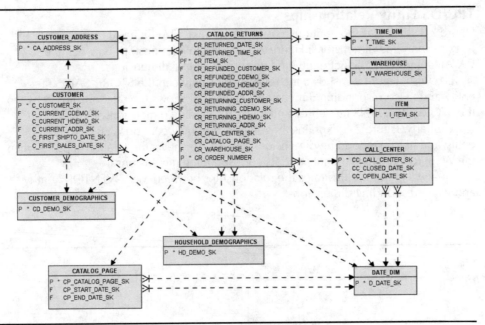

FIGURE 2-2. *CATALOG_RETURNS entity relationship model*

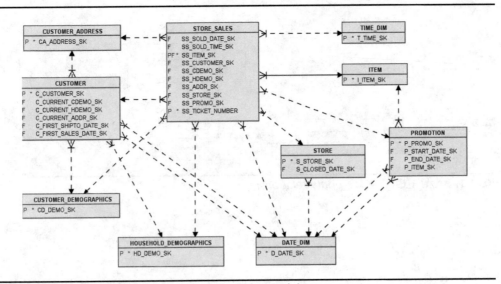

FIGURE 2-3. *STORE_SALES entity relationship model*

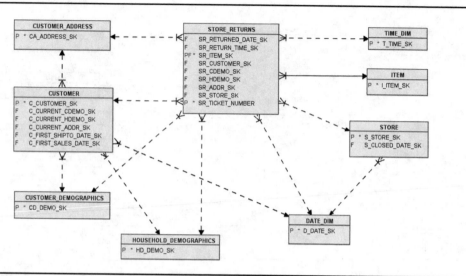

FIGURE 2-4. *STORE_RETURNS entity relationship model*

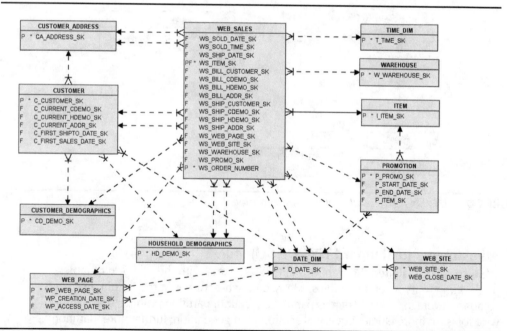

FIGURE 2-5. *WEB_SALES entity relationship model*

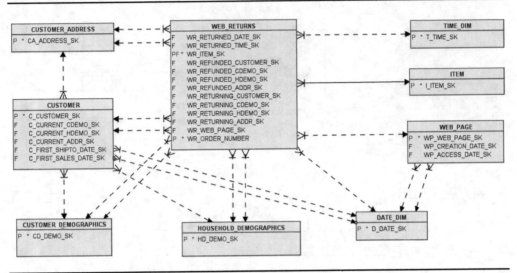

FIGURE 2-6. *WEB_RETURNS entity relationship model*

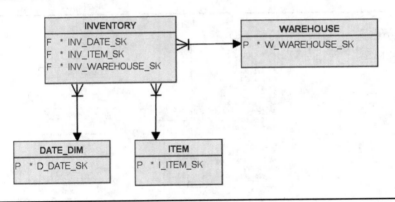

FIGURE 2-7. *INVENTORY entity relationship model*

Adjustments to Standard TPC-DS Schema

We also slightly altered the standard TPC-DS schema with the addition of table partitioning to its seven fact tables. Many data warehouses stored within an Oracle database leverage features such as parallel execution, partition pruning, and partition-wise joins for more efficient query execution plan generation; furthermore, partitioning these tables also enables demonstration of the latest Database In-Memory (DBIM) features first available in Oracle releases 12.1.0.2 and 12.2.0.1, which Chapters 13 and 14 discuss in depth.

NOTE
Implementing partitioned tables within an Oracle database may incur additional licensing costs. Oracle DBAs should check their current licensing agreement to ensure they are in compliance before deciding to implement this modified TPC-DS schema in a testing environment.

To minimize the need to create any new columns for these tables, we leveraged the ability to partition a table based on values obtained through a virtual column—a feature available since Oracle Database 11gR1—to enforce any partitioning schemes. Each of the seven fact tables contains a column that reflects a transaction date for each row (for example, column INV_DATE_SK in table INVENTORY), so we created a virtual column based on that date value. Each transaction date column value is based on the number of days elapsed since January 1, 4712 BCE; for example, January 1, 1900, is day number 2415021. This made it quite simple to calculate a representative calendar date via a scalar function expression. An example for the INVENTORY table is shown in Listing 2-1.

Listing 2-1 *INVENTORY Table DDL showing virtual column generation based on number of days since January 1, 1900*

```
DROP TABLE tpcds.inventory PURGE;
CREATE TABLE tpcds.inventory
(
    inv_date_sk                INTEGER            NOT NULL
   ,inv_item_sk                INTEGER            NOT NULL
   ,inv_warehouse_sk           INTEGER            NOT NULL
   ,inv_quantity_on_hand       INTEGER
   ,inv_dtm                    DATE
    VISIBLE GENERATED ALWAYS
    AS (TO_DATE('1900-01-01','yyyy-mm-dd')+(inv_date_sk-2415021))
    VIRTUAL
)
    TABLESPACE tpcds_data
    STORAGE (INITIAL 8M NEXT 4M)
    PARTITION BY RANGE (inv_dtm)
    INTERVAL(NUMTOYMINTERVAL(3, 'MONTH'))
    (
        PARTITION inv_oldest
            VALUES LESS THAN (TO_DATE('1998-04-01', 'yyyy-mm-dd'))
    );
```

NOTE
These modifications are permitted within the boundaries of the TPC-DS standard model as described within the section on horizontal partitioning (2.5.3.8.3) of the TPC-DS Standard Specification, Version 2.3.0.

TPC-DS Application Workloads

The TPC-DS schema is only half of the model—the most important aspect of TPC-DS is the ability to generate sufficient application workloads against that schema.

TPC-DS Queries

The TPC-DS specification is focused mainly on obtaining business answers from a potentially massive dataset. From that viewpoint, the most important part of the TPC-DS benchmark are the nearly 100 individual queries that attempt to provide answers for these particular business questions. Each of the TPC-DS queries implement varying degrees of analytic complexity; some queries access ten or more fact and dimension tables, thus producing varying and complex execution plans depending upon the values supplied for the query's selection criteria.

TPC-DS Data Refreshes

The TPC-DS benchmark also includes provisions for applying bulk updates to the fact and dimension tables. The corresponding benchmark application code does provide methods to generate additional data for bulk loading of refreshed data into these tables, but otherwise leaves the actual implementation of those methods to the application coder himself. Because this book is focused on detecting application workloads and their underlying SQL statements that need improvement, we have implemented several PL/SQL maintenance routines that refresh data within several of the fact tables using simple random value generation for data maintenance, including addition of new rows, update of existing column values, and deletion of individual rows.

NOTE
The data refresh methods implemented within the chosen load generation tool (Swingbench 2.6.1) are not precisely compliant with the boundaries described within section 5.3 of the TPC-DS Standard Specification, Version 2.3.0. However, the authors consider this a moot point because the intent of the maintenance application workload is to provide sufficient SQL statements and operations as "grist for the mill" of the various Oracle Database testing tools, not to provide an accurate TPC-DS benchmark result.

TPC-DS Data Volume Sizes

The TPC-DS 2.3.1 specification recommends creating a dataset sized no smaller than 1TB in order to generate a sufficiently robust workload. As our experiments in the following chapters show, however, we generated adequate application workloads with a dataset of 100GB or less; in fact, for simple demonstrations of

SQL performance tuning tools, even the smallest possible dataset that can be generated via the TPC-DS DSDGEN utility (1 GB) was more than sufficient to observe how these toolsets work.

Swingbench: Our Tool of Choice for Workload Generation

There are quite literally dozens of tools in the marketplace for generating complex workloads of all kinds against an Oracle database; in fact, we summarize and describe several of them in Appendix A. We have focused this book on detecting and solving performance issues as part of an end-to-end diagnosis, starting at an individual SQL statement, traversing through subset operations of an application workload, and finally plumbing the depths of the Oracle database executing that workload. We therefore decided to select a workload generation method that would create significant query-centric workloads so that we could analyze improved methods for query performance. We also needed to be able to demonstrate several new features of Oracle Database 12cR2, especially the numerous significant improvements to Database In-Memory features. We realized we required a way to generate a workload that consists of a sufficiently robust set of complex queries that access, filter, and aggregate millions of rows to identify truly those potential performance improvements.

We therefore selected the most recent version of Swingbench, a well-known and venerable tool, as our workload generation toolset. Swingbench is a freeware distribution, so any reader can easily replicate our tests at minimal cost with only minimal setup time.

Swingbench can be downloaded free of charge at http://dominicgiles.com/swingbench.html.

Swingbench Overview

Dominic Giles created the original version of Swingbench in 2003, and it quickly became a favorite tool of many Oracle DBAs. It offers a simple installation process, requires only Java to be present on the host, and runs within Windows, Linux, and UNIX environments. Swingbench offers a character-based command-line application workload generator as well as a simple, intuitive GUI that runs in either the X Window System or Microsoft Windows environments. Because the majority of its configuration files use Extended Markup Language (XML) to specify runtime parameters, application workloads, and even database loading and maintenance routines, Swingbench is extremely simple to configure and customize in just about any environment.

Swingbench Improvements in Version 2.6.1

Driven by the need to demonstrate a significant application workload dominated by complex queries against a more robust data warehousing schema, Jim Czuprynski and Dominic Giles collaborated throughout 2016 to produce an improved version of Swingbench that incorporated the slightly modified version of the TPC-DS schema we previously described. This latest version includes the capability to generate an application workload that executes every standard TPC-DS query with various bind variable values for the queries' selection criteria.

In keeping with the current TPC-DS benchmark standard, Swingbench v2.6.1 also includes a fully functional database-loading process that builds the complete TPC-DS schema described previously, loads it with randomized data, creates all indexes and constraints, and gathers Oracle-optimizer statistics. The Swingbench loading process therefore mimics the loading process used by the TPC-DS benchmark's DSDGEN C routines to create flat files suitable for loading directly into the TPC-DS schema via utilities such as Oracle SQL*Loader.

The latest version of Swingbench also incorporates several tweaks and features that Giles had been waiting to add for some time, including

- A brand-new JavaScript Object Notation (JSON) benchmark

- A new declarative approach to creating a user-defined benchmark

- A new SQL Query Editor to create queries for user-defined benchmarks

- An improved chart-rendering engine

- The ability to start Swingbench without a named configuration file, allowing the choice through a new Select Benchmark dialog

- Enhanced statistics collection routines that estimate response time percentiles

- Collected statistics that include transactions per second (TPS) as well as CPU and I/O metrics when available

- Support for remote connectivity to databases in the Oracle Cloud in connection dialogs

- A new sbutil (Swingbench utility) module that validates several of the available Swingbench benchmarks and scales them up appropriately

- A new results2pdf utility to convert benchmark result files into Adobe Portable Document Format (PDF) files

Figure 2-8 shows an example of the workload generation panel while a sample TPC-DS Query Application Workload was being generated against an Oracle 12cR2 test database instance.

We will be leveraging Swingbench v2.6.1 extensively throughout the remaining chapters to generate query application workloads of various intensities as well as for execution of bulk data modification routines so that we can demonstrate repeatable workloads for analysis at the SQL statement, instance, and database level.

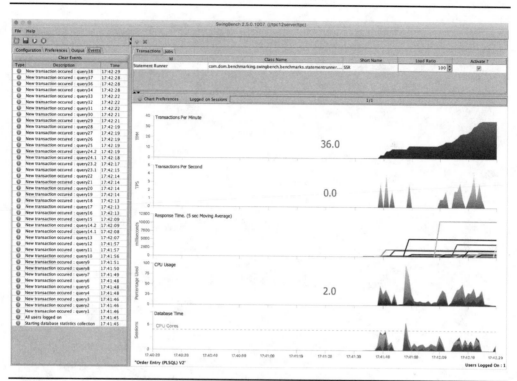

FIGURE 2-8.   *Swingbench TPC-DS workload generation panel*

Summary

In this chapter we outlined the reasons for choosing TPC-DS Benchmark 2.3.0 as the standard benchmark for our application workload performance evaluations—namely, that TPC-DS provides methods to generate and load sufficiently large volumes of data for its nearly 100 complex queries to operate against so that those queries' execution will cause enough stress on a database so that numerous Oracle Database diagnostic and tuning tools can analyze those workloads for performance improvement possibilities.

We also outlined our reasons for leveraging the most recent version of Swingbench (v2.6.1) for application load generation—specifically, because of its ease of installation, its simplicity to configure, and its ability to generate just about any application workload against an Oracle database.

PART II

Digging Deeper: SQL Performance Management Tools

CHAPTER
3

SQL Tuning Sets and Tuning Advisor

P rior to Oracle Database 10g, tuning SQL statements was a complex, repetitive, and time-consuming activity for DBAs. Beginning with version 10g, Oracle Database has included several performance management tools and Advisors that help automate performance management and tuning. Oracle Database includes several Advisors, each one analyzing a specific database aspect and providing specific recommendations.

SQL Tuning Advisor is one of these Advisors; SQL Tuning Advisor helps the DBA resolve problems related to suboptimally performing SQL statements and offers recommendations for improving performance of problematic statements. In Chapter 4, we'll discuss the SQL Access Advisor, which analyzes access paths to determine how each object involved in each SQL statement is being accessed.

We'll start the chapter with a discussion of SQL Tuning Sets (STS), which enable you to group SQL statements and related metadata into a single database object, which you can then use to meet your tuning goals. You can use an STS as input to multiple database Advisors, including SQL Tuning Advisor, SQL Access Advisor, and SQL Performance Analyzer. The information provided in this chapter will serve as the basis upon which other discussions about Advisors and tools will be focused.

SQL Tuning Sets

Each advisor in Oracle Database has different sources from where you can take the SQL statement that you want to tune. Some Advisors can receive the text of a SQL statement as the input, and others take data from the Automatic Workload Repository (AWR), the shared SQL area in the library cache, and other sources. Regardless of the source of the SQL statement, the statement's text is insufficient for tuning and providing performance recommendations; further information is needed regarding the SQL statement, such as information that describes how it is being executed, the time spent, rows processed, the resources used, and, especially, the values used by the SQL statement such as bind variables. All this information is needed to analyze different performance scenarios properly.

It is therefore necessary to obtain a standard input for all Advisors and tools that defines a proper way to serialize a SQL statement along with its execution plans and context in a single object, regardless of the source. Such a standard input would serialize all the information for a whole set of SQL statements—not just for a single statement. This standard would enable the transfer of the serialized object to other databases transparently—for example, to enable the transfer of a set of SQL statements and the information to a test environment where changes and recommendations can be safely implemented, or simply to have the SQL statement and its related information presented.

Fortunately, Oracle added SQL Tuning Set (STS) to Oracle Database 10g. An STS can include one or more SQL statements gathered from different sources. For each

SQL statement, much crucial information is also captured, including the statement's execution plans; execution statistics such as elapsed time, CPU time, rows processed, fetches, and disk reads; bind variables; the parsing schema name; the application module name; compilation parameters; and much more.

NOTE
If you are licensed to use Oracle Database Enterprise Edition, you can use SQL Tuning Sets even if you do not have an Oracle Tuning Pack license.

Constructing SQL Tuning Sets

There are three basic steps involved when working with STS:

1. Create an empty SQL Tuning Set.

2. Load SQL statements into the SQL Tuning Set.

3. Use the SQL Tuning Set:

   - As input for Oracle Advisors

   - To transfer (export/import) a set of SQL statements and corresponding execution information to another database

   - To create a SQL plan baseline

   - To create other SQL Tuning Sets

Creating an Empty SQL Tuning Set

The function `SQL_TUNE.CREATE_SQLSET` is used to create an STS; by default, no SQL statements exist in the function:

```
SQL> exec DBMS_SQLTUNE.CREATE_SQLSET ('STS_QUERY70');

PL/SQL procedure successfully completed.
```

To confirm that the STS has been successfully created, the view `DBA_SQLSET` can be used:

```
SQL> select name, id, created, statement_count from dba_sqlset;

NAME          ID          CREATED    STATEMENT_COUNT
-----------   ----------  ---------  ----------------
STS_QUERY70    2 27-DEC-16                 0
```

The column STATEMENT_COUNT shows how many SQL statements are included in the STS. In this case, there are none, because no SQL statements have been loaded yet—and that is the purpose of the next step.

Sources for Loading SQL Statements into a SQL Tuning Set

An STS can be created from the most useful sources when you are troubleshooting a performance issue. SQL statements that need to be analyzed may have been running days ago, may have run just minutes ago, or perhaps they are still running. For all those scenarios, you have different sources from which the SQL statements can be taken and loaded into an STS. Then the STS can be used as an input to Oracle Advisors or other tools. The Figure 3-1 outlines how different sources can be used to create an STS.

Capturing SQL Statements from the Shared SQL Area

When a DBA receives a notification from application developers that a report or some applications are running too slow, sometimes the problematic SQL statement is still in progress. This means that the SQL statement can be found in the shared SQL area of the database's shared pool memory. In that scenario, you can create an STS with one or more SQL statements from the shared SQL area and use a filter on either SQL_ID or the SQL text of the statement to load those SQL statements; this makes it easy and fast to load the statements while they are in progress or a short time afterward. Use the function DBMS_SQLTUNE.SELECT_CURSOR_CACHE to load the SQL statements into the STS.

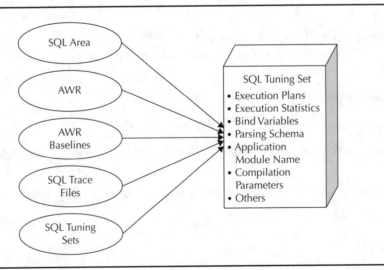

FIGURE 3-1. *SQL Tuning Set sources*

In the following example, the query #70 from the TPC-DS benchmark queries was executed and was registered into the shared SQL area, with `SQL_ID = ''361v8yqfm0hct'`. Finally, the query `STS_QUERY70` was loaded into an STS.

```
DECLARE
cur SYS_REFCURSOR;
BEGIN
OPEN cur FOR
SELECT value(p) FROM table(DBMS_SQLTUNE.SELECT_CURSOR_CACHE('sql_id =
''361v8yqfm0hct''')) p;
DBMS_SQLTUNE.LOAD_SQLSET('STS_QUERY70', cur);
CLOSE cur;
END;
/


PL/SQL procedure successfully completed.
```

Capturing SQL Statements from AWR Snapshots

As its name implies, the Automatic Workload Repository (AWR) captures and retains performance statistics. By default, an Oracle database creates an AWR snapshot every hour and keeps those snapshots for eight days. You can manually change the frequency and the retention of AWR snapshots. If a performance issue in the past needs to be analyzed and the information about the problematic SQL statement is no longer available in the shared SQL area, you can check AWR, which retains performance information up until the specified AWR retention time.

In this case, an STS is created from AWR, filtering the SQL statement by SQL ID, AWR initial snapshot ID, and AWR final snapshot ID. The function `DBMS_SQLTUNE.SELECT_WORKLOAD_REPOSITORY` is used to load the SQL statement into the STS.

```
DECLARE
cur SYS_REFCURSOR;
BEGIN
OPEN cur FOR
SELECT value(p) FROM table(
     DBMS_SQLTUNE.SELECT_WORKLOAD_REPOSITORY(
          begin_snap => 170,
          end_snap => 171,
          basic_filter => 'sql_id = ''6wzu736hx4fcq''')) p;
DBMS_SQLTUNE.LOAD_SQLSET ('STS_QUERY82', cur);
CLOSE cur;
END;
/
```

Capturing SQL Statements from AWR Baselines

An AWR baseline comprises a set of AWR snapshots that you can use as performance references during a time period in which the database performs acceptably well; then, when the database is slow, you can compare several metrics against the AWR baseline to determine which metrics have changed. AWR baselines are not reactive, but proactive, because they are taken when the performance is good.

An AWR baseline's retention time is set according to a number of days to expire, or it may never expire. As AWR snapshots, AWR baselines are useful for analyzing a SQL statement that is no longer available in the shared SQL area. An STS can be created from an AWR baseline to filter the problematic SQL statement by the AWR baseline name and the SQL ID. The function DBMS_SQLTUNE.SELECT_WORKLOAD_ REPOSITORY is used to load the SQL statement into the STS.

Capturing SQL Statements from SQL Trace Files

Starting with Oracle Database 11g, an STS can be created from a 10046 trace file. A trace file contains enough information to create an STS, such as SQL text, parse, execute, and fetch counts; CPU and elapsed times; logical reads; number of rows processed; misses on the shared SQL area; username under which each parse occurred; each commit and rollback; wait event data for each SQL statement in the trace file; a summary of waits; actual execution plan for each SQL statement; the number of rows, consistent reads, physical reads and physical writes; and the time elapsed for each operation.

An Oracle directory must be created using the path of the directory where the trace file is located. The function DBMS_SQLTUNE.SELECT_SQL_TRACE is used to load the SQL statement into the STS; the Oracle directory and the trace filename must be specified as parameters of the function. In the following example, the STS STS_FROMTRACEFILE is created from trace file db1_ora_25267.trc, which is located in the directory /home/oracle:

```
SQL> create directory HOME_ORACLE as '/home/oracle/';

Directory created.

SQL> exec DBMS_SQLTUNE.CREATE_SQLSET('STS_FROMTRACEFILE');

PL/SQL procedure successfully completed.

SQL> DECLARE
cur SYS_REFCURSOR;
BEGIN
OPEN cur FOR
SELECT value(p) FROM table(DBMS_SQLTUNE.SELECT_SQL_
TRACE(directory=>'HOME_ORACLE', file_name=>'db1_ora_25267.trc')) p;
DBMS_SQLTUNE.LOAD_SQLSET ('STS_FROMTRACEFILE', cur);
CLOSE cur;
END;
/

PL/SQL procedure successfully completed.
```

```
SQL>   SELECT       sqlset_name,
                    count(*)
       FROM         dba_sqlset_statements
       WHERE        sqlset_name='STS_FROMTRACEFILE'
       GROUP BY sqlset_name ;


SQLSET_NAME           COUNT(*)
-----------------     ---------
STS_FROMTRACEFILE           5
```

Capturing SQL Statements from Another SQL Tuning Set

The last source from which to create an STS is another STS. In this case, the function DBMS_SQLTUNE.SELECT_SQLSET is used to load the SQL statement into the STS. In the following example, an STS is created with the SQL ID '6wzu736hx4fcq', which is included in another STS called 'STS_QUERY82':

```
DECLARE
cur SYS_REFCURSOR;
BEGIN
OPEN cur FOR
SELECT value(p) FROM table(DBMS_SQLTUNE.SELECT_SQLSET(sqlset_name
=> 'STS_QUERY82', sqlset_owner => 'SYS', basic_filter => 'sql_id =
''6wzu736hx4fcq''')) p;
DBMS_SQLTUNE.LOAD_SQLSET ('STS_FROMSTS', cur);
CLOSE cur;
END;
/
```

Showing SQL Tuning Set Information

After the STS is created and populated, its information can be queried using the function DBMS_SQLTUNE.SELECT_SQLSET; the views (DBA|ALL|USER)_SQLSET* can be also used. In the following example, some execution statistics are queried using DBMS_SQLTUNE.SELECT_SQLSET:

```
SELECT      sql_id,
            elapsed_time,
            buffer_gets,
            cpu_time,
            disk_reads
FROM   table( DBMS_SQLTUNE.SELECT_SQLSET(
                                sqlset_name=>'STS_QUERY70',
                                attribute_list=>'BASIC'));


SQL_ID          ELAPSED_TIME BUFFER_GETS   CPU_TIME DISK_READS
-------------   ------------ -----------   ---------- ----------
361v8yqfm0hct        714047       37587      213968      33326
```

The same execution statistics are displayed using the view `DBA_SQLSET_STATEMENT`:

```
SELECT      sqlset_name,
            sql_id,
            elapsed_time,
            buffer_gets,
            cpu_time,
            disk_reads
FROM dba_sqlset_statements;


SQLSET_NAME SQL_ID         ELAPSED_TIME BUFFER_GETS  CPU_TIME DISK_READS
----------- -------------- ------------ -----------  -------- ----------
STS_QUERY70 361v8yqfm0hct        714047       37587    213968      33326
```

Transporting SQL Tuning Sets to Another Database

A common usage of STS is to transport SQL statements and all their related information to another database to test, evaluate, and fix execution plans so that changes or any Oracle Advisor recommendations are not implemented directly on a production database.

> **NOTE**
> *We strongly recommend that you do not implement a change on a production database before testing it in a test environment.*

Following our proactive approach, a very frequent task will be to transfer errant SQL statements to another database to start the analysis. To do so, follow these steps:

1. Create a stage table.

2. Pack a SQL Tuning Set.

3. Export the SQL Tuning Set.

4. Transfer the dump file to the target database.

5. Import the SQL Tuning Set.

6. Unpack the SQL Tuning Set.

7. Verify successful transferal of SQL Tuning Set.

Create a Staging Table

A staging table is a special table in which all the data related to an STS can be stored. In Oracle Database 12c Release 1, this staging table has 105 columns, enough to store all the information related to an STS, such as the execution plan information, bind variables, execution statistics, and of course the SQL statement itself. This table is basically a merge of the tables WRI$_SQLSET_DEFINITIONS, WRI$_SQLSET_REFERENCES, WRI$_SQLSET_STATEMENTS, WRI$_SQLSET_PLANS, and WRI$_SQLSET_BINDS, and that's why it has several columns. The WRI$_SQLSET* tables are the base of the views (DBA|ALL|USER)_SQLSET*.

In the following example, a staging table called STS_STAGE_TABLE is created in the schema named TPCDS and stored in the USERS tablespace:

```
BEGIN
DBMS_SQLTUNE.CREATE_STGTAB_SQLSET(table_name => 'STS_STAGE_TABLE',
schema_name => 'TPCDS',
tablespace_name => 'USERS');
END;
/

PL/SQL procedure successfully completed.
```

Pack a SQL Tuning Set

In this step, all the information related to an STS is inserted into a staging table, and the function DBMS_SQLTUNE.PACK_STGTAB_SQLSET manages transparently how the STS information is mapped to the staging table. In the following example, the STS called STS_QUERY70 is inserted into the table TPCDS.STS_STAGE_TABLE:

```
BEGIN
DBMS_SQLTUNE.PACK_STGTAB_SQLSET(sqlset_name => 'STS_QUERY70',
sqlset_owner => 'SYS',
staging_table_name => 'STS_STAGE_TABLE',
staging_schema_owner => 'TPCDS');
END;
/

PL/SQL procedure successfully completed.
```

Export a SQL Tuning Set

To export an STS staging table, the EXPDP utility is used. Neither the table statistics nor the index statistics of the staging table itself needs to be exported; only the data (STS) and its metadata required to re-create the staging table in the target database are required.

```
expdp tpcds/tpcds tables=STS_STAGE_TABLE directory=tpcds_dumps
dumpfile=tpcds_sts.dmp exclude=TABLE_STATISTICS,INDEX_STATISTICS
```

Transfer the Dump File to the Target Database

After the STS has been packed into an STS staging table and successfully exported, the export dump file can be transferred to the target database. Any method to transfer files through the network is acceptable, such as secure copy (SCP).

```
scp /home/oracle/tpcds_sts.dmp oracle@testdb:/home/oracle/TPCDS
```

Import the SQL Tuning Set

An STS is imported with the IMPDP utility just as it would be with any other data import:

```
impdp tpcds/tpcds tables=STS_STAGE_TABLE directory=tpcds_dumps
dumpfile=tpcds_sts.dmp
```

Unpack the SQL Tuning Set

After the STS has been imported, the STS staging table is created, but the STS itself will still exist in packed format. Using the function DBMS_SQLTUNE.UNPACK_STGTAB_SQLSET, the STS can be unpacked and registered in the target database:

```
BEGIN
DBMS_SQLTUNE.UNPACK_STGTAB_SQLSET(sqlset_name => 'STS_QUERY70',
sqlset_owner => 'SYS',
replace => TRUE,
staging_table_name => 'STS_STAGE_TABLE',
staging_schema_owner => 'TPCDS');
END;
/

PL/SQL procedure successfully completed.
```

Verify Successful Transferal of SQL Tuning Set

The last step is to verify that the STS is ready to use in the target database by querying view DBA_SQLSET_STATEMENTS:

```
SELECT      sqlset_name,
            sql_id,
            elapsed_time,
            buffer_gets,
            cpu_time,
            disk_reads
FROM dba_sqlset_statements;

SQLSET_NAME SQL_ID          ELAPSED_TIME BUFFER_GETS CPU_TIME DISK_READS
----------- --------------- ------------ ----------- -------- ----------
STS_QUERY70 361v8yqfm0hct         714047       37587   213968      33326
```

SQL Tuning Advisor

The art of improving the performance of a SQL statement manually requires several steps, a high level of SQL performance tuning skills, and—perhaps most importantly—a lot of time, because each component directly or indirectly influencing the statement's execution plan has to be carefully analyzed.

Even when an Oracle DBA has developed sufficient skills to tune SQL statements, he may not have sufficient time to deploy those skills, especially when his application team is complaining loudly about performance degradation that demands immediate action. In this situation, a DBA will often leverage a standard recipe to determine the cause of the performance issue, consisting of verifying whether optimizer statistics for the underlying objects are fresh, checking the statement's execution plan to verify how those objects are being accessed, looking to see if any SQL profiles might influence the execution plan, checking to see if an inappropriate level of parallelism has been specified, and so forth. Conversely, if an Oracle DBA hasn't yet developed sufficient skill and experience in diagnosing performance issues but has enough time to investigate the possible vectors of poor performance, he might arrive at almost the same conclusion drawn by his highly skilled counterpart.

In an effort to answer this paradox, Oracle Database 10g introduced Oracle SQL Tuning Advisor. Instead of reinventing the wheel, an Oracle DBA with high skills can leverage SQL Tuning Advisor to perform all those initial checks he normally invoked as part of his recipe; then, when SQL Tuning Advisor quickly delivers tuning recommendations, he can use his highly developed tuning skills to evaluate and approve them based on his painfully obtained experience. Contrariwise, a DBA with only limited performance tuning expertise may not know exactly where to start his analysis; he can immediately begin using SQL Tuning Advisor to obtain recommendations, evaluate them in a test environment, and then verify the benefit.

NOTE
Using SQL Tuning Advisor requires licensing the
Oracle Tuning Pack.

SQL Tuning Advisor: Analysis Targets

SQL Tuning Advisor can receive SQL statements from the following sources:

- **Text of a SQL statement**   In this case, the Automatic Tuning Optimizer executes the SQL statement provided to gather information about how the SQL statement currently is being executed, such as physical reads, logical reads, CPU consumption, and so forth.

- **An STS**   An existing STS is needed. Since an STS can store several SQL statements, a filter can be also used to select only those SQL statements from the STS that need to be analyzed.

■ **Shared SQL area**   The SQL ID of the SQL statement has to be provided.

■ **AWR**   The starting and ending snapshots and the SQL ID must be provided to filter the problematic SQL statement.

■ **SQL Performance Analyzer (SPA)**   If an SPA task already exists, it can be used as an input to SQL Tuning Advisor. The SPA task owner and name must be provided and optionally a filter applied to select the problematic SQL statement.

In this chapter, STS_QUERY70, the STS that was created earlier in the section "SQL Tuning Set," will be used.

SQL Tuning Advisor uses the Automatic Tuning Optimizer to perform its analysis. For all the SQL statement sources, the execution statistics of how the SQL statement is executed already exist in the data dictionary, except when the SQL statement source is SQL text; in that case, SQL Tuning Advisor also uses Automatic Tuning Optimizer to parse, fetch, and execute the SQL text provided and then perform its analysis. When Automatic Tuning Optimizer is called by SQL Tuning Advisor, it analyzes several aspects of each SQL statement passed as input, such as calculating the benefit of different hints and several modifications of the SQL structure; determining whether objects used in the SQL statement have current, non-stale statistics; determining which access paths are used; determining whether new access paths are valid; and profiling the SQL.

After its analysis is complete, SQL Tuning Advisor will return one or more of the following recommendations:

■ **Gathering Statistics**   SQL Tuning Advisor interacts with the Automatic Tuning Optimizer to analyze the SQL statement's structure, including the predicates, objects, and columns, as part of the plan generation process. For every object it checks, it determines whether the object has missing or stale statistics. Statistics are useful for the cost-based optimizer to generate efficient plans and avoid reliance on the assumption of a uniform data distribution when in fact the data distribution is skewed.

■ **Create a SQL Profile**   Automatic Tuning Optimizer checks out hints, estimations, SQL plan directives, execution history, and optimizer parameters that can be used to create new SQL profiles. Every SQL profile is analyzed to determine its resulting optimizer cost; if it provides sufficient benefit, it is recommended in the final report.

■ **Rewrite the SQL Statement** Because Automatic Tuning Optimizer analyzes the SQL structure and the statement's corresponding access path, it can determine when a SQL statement can be improved by rewriting it in another way without compromising the reliability of the results returned.

■ **Create Indexes on Tables** Automatic Tuning Optimizer analyzes how the data is being accessed, how the indexes are being used, and the predicates used in the SQL statement; based on that information, it generates a list of indexes that hypothetically could improve the access path and then evaluates them. If the estimations indicate that the index being estimated makes the access path faster, that index results in an "index creation recommendation." For every recommendation to create an index, SQL Tuning Advisor also calculates the resulting benefit and the corresponding DDL to create the recommended index.

■ **SQL Plan Baselines** SQL Tuning Advisor looks for alternative plans in the AWR, result cache, SQL Performance Analyzer, or other STSs to compare costs and avoid performance regressions by creating SQL plan baselines.

Figure 3-2 outlines how several SQL statement sources can be used as input for SQL Tuning Advisor and how SQL Tuning Advisor uses Automatic Tuning Optimizer to perform several analyses to create a report with recommendations.

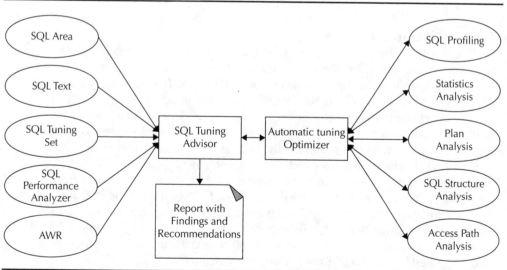

FIGURE 3-2. *SQL Tuning Advisor overview*

A basic algorithm of the analyses performed by SQL Tuning Advisor with Automatic Tuning Optimizer is the following:

```
While (there are SQL Statements pending to analyze)
{
        SQL Profiling analysis(){…}
        Statistics analysis(){…}
        SQL Structural Analysis(){…}

        Access Path Analysis(){…}
        Alternative Plan Analysis(){…}
}
```

Several procedures are called during analysis. The prefix of these procedures indicate what is calling them:

- Procedure names starting with *kesai* are performed by SQL Manageability Infrastructure.

- Procedure names starting with *kests, kestsi, kestsp*, and *kestsa* are performed by SQL Tuning Advisor.

- Procedure names starting with *kesds* are performed by SQL Repair Advisor.

- Procedure names starting with *kkoat* are performed by Automatic Tuning Optimizer.

Modes of Execution

SQL Tuning Advisor can be used on-demand, but it can also execute automatically on a scheduled basis. When SQL Tuning Advisor runs automatically, it uses the Automated Maintenance Tasks infrastructure, also known as AUTOTASK. The advantage of running SQL Tuning Advisor as part of the AUTOTASK regular maintenance schedule is that it has more time to perform an analysis of SQL statements and automatically select the top SQL statements from AWR for analysis; in addition, it can be configured to accept many of its recommendations automatically, or simply store the recommendations so that the DBA can review them later and decide to implement them or not. When SQL Tuning Advisor is executed automatically via AUTOTASK, it has a few downsides: It cannot analyze parallel queries or recursive SQLs, and it does not test the execution of a SQL statement after being SQL profiled if that SQL statement takes too long to be executed. Also be aware that if SQL Tuning Advisor is executed by AUTOTASK, it will run at night by default, and its analyses would consume considerable resources that could be needed by your batch jobs that also run at night.

Package DBMS_SQLTUNE is used to execute SQL Tuning Advisor tasks for an on-demand request, and it can be executed either locally or remotely. When SQL Tuning Advisor is executed locally, it incurs considerable overhead. Based on that, we strongly suggest that you tune SQL statements with SQL Tuning Advisor in a test environment or during off-peak periods when normal production business workloads aren't demanding system resources.

Starting with Oracle Database 12cR2, SQL statements in a physical standby database can be analyzed by SQL Tuning Advisor by using a private database link pointing to the primary database where necessary data regarding the tuning tasks will be captured and retained. In this case, the SQL statement and its related data will be read from the primary database but processed in the standby database, but the findings and recommendations will be stored in the primary database via the database link.

NOTE
In the SQL Tuning Advisor examples in the remainder of this chapter, on-demand SQL Tuning Advisor tasks will be generated locally.

Analysis Scope

The scope of any SQL Tuning Advisor task can be limited to prevent excessive resource consumption:

- **Limited Scope**   SQL Tuning Advisor will perform all the analyses except for SQL Profiler analysis.

- **Comprehensive Scope**   SQL Tuning Advisor will perform all analyses, including SQL profiling.

Example: Tuning a SQL Statement with SQL Tuning Advisor

When a SQL statement requires tuning, we recommend caution over expediency. The following approach involves evaluation and testing of the recommendations against a test database before deciding to execute any recommendations in the corresponding production environment. There will be cases, however, where reactive actions may have to be taken, and SQL Tuning Advisor can be extremely useful to validate a DBA's judgement to take only appropriate actions based on its recommendations.

Creating a SQL Tuning Set

In this step, the SQL statement is identified from its source database, and an STS is created. In this example, we will reuse the SQL Tuning Set named STS_QUERY70 that was created at the beginning of this chapter, which includes query #70 from the TPC-DS benchmark queries run via Swingbench. This query is easily identifiable by the hint /* query70 */. Only the values for some variables were replaced in the query #70 template:

```
select /* query70 */
    sum(ss_net_profit) as total_sum
   ,s_state
   ,s_county
   ,grouping(s_state)+grouping(s_county) as lochierarchy
   ,rank() over (
      partition by grouping(s_state)+grouping(s_county),
      case when grouping(s_county) = 0 then s_state end
      order by sum(ss_net_profit) desc) as rank_within_parent
 from
    store_sales
   ,date_dim        d1
   ,store
 where
    d1.d_month_seq between 1176  and 1224+11
 and d1.d_date_sk = ss_sold_date_sk
 and s_store_sk  = ss_store_sk
 and s_state in
              ( select s_state
                from  (select s_state as s_state,
                       rank() over ( partition by s_state order by
sum(ss_net_profit) desc) as ranking
                       from   store_sales, store, date_dim
                       where  d_month_seq between 1176  and 1224+11
                       and d_date_sk = ss_sold_date_sk
                       and s_store_sk  = ss_store_sk
                       group by s_state
                       ) tmp1
                where ranking <= 5
              )
 group by rollup(s_state,s_county)
 order by
   lochierarchy desc
  ,case when lochierarchy = 0 then s_state end
  ,rank_within_parent;
```

An experienced DBA might be able to imagine at first glance what might be wrong with this SQL statement, but the goal of this example is to demonstrate that SQL Tuning Advisor would be as exact as our experience.

Creating a SQL Tuning Task

A SQL tuning task needs to be created so that the specified STS can be analyzed. The scope of the analysis and a time limit in which the task can run are also included.

```
DECLARE
   stmt_task VARCHAR2(64);
   sta_task  VARCHAR2(64);
BEGIN
   sta_task := DBMS_SQLTUNE.CREATE_TUNING_TASK(
   sqlset_name  => 'STS_QUERY70',
   sqlset_owner => 'SYS',
   task_name    => 'STATASK01_QUERY70',
   scope        => 'COMPREHENSIVE',
   time_limit   => 3600,
   plan_filter  => 'MAX_ELAPSED_TIME');
END;
/

PL/SQL procedure successfully completed.
```

NOTE
If the time limit used for the task is too short, the following error can appear in the alert log or in the SQL Tuning Advisor report:
```
ORA-16957: SQL Analyze time limit
interrupt
ORA-13639: The current operation was
interrupted because it timed out.
```
In that case, the time limit must be increased by using the function DBMS_SQLTUNE.SET_TUNING_
TASK_PARAMETER.

Executing a SQL Tuning Task

After the SQL tuning task has been successfully created, it can be executed:

```
BEGIN
   DBMS_SQLTUNE.EXECUTE_TUNING_TASK(task_name=>'STATASK01_QUERY70');
END;
/

PL/SQL procedure successfully completed.
```

Monitoring a SQL Tuning Task

While the SQL tuning task is running, the task can be monitored to determine how long it will take and the percentage of completion. To do so, the views `DBA_ADVISOR_TASKS` and `V$ADVISOR_PROGRESS` can be used.

Using `DBA_ADVISOR_TASKS`:

```
SQL> select owner, task_id, task_name, status, status_message, pct_completion_time from
dba_advisor_tasks where task_name='STATASK01_QUERY70'

OWNER  TASK_ID       TASK_NAME     STATUS STATUS_MESSAGE PCT_COMPLETION_TIME
-----  --------  ---------------- --------- -------------- -------------------
SYS       228 STATASK01_QUERY70 COMPLETED                                    0
```

Using `V$ADVISOR_PROGRESS`:

```
SELECT      advisor_name,
            opname,
            task_id,
            findings,
            recommendations,
            round((sofar/totalwork)*100,0) pct_completed, time_remaining
FROM v$advisor_progress
WHERE task_id=228;

ADVISOR_NAME       OPNAME  TASK_ID FINDINGS RECOMMENDATIONS PCT_COMPLETED TIME_REMAINING
------------------ ------- ------- -------- --------------- ------------- --------------
SQL Tuning Advisor Advisor     228        0               0           100              0
```

Displaying the Results of a SQL Tuning Task

Once the task has completed without any timeout, the findings and recommendations will be ready for viewing. To display the SQL Tuning Advisor report, the function `DBMS_SQLTUNE.REPORT_TUNING_TASK` is used; the only required parameter to specify is the tuning task ID.

```
SELECT DBMS_SQLTUNE.REPORT_TUNING_TASK('STATASK01_QUERY70') FROM DUAL;
```

A SQL Tuning Advisor report has several sections, and it may have several subsections as well. The report starts with general information and ends with findings and recommendations specific to the SQL statements included within the analysis:

- **General Information section**   This section has information that describes the SQL tuning task, the parameters used, the date of the report, the source of the SQL statements, a count of SQL statements, and other pertinent data.

- **Summary section**   The summary section is the first place to look at, because it will contain findings (if any exist) as well as which kind of findings where observed. If no findings were found, it's best to adjust the parameters for the SQL Tuning task—for example, provide more time for the analysis or use a wider scope (if a limit was used).

- **Global SQL Tuning Result Statistics**   This subsection provides a count of how many SQL statements were analyzed, how many findings applied to those statements, and a classification of the finding types.

```
                    Global SQL Tuning Result Statistics
-------------------------------------------------------------------------------

Number of SQLs Analyzed                        : 1
Number of SQLs in the Report                   : 1
Number of SQLs with Findings                   : 1
Number of SQLs with Alternative Plan Findings  : 1
Number of SQLs with Index Findings             : 1
```

- **SQLs with Findings Ordered by Maximum (Profile/Index) Benefit, Object ID**   This subsection is one of the most important and useful sections in the report. For each SQL ID, it shows statistics findings, SQL profile findings and corresponding benefits, index creation findings and corresponding benefits, and findings suggesting a rewrite of the corresponding statement. When SQL Tuning Advisor recommends new profiles or new indexes, it also provides a benefit, and that is calculated via the following formula:

Benefit % = (old execution time − new time execution) / old time execution

```
-------------------------------------------------------------------------------
object ID SQL ID        statistics profile(benefit) index(benefit) restructure
--------- -------------  ---------- ---------------- -------------- -----------
        2 361v8yqfm0hct                                      90.73%
```

- **Objects with Missing/Stale Statistics (ordered by schema, object, type)**   If there was a count for statistics findings in the previous subsection, this subsection will list all the objects that require statistics to be regenerated because they are stale, or generated because statistics are missing.

```
-------------------------------------------------------------
Schema Name          Object Name     Type   State   Cascade
-------------------- --------------- ------ ------- ---------
             TPCDS DATE_DIM          TABLE MISSING NO
                   STORE             TABLE MISSING YES
```

- **Tables with New Potential Indices (ordered by schema, number of times, table)**   In this subsection, recommendations for any tables that would benefit by the creation of any additional indexes are listed.

```
-------------------------------------------------------------
Schema Name          Table Name      Index Name      Nb Time
-------------------- --------------- --------------- --------
             TPCDS DATE_DIM          IDX$$_00E40001         1
```

■ **Details section** In this subsection, the text of the SQL ID is provided:

```
Statements with Results Ordered by Maximum (Profile/Index) Benefit, Object ID
-------------------------------------------------------------------------------
Object ID  : 3
Schema Name: TPCDS
SQL ID     : 361v8yqfm0hct
SQL Text   : select /* query70 */
               sum(ss_net_profit) as total_sum
             ...
             ...
```

■ **Findings section** This is the most important section of the report. It includes not only every recommendation, but also an explanation of how each recommendation will improve the SQL statement's performance. Here are some examples of typical findings:

■ **Statistics Finding** In this subsection one of the recommendations is to gather statistics for TPCDS dimension tables DATE_DIM and STORE:

```
1- Statistics Finding
---------------------
  Table "TPCDS"."DATE_DIM" was not analyzed.

  Recommendation
  --------------
  - Consider collecting optimizer statistics for this table.
      execute dbms_stats.gather_table_stats(ownname => 'TPCDS', tabname =>
          'DATE_DIM', estimate_percent => DBMS_STATS.AUTO_SAMPLE_SIZE,
          method_opt => 'FOR ALL COLUMNS SIZE AUTO');

  Rationale
  ---------
    The optimizer requires up-to-date statistics for the table in order to
    select a good execution plan.

2- Statistics Finding
---------------------
  Table "TPCDS"."STORE" and its indices were not analyzed.

  Recommendation
  --------------
  - Consider collecting optimizer statistics for this table and its indices.
      execute dbms_stats.gather_table_stats(ownname => 'TPCDS', tabname =>
          'STORE', estimate_percent => DBMS_STATS.AUTO_SAMPLE_SIZE,
          method_opt => 'FOR ALL COLUMNS SIZE AUTO', cascade => TRUE);

  Rationale
  ---------
    The optimizer requires up-to-date statistics for the table and its indices
    in order to select a good execution plan.
```

■ **Index Finding**   In this subsection the index creation recommendations are listed, including a rationale for creating the additional index and a potential benefit for the statement once that index is created. (See "Explain Plan Section" a bit later.)

```
3- Index Finding (see explain plans section below)
--------------------------------------------------

  The execution plan of this statement can be improved by creating one or more
  indices.

  Recommendation (estimated benefit: 89.4%)
  -----------------------------------------

  - Consider running the Access Advisor to improve the physical schema design
    or creating the recommended index.
    create index TPCDS.IDX$$_00E40001 on TPCDS.DATE_DIM("D_MONTH_SEQ","D_DATE_S
    K");


  Rationale
  ---------

    Creating the recommended indices significantly improves the execution plan
    of this statement. However, it might be preferable to run "Access Advisor"
    using a representative SQL workload as opposed to a single statement. This
    will allow to get comprehensive index recommendations which takes into
    account index maintenance overhead and additional space consumption.
```

■ **Alternative Plan Finding**   This subsection lists the findings related to alternative plans found in the shared SQL area or in historical AWR data that appear to offer better performance than the current plan the statement used. It also provides some suggestions to create SQL plan baselines. For the alternative plans, this subsection lists the plan hash, where the alternative plan was found, the last time when it was used, and the elapsed time in seconds.

```
4- Alternative Plan Finding
---------------------------

  Some alternative execution plans for this statement were found by searching
  the system's real-time and historical performance data.

  The following table lists these plans ranked by their average elapsed time.
  See section "ALTERNATIVE PLANS SECTION" for detailed information on each
  plan.

  id plan hash  last seen             elapsed (s)  origin       note
  -- ---------- -------------------   -----------  ------------ -----------
   1 2810692197 2016-12-27/11:10:18       0.102    STS
   2 3332687846 2017-01-16/01:24:56       0.179    Cursor Cache


  Information
  -----------

  - Because no execution history for the Original Plan was found, the SQL
    Tuning Advisor could not determine if any of these execution plans are
```

```
superior to it.  However, if you know that one alternative plan is better
than the Original Plan, you can create a SQL plan baseline for it. This
will instruct the Oracle optimizer to pick it over any other choices in
the future.
execute dbms_sqltune.create_sql_plan_baseline(task_name =>
       'STATASK01_QUERY70', object_id => 3, owner_name => 'SYS',
       plan_hash_value => xxxxxxxx);
```

■ **SQL Profile Finding** This subsection includes findings regarding SQL
profile creations that potentially can improve the execution time of the
SQL statement. It also provides the statement to create such SQL profiles.

Explain Plan Section

In this section, the SQL statement's original execution plan (Figure 3-3) as well as all
the plans that result from a recommendation (Figure 3-4) are shown. This makes it
easy to perform a fast comparison to confirm the benefit. In these examples, the
original plan is compared against the plan that results if the recommended index
was created.

There could be several new execution plans in the new plan (Using New
Indexes) section, each one for each recommendation given. In the example shown
in Figure 3-4, only one new plan is listed for space reasons.

```
1- Original
-----------
Plan hash value: 2938537100

---------------------------------------------------------------------------------------------
| Id  | Operation                     | Name       | Rows  | Bytes | Cost (%CPU)| Time     | Pstart| Pstop |
---------------------------------------------------------------------------------------------
|   0 | SELECT STATEMENT              |            | 1499  |  115K| 2441   (1) | 00:00:01 |       |       |
|   1 |  SORT ORDER BY                |            | 1499  |  115K| 2441   (1) | 00:00:01 |       |       |
|   2 |   WINDOW SORT                 |            | 1499  |  115K| 2441   (1) | 00:00:01 |       |       |
|   3 |    SORT GROUP BY ROLLUP       |            | 1499  |  115K| 2441   (1) | 00:00:01 |       |       |
|*  4 |     HASH JOIN                 |            | 1499  |  115K| 2438   (1) | 00:00:01 |       |       |
|*  5 |      HASH JOIN                |            | 1491  | 79023 | 1315   (1) | 00:00:01 |       |       |
|*  6 |       HASH JOIN SEMI          |            |   12  |   456 | 1226   (1) | 00:00:01 |       |       |
|   7 |        TABLE ACCESS FULL      | STORE      |   12  |   408 |    7   (0) | 00:00:01 |       |       |
|   8 |        VIEW                   | VW_NSO_1   | 1499  |  5996 | 1219   (1) | 00:00:01 |       |       |
|*  9 |         VIEW                  |            | 1499  | 25483 | 1219   (1) | 00:00:01 |       |       |
|* 10 |          WINDOW SORT PUSHED RANK|          | 1499  | 86942 | 1219   (1) | 00:00:01 |       |       |
|  11 |           HASH GROUP BY       |            | 1499  | 86942 | 1219   (1) | 00:00:01 |       |       |
|* 12 |            HASH JOIN          |            | 1499  | 86942 | 1218   (1) | 00:00:01 |       |       |
|* 13 |             HASH JOIN         |            | 1491  | 47712 |   95   (0) | 00:00:01 |       |       |
|  14 |              TABLE ACCESS FULL| STORE      |   12  |   204 |    7   (0) | 00:00:01 |       |       |
|  15 |              PARTITION RANGE ALL|          | 1534  | 23010 |   88   (0) | 00:00:01 |     1 |1048575|
|  16 |               TABLE ACCESS FULL| STORE_SALES| 1534 | 23010 |   88   (0) | 00:00:01 |     1 |1048575|
|* 17 |             TABLE ACCESS FULL | DATE_DIM   | 3543  | 92118 | 1123   (1) | 00:00:01 |       |       |
|  18 |            PARTITION RANGE ALL |           | 1534  | 23010 |   88   (0) | 00:00:01 |     1 |1048575|
|  19 |             TABLE ACCESS FULL | STORE_SALES| 1534  | 23010 |   88   (0) | 00:00:01 |     1 |1048575|
|* 20 | TABLE ACCESS FULL            | DATE_DIM   | 3543  | 92118 | 1123   (1) | 00:00:01 |       |       |
---------------------------------------------------------------------------------------------
```

FIGURE 3-3. *Original execution plan*

```
2- Using New Indices
--------------------
Plan hash value: 2388633030
```

Id	Operation	Name	Rows	Bytes	Cost (%CPU)	Time	Pstart	Pstop
0	SELECT STATEMENT		4811	371K	259 (2)	00:00:01		
1	SORT ORDER BY		4811	371K	259 (2)	00:00:01		
2	WINDOW SORT		4811	371K	259 (2)	00:00:01		
3	SORT GROUP BY ROLLUP		4811	371K	259 (2)	00:00:01		
* 4	HASH JOIN RIGHT SEMI		4811	371K	255 (1)	00:00:01		
5	VIEW	VW_NSO_1	4811	19244	128 (1)	00:00:01		
* 6	VIEW		4811	81787	128 (1)	00:00:01		
* 7	WINDOW SORT PUSHED RANK		4811	272K	128 (1)	00:00:01		
8	HASH GROUP BY		4811	272K	128 (1)	00:00:01		
* 9	HASH JOIN		4811	272K	127 (0)	00:00:01		
10	TABLE ACCESS FULL	STORE	12	204	7 (0)	00:00:01		
* 11	HASH JOIN		4949	198K	120 (0)	00:00:01		
12	PARTITION RANGE ALL		1534	23010	88 (0)	00:00:01	1	1048575
13	TABLE ACCESS FULL	STORE_SALES	1534	23010	88 (0)	00:00:01	1	1048575
* 14	INDEX RANGE SCAN	IDX$$_00E40001	5404	137K	32 (0)	00:00:01		
* 15	HASH JOIN		4811	352K	127 (0)	00:00:01		
16	TABLE ACCESS FULL	STORE	12	408	7 (0)	00:00:01		
* 17	HASH JOIN		4949	198K	120 (0)	00:00:01		
18	PARTITION RANGE ALL		1534	23010	88 (0)	00:00:01	1	1048575
19	TABLE ACCESS FULL	STORE_SALES	1534	23010	88 (0)	00:00:01	1	1048575
* 20	INDEX RANGE SCAN	IDX$$_00E40001	5404	137K	32 (0)	00:00:01		

FIGURE 3-4. *New execution plan with indexes*

NOTE
The authors strongly recommend that you first test any recommendations that SQL Tuning Advisor provides against a test or staging database system, and even then evaluate the viability of the recommendations based on personal judgment instead of blindly implementing those recommendations against a production system.

Using SQL Tuning Advisor in Enterprise Manager Cloud Control

SQL Tuning Advisor can also be executed from almost any version of Oracle Enterprise Manager Cloud Control. In this chapter, EM Cloud Control version 13c was used. EM Cloud Control allows a faster way to capture SQL statements, to analyze them with SQL Tuning Advisor, to review the recommendation, and to implement them with few clicks. To access SQL Tuning Advisor in EM Cloud Control 13c, go to the home page of the desired database and, from the Performance menu, choose SQL and then SQL Tuning Advisor. Once in SQL Tuning Advisor, you will see three main sources for SQL Tuning Advisor: Top Activity, Historical SQL (AWR), and SQL Tuning Sets.

For this example, select the Top Activity source. Next, you'll see a performance chart with the top activity shown, which includes the Top Sessions and the Top SQL Statements. In this page, you select the problematic SQL statements, select Schedule SQL Tuning Advisor, and then click the Go button to go to the Schedule SQL Tuning Advisor configuration area.

Some parameters will be required to configure the SQL Tuning Advisor, such as the Total Time Limit, the Scope Of Analysis, and when the task will run, either Immediately or Later (see Figure 3-5).

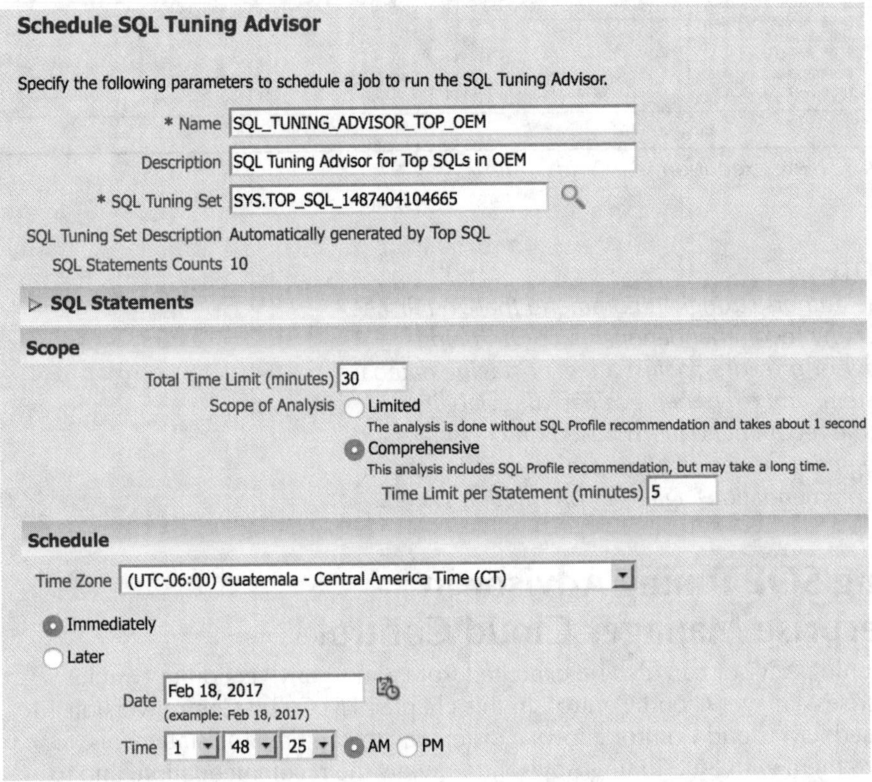

FIGURE 3-5. *Parameters to configure the SQL Tuning Advisor task*

SQL Tuning Advisor Results in EM Cloud Control 13c

Once the SQL Tuning Advisor task is completed, the recommendations are displayed. One of the advantages to using EM Cloud Control 13c to execute SQL Tuning Advisor is that the real benefit of the recommendations are shown in charts, which make it easier to understand how the SQL statements will improve after implementing the recommendations. In this example, Figure 3-6 shows a pie chart and a bar chart to summarize the analysis of the SQL profiles, to show statistics, and to show recommendations on the restructuring SQL statements.

The Figure 3-7 shows the second part of the summary of a SQL Tuning Advisor analysis. Here a bar chart shows the benefits if the recommendations are implemented, before and after.

The dramatic improvement can be confirmed if you click the Show All Results button (Figure 3-6). You'll see that a SQL profile creation results in a 99 percent performance benefit, as shown in Figure 3-8.

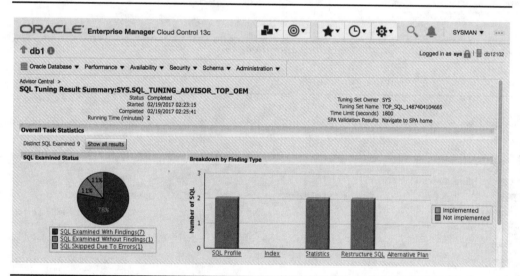

FIGURE 3-6. *Summary of a SQL Tuning Advisor analysis*

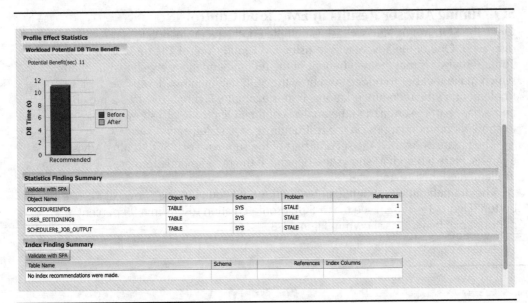

FIGURE 3-7. *Bar chart showing the before and after execution time*

Advisor Central > SQL Tuning Summary:SYS.SQL_TUNING_ADVISOR_TOP_OEM >

SQL Tuning Result Details: All Analyzed SQLs

Status	Completed	Tuning Set Owner	SYS
Started	02/19/2017 02:23:15	Tuning Set Name	TOP_SQL_1487404104665
Completed	02/19/2017 02:25:41	Time Limit (seconds)	1800
Running Time (minutes)	2		

Recommendations

Only profiles that significantly improve SQL performance were implemented.

View Recommendations   Implement All SQL Profiles   Validate All Profiles with SPA

Select	SQL Text	Parsing Schema ▼	SQL ID	Cumulative DB Time Benefit(sec)	Per-Execution % Benefit	Statistics	SQL Profile	Index	Restructure SQL	Alternative Plan	Miscellaneous	Timed Out	Error
●	WITH MONITOR_DATA AS (SELECT INST_ID, KE...	SYS	dfffkcnqfystw	10.49	99	✓	(99%) ✓						
○	SELECT /*+ OPT_PARAM('_fix_control' '163...	SYS	8mdz49zkajhw3										✓
○	with last_run as (SELECT all_runs.OWNE...	SYS	4d43by1zzjfna			✓					✓		
○	SELECT COUNT(1) FROM SYS.DBA_CAPTURE	SYS	1dbtz6cfqk1t1						✓		✓		
○	DECLARE shared_free_pct NUMBER; large_...	SYS	3z5dy8u30qmjf								✓		
○	SELECT m.tablespace_name, ROUND(m.used_...	SYS	5qdptu5gnkayq						✓		✓		
○	SELECT event#, sql_id, sql_plan_hash_val...	SYS	8d62ttmswmy01								✓		
○	SELECT TO_CHAR(END_TIME, 'YYYY-MM-DD HH2...	SYS	a39ac8w0f0fhh	0.05	24		(24%) ✓						
○	select open_mode from v$database	SYS	2nhzyn560xyhs										

Legend   ✓ Recommended   🄸 Implemented

FIGURE 3-8. *Details of each recommendation*

Summary

In this chapter, we discussed each kind of input and output that SQL Tuning Sets and SQL Tuning Advisor use, so that DBAs can know clearly what to expect from SQL Tuning Advisor and will see the differences among the recommendations given by SQL Tuning Advisor with other advisors in the database. We outlined a process DBAs can follow whenever they encounter performance issues in the database. Using these guidelines, DBAs can directly analyze SQL tuning statements without having to read hundreds of pages in the documentation. At the end of the chapter, we discussed how to interpret every section of the SQL Tuning Advisor report so that DBAs can learn about the reasons behind recommendations, their benefit, and how to implement them.

CHAPTER
4

SQL Access Advisor

In this chapter, you'll learn about the Oracle SQL Access Advisor, which is useful when you need to analyze how an object is being accessed and how to improve that access path to reduce the optimizer cost.

Oracle SQL Access Advisor, introduced in Oracle Database 10g, receives a real or hypothetical workload as input and then analyzes how each object involved in each SQL statement is being accessed. It uses Automatic Tuning Optimizer to perform the analysis of several hypothetical improvements and calculates the resulting optimizer cost of each improvement. It lists all improvements that offer considerable benefits compared with the optimizer cost of the original execution plan as recommendations that can be executed using a script.

Using SQL Access Advisor

SQL Access Advisor is customizable; the DBA can enable or disable a specific type of analysis to limit the type of recommendations it offers. The recommended scripts are also customizable, since the owner of each object can be provided, plus the tablespace name where each object (per type) should be created; in this way, after viewing the Advisor's script recommendations, the DBA can make modifications by providing metadata information to adapt the script to a specific database environment.

In Chapter 3, you used the package DBMS_SQLTUNE, which is a package specific to SQL Tuning Advisor. Other advisors have their own packages: Automatic Database Diagnostic Monitor (DBMS_ADDM), SQL Performance Analyzer (DBMS_SQLPA), and SQL Repair Advisor (DBMS_SQLDIAG). SQL Access Advisor and Segment Advisor share the package DBMS_ADVISOR.

NOTE
Using SQL Access Advisor requires licensing the Oracle Tuning Pack.

Analysis Sources

SQL Access Advisor can receive SQL statements from several sources, as shown in Figure 4-1.

Shared SQL Area

When the shared SQL area is used as the input for SQL Access Advisor, the function `DBMS_ADVISOR.IMPORT_SQLWKLD_SQLCACHE` is used. The function creates a workload object. A workload is a SQL statement or a set of SQL statements with execution statistics. After the workload is created, the function `DBMS_ADVISOR.ADD_SQLWKLD_REF` is used to link that workload to a SQL Access Advisor task.

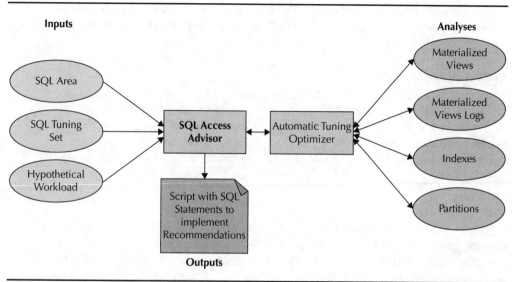

FIGURE 4-1. *SQL Access Advisor overview*

A SQL Tuning Set
By using SQL Tuning Sets (STS), several SQL statements can be included in a single object. To link an STS to a SQL Access Advisor task, use the function DBMS_ADVISOR .ADD_STS_REF. The function accepts the SQL Access Advisor task name, the owner of the STS, and the STS name.

Hypothetical Workload
This input is used when a real workload doesn't yet exist. In this case, the function DBMS_ADVISOR.SET_SQLWKLD_PARAMETER is used to set the schema that will be used to create the hypothetical workload. Then the function DBMS_ADVISOR .IMPORT_SQLWKLD_SCHEMA is used to create the hypothetical workload. With this method, the schema must contain dimensions.

Analysis Recommendations
After its analysis is complete, SQL Access Advisor will return one or more of the following recommendations.

Materialized Views
SQL Access Advisor can recommend that materialized views be retained, created, or dropped after its analysis. It also uses DBMS_ADVISOR.TUNE_MVIEW to optimize the existing materialized views to make them fast refreshable and to take advantage

of query rewrite. SQL Access Advisor also can recommend dropping materialized views if they are not used or if the benefit they offer is insufficient when compared with maintenance requirements.

Materialized View Logs

The materialized view log tracks all the changes performed by data manipulation languages (DMLs) on a base table, or master table. SQL Access Advisor can recommend that materialized view logs be created as part of its optimization for materialized views, because the logs are required to make the materialized views fast refreshable. SQL Access Advisor also can recommend dropping materialized view logs.

Indexes

SQL Access Advisor uses Automatic Tuning Optimizer to estimate the benefit of new indexes, to drop indexes, or to change the type of an existing index, such as changing from a B-Tree to a bitmap index. SQL Access Advisor can recommend bitmap, function-based, and B-Tree index types. SQL Access Advisor also analyses whether indexes are being used, and based on that information, it can recommend retaining or dropping them.

Partitions

In Oracle Database 10*g*, SQL Access Advisor was not able to make recommendations regarding partitions, but starting with Oracle Database 11*g*R2, SQL Access Advisor was enhanced with the analysis of the partitions, and since then it can recommend creation of new partitioned indexes on a table and on a materialized view, creation of a partition on an nonpartitioned table or an nonpartitioned index, or creation of a partition on a materialized view. When SQL Access Advisor recommends to partition a nonpartitioned table, it creates all the required steps, but it doesn't use `DBMS_REDEFINITION`—instead, it uses `INSERT AS SELECT` from the nonpartitioned table to the new partitioned table. Note that the SQL Access Advisor script doesn't drop the former nonpartitioned table; it has to be dropped manually, or the script has to be modified with the `DROP TABLE` statement.

Limiting the Analysis

In some situations, the DBA will decide not to follow the recommendations provided by SQL Access Advisor. To accommodate those situations, the scope of the SQL Access Advisor task must be updated to exclude those specific analyses. It's not possible to remove SQL statements from the script generated by SQL Access Advisor, because the script is created to be executed in its entirety. If some SQL statements are removed from the script, the remaining SQL statements would fail because of dependencies.

The correct approach is to limit the analysis of SQL Access Advisor before executing the advisor task. This is done using the function `DBMS_ADVISOR.SET_TASK_PARAMETER` with the parameter name `ANALYSIS_SCOPE`, which is a string of values separated by commas. The values can be the following:

- **ALL**   The default, which considers all kind of recommendations.

- **EVALUATION**   It estimates which access structures are candidates to be retained. It doesn't recommend new structure creations.

- **INDEX**   Considers recommendations related to indexes.

- **MVIEW**   Considers recommendations related to materialized view.

- **PARTITION**   Considers recommendations related to all kinds of partitions.

- **TABLE**   Considers recommendations related to tables, such as partitioning an nonpartitioned table.

Modes of Execution

SQL Access Advisor also can run in two execution modes, evaluation mode and problem-solving mode, which makes it even more customizable.

Evaluation Mode

In evaluation mode, SQL Access Advisor uses Automatic Tuning Optimizer to estimate which access structures in use are candidates to be retained. However, this mode doesn't analyze whether new access structures could be created to improve the optimizer cost or data access.

Every application goes through several changes throughout its life cycle; some access structures are created when an application is deployed, and other new access structures are created because tuning is a constant process. It is not unusual for a DBA to create a new index or structure to accommodate new WHERE clauses, SELECT statements, or DMLs that have been included, but often existing index or other access structures do not need to be retained later on. Throughout the application's life cycle, these access structures, which were once needed, are no longer required and can actually slow performance; in such cases, if the SQL statement structures were retained, instead of being beneficial to the application, they would reduce the application's performance, because even though they are no longer needed, they still have to be maintained by the database.

Consider, for example, redundant indexes. Suppose a DBA is planning to analyze which access structures are no longer needed, either because they are no longer used by the optimizer or because the maintenance overhead is too great. Running SQL Access Advisor in evaluation mode is a good practice in such cases.

Problem-Solving Mode

This mode performs the same analysis as evaluation mode, but it also analyzes the creation of new access structures that improve the optimizer cost, such as new indexes, new materialized views, and so on. This mode is recommended when a DBA is looking for improvements to the SQL statements that would entail removing unnecessary access structures as well as creating new access structures. For every recommendation delivered by SQL Access Advisor, the pre-optimizer and post-optimizer costs are provided as well, so that the DBA can determine whether implementing the recommendations is worth the effort.

Analysis Scope

The scope of any SQL Access Advisor task can be limited to prevent excessive resource consumption:

- **Limited scope**   When limited scope is used, SQL Access Advisor performs an analysis that focuses on improving problematic SQL statements instead of performing maintenance tasks, such as dropping an unused index. Basically, the analysis focuses on highest-cost SQL statements.

- **Comprehensive scope**   When SQL Access Advisor uses this scope, it performs all the analyses for maintenance tasks as well as tasks to improve SQL statements. It is the full mode.

The following table lists the features that are enabled in each Scope:

Recommendation	Comprehensive	Limited
Add new [partitioned] index on a table	Yes	Yes
Add a new [partitioned] index on a materialized view	Yes	Yes
Add a new [partitioned] materialized view	Yes	Yes
Drop an unused index	Yes	No
Change an index type	Yes	No
Add columns at the end of an index	Yes	Yes
Drop unused materialized view	Yes	No
Drop unused materialized view log	Yes	No
Add new materialized view log	Yes	Yes
Add more columns or clauses to a materialized view log	Yes	Yes
Partition a nonpartitioned table	Yes	Yes
Partition a nonpartitioned index	Yes	Yes

Example: Tuning a SQL Statement with SQL Access Advisor

As we did in Chapter 3, our approach is always to test the recommendations on a test database before deciding to execute any recommendations in the corresponding production environment. In reactive situations, every recommendation provided by SQL Access Advisor must be validated by the DBA, who will take only appropriate actions.

Creating a SQL Tuning Set

In this example, we will use an STS as the input and reuse the STS named STS_QUERY82 that was created in Chapter 3, which includes query #82 from the TPC-DS benchmark queries run via Swingbench. This query is easily identifiable by the hint /* query82 */. Only the values for some variables were replaced in the query #82 template:

```
select /* query82 */  i_item_id
        ,i_item_desc
        ,i_current_price
 from item, inventory, date_dim, store_sales
 where i_current_price between 30 and 60
 and inv_item_sk = i_item_sk
 and d_date_sk=inv_date_sk
 and d_date between '30-MAY-95' and '30-JUL-03'
 and i_manufact_id in (437,191,515,649,129,727,663)
 and inv_quantity_on_hand between 10 and 50000
 and ss_item_sk = i_item_sk
 group by i_item_id,i_item_desc,i_current_price
 order by i_item_id;
```

An experienced DBA might be able to point out what should be the first things to review to determine what's wrong with this SQL statement and confirm in some minutes the root cause. The goal here, as in the previous chapter, is to prove that SQL Access Advisor would be as exact as our experience and will deliver the same root cause (or a deeper root cause), with the same recommendations, better recommendations, or more recommendations.

Creating a SQL Tuning Task

A SQL Access Advisor task must be created so that the specified STS can be analyzed:

```
SQL> VARIABLE task_id NUMBER
SQL> VARIABLE task_name VARCHAR2(255);
SQL> EXECUTE :task_name := 'SQLAccessAdvisorTask';

PL/SQL procedure successfully completed.
```

```
SQL> EXECUTE DBMS_ADVISOR.CREATE_TASK('SQL Access Advisor', :task_id, :task_name);

PL/SQL procedure successfully completed.
```

Linking the SQL Access Advisor Task with the STS

Once the task is created, it must be linked to the STS so that the analysis can
be performed:

```
SQL> EXECUTE DBMS_ADVISOR.ADD_STS_REF('SQLAccessAdvisorTask', 'SYS', 'STS_QUERY82');

PL/SQL procedure successfully completed.
```

Configuring the Task

In this step, several parameters are set for the task; this is where the scope, the mode,
and the types of analyses are set. Most of those parameters have a default value.

```
EXECUTE DBMS_ADVISOR.SET_TASK_PARAMETER('SQLAccessAdvisorTask', 'TIME_LIMIT', 3000);
EXECUTE DBMS_ADVISOR.SET_TASK_PARAMETER('SQLAccessAdvisorTask', 'ANALYSIS_SCOPE', 'ALL');
EXECUTE DBMS_ADVISOR.SET_TASK_PARAMETER('SQLAccessAdvisorTask', 'MODE', 'COMPREHENSIVE');
EXECUTE DBMS_ADVISOR.SET_TASK_PARAMETER('SQLAccessAdvisorTask', 'CREATION_COST', 'TRUE');
EXECUTE DBMS_ADVISOR.SET_TASK_PARAMETER('SQLAccessAdvisorTask', 'MAX_NUMBER_PARTITIONS', 10);
EXECUTE DBMS_ADVISOR.SET_TASK_PARAMETER('SQLAccessAdvisorTask', 'DEF_INDEX_OWNER', 'TPCDS');
EXECUTE DBMS_ADVISOR.SET_TASK_PARAMETER('SQLAccessAdvisorTask', 'DEF_INDEX_TABLESPACE', 'TPCDS_IDX');
EXECUTE DBMS_ADVISOR.SET_TASK_PARAMETER('SQLAccessAdvisorTask', 'DEF_MVIEW_OWNER', 'TPCDS');
EXECUTE DBMS_ADVISOR.SET_TASK_PARAMETER('SQLAccessAdvisorTask', 'DEF_MVIEW_TABLESPACE', 'TPCDS_DATA');
EXECUTE DBMS_ADVISOR.SET_TASK_PARAMETER('SQLAccessAdvisorTask', 'DEF_MVLOG_TABLESPACE', 'TPCDS_DATA');
EXECUTE DBMS_ADVISOR.SET_TASK_PARAMETER('SQLAccessAdvisorTask', 'DEF_PARTITION_TABLESPACE', 'TPCDS_DATA');
```

Executing a SQL Tuning Task

Now that the task has been successfully created and configured, it's time to
execute it:

```
SQL> EXECUTE DBMS_ADVISOR.EXECUTE_TASK('SQLAccessAdvisorTask');

PL/SQL procedure successfully completed.
```

Monitoring a SQL Tuning Task

While the task is running, it can be monitored to know how long it will take and
the percentage of completion. To do so, the views DBA_ADVISOR_TASKS and
V$ADVISOR_PROGRESS can be used.

Here is an example using `DBA_ADVISOR_TASKS`:

```
SQL> select owner, task_id, task_name, status, status_message, pct_completion_time
from dba_advisor_tasks where task_name='SQLAccessAdvisorTask';

OWNER TASK_ID TASK_NAME            STATUS    STATUS_MESSAGE       PCT_COMPLETION_TIME
----- ------- -------------------- --------- -------------------- -------------------
SYS       280 SQLAccessAdvisorTask EXECUTING Generating materiali                   0
                                             zed view candidates
                                             (0%)
```

NOTE
The view `DBA_ADVISOR_LOG` *also can be used.*

Displaying the Results of a SQL Tuning Task

Once the task has completed without any timeouts, the findings and recommendations will be ready for viewing. The view `DBA_ADVISOR_ACTIONS` has all the recommendations. The column `REC_ID` identifies the number of the recommendation. SQL Access Advisor can provide several recommendations in a single execution. The column `ACTION_ID` shows the unique identifier of the action of one specific recommendation (`REC_ID`):

```
SQL> SELECT rec_id, action_id, command FROM DBA_ADVISOR_ACTIONS  WHERE
task_name = 'SQLAccessAdvisorTask' ORDER BY rec_id, action_id;

    REC_ID ACTION_ID COMMAND
---------- --------- ----------------------------
         1         1 PARTITION TABLE
         1         2 CREATE MATERIALIZED VIEW LOG
         1         4 CREATE MATERIALIZED VIEW LOG
         1         6 CREATE MATERIALIZED VIEW LOG
         1         8 CREATE MATERIALIZED VIEW LOG
         1        10 CREATE MATERIALIZED VIEW
         1        11 GATHER TABLE STATISTICS
         1        12 CREATE INDEX

8 rows selected.
```

To know how the SQL statements in the STS will be improved, the view `DBA_ADVISOR_SQLA_WK_STMTS` can be used:

```
SQL> SELECT sql_id, rec_id, precost, postcost, round((precost-
postcost)*100/precost,3) AS per_benefit  FROM DBA_ADVISOR_SQLA_WK_STMTS
WHERE task_name = 'SQLAccessAdvisorTask' ;

SQL_ID        REC_ID PRECOST POSTCOST PER_BENEFIT
------------- ------ ------- -------- -----------
6wzu736hx4fcq      1  591116       28      99.995
```

Creating a Script with the Recommendations

All the SQL statements to implement the recommendations can be sent to a script. To create the script, an Oracle directory object must first be created:

```
SQL> create directory SQLAccessAdvisorOutput as '/home/oracle/
SQLAccessAdvisorOutput';

Directory created.
```

Then the function `DBMS_ADVISOR.CREATE_FILE` is called to send out all SQL statements to implement all the recommendations:

```
SQL> exec DBMS_ADVISOR.CREATE_FILE(
        buffer => DBMS_ADVISOR.GET_TASK_SCRIPT('SQLAccessAdvisorTask'),
-- Task Name
        location =>'SQLACCESSADVISOROUTPUT', -- Directory
        filename =>'SQLAccessAdvisor_Script.sql'); -- Name of the file

PL/SQL procedure successfully completed.
```

Once the procedure is completed, the script with all the SQL statements to implement the recommendations can be reviewed:

```
cat /home/oracle/SQLAccessAdvisorOutput/SQLAccessAdvisor_Script.sql

Rem   SQL Access Advisor: Version 12.1.0.2.0 - Production
Rem
Rem   Username:         SYS
Rem   Task:            SQLAccessAdvisorTask
Rem   Execution date:
Rem


Rem
Rem   Repartitioning table "TPCDS"."ITEM"
Rem

SET SERVEROUTPUT ON
SET ECHO ON

Rem
Rem Creating new partitioned table
Rem
  CREATE TABLE "TPCDS"."ITEM1"
    (   "I_ITEM_SK" NUMBER(*,0),
        "I_ITEM_ID" CHAR(16),
        "I_REC_START_DATE" DATE,
        "I_REC_END_DATE" DATE,
        "I_ITEM_DESC" VARCHAR2(200),
        "I_CURRENT_PRICE" NUMBER(7,2),
```

```
          "I_WHOLESALE_COST" NUMBER(7,2),
          "I_BRAND_ID" NUMBER(*,0),
          "I_BRAND" CHAR(50),
          "I_CLASS_ID" NUMBER(*,0),
          "I_CLASS" CHAR(50),
          "I_CATEGORY_ID" NUMBER(*,0),
          "I_CATEGORY" CHAR(50),
          "I_MANUFACT_ID" NUMBER(*,0),
          "I_MANUFACT" CHAR(50),
          "I_SIZE" CHAR(20),
          "I_FORMULATION" CHAR(20),
          "I_COLOR" CHAR(20),
          "I_UNITS" CHAR(10),
          "I_CONTAINER" CHAR(10),
          "I_MANAGER_ID" NUMBER(*,0),
          "I_PRODUCT_NAME" CHAR(50)
     )
PARTITION BY RANGE ("I_ITEM_SK") INTERVAL( 18) STORE IN ( "TPCDS_DATA" ) ( PARTITION
        VALUES LESS THAN (18) );


Rem
Rem Copying constraints to new partitioned table
Rem
   ALTER TABLE "TPCDS"."ITEM1" ADD CONSTRAINT "ITEM_PK1" PRIMARY KEY ("I_ITEM_SK") DISABLE;
   ALTER TABLE "TPCDS"."ITEM1" MODIFY ("I_ITEM_ID" NOT NULL ENABLE);
   ALTER TABLE "TPCDS"."ITEM1" MODIFY ("I_ITEM_SK" NOT NULL ENABLE);
Rem
Rem Copying indexes to new partitioned table
Rem
   CREATE UNIQUE INDEX "TPCDS"."ITEM_PK_IDX1" ON "TPCDS"."ITEM1" ("I_ITEM_SK")
   PCTFREE 10 INITRANS 2 MAXTRANS 255 COMPUTE STATISTICS
   TABLESPACE "TPCDS_IDX" ;
   ALTER INDEX "TPCDS"."ITEM_PK_IDX1"  UNUSABLE;
Rem
Rem Populating new partitioned table with data from original table
Rem
INSERT /*+ APPEND */ INTO "TPCDS"."ITEM1"
    SELECT * FROM "TPCDS"."ITEM";
COMMIT;


begin
  dbms_stats.gather_table_stats('"TPCDS"', '"ITEM1"', NULL, dbms_stats.auto_sample_size);
end;
/


Rem
Rem Renaming tables to give new partitioned table the original table name
Rem
ALTER TABLE "TPCDS"."ITEM" RENAME TO "ITEM11";
ALTER TABLE "TPCDS"."ITEM1" RENAME TO "ITEM";
```

```
CREATE MATERIALIZED VIEW LOG ON
    "TPCDS"."STORE_SALES"
    TABLESPACE "TPCDS_DATA"
    WITH ROWID, SEQUENCE("SS_SOLD_DATE_SK","SS_ITEM_SK","SS_CUSTOMER_SK","SS_ADDR_SK","SS_
TICKET_NUMBER")
    INCLUDING NEW VALUES;

CREATE MATERIALIZED VIEW LOG ON
    "TPCDS"."INVENTORY"
    TABLESPACE "TPCDS_DATA"
    WITH ROWID, SEQUENCE("INV_DATE_SK","INV_ITEM_SK","INV_QUANTITY_ON_HAND")
    INCLUDING NEW VALUES;

CREATE MATERIALIZED VIEW LOG ON
    "TPCDS"."ITEM"
    TABLESPACE "TPCDS_DATA"
    WITH ROWID, SEQUENCE("I_ITEM_SK","I_ITEM_ID","I_ITEM_DESC","I_CURRENT_PRICE","I_BRAND_
ID","I_BRAND","I_CLASS_ID","I_CLASS","I_CATEGORY_ID","I_CATEGORY","I_MANUFACT_ID")
    INCLUDING NEW VALUES;

CREATE MATERIALIZED VIEW LOG ON
    "TPCDS"."DATE_DIM"
    TABLESPACE "TPCDS_DATA"
    WITH ROWID, SEQUENCE("D_DATE_SK","D_DATE","D_YEAR","D_QOY")
    INCLUDING NEW VALUES;

CREATE MATERIALIZED VIEW "TPCDS"."MV$$_01180000"
    TABLESPACE "TPCDS_DATA"
    REFRESH FAST WITH ROWID
    ENABLE QUERY REWRITE
    AS SELECT TPCDS.INVENTORY.INV_QUANTITY_ON_HAND C1, TPCDS.ITEM.I_MANUFACT_ID C2,
        TPCDS.ITEM.I_CURRENT_PRICE C3, TPCDS.ITEM.I_ITEM_DESC C4, TPCDS.ITEM.I_ITEM_ID
        C5, TPCDS.DATE_DIM.D_DATE C6, COUNT(*) M1 FROM TPCDS.STORE_SALES, TPCDS.INVENTORY,
        TPCDS.ITEM, TPCDS.DATE_DIM WHERE TPCDS.ITEM.I_ITEM_SK = TPCDS.STORE_SALES.SS_ITEM_SK
        AND TPCDS.ITEM.I_ITEM_SK = TPCDS.INVENTORY.INV_ITEM_SK AND TPCDS.DATE_DIM.D_DATE_SK
        = TPCDS.INVENTORY.INV_DATE_SK AND (TPCDS.ITEM.I_CURRENT_PRICE <= 60) AND
        (TPCDS.ITEM.I_CURRENT_PRICE >= 30) AND (TPCDS.ITEM.I_MANUFACT_ID IN (727,
        663, 649, 515, 437, 191, 129)) AND (TPCDS.INVENTORY.INV_QUANTITY_ON_HAND
        <= 50000) AND (TPCDS.INVENTORY.INV_QUANTITY_ON_HAND >= 10) GROUP BY TPCDS.INVENTORY.
INV_QUANTITY_ON_HAND,
        TPCDS.ITEM.I_MANUFACT_ID, TPCDS.ITEM.I_CURRENT_PRICE, TPCDS.ITEM.I_ITEM_DESC,
        TPCDS.ITEM.I_ITEM_ID, TPCDS.DATE_DIM.D_DATE;

begin
  dbms_stats.gather_table_stats('"TPCDS"','"MV$$_01180000"',NULL,dbms_stats.auto_sample_
size);
end;
/

CREATE INDEX "TPCDS"."MV$$_01180000_IDX$$_01180000"
    ON "TPCDS"."MV$$_01180000"
    ("C6")
    COMPUTE STATISTICS
    TABLESPACE "TPCDS_IDX";
```

Unfortunately, `DBMS_ADVISOR.GET_TASK_REPORT` and `DBMS_SQLTUNE` `.REPORT_TUNING_TASK` don't work for SQL Access Advisor tasks; if you try to use these functions, you will get the error ORA-13699 and ORA-13785, respectively. The views `DBA_ADVISOR_FINDINGS` and `DBA_ADVISOR_RATIONALE` also don't get populated by SQL Access Advisor. So we cannot get a detailed report with rationales for every finding. In this example, the first recommendation that will be implemented by the script is to convert the nonpartitioned table TPCDS.ITEM to a new partitioned table, probably because it speeds up the access for queries that filter the result by the column `I_ITEM_SK`. There are also four recommendations to create materialized view logs with the clause `WITH ROWID, SEQUENCE (...)` `INCLUDING NEW VALUES`, which provides fast refresh of materialized views, since it records changes on the `ROWID` of the master table (old values and new values) plus additional ordering information. Then a fast refreshable materialized view is recommended that takes advantage from the previous materialized view logs. At the end, an index on the materialized view is recommended.

As you can see, all the recommendations are considered as a whole, and that's why previously we highlighted that just removing a SQL statement from the result script would make the other SQL statements fail because of dependencies. With these recommendations, the access to the objects in the TPC-DS query #82 will be improved, and the query will benefit by 99.99 percent.

Using SQL Access Advisor in Enterprise Manager Cloud Control

Oracle Enterprise Manager Cloud Control also provides all the SQL Access Advisor functionality. In this chapter, Oracle Enterprise Manager Cloud Control 13c is used to run SQL Access Advisor to analyze the top activity of a database.

To access the SQL Access Advisor, log in into EM Cloud Control and go to the home page of the desired database. Then, from the Performance menu, choose SQL and then SQL Access Advisor. Two options are shown (see Figure 4-2): The first option is to verify only if some structures are being used but the creation of new structures won't be analyzed. This is analogous to using the evaluation mode described earlier in the chapter. The second option is to analyze the creation of new structures. Depending on what you need, select the desired option.

The SQL statements will be taken from the three sources listed in Figure 4-3: Current And Recent SQL Activity takes all the SQL statements from the shared SQL area. Use An Existing SQL Tuning Set enables you to select an already created SQL Tuning Set. Create A Hypothetical Workload From The Following Schemas And Tables enables you to select tables from a schema and create a custom workload to analyze. If a problematic SQL statement is running at the time, your best option is Current And Recent SQL Activity.

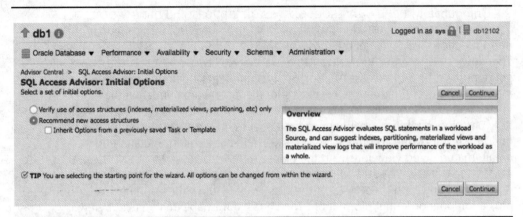

FIGURE 4-2. *SQL Access Advisor: Initial Options*

If the mode Recommend New Access Structures was selected in the first step (shown in Figure 4-2), the Recommendation Options page will be displayed, where the DBA can check or uncheck the structures to get recommendations (see Figure 4-4). The scope of the analysis is also selected on this page: Limited or Comprehensive.

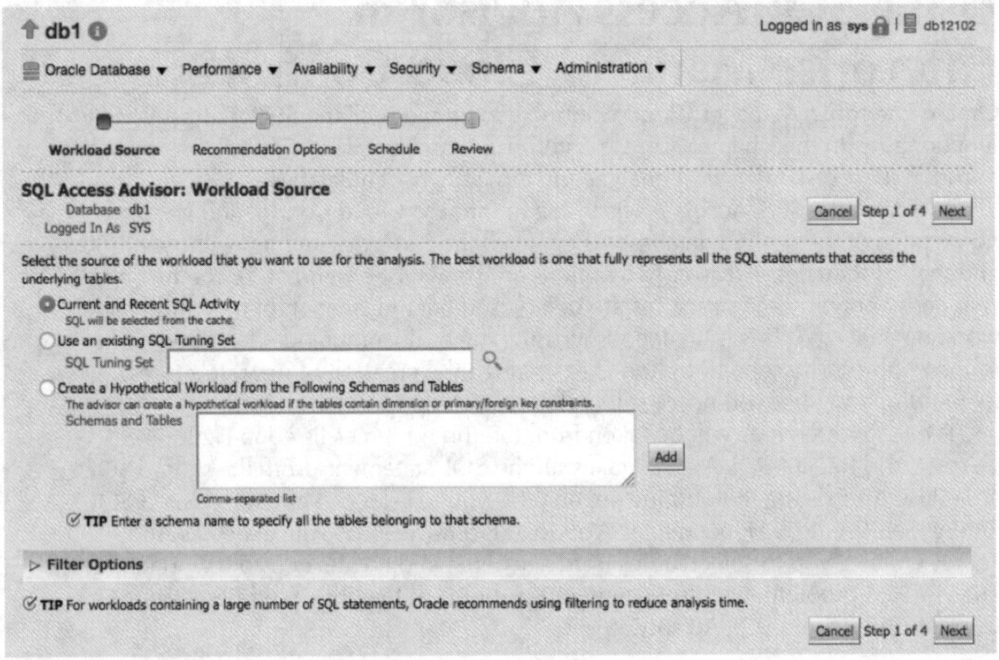

FIGURE 4-3. *SQL Access Advisor: Workload Source step*

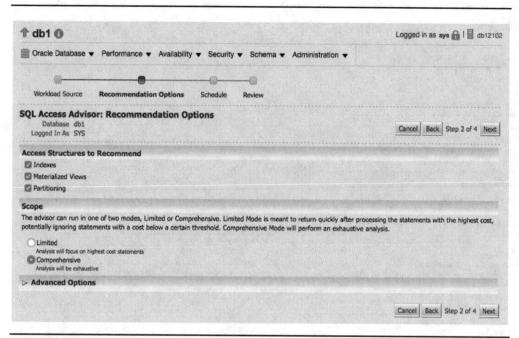

FIGURE 4-4. *SQL Access Advisor: Recommendation Options*

You can expand the Advanced Options (see Figure 4-5) tab to show several other options that the DBA can modify, such as where to store the new structures in case the recommendations are implemented, how to prioritize SQL statements, and so on.

In the next step, Schedule (see Figure 4-6), you enter several options regarding the SQL Access Advisor task, such as the name of the task, when the task will be executed, how long the task should run, the time zone, and other information. In this example, the task name is SQLACCESS883452, the time zone is Guatemala, the task will run immediately, and it will run for 30 minutes.

All the recommendations are available when the task is completed; however, even if the task is still running, some recommendations are shown (Figure 4-7), but we recommend that you review the complete result when the task is completed and all the recommendations are listed. In Figure 4-7, you can see several recommendations already listed by SQL Access Advisor—for example, creation of 198 Indexes, 129 Materialized Views, and 57 Materialized View Logs. An advantage to seeing the result of SQL Access Advisor in EM Cloud Control is that it offers a comparison between the original cost and the new cost if the recommendations are implemented, and it also includes a histogram style chart, in which a bar shows how many SQL statements will be improved—2x, 4x, 6x, 8x, 10x, or even more.

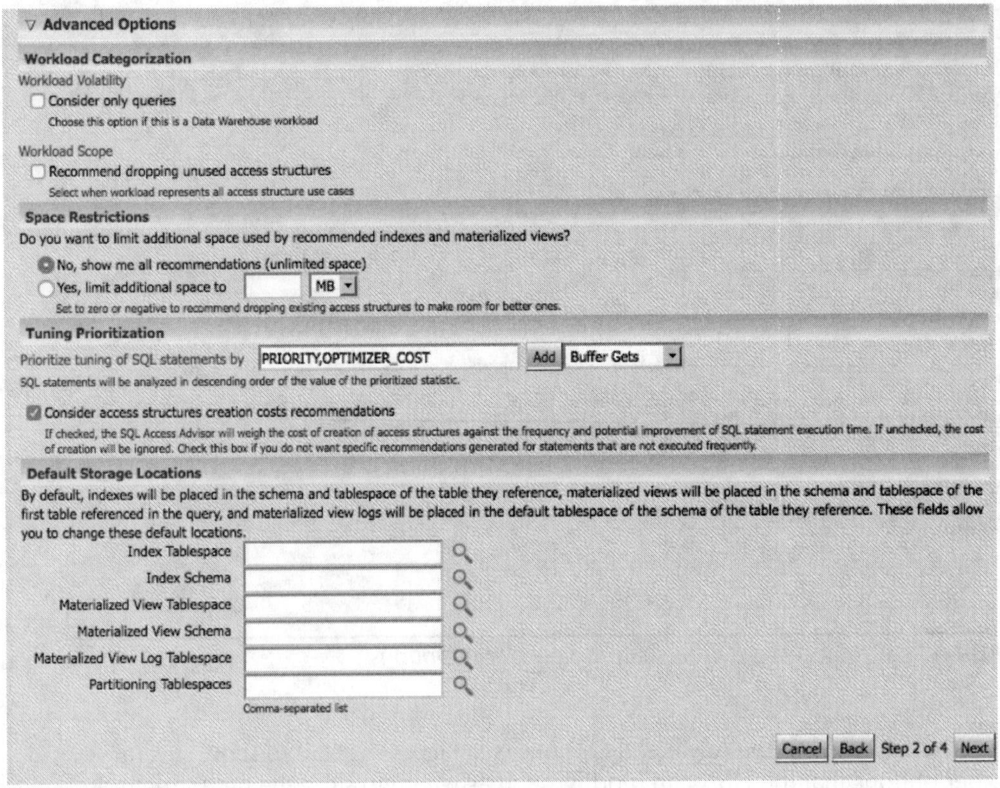

FIGURE 4-5. *SQL Access Advisor: Advanced Options*

Select the Recommendations tab to see more details for every recommendation, as shown in Figure 4-8. This is really useful because it enables you to see the big picture of the all analyses performed by SQL Access Advisor. In the column Action Types, there are squares of specific colors, with each color representing a type of recommendation, such as Index, Materialized Views, Materialized View Logs, Partitions, and others.

Click the button Recommendation Details to see another page with other details for every recommendation, as shown in Figure 4-9. This page is also useful because enables you to see a comparison between the original cost and the new cost after implementing a recommendation, plus a percentage of the improvement.

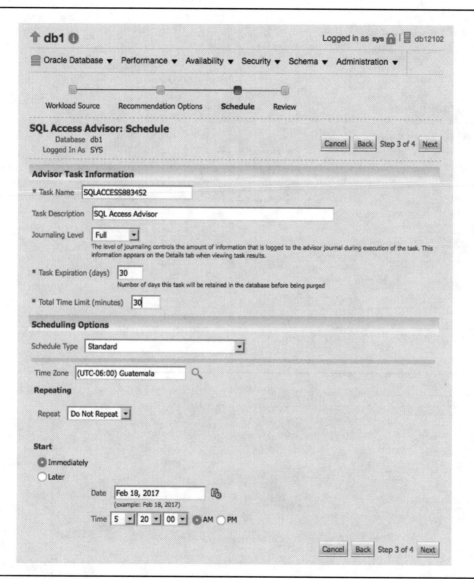

FIGURE 4-6.   *SQL Access Advisor: Schedule*

The last step is to implement the recommendations—but we strongly recommend that you implement all those changes in a test environment first to verify the performance improvements and then safely implement them in a production environment.

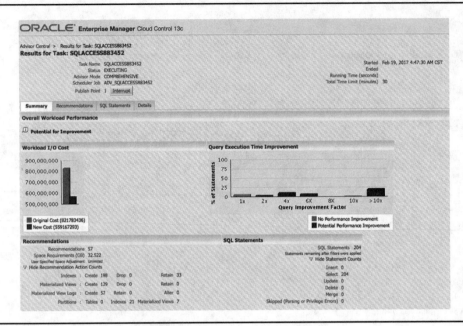

FIGURE 4-7. *SQL Access Advisor: Summary*

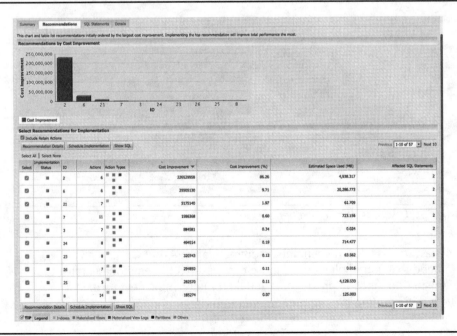

FIGURE 4-8. *SQL Access Advisor: Recommendations*

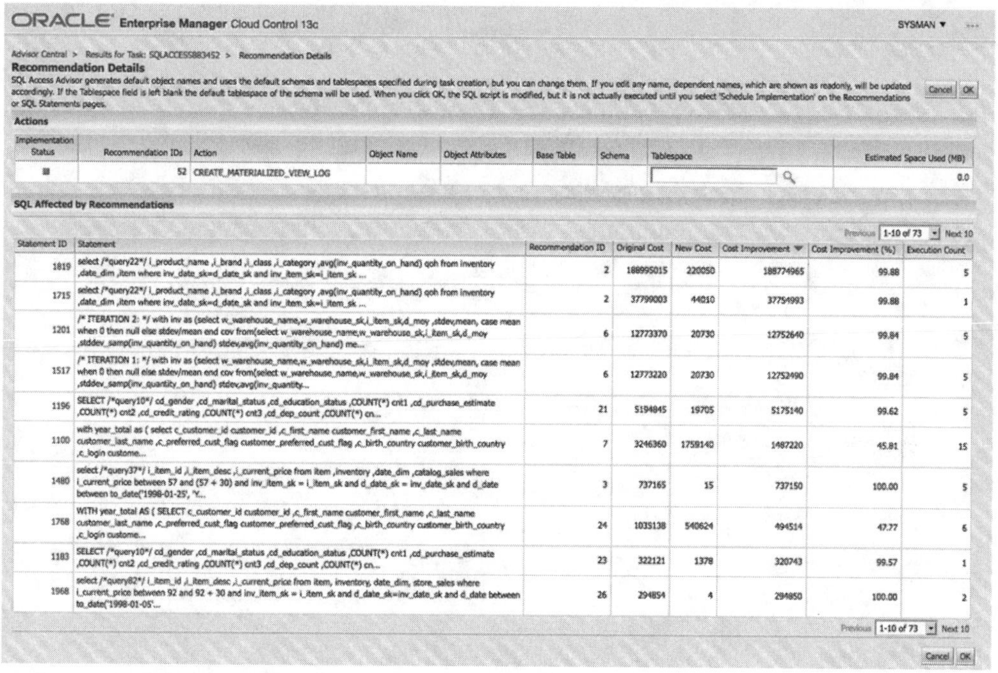

FIGURE 4-9.   *SQL Access Advisor: Recommendation Details*

Summary

In this chapter we outlined all the inputs and outputs used with SQL Access Advisor so that the DBA can know exactly what to expect from it. We also described in detail which scenarios should require a limited scope of SQL Access Advisor and in which scenarios it's better to use a comprehensive scope. DBAs can use SQL procedures to execute SQL Access Advisor but also have the option of using EM Cloud Control, and we described some advantages of using one over the other. At the end of the chapter, we explained the results provided by SQL Access Advisor when it was executed via console and via EM Cloud Control. Every recommendation type was explained by SQL Access Advisor. When SQL Access Advisor is executed, not only are recommendations listed, but other useful information also is provided—such as a comparison between original costs and the new costs to implement recommendations—so that the DBA will be able to know whether to follow or disregard recommendations.

CHAPTER
5

SQL Plan Management

Oracle DBAs and database developers have for many years counted on tuning SQL statements by examining and refining the internal database engine's SQL optimizer *execution plans*, which are often colloquially referred to as "explain plans," even though "execution plans" is a far more accurate name. Since it's generally accepted that many, if not most, database performance issues result from executing inefficient or resource-intensive SQL code, execution plan understanding has become a central tuning technique. As such, execution plans are often analyzed as part of development unit testing, peer code reviews, stress testing, and acceptance testing. Moreover, when database performance varies widely because of resource consumption or contention issues, after discarding the instance and OS, DBAs look for the offending SQL statement and examine the aberrant execution plan.

However, one major challenge has always existed with most execution plans—they can and do change over time, often without warning and sometimes with suboptimal performance ramifications. Much like Global Positioning System (GPS) with the trip selection mode set to the shortest route that avoids any construction, the normal itinerary traveled may suddenly change, increasing both the distance and duration. What's needed is a mechanism to "lock in" an execution plan so that neither natural database evolution nor routine DBA activities adversely affect SQL runtime. SQL Plan Management helps DBAs manage and control the regression behavior of their applications' SQL statements runtime over time.

What Affects Execution Plans

What changes can affect an execution plan? The obvious answers are DBA-initiated alterations of the database software itself or contained persistent database structures such as tables and indexes. But this very concise and digestible answer is an oversimplification of what changes can affect an execution plan. A considerably more comprehensive but still incomplete list of database and operating system changes that can affect database performance includes four major categories, each spanning numerous contributors:

Database Software

- Minor version upgrade
- Major version upgrade
- Bundle patch (BP), as it may contain Cost Based Optimizer (CBO) fixes

Database Configuration

- Initialization parameter changes

- Database or tablespace block size changes

- Temp or undo tablespace changes

Database Objects

- Index creation, removal, or alteration

- Table extended properties alteration

- Statistics and/or histogram changes

- Table major reorganization changes

Natural Data Evolution (via dynamic sampling)

- Row count reduction or growth

- Data skew introduction or growth

- Partition count increase resulting from data growth

- Overall database size reduction or growth

The crucial point is that many factors can radically affect overall database performance—including a great many that can also negatively affect execution plans over time. Since change is natural and inevitable, Oracle DBAs and database developers should not expect that a SQL statement's runtime performance will persist over time without some mechanism to, at least, lock in a specific execution plan—hence the need for SQL Plan Management. But note, however, that although the execution plan may remain relatively constant under SQL Plan Management, the actual runtime performance can still take longer for understandable reasons (such as data growth).

Evolution of Execution Plan Improvements

Because any execution plan's resulting runtime performance is of such paramount importance, Oracle has offered several noteworthy features for improvement over time. Although the older solutions such as stored outlines and SQL profiles should generally not be used (or at least not first), possessing a basic understanding of all such deprecated or out-of-favor methods is worthwhile for several reasons. First, knowing this historical background information provides a useful context for understanding and appreciating the current approach of SQL Plan Management. Second, this background shows how important the issue really is, since Oracle has worked so hard to find an optimal solution. In fact, Oracle should be commended for having the intelligence and courage to evolve its solution while deprecating those that failed to deliver reliably.

Starting with Oracle 8i (and improved in Oracle 9i), the execution plan improvement mechanism was called *stored outlines*, sometimes abbreviated to *outlines*. Basically, this approach stores a collection of optimizer hints to be applied to a specific SQL statement that shouldn't permit the optimizer much (if any) flexibility to come up with an alternative plan. Originally, the recorded SQL statement and the target SQL statement had to match character-for-character. Later, the SQL statement matching algorithm was relaxed to ignore white space. Note that stored outlines are not guaranteed to provide 100 percent plan stability due to the general and universal limitations of optimizer hints. That shortcoming is rather easy to overlook since stored outlines do not require any additional licensing. They were considered useful in two key scenarios: with third-party applications, where it's often impossible to change source code, and to mitigate plan variation due to bind variable peeking.

Beginning with Oracle 10g (and improved in Oracle 11g), the next step of execution plan improvement was a mechanism called *SQL profiles*. Essentially, this approach stores a collection of special-purpose hints; these do not suggest a specific plan or plan step, but instead provide auxiliary statistics to assist the SQL query optimizer in picking an optimal execution plan (and also to avoid certain recognized SQL optimizer troubles). Because of this rather unique approach, SQL profiles were never intended to provide plan stability; in fact, based upon evolving statistics, the resulting execution plan could change quite frequently. Moreover, existence of SQL profiles overrides any optimizer hints in the SQL statement itself. Nonetheless, they were considered very useful, because they are entirely transparent to the user and require no coding changes whatsoever. Furthermore, profiles are generally immune to the changes that can affect an execution plan (covered in the prior section). However, since profiles require the SQL Tuning Advisor, it is necessary to license Oracle Enterprise Edition as well as the optional Diagnostic and Tuning Packs. Many DBAs would argue that these packs are must-haves and should always be purchased. Once you have experienced what these optional packs offer, you may well agree; it's hard to function successfully without them.

With Oracle 11g and beyond, SQL Plan Management relies on *SQL plan baselines*, sometimes abbreviated to *SQL baselines*. The remainder of this chapter will cover in detail the setup and usage of SQL baselines. This approach offers a key advantage over prior techniques because it can almost guarantee that SQL statement runtime performance will not regress over time (unless there are substantial data size increases). Once the DBA or database developer manually accepts—or allows the database itself to accept automatically—an execution plan as superior and thus preferred (a process referred to as "evolution with the verify flag set to true"), only then can an execution plan with a legitimately recognized improved runtime escalate to preferred status versus the existing pool of SQL baselines. The end result: performance should always be equal or better.

NOTE
If you want to use SQL Tuning Sets (STS) from the SQL Tuning Advisor as an input source for SQL plan baselines, licensing Oracle Enterprise Edition with the optional Diagnostic and Tuning Packs is also required.

Understanding Plan Stability Internals

Before we can work successfully with plan stability, we need a thorough understanding of how the internals are stored and the processing occurs. Once we can naturally visualize these, using plan management is far easier.

Plan Management Storage

SQL plan management consumes space in the SYSAUX tablespace. It is stored in the SQL management base (SMB), which comprises two key areas: the SQL statement log, where the database records SQL IDs in order to recognize those SQL statements that repeat, and the SQL plan history, where prior to Oracle 12c only repeatedly executed SQL IDs were stored along with corresponding execution plans of various statuses; starting with version 12c, this information is captured for all SQL statements (even if they do not repeat). This basic structure is shown in Figure 5-1.

NOTE
Most Oracle documentation and content available on the Web show the same basic information in Figure 5-1 as Venn diagrams (of a sort), with circles inside of circles. That presentation style, however, does not make as clear the concept of plan statuses (accepted, fixed, and enabled) and what actually constitutes a baseline. We will discuss how plans get into the plan history as baselines and how their various statuses are set in the next section, which covers the processing aspects.

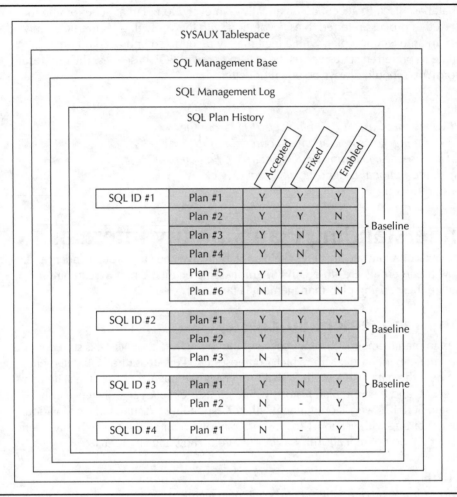

FIGURE 5-1. *Storage of SQL plan management*

The SQL statement log is used to detect whether a SQL statement repeats by comparing its SQL signature with the SQL signatures already stored in SQLLOG$. These SQL signature comparisons ignore SQL text case (that is, are case-insensitive), ignore extra white space, and apply some other text normalizations. If the configuration and/or session parameter OPTIMIZER_USE_SQL_PLAN_BASELINES is set to true (which is the configuration parameter default), the optimizer adds a step of checking the SQL plan history for a baseline to use. To accomplish that, however, the database must first record some additional key metadata. First, the SQL IDs for executed statements are recorded in the SQL statement log so that those with repeated executions can be identified. Second, upon repeated (for versions previous to 12c) execution of a SQL ID, the plan is recorded into the SQL plan history with a status of UNACCEPTED when a baseline already exists (for example, in Figure 5-1, SQL ID #1 plans #5 and #6). Until such time as a plan is marked as ACCEPTED (such as in Figure 5-1, SQL ID #1 plans #1, #2, #3, and #4 highlighted in gray), it will not be considered a baseline and thus cannot be selected to override the statement's default plan.

So how do plans get accepted and thus be considered as part of the baseline? And what purposes do the FIXED and ENABLED statuses fulfill? That leads us into the next section.

Plan Management Internal Processing Logic

SQL plan management internal processing logic is relatively complex, however externally it offers DBAs just two simple modes of operation: automatic and manual. The automatic mode relies on the execution of a default system management task to accept plans as baselines automatically, whereas the manual mode relies on the DBA routinely performing SQL tuning tasks imported from various sources to accept plans manually as baselines. Setting initialization parameter OPTIMIZER_CAPTURE_SQL_ PLAN_BASELINES to TRUE enables automatic processing mode, while setting it to FALSE (default) enables manual processing mode.

Let's begin with disabling plan management entirely, which is the mode many people naturally envision when thinking about plan execution. No plan management occurs when both parameters controlling plan management are set to false:

- OPTIMIZER_USE_SQL_PLAN_BASELINES = FALSE

- OPTIMIZER_CAPTURE_SQL_PLAN_BASELINES = FALSE

Then we follow the very simple plan execution path highlighted in gray in Figure 5-2. As you would expect, the optimizer simply generates a plan and then executes it.

Next, let's examine automatic mode, where we want the database to capture plans automatically and promote some to the baseline (ACCEPTED). Automatic plan management occurs when both parameters controlling plan management are set to true:

- OPTIMIZER_USE_SQL_PLAN_BASELINES = TRUE

- OPTIMIZER_CAPTURE_SQL_PLAN_BASELINES = TRUE

The database is now going to do all the heavy lifting automatically. It will record SQL IDs, identify repeated SQL IDs, and then promote some plans according to the

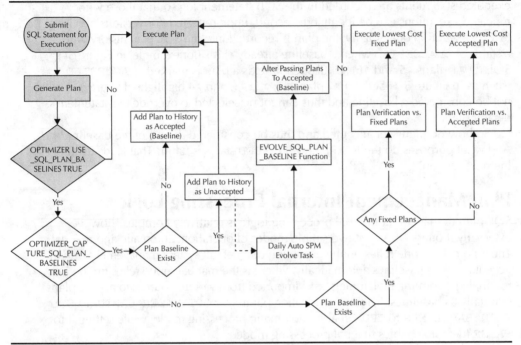

FIGURE 5-2. *Plan management fully disabled*

same criteria as the baseline, shown highlighted in gray in Figure 5-3. If there are no baselines yet, then it simply accepts the plan into the baseline, thus creating the initial baseline plan. When there already is a baseline, it adds the plan to the SQL plan history as unaccepted. Then, when the system management task SYS_AUTO_SPM_EVOLVE_TASK next executes in its daily run schedule, it calls the DBMS_SPM.EVOLVE_SQL_PLAN_BASELINE function to verify the unaccepted plan. If the plan being verified by the evolution function has a lower cost, it is also added to the baseline. The evolution task attempts to process as many unaccepted plans as possible during its limited time window, so it is not unusual for plan evaluations to span multiple days to process all the candidates.

The evolution process offers three modes of verifying that a plan performs as well as or better than the current baseline plan(s). In automatic mode, however, the evolution task uses the simple metric that the new plan must be lower in cost to the existing baseline. In manual mode, the other options are to accept the plan always (by skipping verification) or to run verification (of runtime performance improvements) and produce a report without accepting the plan. Finally, note that you can either enable or disable the system task for the plan evolution process through procedures DBMS_AUTO_TASK_ADMIN.ENABLE and DBMS_AUTO_TASK_ADMIN.DISABLE, respectively.

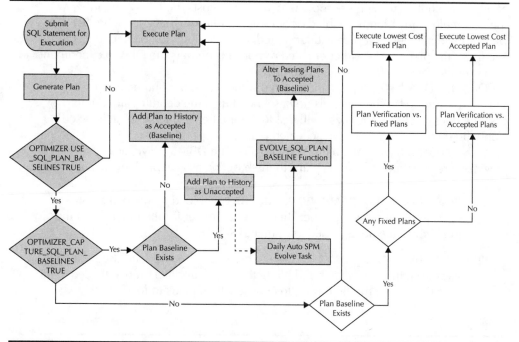

FIGURE 5-3. *Automatic mode plan management*

Lastly, let's examine manual mode, where the DBA is responsible for reviewing all the captured unaccepted plans and choosing to promote some to the baseline manually (accepted). The optimizer will have no choice but to use the default plan until the DBA accepts at least one plan. Manual plan management occurs when the parameters controlling plan management are set as follows:

- `OPTIMIZER_USE_SQL_PLAN_BASELINES = TRUE`

- `OPTIMIZER_CAPTURE_SQL_PLAN_BASELINES = FALSE`

In this mode, the optimizer will look for a baseline plan (assuming any exist) to use instead of the SQL's default plan, but even though the database is collecting plans in the SQL plan history, all those plans are added as unaccepted (and thus not part of the baseline). Therefore, the DBA must manually verify and promote plans into the baseline. This process is known as *plan evolution* or *evolving plans*.

Now we finally reach the point where we can define those additional statuses highlighted in Figure 5-1 (FIXED and ENABLED). Simply put, a fixed plan in the baseline is a *preferred* plan; this forces the optimizer to pick a fixed plan over the others accepted and enabled plans. When there are several fixed plans in the baseline, the optimizer will use the one with lowest cost. The DBA can further specify whether any plan is enabled or not. Again, referring back to Figure 5-1, we can see that whether a plan is unaccepted, accepted but not fixed, or accepted and fixed, the plan can be either enabled or not. This permits the DBA to experiment with various plans, preferences, and statuses.

Once the DBA has accepted and/or fixed some plans, the optimizer operates as shown in Figure 5-4. When there is no baseline, it uses the default plan. But if a baseline does exist, the optimizer will first look for a better plan among the fixed plans and then search among the accepted plans.

So how does the DBA manually accept plans? The DBMS_SPM package provides three methods of adding plans to the baseline as accepted (by default):

- `DBMS_SPM.LOAD_PLANS_FROM_SQLSET` will load all the plans from an existing STS into the baseline. There is a parameter for filtering to limit the number of statements added from that STS.

- `DBMS_SPM.LOAD_PLANS_FROM_CURSOR_CACHE` will load used selected plans from the cursor cache. The function has four different overloaded definitions, with multiple ways to choose which plans to load.

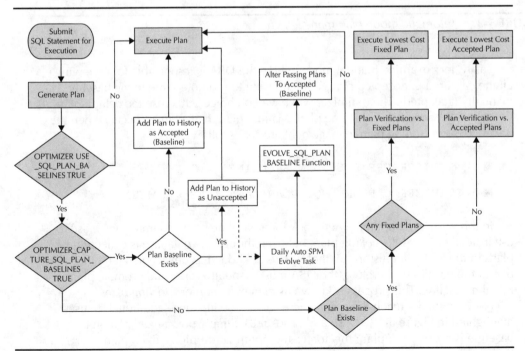

FIGURE 5-4. *Manual mode plan management*

- DBMS_SPM.MIGRATE_STORED_OUTLINE will migrate stored outlines from Oracle versions prior to 10gR2 into baselines.

- The DBA can export baselines from one environment via DBMS_SPM.PACK_ STGTAB_BASELINE and then import them into another environment via DBMS_SPM.UNPACK_STGTAB_BASELINE. This is done using a staging table created by DBMS_SPM.CREATE_STGTAB_BASELINE.

Plan Management Cleanup

Remember that the SQL management base has two areas, the SQL statement log and SQL plan history (Figure 5-1), which consume space in the SYSAUX tablespace. Moreover, no matter what method of baseline creation you are using (manual or automatic), both the unaccepted and accepted plans consume space in the SYSAUX tablespace. So at some point the DBA may want to run the procedure DBMS_SPM.DROP_SQL_PLAN_BASELINE to reclaim or free up some space. By default, baselines can consume up to 10 percent of SYSAUX and are retained for 53 weeks. When total stored cumulative baseline space consumption exceeds the defined space budget limit, a weekly database alert is generated. To increase the baseline space budget limit to its maximum of 50 percent and the retention period to its maximum of 523 weeks, you would issue the following commands:

```
-- filename: max-baselines.sql
-- script to increase baseline limits to their max

DBMS_SPM.CONFIGURE (parameter_name=>'space_budget_percent',
                    parameter_value=>50);

DBMS_SPM.CONFIGURE (parameter_name=>'plan_retention_weeks',
                    parameter_value=>523);
```

SQL Plan Management Example Using TPC-DS

Now let's examine a practical example of SQL plan management at work against one of the TPC-DS benchmark queries to see the command required, how it operates, and what kind of results it can achieve. TPC-DS query #6 is shown next. It was chosen for several reasons:

- It is only 20 lines long and is small enough to visualize and comprehend.

- There is a single full table scan on a very large table (STORE_SALES) that accounts for nearly the entire cost of the plan.

- The plan cost is fairly high at 469K (which in and of itself is OK), so there may possibly be a better plan with a lesser cost.

Note that most of the TPC-DS queries are much longer and far more complex than query #6. Also note that TPC-DS queries run by Swingbench are readily identifiable via a hint with its name, as delineated in this case by the hint of /*query6*/.

```
-- filename: query6.sql
-- script to execute TPC-DS query #6
set timing on
SELECT /*query6*/ a.ca_state state, COUNT(*) cnt
FROM   tpcds.customer_address a ,
       tpcds.customer c ,
       tpcds.store_sales s ,
       tpcds.date_dim d ,
       tpcds.item i
WHERE a.ca_address_sk    = c.c_current_addr_sk
  AND c.c_customer_sk    = s.ss_customer_sk
  AND s.ss_sold_date_sk  = d.d_date_sk
  AND s.ss_item_sk       = i.i_item_sk
  AND d.d_month_seq      = (SELECT DISTINCT (d_month_seq)
                              FROM  tpcds.date_dim
                             WHERE d_year = 2001
                               AND d_moy   = 6)
  AND i.i_current_price > 1.2 * (SELECT AVG(j.i_current_price)
                                   FROM  tpcds.item j
                                  WHERE j.i_category = i.i_category)

GROUP BY a.ca_state
HAVING COUNT(*)  >= 10
ORDER BY cnt;
set timing off
```

When query6.sql is executed without any preexisting plan baselines and without any extra optimizer hints as shown earlier, we obtain the following execution plan. Note that the operation in line 17—a full table scan of STORE_SALES, one of the largest tables in the TPC-DS schema—is responsible for consuming the vast majority of the execution runtime, so if we want to improve performance, we should focus our attention on that step.

Id	Operation	Name	Rows	Bytes	Cost (%CPU)	Time
0	SELECT STATEMENT		3	507	469K (1)	00:00:19
1	SORT ORDER BY		3	507	469K (1)	00:00:19
* 2	FILTER					
3	HASH GROUP BY		3	507	469K (1)	00:00:19
4	NESTED LOOPS		7021	1158K	469K (1)	00:00:19
5	NESTED LOOPS		7021	1158K	469K (1)	00:00:19
6	NESTED LOOPS		7021	1103K	468K (1)	00:00:19
* 7	HASH JOIN		7021	1028K	466K (1)	00:00:19
* 8	TABLE ACCESS FULL	DATE_DIM	30	300	264 (1)	00:00:01
9	HASH UNIQUE		30	330	265 (1)	00:00:01
* 10	TABLE ACCESS FULL	DATE_DIM	30	330	264 (1)	00:00:01
* 11	HASH JOIN		8565K	1143M	466K (1)	00:00:19
* 12	HASH JOIN		6210	745K	2716 (1)	00:00:01

13	VIEW	VW_SQ_1		10	640	1360	(1)	00:00:01
14	HASH GROUP BY			10	540	1360	(1)	00:00:01
15	TABLE ACCESS FULL	ITEM		124K	6549K	1356	(1)	00:00:01
16	TABLE ACCESS FULL	ITEM		124K	7156K	1356	(1)	00:00:01
17	TABLE ACCESS FULL	STORE_SALES		172M	2801M	463K	(1)	00:00:19
18	TABLE ACCESS BY INDEX ROWID	CUSTOMER		1	11	1	(0)	00:00:01
* 19	INDEX UNIQUE SCAN	CUSTOMER_PK_IDX		1		1	(0)	00:00:01
* 20	INDEX UNIQUE SCAN	CA_ADDRESS_PK_IDX		1		1	(0)	00:00:01
21	TABLE ACCESS BY INDEX ROWID	CUSTOMER_ADDRESS		1	8	1	(0)	00:00:01

Next, we need a script to query DBA_SQL_PLAN_BASELINES to display only those plan baselines created for a TPC-DS query (by filtering on the embedded query hint). Note that the ORIGIN column will show how the plan baseline was created, which must be one of four methods: MANUAL-LOAD, AUTO-CAPTURE, MANUAL-SQLTUNE, or AUTO-SQLTUNE. Also note that the script checks for any optimizer hints used for that query's execution for that plan baseline, so we now know that TPC-DS query #6 executed, its plan cost, and applied hints.

```
-- filename: spm_show_tpcds.sql
-- script to display plan baselines for TPC-DS queries
set linesize 256
set pagesize 40
set trimout on
set trimspool on
set wrap on
set long 8000
col sql_handle format a25
col plan_name format a35
col optimizer_cost format 999,999 heading COST
col sql_text format a70
col query# format a10
col optihint format a25
SELECT sql_handle, plan_name, origin, enabled, accepted, fixed,
       SUBSTR(sql_text,INSTR(sql_text, '/*', 1, 1),
              INSTR(sql_text, '*/', 1, 1)-
              INSTR(sql_text, '/*', 1, 1)+2) as "QUERY#",
       optimizer_cost,
       CASE
         WHEN INSTR(sql_text, '/*+', 1, 1) = 0 THEN null
         ELSE SUBSTR(sql_text,INSTR(sql_text, '/*+', 1, 1),25)
         END  as "OPTIHINT"
FROM dba_sql_plan_baselines
WHERE LOWER(SUBSTR(sql_text,INSTR(sql_text, '/*', 1, 1),
                   INSTR(sql_text, '*/', 1, 1)-
                   INSTR(sql_text, '/*', 1, 1)+2)) LIKE '%query%'
ORDER BY last_executed;
```

Finally, we need a script to query DBA_SQL_PLAN_BASELINES to drop all those plan baselines created for a TPC-DS query. This script will enable us to reset the database state to a clean starting position so that we can repeat the testing steps to reproduce the results. Note that this script uses an advanced technique often referred to as *dynamic scripting*—that is, a script to generate a script. It queries the SQL plan baseline table to create statements to drop each appropriate baseline, spools them to a temp file, and finally executes that temp file's contents—a powerful technique:

```
-- filename: spm_drop_tpcds.sql
-- script to drop plan baselines for TPC-DS queries
set echo off
set verify off
set pagesize 0
set feedback off
@spm_show_tpcds
prompt
prompt **** PLANS BEFORE CLEANUP
spool spm_drop_tpcds.tmp
SELECT
'declare x PLS_INTEGER; begin x := DBMS_SPM.DROP_SQL_PLAN_
BASELINE('''||SQL_HANDLE||'''); end;'||CHR(10)||'/'
FROM dba_sql_plan_baselines
WHERE LOWER(SUBSTR(sql_text,INSTR(sql_text, '/*', 1, 1),
                   INSTR(sql_text, '*/', 1, 1)-
                   INSTR(sql_text, '/*', 1, 1)+2)) LIKE '%query%';
spool off
@spm_drop_tpcds.tmp
prompt
prompt **** PLANS AFTER CLEANUP
@spm_show_tpcds
```

We can now construct a complete test scenario using these three SQL scripts and a few additional versions of query6.sql in which different optimizer hints are added in an effort to find a better plan baseline. Since we know from the base execution plan that the full table scan operation in line 17 against a very large table is responsible for the majority of the runtime, we will try two very simple hints: PARALLEL and DYNAMIC SAMPLING (at level 5 of 10). We chose the parallel hint because sometimes a parallel full table scan is a reasonable choice for large tables. We chose the dynamic sampling hint because it's a reasonable sanity check to make sure that table growth has not caused unforeseen performance ramifications (that is, in case the statistics are stale). (These are not universal recommendations or a best practice approach of any kind. We just wanted to demonstrate a couple simple yet reasonable alternatives to showcase how you might try to find a better execution plan.)

```
-- filename: run_test.sql
-- script to try several versions of query 6
-- and to automatically create a plan baseline
-- for each where a hint may result in lower cost

connect dbauser/dbauser
@spm_drop_tpcds
```

```
connect tpcds/tpcds
alter session set optimizer_use_sql_plan_baselines=true;
alter session set optimizer_capture_sql_plan_baselines=true;
set term off
spool run_test.log
@query6
@query6_parallel
@query6_dynsampling
spool off
set term on

connect dbauser/dbauser
@spm_show_tpcds
```

The output from spm_show_tpcds.sql after executing the run_test.sql script is as follows:

```
SQL> @spm_show_tpcds

SQL_HANDLE              PLAN_NAME                        ORIGIN ENA ACC FIX QUERY#       COST OPTIHINT
-------------------    ------------------------------   ------ --- --- --- ----------  -------- --------------------
SQL_f00ec562f2e31bb0   SQL_PLAN_g03q5cbtf66xh87f12331   AUTO-C YES YES NO  /*query6*/  469,728
SQL_20f127b92cb73327   SQL_PLAN_21w97r4qbfct7ea12eb73   AUTO-C YES YES NO  /*query6*/  132,685 /*+parallel(s 4)*/ a
SQL_f691b44898a1745f   SQL_PLAN_gd4dn92ca2x2z87f12331   AUTO-C YES YES NO  /*query6*/  469,728 /*+ dynamic_sampling
```

You can see that the PARALLEL hint resulted in a 71.8 percent lower plan cost, but we all know that a lower plan cost does not necessarily translate into better actual runtime performance. However, the execution runtime also improved in a very similar fashion, from 19 seconds to just 6 seconds, a 68.4 percent decrease. We therefore might want to consider marking that baseline as preferred (FIXED).

NOTE
It is possible, or even likely, that using parallel query only reduced the measured runtime without any reduction in database time (DB time)—and possibly even an increase. In effect, we may have simply traded a shorter elapsed time for higher resource consumption (DB time). That may be an OK tradeoff on my test isolated environment, but it might not be a good deal on an actual system with multiple concurrent processing requests. So weigh this type of choice accordingly.

Up to this point, we have been using PL/SQL commands to implement all aspects of SQL plan management. But for DBAs who prefer a graphical tool for working with plan baselines, the Oracle Enterprise Manager (OEM) SQL Plan Control screen, shown in Figure 5-5, operates without the user having to call the `DBMS_SPM` package or query `DBA_SQL_PLAN_BASELINES`. From here, we could quite easily evolve the third baseline for the parallel hint to a status of fixed.

However, we're not done yet—we can improve upon this using Oracle's SQL Tuning Advisor to complement SQL plan management. Since many database application developers employ Oracle SQL Developer, we'll use that tool to invoke the SQL Tuning Advisor.

Figure 5-6 shows that creating three additional indexes will reduce the cost from the previously, as shown by the output from the spm_show_tpcds script, attained 469K or 132K down to 32K. However, as before, we again know that reduced plan cost does not necessarily mean improved runtime. But the database runtime for the query after adding these three new indexes was also reduced by 66.7 percent, from 00:00:06 to 00:00:02 seconds. Of course, creating any new index should be carefully considered, as there may be additional unexpected overhead for other workloads; however, let's assume they are warranted here and thus create them.

Once the recommended indexes are created, we can rerun our three versions of query6.sql (with and without hints). The output from spm_show_tpcds.sql will now show that there are three new plan baselines that are not yet accepted, as shown

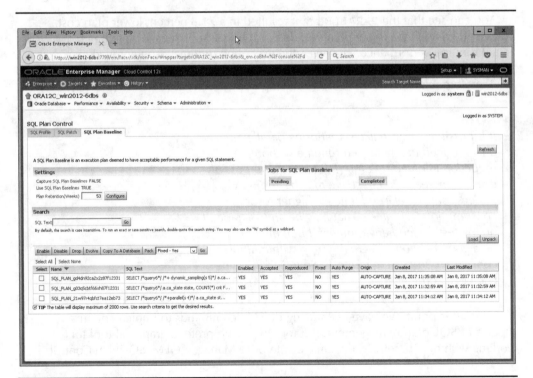

FIGURE 5-5. *OEM SQL Plan Control screen*

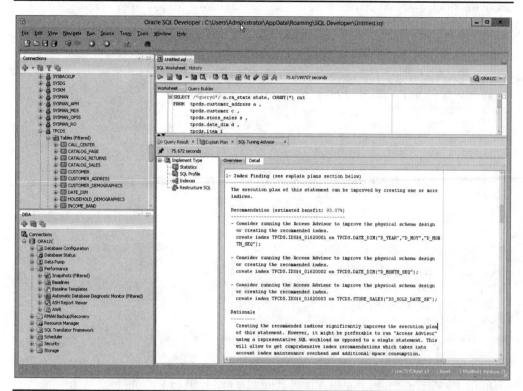

FIGURE 5-6. *SQL Developer Tuning Advisor*

next highlighted in gray. So why did these three new plan baselines show up as not accepted? Refer back to Figure 5-4: when using automatic mode and a plan baseline exists, then any new baselines are added as unaccepted.

```
SQL> @spm_show_tpcds

SQL_HANDLE            PLAN_NAME                           ORIGIN ENA ACC FIX QUERY#        COST OPTIHINT
-------------------   ---------------------------------   ------ --- --- --- ----------   -------- --------------------
SQL_f00ec562f2e31bb0  SQL_PLAN_g03q5cbtf66xh87f12331      AUTO-C YES YES NO  /*query6*/    469,728
SQL_20f127b92cb73327  SQL_PLAN_21w97r4qbfct7ea12eb73      AUTO-C YES YES NO  /*query6*/    132,685 /*+parallel(s 4)*/ a
SQL_f691b44898a1745f  SQL_PLAN_gd4dn92ca2x2z87f12331      AUTO-C YES YES NO  /*query6*/    469,728 /*+ dynamic_sampling
SQL_20f127b92cb73327  SQL_PLAN_21w97r4qbfct7addebcc2      AUTO-C YES NO  NO  /*query6*/     53,392 /*+parallel(s 4)*/ a
SQL_f00ec562f2e31bb0  SQL_PLAN_g03q5cbtf66xhaddebcc2      AUTO-C YES NO  NO  /*query6*/    105,409
SQL_f691b44898a1745f  SQL_PLAN_gd4dn92ca2x2zaddebcc2      AUTO-C YES NO  NO  /*query6*/    105,409 /*+ dynamic_sampling
```

To accept all the unaccepted plan baselines, we must run the following script three times and pass in the corresponding SQL handle for each statement (SQL_20f127b92cb73327). This script will accomplish several other things: it will verify the plan, promote it as accepted if more efficient, and even produce a report about the findings. Note that running this script will take a while—in this case, it took more than 20 minutes per SQL handle being checked. Furthermore, note that not one of these three new SQL plan baselines were accepted because none of them actually turned out to be better than the existing plan:

```
-- filename: spm_evolve.sql
-- script to evolve/accept/verify a plan baseline
SET SERVEROUTPUT ON
SET LONG 8000
DECLARE
  report clob;
BEGIN
  report := DBMS_SPM.EVOLVE_SQL_PLAN_BASELINE(sql_handle => '&1');
  DBMS_OUTPUT.PUT_LINE(report);
END;
/
```

Cloud Considerations: Caveat Emptor *Nubes*

With the major push toward leveraging cloud technology these days, DBAs would do well to understand and appreciate that their primary focus may shift somewhat under the new paradigm.

For example, because CPU, memory, and disk space are all essentially elastic and merely metered for usage, DBAs now need to focus more than in the past upon the performance of their applications' SQL statements. With on-premises hardware, slow runtimes might be resolved by shifting jobs in the scheduler, assigning more resources to a virtual machine, moving a virtual machine to a less constrained host, or by moving a poorly performing database from one physical server to another more powerful server. In other words, there may not have been any easily measurable monthly cost of a slow-running SQL.

In a cloud environment, however, slow-running SQL might actually result in either a manual or dynamic upgrade of the database's corresponding cloud tier or service level, and operating within that new tier may cost dramatically more than the prior tier. Depending on the type of cloud computing environment that an Oracle DBA's organization has selected, inefficient SQL statements could therefore add dramatically to monthly cloud subscription costs, and these increased costs may not necessarily become apparent until the accounting department presents that bill to the CIO. So, in the future, keeping your organization's SQL statements executing as efficiently as possible becomes a far more critical task, because it will not only be upset end users calling when a system is running slow—it could be the proverbial "bean counters" asking why cloud costs are rising when your CIO had promised they would actually decrease.

Summary

SQL plan management in Oracle Database 12c makes the task of achieving plan stability over time and even across database patches or versions far simpler than in earlier database releases. Plus, it does not require additional licensing unless using SQL Tuning Sets (STS) as an input source. Prior versions of Oracle offered older, less effective techniques such as stored outlines and SQL profiles, but neither was the ideal solution, so Oracle 11g implemented a mature replacement—SQL plan baselines. Any Oracle DBA using SQL plan baselines should be able to achieve and maintain satisfactory SQL runtime performance for just about any application workload. Hopefully gone are the days of major surprises from SQL statements that once ran quickly but unexpectedly take inordinate amounts of time to run, when everyone claims nothing has changed.

PART III

It's Running Slow: Database Performance Evaluation

CHAPTER
6

SQL Monitor

Oracle DBAs and database developers have always needed to locate and identify any poorly performing SQL code that has been rolled out into production. But no matter how carefully developers and DBAs try to implement the best code possible, at some point a bad SQL statement or two are going to slip by into production and negatively impact performance at the least opportune time. For some reason, it seems that poorly performing code tends to happen in the wee hours of the night, and ironically not as much during the daytime when DBAs and developers are close at hand to react.

When this occurs, DBAs need an easy and quick way to decipher everything that's going on inside the database and focus on the true problem areas. Fortunately, Oracle 11*g*R1 introduced a great new feature to simplify that process, called SQL Monitor. In short, SQL Monitor does exactly what its name says—it monitors SQL statements, especially long-running and excessively expensive SQL statements—and it accomplishes all this with little to no overhead. Let's dig deeper.

NOTE
This feature requires the optional Diagnostic and Tuning Packs. Furthermore, the database configuration parameter for STATISTICS_LEVEL must be set to ALL or TYPICAL.

Which SQL Statements Are Monitored?

The first and logical question is how exactly does SQL Monitor work—in other words, what SQL statements does it monitor? The answer is actually quite simple: Serially executed SQL statements that consume 5 or more seconds of either CPU or I/O in a single execution and all SQL statements executed in parallel qualify as candidates. In short, any and all resource-intensive long-running and parallel SQL statements are automatically monitored. Moreover, you can force any statement to be monitored by SQL Monitor by specifying the /*+MONITOR*/ optimizer hint. However, there are limits to how many SQL statements a database can monitor; by default, the concurrent SQL statement monitoring limit is 20 times the value in initialization parameter CPU_COUNT. This limit can be modified (using caution, of course) via the hidden database initialization parameter _SQLMON_MAX_PLAN. Likewise, there is also a limit on the number of execution plan lines allowed within a single monitored SQL statement. The default is 300 lines, but this can be modified via the hidden database initialization parameter _SQLMON_MAX_PLANLINES.

SQL Monitor: Division of Labor

The two key goals of SQL Monitor are simple and direct: First, identify which SQL statements of interest are executing or have recently been executed, as well as which sessions are executing them; and second, capture all pertinent information about those SQL statements of interest. This division of labor is reflected in the two data dictionary views that capture this information: V$SQL_MONITOR and V$SQL_PLAN_MONITOR.

V$SQL_MONITOR: Identifying Statements of Interest

V$SQL_MONITOR contains information about SQL statements whose execution have been or are currently being monitored. The data is refreshed in near real time, at least once a second. Here is a simple script to display the V$SQL_MONITOR data for a specified user and its output in Figure 6-1 (which shows once again that multiple TPC-DS queries are executing; note that we're specifically interested in the first instance of query 6 being executed by session ID 779):

```
-- filename: sql_monitor.sql
-- script to display all SQL statements being monitored

    SET HEADING ON
    SET LINESIZE 200
    SET PAGESIZE 100

    define v_username=&1

    COLUMN sql_text FORMAT A120

    SELECT sql_id, sid, status, sql_text
    FROM    v$sql_monitor
    WHERE   username LIKE upper('%&v_username%');
```

V$SQL_PLAN_MONITOR: Pertinent Information for Statements of Interest

The data dictionary view V$SQL_PLAN_MONITOR contains the actual plan steps and their costs—plus a multitude of other data—for a given SQL ID and session ID. Supplying a given SQL ID and session ID from Figure 6-1 as input parameters to the following SQL script creates the output shown in Figure 6-2:

```
-- filename: sql_plan_monitor.sql
-- script to display a monitored SQL statement plan

    SET HEADING ON
    SET LINESIZE 200
    SET PAGESIZE 100

    define v_sql_id=&1
    define v_sid=&2

    COLUMN operation format a20
    COLUMN plan_cpu_cost format 999,999,999,999,999
```

```
COLUMN plan_io_cost format 999,999
COLUMN output_rows format 999,999,999,999

SELECT sid, sql_id, status, plan_line_id, plan_cpu_cost, plan_io_cost,
plan_operation || ' ' || plan_options operation, output_rows
FROM v$sql_plan_monitor
WHERE sql_id='&v_sql_id'
  AND sid='&v_sid'
  ORDER BY 1,4;
```

NOTE
*The output in Figure 6-2 shows extremely basic
information because there is an enormous amount
of performance metadata present within V$SQL_
PLAN_MONITOR. Rather than develop a more
complex script with far more detailed output that
won't fit on a single page, we've shown just the
basics so that the reader can appreciate just how
much information is contained in this view.*

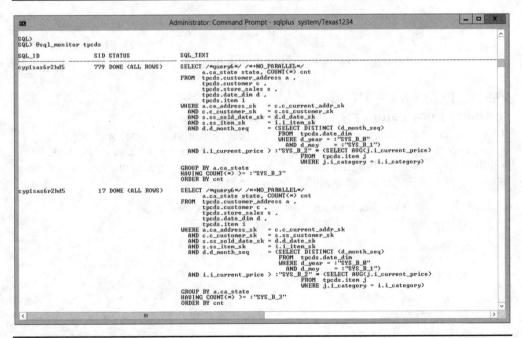

FIGURE 6-1. *Query V$SQL_MONITOR*

```
Administrator: Command Prompt - sqlplus system/Texas1234

SQL> @sql_plan_monitor cyp1sas6r2hd5 779

  SID SQL_ID        STATUS          PLAN_LINE_ID     PLAN_CPU_COST PLAN_IO_COST OPERATION                OUTPUT_ROWS
  779 cyp1sas6r2hd5 DONE (ALL ROWS)            0                 0            0 SELECT STATEMENT                  50
  779 cyp1sas6r2hd5 DONE (ALL ROWS)            1 2,588,691,259,150       44,864 SORT ORDER BY                     50
  779 cyp1sas6r2hd5 DONE (ALL ROWS)            2                               FILTER
  779 cyp1sas6r2hd5 DONE (ALL ROWS)            3 2,588,691,259,150       44,864 HASH GROUP BY                     50
  779 cyp1sas6r2hd5 DONE (ALL ROWS)            4 2,588,596,489,056       44,864 VIEW                          55,756
  779 cyp1sas6r2hd5 DONE (ALL ROWS)            5                               FILTER                        55,756
  779 cyp1sas6r2hd5 DONE (ALL ROWS)            6 2,588,596,489,056       44,864 HASH GROUP BY                139,609
  779 cyp1sas6r2hd5 DONE (ALL ROWS)            7   176,203,600,469       44,864 HASH JOIN              1,733,996,294
  779 cyp1sas6r2hd5 DONE (ALL ROWS)            8       104,056,446        1,354 TABLE ACCESS FULL            124,200
  779 cyp1sas6r2hd5 DONE (ALL ROWS)            9     1,642,264,631       41,947 HASH JOIN                    139,609
  779 cyp1sas6r2hd5 DONE (ALL ROWS)           10       104,056,446        1,354 TABLE ACCESS FULL            124,200
  779 cyp1sas6r2hd5 DONE (ALL ROWS)           11     1,477,955,702       39,395 HASH JOIN                    139,609
  779 cyp1sas6r2hd5 DONE (ALL ROWS)           12     1,004,999,336       35,215 HASH JOIN                    139,609
  779 cyp1sas6r2hd5 DONE (ALL ROWS)           13       210,329,142       27,919 HASH JOIN                          1
  779 cyp1sas6r2hd5 DONE (ALL ROWS)           14       210,329,142       27,919 NESTED LOOPS                 139,609
  779 cyp1sas6r2hd5 DONE (ALL ROWS)           15       210,329,142       27,919 NESTED LOOPS                 139,609
  779 cyp1sas6r2hd5 DONE (ALL ROWS)           16                               STATISTICS COLLECTOR              30

  779 cyp1sas6r2hd5 DONE (ALL ROWS)           17             5,561            1 TABLE ACCESS BY INDE              30
                                                                                X ROWID BATCHED

  779 cyp1sas6r2hd5 DONE (ALL ROWS)           18             2,834            1 INDEX RANGE SCAN                  30
  779 cyp1sas6r2hd5 DONE (ALL ROWS)           19        46,822,681            1 SORT UNIQUE NOSORT                 1
  779 cyp1sas6r2hd5 DONE (ALL ROWS)           20             4,049            1 INDEX RANGE SCAN                  30
  779 cyp1sas6r2hd5 DONE (ALL ROWS)           21           187,980            1 INDEX RANGE SCAN             139,609
  779 cyp1sas6r2hd5 DONE (ALL ROWS)           22         7,010,786          931 TABLE ACCESS BY INDE         139,609
                                                                                X ROWID

  779 cyp1sas6r2hd5 DONE (ALL ROWS)           23         7,010,786          931 TABLE ACCESS FULL                  0
  779 cyp1sas6r2hd5 DONE (ALL ROWS)           24       489,912,014        4,756 TABLE ACCESS FULL          1,280,000
  779 cyp1sas6r2hd5 DONE (ALL ROWS)           25       306,745,588        2,636 TABLE ACCESS FULL            640,000

26 rows selected.
SQL> _
```

FIGURE 6-2. *Query V$SQL_PLAN_MONITOR*

Interacting with SQL Monitor

SQL Monitor is such a useful feature that Oracle provides an interface to it through just about every graphical user interface (GUI) that accesses an Oracle database, as well as via simple scripting with command line tools. We will illustrate how to access SQL Monitor using these interfaces in the following sections of this chapter.

NOTE
For completeness, we have presented all the various interfaces and methods for working with SQL Monitor. Of course, every Oracle DBA is free to choose the one that best suits his needs. We do not profess that any of these methods is superior to the others—each one will get the job done.

Invoking SQL Monitor via PL/SQL

For those Oracle DBAs who still prefer to leverage a scripted approach rather than a GUI, Oracle provides a PL/SQL API for SQL Monitor.

NOTE
In Oracle 11g, these functions were part of package DBMS_SQLTUNE, but in Oracle 12c they are now part of package DBMS_SQL_MONITOR. Other than their relocation, however, there were basically no other major changes; apparently, the DBMS_ SQLTUNE package was simply getting too large and complex.

Accomplishing our first goal—identifying all SQL statements of interest that are currently being monitored or recently have been monitored (and have not aged out or been replaced yet in the library cache)—is provided through the much cleaner and more navigable HTML output shown in Figure 6-3, which we generated through this SQL script:

```
-- filename: report_sql_monitor_list.sql
-- script to display SQL statements being monitored

      SET LONG 1000000
      SET LONGCHUNKSIZE 1000000
      SET LINESIZE 1000
      SET PAGESIZE 0
      SET TRIM ON
      SET TRIMSPOOL ON
      SET ECHO OFF
      SET FEEDBACK OFF

      SPOOL C:\Temp\report_sql_monitor_list.htm
      SELECT DBMS_SQL_MONITOR.REPORT_SQL_MONITOR_LIST(
        type          => 'HTML',
        report_level => 'ALL') AS report
      FROM dual;
      SPOOL OFF
```

Accomplishing our second goal—drilling down into actual performance data for the SQL statement of interest—is illustrated next, using the given SQL ID and session ID obtained from Figure 6-3. The following simple SQL script, which accepts a given SQL ID and session ID as its input parameters, produces the much cleaner and more navigable HTML output shown in Figure 6-4:

```
-- filename: report_sql_monitor.sql
-- script to display specific SQL statements being monitored

      SET LONG 1000000
      SET LONGCHUNKSIZE 1000000
      SET LINESIZE 1000
```

```
SET PAGESIZE 0
SET TRIM ON
SET TRIMSPOOL ON
SET ECHO OFF
SET FEEDBACK OFF

define v_sql_id=&1

SPOOL C:\Temp\report_sql_monitor.htm
SELECT DBMS_SQL_MONITOR.REPORT_SQL_MONITOR(
  sql_id        => '&v_sql_id',
  type          => 'HTML',
  report_level  => 'ALL') AS report
FROM dual;
SPOOL OFF
```

SQL Monitoring List

Status	Duration	SQL Id or DBOP Name	User	Dop	DB Time	IOs	Start	End	SQL Text
DONE (ALL ROWS)	754s	cyp1sas6r2hd5	TPCDS		754s	27621	02/03/2017 16:56:13	02/03/2017 17:08:47	SELECT /*query6*/ /*+NO_PARALLEL*/ a.ca_state state, COUNT(*) cnt FROM tp...
DONE (ALL ROWS)	754s	cyp1sas6r2hd5	TPCDS		754s	34301	02/03/2017 16:56:13	02/03/2017 17:08:47	SELECT /*query6*/ /*+NO_PARALLEL*/ a.ca_state state, COUNT(*) cnt FROM tp...
DONE (ALL ROWS)	753s	cyp1sas6r2hd5	TPCDS		753s	37714	02/03/2017 16:56:13	02/03/2017 17:08:46	SELECT /*query6*/ /*+NO_PARALLEL*/ a.ca_state state, COUNT(*) cnt FROM tp...
DONE (ALL ROWS)	750s	5usq97szqtj08	TPCDS		669s	91999	02/03/2017 16:56:13	02/03/2017 17:08:43	WITH all_sales AS (SELECT d_year ,i_brand_id ,i_class_id ...
DONE (ALL ROWS)	750s	5usq97szqtj08	TPCDS		667s	92019	02/03/2017 16:56:13	02/03/2017 17:08:43	WITH all_sales AS (SELECT d_year ,i_brand_id ,i_class_id ...
DONE (ALL ROWS)	749s	cyp1sas6r2hd5	TPCDS		750s	34508	02/03/2017 16:56:13	02/03/2017 17:08:42	SELECT /*query6*/ /*+NO_PARALLEL*/ a.ca_state state, COUNT(*) cnt FROM tp...
DONE (ALL ROWS)	357s	1qjztdqwyz5d8	TPCDS		330s	137K	02/03/2017 16:56:13	02/03/2017 17:02:10	ss ss as (select s_store_sk, sum(ss_ext_sales_price) as sales, ...
DONE (ALL ROWS)	348s	1qjztdqwyz5d8	TPCDS		329s	172K	02/03/2017 16:56:13	02/03/2017 17:02:01	with ss as (select s_store_sk, sum(ss_ext_sales_price) as sales, ...
DONE	82s	fhf8upax5cxsz			82s	604	02/03/2017 16:59:46	02/03/2017 17:01:08	BEGIN sys.dbms_auto_report_internal.i_save_report (:rep_ref, :snap_id, :pr_class...
DONE (ALL ROWS)	80s	5k5207588w9ry			80s	589	02/03/2017 16:59:46	02/03/2017 17:01:06	SELECT DBMS_REPORT.GET_REPORT(:B1) FROM DUAL
DONE	6.0s	c3hjkha2s5q42	SYSMAN		6s	1444	02/03/2017 16:41:29	02/03/2017 16:41:35	DECLARE job BINARY_INTEGER := :job; next_date TIMESTAMP WITH TIME ZONE := :myda...
DONE (FIRST N ROWS)	5.0s	f6cz4n8y72xdc			5s	1175	02/03/2017 16:18:59	02/03/2017 16:19:04	SELECT space_usage_kbytes FROM v$sysaux_occupants WHERE occupant_name = 'SQL_...
DONE (ALL ROWS)	12s	b9p45hkcx0pwh			20s	225	02/03/2017 16:18:47	02/03/2017 16:18:59	select dbms_qopatch.get_opatch_lsinventory() from dual
DONE	6.0s	2t8b8vn1b7ap3	SYSMAN		6s	1078	02/03/2017 16:18:47	02/03/2017 16:18:53	DECLARE job BINARY_INTEGER := :job; next_date TIMESTAMP WITH TIME ZONE := :myda...

FIGURE 6-3. *DBMS_SQL_MONITOR.report_sql_monitor_list*

SQL Monitoring Report

SQL Text

SELECT /*query6*/ /*+NO_PARALLEL*/ a.ca_state state, COUNT(*) cnt FROM tpcds.customer_address a , tpcds.customer c , tpcds.store_sales s , tpcds.date_dim d , tpcds.item i WHERE a.ca_address_sk = c.c_current_addr_sk AND c.c_customer_sk = s.ss_customer_sk AND s.ss_sold_date_sk = d.d_date_sk AND s.ss_item_sk = i.i_item_sk AND d.d_month_seq = (SELECT DISTINCT (d_month_seq) FROM tpcds.date_dim WHERE d_year = :"SYS_B_0" AND d_moy = :"SYS_B_1") AND i.i_current_price > :"SYS_B_2" * (SELECT AVG(j.i_current_price) FROM tpcds.item j WHERE j.i_category = i.i_category) GROUP BY a.ca_state HAVING COUNT(*) >= :"SYS_B_3" ORDER BY cnt

Global Information: DONE (ALL ROWS)

Instance ID	: 1
Session	: TPCDS (1173:58554)
SQL ID	: cyp1sas6r2hd5
SQL Execution ID	: 16777217
Execution Started	: 02/03/2017 16:56:13
First Refresh Time	: 02/03/2017 16:56:17
Last Refresh Time	: 02/03/2017 17:08:47
Duration	: 754s
Module/Action	: SQL*Plus/-
Service	: SYS$USERS
Program	: sqlplus.exe
Fetch Calls	: 5

Buffer Gets	IO Requests	Database Time	Wait Activity
197K	34301	754s	

Binds

Name	Position	Type	Value
:SYS_B_0	1	NUMBER	2001
:SYS_B_1	2	NUMBER	6
:SYS_B_2	3	NUMBER	1.2
:SYS_B_3	4	NUMBER	10

SQL Plan Monitoring Details (Plan Hash Value=1451698235)

Id	Operation	Name	Estimated Rows	Cost	Active Period (754s)	Execs	Rows	Memory (Max)	Temp (Max)	IO Requests	CPU Activity	Wait Activity
0	SELECT STATEMENT					1	50					
1	SORT ORDER BY		3	100K		1	50	2.0KB				
2	FILTER					1	50					
3	HASH GROUP BY		3	100K		1	50	2.4MB				
4	VIEW	VM_NWVW_2	1238	100K		1	55756					
5	FILTER					1	55756					
6	HASH GROUP BY		1238	100K		1	140K	73.7MB				
7	HASH JOIN		2G	48628		1	2G	14.9MB				
8	TABLE ACCESS FULL	ITEM	124K	1356		1	124K			19 (<0.1%)		
9	HASH JOIN		140K	41982		1	140K	15.3MB				
10	TABLE ACCESS FULL	ITEM	124K	1356		1	124K					
11	HASH JOIN		142K	39427		1	140K	16.2MB				
12	HASH JOIN		142K	35236		1	140K	14.5MB				
13	HASH JOIN		142K	27923		1	1					
14	NESTED LOOPS		142K	27923		1	140K					
15	NESTED LOOPS		142K	27923		1	140K					
16	STATISTICS COLLECTOR					1	30					
17	TABLE ACCESS BY INDEX ROWID BATCHED	DATE_DIM	30	1		1	30					
18	INDEX RANGE SCAN	NEW_IDX1	30	1		1	30			3 (<0.1%)		
19	SORT UNIQUE NOSORT		30	2		1	1					
20	INDEX RANGE SCAN	NEW_IDX2	30	1		1	30			1 (<0.1%)		
21	INDEX RANGE SCAN	NEW_IDX3	4656	1		295	140K			15 (<0.1%)		
22	TABLE ACCESS BY INDEX ROWID	STORE_SALES	4656	931		280K	140K			33932 (98%)		
23	TABLE ACCESS FULL	STORE_SALES	4656	931		1	1					
24	TABLE ACCESS FULL	CUSTOMER	1M	4766		1	1M			211 (.6%)		
25	TABLE ACCESS FULL	CUSTOMER_ADDRESS	640K	2643		1	640K			120 (.3%)		

FIGURE 6-4. *DBMS_SQL_MONITOR.report_sql_monitor*

NOTE
Choosing HTML as the report type as in this example script generates only the simple version of the HTML report. The ACTIVE option for database activity will also generate an HTML report, but will also include additional information such as the explain plan, activity_histogram, metrics, and plan_histogram. Hence you may want to choose ACTIVE.

Invoking SQL Monitor from SQL Developer

SQL Developer was first introduced in Oracle 11g and has rapidly grown in popularity as each successive release has expanded its feature set. Not only is it easy to use, but it's a simple fat client Java application that's easily installed. Best of all, SQL Developer is provided free without any Oracle licensing cost, regardless of whether a database is licensed.

We accomplish our first goal—identifying SQL statements of interest—by choosing Tools | Monitor SQL from the main menu to display the Real Time SQL Monitoring screen, shown in Figure 6-5.

Our second goal—drilling down into a detailed performance analysis breakdown for a specific SQL ID and session ID—is accomplished by navigating to a row of interest in the Real Time SQL Monitoring screen, right-clicking it, and selecting Show SQL Details. An example of this for one SQL statement of interest that is still executing—SQL ID cyp1sas6r2hd5—is shown in Figure 6-6.

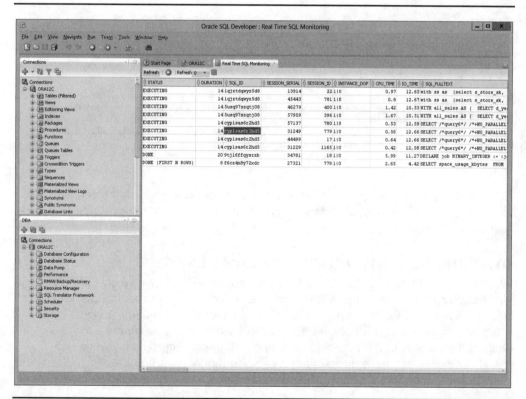

FIGURE 6-5. *SQL Developer monitored SQL overview*

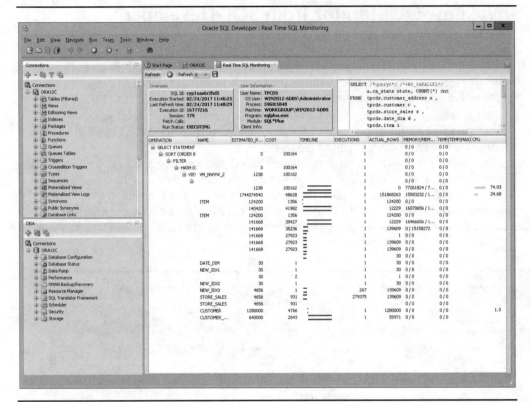

FIGURE 6-6. *SQL Developer monitored SQL drilldown*

Note that the early adopter version of SQL Developer has greatly improved its SQL Monitor interface to look a lot more like Oracle Enterprise Manager (OEM), as shown in Figure 6-7.

Invoking SQL Monitor from OEM Express

Introduced with Oracle 12.1.0.1, OEM Express is a simple and lightweight client web browser, flash-based utility. OEM Express can't do everything that its full-blown cousin, OEM Cloud Control, can do—for example, it can't be used to manage a database instance—but it is nonetheless a notably worthwhile tool for most any Oracle DBA's tool belt. With the features and capabilities it offers, it can do the job quickly and without the overhead of a server-based tool or repository.

FIGURE 6-7. *SQL Developer early adopter improvements*

NOTE
Over the past 30 years, Oracle has offered several DBA tools, some of which were quite good and had passionate followers. When OEM emerged, many, if not all of those tools, were deprecated—and often sorely missed. Our hope is that Oracle will remain committed to OEM Express over the coming years. It's wonderful to have all three tools: SQL Developer for the more developer-oriented and some DBA tasks, OEM Express for DBA tasks that don't require the full weight of a server-based tool with a repository, and of course OEM Cloud Control for all remaining work.

Accomplishing our first goal—identifying SQL statements of interest—is fulfilled by choosing, from the main toolbar, Performance Hub | Monitored SQL to display the screen shown in Figure 6-8.

Accomplishing our second goal—obtaining a detailed performance analysis breakdown for a specific SQL ID and session ID—is as easy as navigating to the desired row and then either clicking the Execution Details button or clicking the SQL ID link to display the screen shown in Figure 6-9.

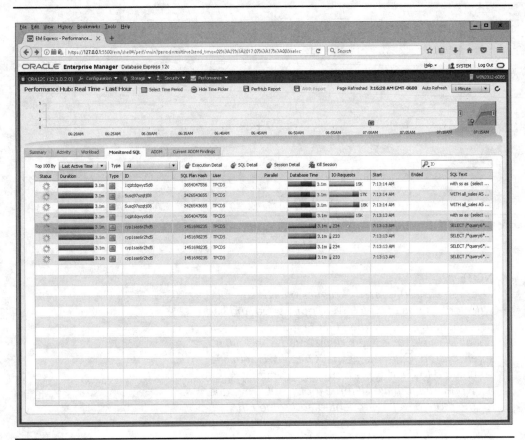

FIGURE 6-8. *OEM Express monitored SQL overview*

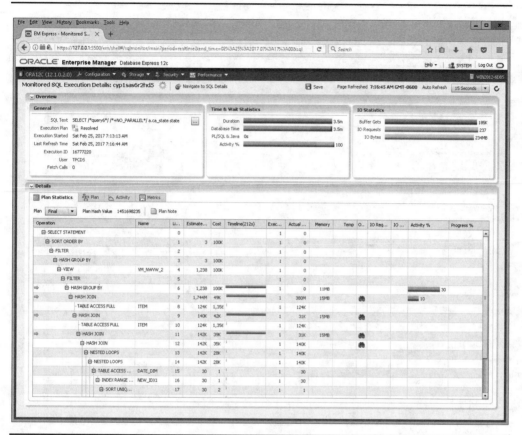

FIGURE 6-9.   *OEM Express monitored SQL drilldown*

NOTE
The report shown in Figure 6-9 is the ACTIVE version of the report, and not the simple HTML version as shown by the earlier script.

Finally, OEM Express offers one more location from which to monitor SQL statements: its Home page, shown in Figure 6-10. The lower-right corner of the screen displays all the SQL monitored for the past hour—up to a maximum of 20—so from the moment that OEM Express is launched, there is an overview of monitored SQL statements. One simple click of the SQL ID link for any row displayed in this panel will launch the execution details screen.

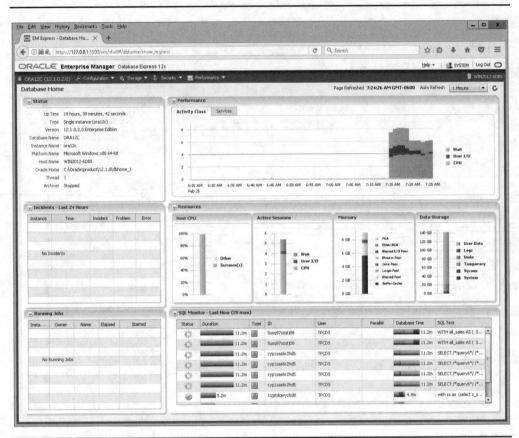

FIGURE 6-10. *OEM Express Home page*

Invoking SQL Monitor from OEM Cloud Control

Many IT shops these days have adopted OEM 13c Cloud Control as their de facto standard for monitoring and maintaining their Oracle database infrastructure, including their virtualized as well as "bare metal" hardware platforms. OEM 13c Cloud Control is also well-suited for managing Oracle enterprise computing systems such as Exadata Database Machine, SPARC SuperCluster, Oracle Database Appliance (ODA), and ZFS Storage Appliance. With the simplicity of a hybrid agent, OEM 13c Cloud Control can also monitor database environments in the Oracle Public Cloud. It's therefore the natural choice for SQL monitoring for an Oracle DBA whose applications are leveraging any of these platforms.

OEM 13*c* Cloud Control offers a fairly simple yet comprehensive GUI for SQL monitoring. Once the Oracle DBA has navigated to the desired database instance, any SQL statements of interest can be identified by choosing Tools | Monitor SQL from the main menu, as Figure 6-11 illustrates.

Just as with the previous GUI-based methods, our second goal—obtaining a detailed performance analysis for a single SQL ID and session ID—is accomplished by navigating to a row of interest on the screen shown in Figure 6-11 and then either clicking the Execution Details button or clicking the link to its SQL ID, which displays the screen shown in Figure 6-12.

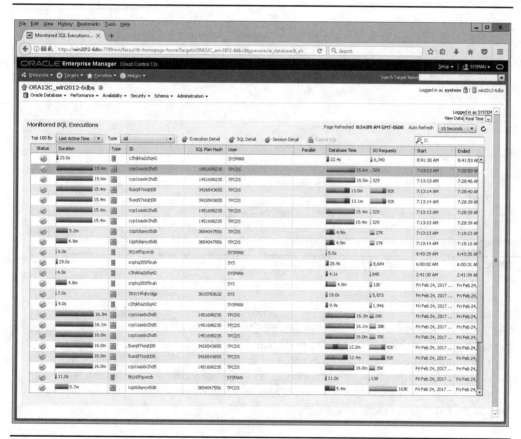

FIGURE 6-11.   *OEM monitored SQL overview*

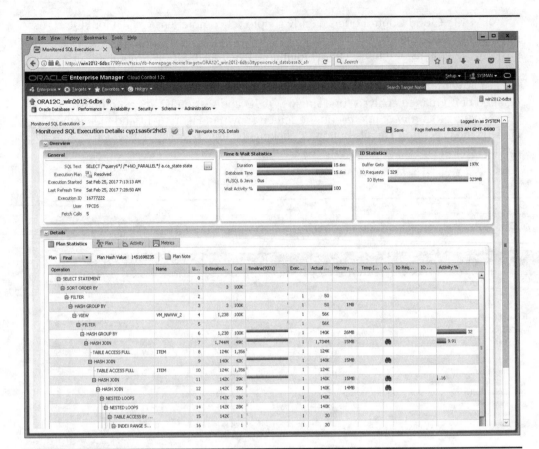

FIGURE 6-12. *OEM monitored SQL drilldown*

Finally, OEM 13c Cloud Control offers one more location from which to monitor SQL—the Database Home page (which many Oracle DBAs set as their default starting page), shown in Figure 6-13. The screen displays all the SQL monitored for the past hour (without any stated maximum number of statements), so from the moment that OEM 13c Cloud Control has been launched, a comprehensive overview of the SQL monitored is available. Clicking the SQL ID for any row displayed in that panel will launch the execution details screen.

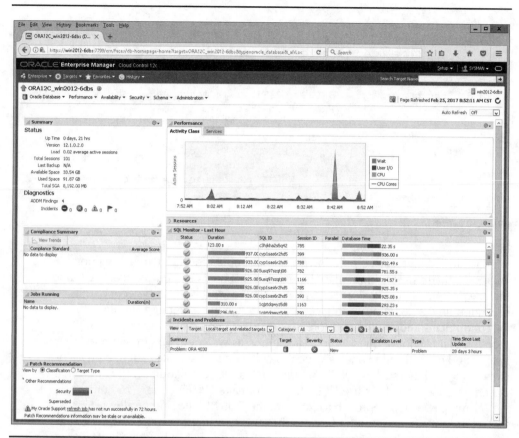

FIGURE 6-13. *OEM Database Home page*

Interpreting SQL Monitor Performance Data

After obtaining a SQL Monitor detailed view for a SQL statement of interest, what do we do next? Let's take another look at TPC-DS query #6 as an example, since it is only 20 lines long and is small enough to visualize and comprehend:

```
-- filename: query6.sql
-- script to execute TPC-DS query #6
set timing on
SELECT /*query6*/ a.ca_state state, COUNT(*) cnt
FROM  tpcds.customer_address a ,
      tpcds.customer c ,
      tpcds.store_sales s ,
```

```
       tpcds.date_dim d ,
       tpcds.item i
WHERE a.ca_address_sk    = c.c_current_addr_sk
  AND c.c_customer_sk    = s.ss_customer_sk
  AND s.ss_sold_date_sk  = d.d_date_sk
  AND s.ss_item_sk       = i.i_item_sk
  AND d.d_month_seq      = (SELECT DISTINCT (d_month_seq)
                             FROM  tpcds.date_dim
                             WHERE d_year = 2001
                               AND d_moy   = 6)
  AND i.i_current_price > 1.2 * (SELECT AVG(j.i_current_price)
                                  FROM  tpcds.item j
                                  WHERE j.i_category = i.i_category)
GROUP BY a.ca_state
HAVING COUNT(*) >= 10
ORDER BY cnt;
set timing off
```

Back in Chapter 5 we tried applying a few simple hints (and arguably poor choices at that) as shots in the dark to improve this query's performance. We found that the PARALLEL hint both reduced the optimizer cost by 71.8 percent and its execution time by 68.4 percent. However, since we were working simply with execution plans and not the far more advanced and complete output from SQL Monitor, that may have been as good a solution as we could obtain without doing a deeper and more detailed analysis such as collecting a trace file. But that's a lot of extra work, and that's why SQL Monitor is such a welcome addition to our arsenal of performance tools. Let's use SQL Monitor to make TPC-DS query #6 hum.

A simple two-step approach to interpret the SQL Monitor data follows. First, look at the left-side execution plan information focusing on just the leaf nodes (for now) for any generally expensive (that you believe that could be done better) or concerning operations such as full table scans or nested loops. If you find any, record those line numbers as possible candidates for concern.

■ Examining Figure 6-14, note the following lines: 4, 5, 6, 8, 10, 15, 16, and 17.

■ Of those lines, three are nested loops and five are full table scans. Although nested loops and full table scans are not bad, lots of them showing here and nothing else hints at the possibility of something better.

■ Moreover, line 17 (which contributes to line 11, which has the highest reported activity) is a full table scan on the largest table in the TPC-DS schema, with some 173 million rows. Because we happen to know the size of this table, this makes it easier to spot the issue; however, if table sizes were not know beforehand, the Estimated Rows and Actual Rows columns in Figure 6-14 would serve as an accurate gauge.

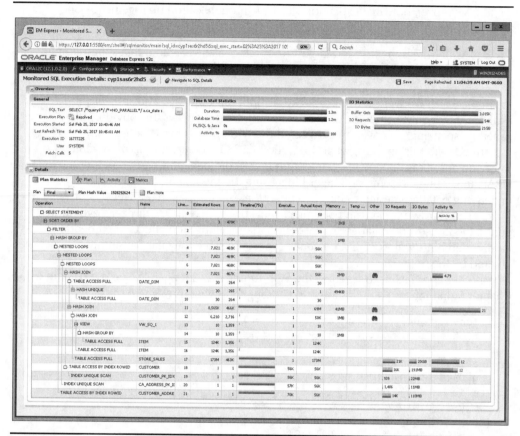

FIGURE 6-14. *Dissecting SQL monitoring details*

Therefore, from this simple execution plan–oriented cursory review, it seems that there are too many expensive plan steps, and in particular, line 17 appears to be the highest contributing resource consumer to line 11, which reports the most activity. Although this first step is fairly subjective and basically how most Oracle DBAs normally would have interpreted an execution plan, nothing really new is revealed here; but it is still helpful to gather these observations.

The second step is far more objective and based upon runtime performance data provided by SQL Monitor. Let's examine Figure 6-14 again, but this time focus attention on the right side of the data—most notably the columns for Activity %, Actual Rows, IO Requests, and IO Bytes:

■ Using this approach initially focuses our attention on lines 11, 17, and 18.

■ However, we can safely eliminate line 18, as its 56K rows and 191MB of I/O are orders of magnitude smaller than the others.

- Moreover, note that execution steps 11 through 17 roll up together as one major execution plan subgrouping.

- As line 17 is the first and largest resource consumer within that subgrouping, it's the logical focal point.

In this case, we were extremely lucky, as both our objective and subjective analyses yielded the same line as the pain point. It's not always this obvious, but generally speaking, any overlap between these two approaches is noteworthy.

Armed with this analysis, what do we do next? Of course, the simplest yet least satisfying answer is, It depends. Sometimes (as we did back in Chapter 5), an Oracle DBA can simply add some optimizer hints using the intimate knowledge of the underlying database design to improve upon the execution plan. However, some Oracle shops frown upon using optimizer hints because of the optimizer's evolution during the last several database releases and the resulting side-effects of embedding hard-coded hints within SQL statements, especially since they can be simply ignored by the optimizer.

Another approach is to leverage the SQL Tuning Advisor again as we did back in Chapter 5. In that case, it recommended adding following three indexes:

```
-- filename: query6_sqltuning_indexes.sql
-- script to index TPC-DS query #6 for speed

create index new_idx1
    on DATE_DIM(D_MONTH_SEQ);
create index new_idx2
    on DATE_DIM(D_YEAR,D_MOY,D_MONTH_SEQ);
create index new_idx3
    on STORE_SALES(SS_SOLD_DATE_SK);
```

Interestingly, in this case the SQL Tuning Advisor's suggestions to add these three indexes actually increased the query's runtime from 75 seconds to 954 seconds.

In most cases, the informed DBA can use her knowledge of the database design to modify the underlying database objects' structure, or her intuition about the nature of the query to improve upon the SQL code. In our case and for many people using third-party database applications, we cannot change the SQL code for a query. So very often we must find a database object change to make the difference. We looked at the query and realized that other than the basic join condition columns, the query did a count of orders per state. In other words, with adding proper indexes, the query could be satisfied entirely with just the indexes. So we added the following five indexes:

```
-- filename: query6_berts_indexes.sql
-- script to index TPC-DS query #6 for speed

create index bert_idx1
    on DATE_DIM(D_DATE_SK,D_MONTH_SEQ,D_YEAR);
create index bert_idx2
    on ITEM(I_ITEM_SK,I_CURRENT_PRICE,I_CATEGORY);
create index bert_idx3
    on CUSTOMER_ADDRESS(CA_ADDRESS_SK,CA_STATE);
create index bert_idx4
    on CUSTOMER(C_CUSTOMER_SK,C_CURRENT_ADDR_SK);
create index bert_idx5
    on STORE_SALES(SS_ITEM_SK,SS_CUSTOMER_SK,SS_SOLD_DATE_SK);
```

The results shown in Figure 6-15 confirm the intuition. With these new indexes, the runtime went from 8.3 minutes (see row with hint query 6-1) down to just 22 seconds (see row with hint 6-2). Remember we're not saying that nest loops or full table scans are necessarily a bad thing. But for this query, they kind of stuck out as interesting. In the proper environment, those operations could very well have been just fine.

Furthermore, the SQL Monitor data shown in Figure 6-16 revealed that we reduced the nested loop count from five down to one, eliminated all the full table scans, and reduced the total I/O Bytes by a factor of 10! Oh, and did you notice it used all the new indexes? While there may still be room for improvement, we decided this was sufficient.

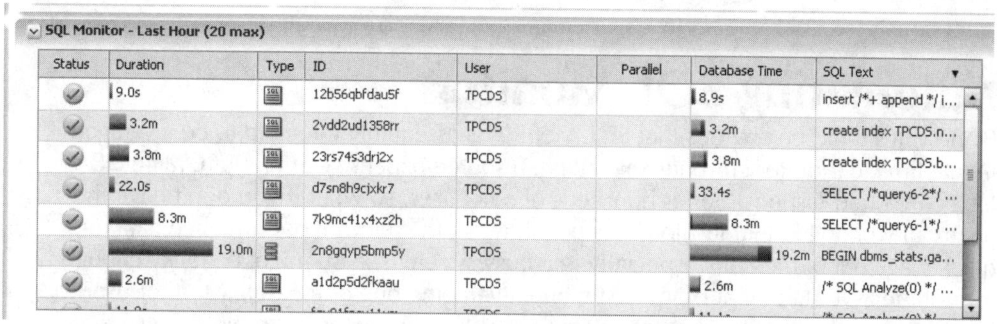
SQL Monitor - Last Hour (20 max)

Status	Duration	Type	ID	User	Parallel	Database Time	SQL Text
	9.0s		12b56qbfdau5f	TPCDS		8.9s	insert /*+ append */ i...
	3.2m		2vdd2ud1358rr	TPCDS		3.2m	create index TPCDS.n...
	3.8m		23rs74s3drj2x	TPCDS		3.8m	create index TPCDS.b...
	22.0s		d7sn8h9cjxkr7	TPCDS		33.4s	SELECT /*query6-2*/ ...
	8.3m		7k9mc41x4xz2h	TPCDS		8.3m	SELECT /*query6-1*/ ...
	19.0m		2n8gqyp5bmp5y	TPCDS		19.2m	BEGIN dbms_stats.ga...
	2.6m		a1d2p5d2fkaau	TPCDS		2.6m	/* SQL Analyze(0) */ ...

FIGURE 6-15. *Query #6 runtime greatly reduced*

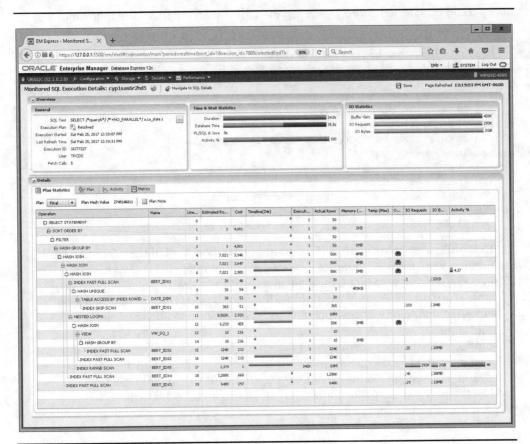

FIGURE 6-16. *Improved SQL Monitor results*

Automating SQL Monitor

By now, it should be obvious that SQL Monitor is essentially intended to be leveraged in real time to monitor currently executing, resource-expensive SQL. But Oracle DBAs today are often responsible for hundreds of databases, so what if you don't have the luxury of working in that fashion? It is possible that the relevant performance data may quickly age out of memory, especially in a busy system, so you might be lucky enough to spot the SQL statement of interest while leveraging one of the SQL Monitor user interfaces covered in this chapter or continuously running the example scripts provided—or you might miss it completely.

Luckily, starting in Oracle 12cR1, there is now a facility (DBMS_AUTO_REPORT) to automate collection of the SQL Monitor data into Automatic Workload Repository (AWR) for the activity over a user-controlled period of time. From that data collection, it's a simple matter of running a listing report of the SQL activity captured, and then detailed SQL Monitor reports for any of those captured SQL statements; that means there's no longer a need to watch things running live, hoping to spot correctly and dissect in real time the activity of interest.

Let's examine a relatively simple yet typical and extremely useful use case: An Oracle DBA starts a SQL Monitor data collection with DBMS_AUTO_REPORT, allows some application workload activity to occur, and then stops that data collection.

```
-- filename: auto_report_demo.sql
-- script to auto collect SQL Monitor data for defined workload

        CONNECT sys/bert1234 as sysdba
        BEGIN
            DBMS_AUTO_REPORT.START_REPORT_CAPTURE;
        END;
        /


        . . .
        << application workload occurs >>
        . . .

        CONNECT tpcds/tpcds
        @tpcds_queries.sql

        CONNECT sys/bert1234 as sysdba

        BEGIN
            DBMS_AUTO_REPORT.FINISH_REPORT_CAPTURE;
        END;
        /
```

NOTE
By default, the DBMS_AUTO_REPORT package is granted only to SYS, so it will be necessary to grant execute explicitly to any DBA account(s) that need to have access to use this feature. However, note that often when Oracle restricts access to DBMS packages like this, there could be valid security concerns or reasons for the restriction, so be conservative with any such grants.

Once the Oracle DBA has successfully collected the SQL Monitor data for the activity or period desired, she must first list the captured inventory (stored in DBA_HIST_REPORTS). There are two ways to extract such a listing, shown by these two SQL scripts:

```
-----
-- Show recently-executed SQL Monitor reports (directly from key values)
-----
COL report_id      FORMAT 999999    HEADING "Report|ID"
COL sql_id         FORMAT A15       HEADING "SQL ID"
COL sql_exec_id    FORMAT A15       HEADING "SQL EXEC ID"
COL sql_exec_start FORMAT A19       HEADING "SQL EXEC Start"
TTITLE "Recently-Executed SQL Monitor Report Tasks|(from DBA_HIST_REPORTS)"
SELECT
     report_id
    ,key1 sql_id
    ,key2 sql_exec_id
    ,key3 sql_exec_start
  FROM dba_hist_reports
 WHERE component_name = 'sqlmonitor';
TTITLE OFF


-----
-- Show recently-executed SQL Monitor reports (via XML decoding)
-----
COL report_id      FORMAT 999999    HEADING "Report|ID"
COL sql_id         FORMAT A15       HEADING "SQL ID"
COL sql_exec_id    FORMAT A15       HEADING "SQL EXEC ID"
COL sql_exec_start FORMAT A19       HEADING "SQL EXEC Start"
TTITLE "Recently-Executed SQL Monitor Report Tasks|(from DBA_HIST_REPORTS)"
SELECT
     report_id
    ,EXTRACTVALUE(XMLType(report_summary),'/report_repository_summary/sql/@sql_id') sql_id
    ,EXTRACTVALUE(XMLType(report_summary),'/report_repository_summary/sql/@sql_exec_id') sql_exec_id
    ,EXTRACTVALUE(XMLType(report_summary),'/report_repository_summary/sql/@sql_exec_start') sql_exec_start
  FROM dba_hist_reports
 WHERE component_name = 'sqlmonitor';
TTITLE OFF
```

The output is rather simple, as shown here:

```
Thu Mar 09                                          page      1
          Recently-Executed SQL Monitor Report Tasks
                   (from DBA_HIST_REPORTS)


    Report
        ID SQL ID          SQL EXEC ID      SQL EXEC Start
   ------- --------------- ---------------- -------------------
      1783 71x8xp9byq9cy   16777216         02:24:2017 01:59:04
      1784 05s9358mm6vrr   16777216         02:24:2017 01:58:15
      1785 7h1yzj6ymv9q2   16777216         02:24:2017 01:58:55
      1788 9tj16ffqysrzb   16777216         02:24:2017 11:45:09
      1790 f6cz4n8y72xdc   16777216         02:24:2017 11:45:21
      1794 cyp1sas6r2hd5   16777219         02:24:2017 11:46:25
      1833 2vdd2ud1358rr   16777216         02:25:2017 23:39:04
      1825 b2naawfzu7huu   16777216         02:25:2017 11:49:20
```

```
1933 c3hjkha2s5q42     16777216          03:09:2017 20:43:51
1936 d95mwqjmf1y0r     16777216          03:09:2017 20:49:13
...
 964 ddwr7w813xk07     16777219          03:09:2017 22:03:40
1965 1rgwqqsynkqm6     16777216          03:09:2017 22:05:17
1952 381t19fqhxdgp     16777216          03:09:2017 22:00:15
1953 2jzsdwqxbta4u     16777216          03:09:2017 22:00:08
1945 cyp1sas6r2hd5     16777216          03:09:2017 21:19:05
1946 cyp1sas6r2hd5     16777219          03:09:2017 21:19:05
1948 1qjztdqwyz5d8     16777218          03:09:2017 21:22:48
1949 1qjztdqwyz5d8     16777219          03:09:2017 21:22:49
1950 5usq97szqtj08     16777218          03:09:2017 21:22:48
1951 5usq97szqtj08     16777219          03:09:2017 21:22:49
```

```
179 rows selected.
```

The detailed SQL Monitor report itself for a specific SQL ID is stored in XML format in DBA_HIST_REPORTS_DETAILS and is referenced by the Report ID. There are multiple ways to extract the report (TEXT and HTML), as shown by the following two SQL scripts (using Report ID 1951 from the prior listing, which is the SQL ID and report desired):

```
-----
-- Extract a text-only (non-HTML) report for a past SQL Monitor session
-----
SET LONG 10000000
SET LONGCHUNKSIZE 10000000
SET PAGESIZE 0
SELECT
    DBMS_AUTO_REPORT.REPORT_REPOSITORY_DETAIL(RID => 1951, TYPE => 'text')
  FROM dual;


-----
-- Generate an HTML format report for a past SQL Monitor session
-----
SET TRIMSPOOL ON
SET TRIM ON
SET PAGESIZE 0
SET LINESIZE 1000
SET LONG 1000000
SET LONGCHUNKSIZE 1000000
SPOOL /home/oracle/historical_sqlmon.sql
SELECT
    DBMS_AUTO_REPORT.REPORT_REPOSITORY_DETAIL(RID => 1951, TYPE => html)
  FROM dual;
```

The resulting report, shown in Figure 6-17, is very similar to the one shown earlier in Figure 6-4. So we have, in fact, been able to perform detailed SQL monitoring without having to sit online in front of a screen mining manually for the SQL statement that was causing performance issues.

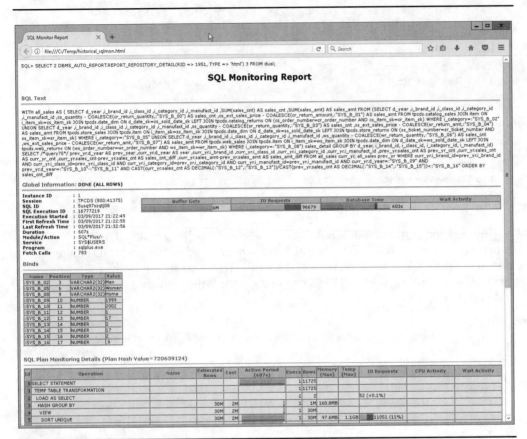

FIGURE 6-17. *SQL monitoring report from automated run*

Summary

Since its introduction in Oracle 11gR1, SQL Monitor is probably one of the most valuable new features that Oracle has introduced. This feature has advanced the art of obtaining SQL runtime improvements to a science. Furthermore, it has made the process far more straightforward, and as we have demonstrated, interfaces are provided in just about every conceivable tool an Oracle DBA is likely to use, including a PL/SQL API for scripting, SQL Developer, OEM Express, and OEM Cloud Control. Finally, we showed that even the SQL Tuning Advisor sometimes cannot automatically provide a solution that's superior to a simple SQL Monitor review for potential improvements.

CHAPTER
7

Real-Time Operations Monitoring

The previous chapter made the case for leveraging the extensive features of SQL Monitor as one of the most powerful tools on any Oracle DBA's tool belt. Although SQL Monitor is definitely a flexible and wide-ranging tool for detecting and monitoring the most expensive individual SQL statements, it offers only two modes of operation: either live, ad-hoc monitoring, or automated capture and reporting during a time period of the Oracle DBA's choosing. Since most performance tuning situations are often focused on *individual* SQL statements, either of these two operation modes is quite sufficient.

In most real-world database applications, however, business requirements are implemented and deployed as a set of batched tasks that, for the sake of simplicity, we will call a *job*. Jobs can be executed manually, but more often a job is executed using either an Oracle-provided scheduling tool such as DBMS_SCHEDULER, DBMS_JOB, or Oracle Enterprise Manager; some Oracle shops leverage a third-party scheduling tool or even an OS-based scheduler such as CRON. To make matters even more complex, there are often dependencies between jobs that must be honored so that regularly scheduled business logic can be implemented with only limited human intervention.

When an Oracle DBA investigates actual performance problems in these situations, it is crucial to expand the scope of the inquiry beyond just a single SQL statement. What is needed instead is a guaranteed way to group together and collect performance data from only the SQL statements for a specific given job—in other words, applying SQL Monitor to a *defined collection* of individual SQL statements.

Fortunately, Oracle 12cR1 introduced the concept of *Real Time Operation Monitoring*, which is exactly what's needed (to augment SQL Monitoring). A database operation is simply the name given to a specific collection of SQL statements, including all PL/SQL calls containing SQL statements. There are two classes of real-time database operations:

- Simple, which encompasses just a single SQL statement (as with SQL Monitor)

- Composite, which comprises multiple SQL or PL/SQL statements

Since this latter composite case best matches the concept of a job, that's what we will pursue in the remainder of this chapter.

NOTE
This feature requires the optional diagnostics and tuning packs. Furthermore, the database configuration parameter for STATISTICS_LEVEL must be set to ALL or TYPICAL.

Defining a Simple Operation: The +MONITOR Hint

A reasonable question at this point might be, why does an Oracle DBA ever need to define a simple operation—that is, one that contains just a single SQL statement? After all, doesn't SQL Monitor already provide this capability?

The answer is that SQL Monitor *automatically* chooses candidate SQL statements based upon its default scope: any serially executed SQL statement that consumes five or more seconds of CPU or I/O in a single execution, as well as any parallelized SQL statement. Moreover, recall that an Oracle Database can monitor only a certain number of statements concurrently—20 times the number of CPUs. So if a single SQL statement doesn't meet the resource consumption criteria, SQL Monitor will simply ignore it. Fortunately, there's a simple way to override this behavior and force SQL Monitor to treat a specific SQL statement as a simple operation—simply add the +MONITOR optimizer hint to the statement, as shown here:

```
-- filename: query6.sql
-- script to execute TPC-DS query #6

set timing on
SELECT /*query6*/ /*+MONITOR*/
      a.ca_state state, COUNT(*) cnt
FROM  tpcds.customer_address a ,
      tpcds.customer c ,
      tpcds.store_sales s ,
      tpcds.date_dim d ,
      tpcds.item i
WHERE a.ca_address_sk   = c.c_current_addr_sk
  AND c.c_customer_sk   = s.ss_customer_sk
  AND s.ss_sold_date_sk = d.d_date_sk
  AND s.ss_item_sk      = i.i_item_sk
  AND d.d_month_seq     =
      (SELECT DISTINCT (d_month_seq)
         FROM  tpcds.date_dim
        WHERE d_year = 2001
          AND d_moy   = 6)
          AND i.i_current_price > 1.2 * (SELECT AVG(j.i_current_price)
                                           FROM  tpcds.item j
                                          WHERE j.i_category = i.i_category)
GROUP BY a.ca_state
HAVING COUNT(*) >= 10
ORDER BY cnt;
set timing off
exit
```

Otherwise, locating the SQL statements and then examining the detailed report for a simple operation is handled no differently than using SQL Monitor in Chapter 6. It's up to the Oracle DBA to choose whichever of the five methods described in that chapter to complete the diagnosis of the SQL statement.

Defining a Composite Operation

The second and far more important question is, how does one define a *composite operation* (that is, an operation that contains multiple SQL or PL/SQL statements)? Remember that this is the use case that more closely matches the real-world concept of a job. The process is actually quite easy: we encapsulate a composite operation by calling the DBMS_SQL_MONITOR package's BEGIN_OPERATION and END_ OPERATION procedures, respectively.

Let's examine a relatively simple, yet typical and extremely useful, scenario: The DBA starts a SQL Monitor data collection, runs some activity, and then stops that data collection as shown in the following script. Note that any existing job simply needs these two additional statements added to instrument the job: In this example the operation is named top_4_queries, which is a simple and easy-to-remember name for grouping together these four queries (5, 6, 75, and 77) of interest. Choose a name that holds meaning for you, that will be easy to remember, and that will be easy to spot.

```
-- filename: composite_operation.sql
-- script to run 4 tpc-ds queries as a composite operation

var composite_id number

exec :composite_id := DBMS_SQL_MONITOR.BEGIN_OPERATION('top_4_queries');

@query5.sql
@query6.sql
@query75.sql
@query77.sql

exec DBMS_SQL_MONITOR.END_OPERATION('top_4_queries',:composite_id);
```

After the job has been executed as a composite operation, it's time to see exactly how it consumed resources while it was running. To demonstrate, let's leverage the exact same process and tools that we did in Chapter 6. We'll show just two methods here for brevity—*PL/SQL scripting* and *OEM Express*.

> **NOTE**
> *This function associates a session with a database operation. Starting in Oracle Database 12c Release 2 (12.2), you can use* `session_id` *and* `session_num` *to indicate the session in which to start monitoring.*

Examining a Composite Operation via PL/SQL

Just as we did in Chapter 6, we'll start by looking at the list of operations that have recently executed. Running the SQL Monitor listing script, shown next, generates the HTML output shown in Figure 7-1. (Once again, changing the value for the `TYPE` variable from `HTML` to `TEXT` in the call to the `REPORT_SQL_MONITOR_LIST` procedure will produce the report in a text-only format if desired.) Note that the last row of output shows the `top_4_queries` database operation.

```
-- filename: report_sql_monitor_list.sql
-- script to display SQL statements being monitored

SET LONG 1000000
SET LONGCHUNKSIZE 1000000
SET LINESIZE 1000
SET PAGESIZE 0
SET TRIM ON
SET TRIMSPOOL ON
SET ECHO OFF
SET FEEDBACK OFF

SPOOL C:\Temp\report_sql_monitor_list.htm
SELECT DBMS_SQL_MONITOR.REPORT_SQL_MONITOR_LIST(
  type => 'HTML',
  report_level => 'ALL') AS report
FROM dual;
SPOOL OFF
```

Status	Duration	SQL Id or DBOP Name	User	Dop	DB Time	IOs	Start	End	SQL Text
DONE (ALL ROWS)	95s	1qjztdqwyz5d8	SYSTEM		94s	47509	03/11/2017 15:52:11	03/11/2017 15:53:46	with ss as (select s_store_sk, sum(ss_ext_sales_price) as sales,
DONE (ALL ROWS)	23s	cyp1sas6r2hd5	SYSTEM		35s	292K	03/11/2017 15:51:48	03/11/2017 15:52:11	SELECT /*query6*/ /*+NO_PARALLEL*/ a.ca_state state, COUNT(*) cnt FROM tp...
DONE (ALL ROWS)	180s	f42520uhfta6v	SYSTEM		165s	61009	03/11/2017 15:48:48	03/11/2017 15:51:48	WITH ssr as (SELECT s_store_id, SUM(sales_price) AS sale...
DONE	6.0s	9tj16ffqysrzb	SYSMAN		6s	393B	03/11/2017 15:47:30	03/11/2017 15:47:36	DECLARE job BINARY_INTEGER := :job; next_date TIMESTAMP WITH TIME ZONE := :myda...
DONE	8.0s	9tj16ffqysrzb	SYSMAN		7s	1367	03/11/2017 15:46:30	03/11/2017 15:46:38	DECLARE job BINARY_INTEGER := :job; next_date TIMESTAMP WITH TIME ZONE := :myda...
DONE (FIRST N ROWS)	7.0s	f6cz4n8y72xdc			7s	1510	03/11/2017 15:45:36	03/11/2017 15:45:43	SELECT space_usage_kbytes FROM v$sysaux_occupants WHERE occupant_name = 'SQL_...
DONE	4.0s	c2p32r5mzv8hb			3s	676	03/11/2017 15:45:36	03/11/2017 15:45:40	BEGIN prvt_advisor.delete_expired_tasks; END;
DONE	298s	top_4_queries	SYSTEM		282s	401K	03/11/2017 15:48:48	03/11/2017 15:53:46	

FIGURE 7-1. *SQL Monitoring List showing database operation*

We can now drill into the details for the top_4_queries database operation using the following script that generates the HTML output shown in Figure 7-2. Again, changing the value for the TYPE variable from HTML to TEXT in the call to the REPORT_SQL_MONITOR procedure will produce a text-only format report if so desired. Note that the DBOP_NAME parameter—which specifies the name of the database operation whose data output is requested—essentially replaces the SQL_ID parameter call to the same procedure we used in Chapter 6 to identify just a single SQL statement.

```
-- filename: report_sql_monitor_operation.sql
-- script to display specific db operation being monitored

SET LONG 1000000
SET LONGCHUNKSIZE 1000000
SET LINESIZE 1000
SET PAGESIZE 0
SET TRIM ON
SET TRIMSPOOL ON
SET ECHO OFF
SET FEEDBACK OFF

SPOOL C:\Temp\report_sql_monitor_operation.htm
SELECT DBMS_SQL_MONITOR.REPORT_SQL_MONITOR(
   dbop_name    => '&1',
   type         => 'HTML',
   report_level => 'ALL') AS report
FROM dual;
SPOOL OFF
```

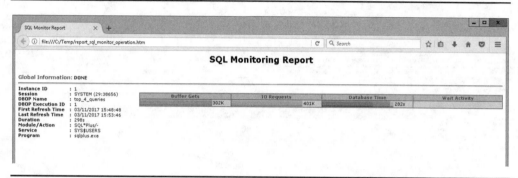

FIGURE 7-2. *SQL Monitoring Report for* `top_4_queries` *problem queries*

Finally, observe that the HTML output in Figure 7-2 is very brief, but this makes sense, because a database operation is just a grouping of related SQL and PL/SQL statements that encompass other SQL statements. To see details for any SQL statement of interest that are encapsulated within the database operation, we would simply drill down into a specific `sql_id` using the following script. The output from this script would be essentially identical to Figure 6-4 in Chapter 6 and is reproduced again here as Figure 7-3.

```
-- filename: report_sql_monitor.sql
-- script to display specific SQL statement being monitored

SET LONG 1000000
SET LONGCHUNKSIZE 1000000
SET LINESIZE 1000
SET PAGESIZE 0
SET TRIM ON
SET TRIMSPOOL ON
SET ECHO OFF
SET FEEDBACK OFF

SPOOL C:\Temp\report_sql_monitor.htm
SELECT DBMS_SQL_MONITOR.REPORT_SQL_MONITOR(
    sql_id       => '&1',
    type         => 'HTML',
    report_level => 'ALL') AS report
FROM dual;
SPOOL OFF
```

SQL Monitoring Report

SQL Text

SELECT /*query6*/ /*+NO_PARALLEL*/ a.ca_state state, COUNT(*) cnt FROM tpcds.customer_address a , tpcds.customer c , tpcds.store_sales s , tpcds.date_dim d , tpcds.item i WHERE a.ca_address_sk = c.c_current_addr_sk AND c.c_customer_sk = s.ss_customer_sk AND s.ss_sold_date_sk = d.d_date_sk AND s.ss_item_sk = i.i_item_sk AND d.d_month_seq = (SELECT DISTINCT (d_month_seq) FROM tpcds.date_dim WHERE d_year = :"SYS_B_0" AND d_moy = :"SYS_B_1") AND i.i_current_price > :"SYS_B_2" * (SELECT AVG(j.i_current_price) FROM tpcds.item j WHERE j.i_category = i.i_category) GROUP BY a.ca_state HAVING COUNT(*) >= :"SYS_B_3" ORDER BY cnt

Global Information: DONE (ALL ROWS)

Instance ID	: 1
Session	: TPCDS (1173:58554)
SQL ID	: cyp1sas6r2hd5
SQL Execution ID	: 16777217
Execution Started	: 02/03/2017 16:56:13
First Refresh Time	: 02/03/2017 16:56:17
Last Refresh Time	: 02/03/2017 17:08:47
Duration	: 754s
Module/Action	: SQL*Plus/-
Service	: SYS$USERS
Program	: sqlplus.exe
Fetch Calls	: 5

Buffer Gets		IO Requests		Database Time		Wait Activity	
	197K		34301		754s		

Binds

Name	Position	Type	Value
:SYS_B_0	1	NUMBER	2001
:SYS_B_1	2	NUMBER	6
:SYS_B_2	3	NUMBER	1.2
:SYS_B_3	4	NUMBER	10

SQL Plan Monitoring Details (Plan Hash Value=1451698235)

Id	Operation	Name	Estimated Rows	Cost	Active Period (754s)	Execs	Rows	Memory (Max)	Temp (Max)	IO Requests	CPU Activity	Wait Activity
0	SELECT STATEMENT					1	50					
1	SORT ORDER BY		3	100K		1	50	2.0KB				
2	FILTER					1	50					
3	HASH GROUP BY		3	100K		1	50	2.4MB				
4	VIEW	VM_NWVW_2	1238	100K		1	155756					
5	FILTER					1	155756					
6	HASH GROUP BY		1238	100K		1	140K	73.7MB				
7	HASH JOIN		2G	48628		1	2G	14.9MB				
8	TABLE ACCESS FULL	ITEM	124K	1356		1	124K			19 (<0.1%)		
9	HASH JOIN		140K	41982		1	140K	15.3MB				
10	TABLE ACCESS FULL	ITEM	124K	1356		1	124K					
11	HASH JOIN		142K	39427		1	140K	16.2MB				
12	HASH JOIN		142K	35236		1	140K	14.5MB				
13	HASH JOIN		142K	27923		1	1					
14	NESTED LOOPS		142K	27923		1	140K					
15	NESTED LOOPS		142K	27923		1	140K					
16	STATISTICS COLLECTOR					1	30					
17	TABLE ACCESS BY INDEX ROWID BATCHED	DATE_DIM	30	1		1	30					
18	INDEX RANGE SCAN	NEW_IDX1	30	1		1	30			3 (<0.1%)		
19	SORT UNIQUE NOSORT		30	2		1	1					
20	INDEX RANGE SCAN	NEW_IDX2	30	1		1	30			1 (<0.1%)		
21	INDEX RANGE SCAN	NEW_IDX3	4656	1		295	140K			15 (<0.1%)		
22	TABLE ACCESS BY INDEX ROWID	STORE_SALES	4656	931		280K	140K			33932 (98%)		
23	TABLE ACCESS FULL	STORE_SALES	4656	931								
24	TABLE ACCESS FULL	CUSTOMER	1M	4766		1	1M			211 (.6%)		
25	TABLE ACCESS FULL	CUSTOMER_ADDRESS	640K	2643		1	640K			120 (.3%)		

FIGURE 7-3. *Report for SQL ID from an operation*

Examining a Composite Operation via OEM Express

Since we don't have to worry about the ad hoc nature of spotting the SQL statement of interest while it's running, because the creation of the database operation has forced that data into the AWR repository, we can instead use the graphical user interface as a quicker and easier method to see an overview and then drill down into various SQL statements to pinpoint the performance problem areas. So, looking at OEM Express, we can see that the second row of the SQL Monitor area (bottom right) displays the `top_4_queries` database operation, as shown in Figure 7-4.

If we click the `top_4_queries` database operation/ID link, we'll see the detailed report information shown in Figure 7-5. Note three things: the SQL IDs we'll need to use to drill down into particular SQL statements, their relative order, and their respective CPU resource usage.

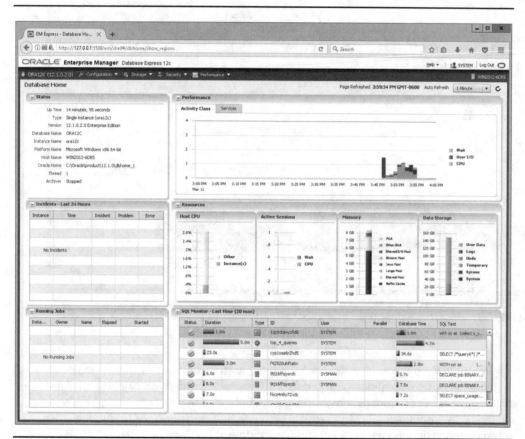

FIGURE 7-4. *Dashboard showing database operation*

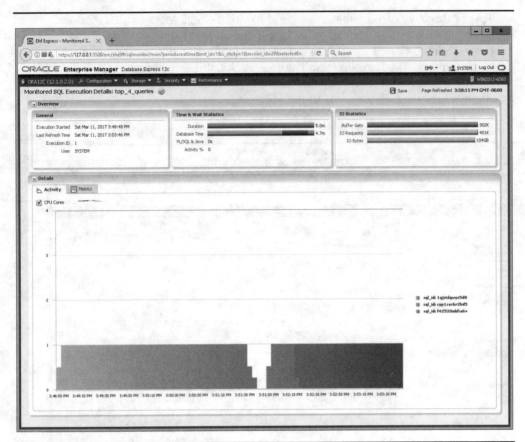

FIGURE 7-5. *Database operation SQL IDs and ordering*

Before leaving this screen, take a look at the Metrics tab, because it contains an extremely useful breakdown of four major resource consumption categories for the entire database operation, as shown in Figure 7-6. Note that you can use the relative timing order from Figure 7-5 to correlate which SQL ID corresponds to the peak resource usage. In this case, it seems that the middle SQL ID (cyp1sas6r2hd5) is worth primary attention. From a timing perspective, it appears to be the one running at 3:51 P.M., when spikes in both memory and IO requests occurred.

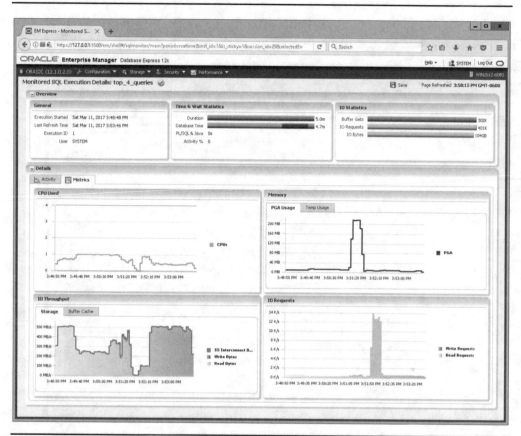

FIGURE 7-6. *Database operation detailed resource usage*

Now that we know the SQL IDs of interest, we can drill down into them individually by returning to the dashboard and clicking the ID URL of interest. For example, Figure 7-7 shows the detailed report information for the first SQL ID (1qjzdqwyz5d8). As you can see, it's doing a full table scan on the STORE_SALES table, which is consuming 35 percent of the overall time. Since that's the largest table in the query, this is not at all surprising.

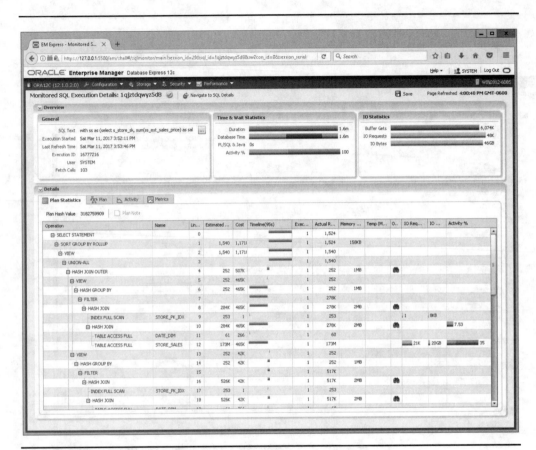

FIGURE 7-7. *Database operation-specific SQL Monitor report*

Finally, we can correlate the SQL statements metrics against those for the entire operation by choosing to display the Metrics tab, shown in Figure 7-8, and comparing that against the results shown in Figure 7-5. Thus we see that the query is doing 500 MB/second of storage reads, which confirms that this full table scan of our largest table is the most expensive. In this case, it's close to the maximum possible limit for the I/O subsystem on this database server. If the I/O subsystem could handle such a load, then an analysis of DB time would be a good place to start.

FIGURE 7-8. *Database operation-specific SQL resource use*

Summary

This chapter built upon the foundations we established in Chapter 6 for SQL Monitor to demonstrate how to collect performance data for database operations, a grouping of one or more SQL and PL/SQL statements. Because most Oracle DBAs are likely to encounter composite database operations—typically known in the parlance of real-world database applications as *jobs*—this extension of SQL Monitor's capability is likely to become one of the single most useful tools that an Oracle DBA can deploy from his tool belt to instrument their application code quickly and easily. This toolset becomes especially valuable when a single SQL statement or operation within a job stream suddenly and unexpectedly begins to perform poorly and needs to be identified, analyzed, and corrected.

CHAPTER
8

Real-Time ADDM and Emergency Monitoring

The previous two chapters focused on monitoring SQL statements on an individual basis as well as conjointly when they are part of a larger group of statements, and both techniques are quite useful under most circumstances. But when a database instance becomes heavily overloaded, begins running miserably slow as compared to expected norms, or even appears to be in a "hung" state, these techniques may be essentially useless, because the overloaded system may become so unresponsive that it's impossible even to initiate a database connection to diagnose the problem.

In the past, an Oracle DBA may have resorted to restarting or "bouncing" the database instance to regain control; however, because many production application systems today demand extreme availability, this solution is simply unacceptable, and not just from a business perspective. For example, bouncing a database instance that supports healthcare, intelligence-gathering, or financial applications may actually require *reporting* that outage—no matter how well intentioned—as part of complying with the corresponding industry's regulatory requirements.

In these situations, an Oracle DBA clearly needs some better alternatives, so starting with Oracle 12cR1, two new feature sets were introduced that provide the ability to diagnose performance problems when a database instance is nearly completely unresponsive: *Real-Time Automatic Database Diagnostic Monitoring (Real-Time ADDM)* and *Emergency Monitoring*.

NOTE
These features do require licensing the optional Diagnostics and Tuning packs. Furthermore, the database configuration parameter for STATISTICS_LEVEL *must be set to* ALL *or* TYPICAL. *Finally, the configuration parameter for* CONTROL_MANAGEMENT_PACK_ACCESS *must be set to* DIAGNOSTIC *or* DIAGNOSTIC+TUNING.

Real-Time ADDM

To appreciate how Real-Time ADDM features work, let's run through a quick refresh on how an Oracle DBA would leverage a standard ADDM reporting workflow in earlier database releases. To simulate the scenario we've just described, we'll use both methods to diagnose potential reasons for extremely poor database performance while the Swingbench utility generates an intense TPC-DS query benchmark.

Standard ADDM: A Review

Prior to Oracle 12cR1, an Oracle DBA would run an ADDM report by selecting a beginning and ending AWR snapshot range that encompassed the critical time when the performance of the database in question had degraded noticeably.

Here's an example scenario: As Swingbench unwound its workload against the database, we observed that the database instance became unresponsive just around 11:15 A.M. as the server became less responsive and the average transaction time increased significantly. At that time, users started complaining about a system slowdown, so we will focus our ADDM analysis tool against that period.

The following script first displays the AWR snapshot IDs for the past eight hours to allow selection of the starting and ending AWR snapshot ID range. Then it generates an ADDM report, spooling the report output in text format to a file:

```
-- filename: addm_report.sql
-- script to run standard addm report

column begin_interval_time format a25
column end_interval_time format a25

select snap_id, begin_interval_time, end_interval_time
  from dba_hist_snapshot
  where end_interval_time >= systimestamp-(8/24)
  order by snap_id desc;

var task_name varchar2(40)
exec task_name   := 'addm_report'
exec dbms_addm.analyze_db(:task_name,&begin_snapshot,&end_snapshot)

SET LONG 1000000 LONGCHUNKSIZE 1000000
SET LINESIZE 1000 PAGESIZE 0
SET TRIM ON TRIMSPOOL ON
SET ECHO OFF FEEDBACK OFF

spool addm_report.txt
SELECT dbms_addm.get_report(:task_name) FROM dual;
spool off
```

When performance levels normalized, we could then run the script and select the appropriate two snapshots—in this case, snapshot IDs 770 and 771—which encompassed the time period of particularly poor performance. (Although it is certainly possible to run an ADDM report using the same snapshot ID for both starting and ending periods, it's generally not advisable, because we want to see a delta over some time period to understand truly what's going on.) Since we only knew the approximate time range to analyze, the only choice was to err on the side of caution by including a longer time period that encapsulated the brief period of unresponsiveness.

```
SQL> @addm_report

   SNAP_ID BEGIN_INTERVAL_TIME        END_INTERVAL_TIME
---------- -------------------------  -------------------------
       772 19-MAR-17 11.37.09.336 AM  19-MAR-17 01.00.43.225 PM
       771 19-MAR-17 11.00.16.251 AM  19-MAR-17 11.37.09.336 AM
       770 19-MAR-17 10.00.03.382 AM  19-MAR-17 11.00.16.251 AM
       769 19-MAR-17 09.00.49.587 AM  19-MAR-17 10.00.03.382 AM
       768 19-MAR-17 08.00.38.289 AM  19-MAR-17 09.00.49.587 AM
       767 19-MAR-17 07.00.27.329 AM  19-MAR-17 08.00.38.289 AM
       766 19-MAR-17 06.00.16.079 AM  19-MAR-17 07.00.27.329 AM
       765 19-MAR-17 05.00.04.591 AM  19-MAR-17 06.00.16.079 AM

8 rows selected.
PL/SQL procedure successfully completed.

Enter value for begin_snapshot: 770
Enter value for end_snapshot: 771

PL/SQL procedure successfully completed.
```

The real issue here, of course, is that we're essentially working backward to solve this particular database performance issue, because we were forced to wait until *after* automatic AWR snapshots had been gathered to cover the targeted time period. Of course, it might have been possible to force the generation of an AWR snapshot manually at 11:15 A.M. when we first encountered excruciatingly slow performance—but what if it was impossible to create a connection to the database in time to generate the snapshot? Or what if generating the snapshot would have taken too long due to the overload?

Put simply, the best solution in this scenario is to leverage Real-Time ADDM.

Real-Time ADDM to the Rescue

Now let's take a look at how Real-Time ADDM is used to probe this apparent database slowdown for its potential root causes. We know there was a major performance slowdown at right 11:15 A.M., so we can focus Real-Time ADDM at that very moment to investigate even though no automatic ending period AWR snapshot had yet been taken.

What changed in Oracle 12cR1 to make such an option possible? The secret is that Real-Time ADDM does not use AWR snapshots performance data; instead, the Oracle Management Monitor (MMON) background process runs every three seconds and uses in-memory data to diagnose any performance spikes in the database.

Real-Time ADDM then concentrates on finding any of the performance issue conditions shown in Table 8-1.

This monitoring and diagnosis is done without any latch or lock overhead. If a condition is observed, it automatically creates a Real-Time ADDM report and stores it within the AWR. The metadata for this report is captured in view DBA_HIST_REPORTS and the actual report itself is retained in view DBA_HIST_REPORT_DETAILS. Even better, to ensure that this automatic process does not contribute to the issue at hand by

Trigger	Triggers Real-Time ADDM When
High System Load	Average active sessions exceeds some threshold that you define based upon your own acceptance criteria: Oracle suggests when >= 3 × # CPU cores
I/O Bound System	Single-block read performance exceeds some threshold that you define based upon your own acceptance criteria: for example, when >= 10ms
CPU Bound System	CPU utilization exceeds some threshold that you define based upon your own acceptance criteria: Oracle suggests when >= 50% of DB Time
Memory Over-Allocation	Memory allocation exceeds some threshold that you define based upon your own acceptance criteria: Oracle suggests when >= 95%
Network Inter-Connect Bound	Single-block interconnect transfer time exceeds some threshold you define based upon your own acceptance criteria
Session Limit Exceeded	Session count exceeds some threshold that you define based upon your own acceptance criteria: for example, session count >= 90% of config parameter PROCESSES
Process Limit Exceeded	Process count exceeds some threshold that you define based upon your own acceptance criteria: for example, session count >= 90% of config parameter SESSIONS
Hung Session Detected	Hung session count exceeds some threshold you define based upon your own acceptance criteria: Oracle suggests when >= 10% of total sessions are hung
Deadlock Detected	Any deadlock condition detected

TABLE 8-1. *Real-Time ADDM: Triggering Conditions*

repeatedly capturing and reporting the same information needlessly, the database limits itself to one such collection in any 5-minute interval, and never performs more than one such collection in a 45-minute period unless the newer occurrence increases the impact at least 100 percent.

NOTE
Not all triggering conditions can be measured as a percentage increase in the impact, so not all triggering conditions can follow the 45-minute filtering rule. For example, deadlock either exists or does not.

Real-Time ADDM via Scripts

Oracle provides multiple methods for performing a Real-Time ADDM analysis. The simplest method, which by default displays the last hour of Real-Time ADDM reports captured, is to execute script rtaddmrpt.sql and select the Real-Time ADDM report ID of interest (2277, as shown here):

```
C:\scripts>sqlplus system/Texas1234 @?/rdbms/admin/rtaddmrpt.sql
SQL*Plus: Release 12.1.0.2.0 Production on Sun Mar 19 11:46:08 2017
Copyright (c) 1982, 2016, Oracle.  All rights reserved.
Last Successful login time: Sun Mar 19 2017 11:46:38 -05:00
Connected to:
Oracle Database 12c Enterprise Edition Release 12.1.0.2.0 - 64bit Production
With the Partitioning, OLAP, Advanced Analytics and Real Application Testing options
Current Database
~~~~~~~~~~~~~~~~~
     DB Id
----------
 309585722
Instances in this Report repository
~~~~~~~~~~~~~~~~~~~~~~~~~~~~~~~~~~~~~~
     Db Id Inst Num
---------- --------
 309585722        1
Default to current database
Using database id:              309585722
Enter begin time for report:
--    Valid input formats:
--       To specify absolute begin time:
--          [MM/DD[/YY]] HH24:MI[:SS]
--          Examples: 02/23/03 14:30:15
--                    02/23 14:30:15
--                    14:30:15
--                    14:30
--       To specify relative begin time: (start with '-' sign)
--          -[HH24:]MI
--          Examples: -1:15 (SYSDATE - 1 Hr 15 Mins)
--                    -25   (SYSDATE - 25 Mins)
```

```
Default to -60 mins
Report begin time specified:
Enter duration in minutes starting from begin time:
Defaults to SYSDATE - begin_time
Press Enter to analyze till current time
Report duration specified:
Using 19/03/2017 10:12:18 as report begin time
Using 19/03/2017 11:12:18 as report end time
Report ids in this workload repository.
~~~~~~~~~~~~~~~~~~~~~~~~~~~~~~~~~~~~~~~~~~~~~~~~
    DB Id REPORT_ID TIME                 trigger_cause impact
---------- --------- ------------------- ------------- ------
 309585722     2277 19/03/2017 11:46:12 I/O Bound        5.1
Select a report id from the list. If the report id list is empty,
please select a different begin time and end time.
Enter value for report_id: 2277
Report id specified : 2277
Specify the Report Name
~~~~~~~~~~~~~~~~~~~~~~~~~
The default report file name is rtaddmrpt_0319_1146.html. To use this name, press
<return> to continue, otherwise enter an alternative.
Enter value for report_name:
```

Isolating the Problem: Activity Summary

The resulting HTML output file looks remarkably like what the OEM Express utility provides; likewise, just as with OEM Express, the HTML file requires only that the Adobe Flash plug-in be installed for the browser selected. Figure 8-1 shows the Activity tab from the resulting report; this clearly shows that around 11:12 A.M., values for both CPU utilization and User IO spiked substantially. Although this is not particularly surprising—after all, the queries that the TPC-DS query benchmark generator executes often consume extremely large amounts of physical IO—we now know *precisely* when the performance bottleneck started.

Real-Time ADDM produces valuable output on the other tabs of the report as well, but for now we'll focus on ADDM findings presented within the Current ADDM Findings tab, shown in Figure 8-2.

Once again, this section of the report revealed no major surprises; the findings reflect that an excessive number of resource-intensive queries are executing simultaneously, which more clearly indicates the predominance of User I/O as compared to System I/O and CPU utilization. Had there been some other issue such as a deadlock between two sessions, the findings would indicate and elaborate on that issue as well; this reflects the fact that Real-Time ADDM has been designed to look for multiple simultaneous vectors of performance issues.

Real-Time ADDM Analysis in XML Format

Finally, there is one other scripting option for Real-Time ADDM reporting. We can run the script shown here, which calls the DBMS_ADDM.REAL_TIME_ADDM_REPORT

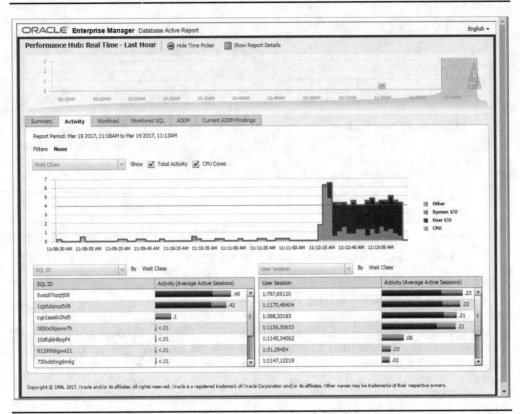

FIGURE 8-1. *Real-Time ADDM report: Activity tab*

function that returns an XML file containing some fairly basic performance metadata for the past five minutes:

```
-- filename: realtimeaddm.sql
-- script to run Real-Time ADDM report for last 5 minutes

SET LONG 1000000 LONGCHUNKSIZE 1000000
SET LINESIZE 1000 PAGESIZE 0
SET TRIM ON TRIMSPOOL ON
SET ECHO OFF FEEDBACK OFF

spool realtimeaddm.xml
select DBMS_ADDM.REAL_TIME_ADDM_REPORT from dual;
spool off
```

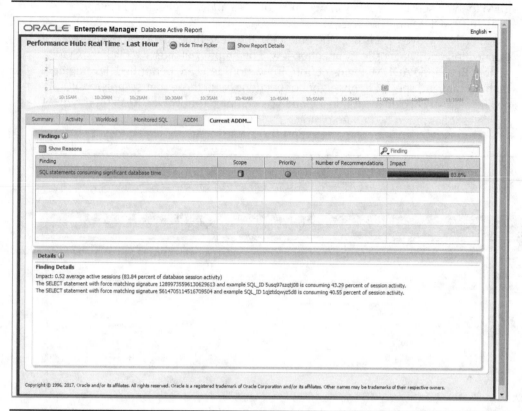

FIGURE 8-2. *Real-Time ADDM analysis: Findings*

Real-Time ADDM via OEM Cloud Control 13cR2

Like many of the analytic tools we demonstrate in this book, we have illustrated that Real-Time ADDM can definitely be leveraged using a scripted approach. But there are times when a GUI tool actually offers an excellent alternative, and Real-Time ADDM is definitely one such tool, especially if the underperforming database is so overwhelmed that a normal connection isn't possible.

Let's retrace the same database performance issue—an unexpected spike in horrendous database response time at 11:15 A.M.—using Oracle Enterprise Manager (OEM) Cloud Control, this time attacking the apparent problem in real time. After launching OEM Cloud Control, selecting the appropriate database, and then connecting to it, we'll select the menu option Performance | Real-Time ADDM.

OEM then presents the screen shown in Figure 8-3 and we're ready to engage a Real-Time ADDM analysis session.

Initially, the two panels near the bottom of the Real-Time ADDM screen—Normal Connection and Diagnostic Connection—will be empty, but after we click the Start button, Real-Time ADDM begins performing various tests are performed, leveraging both normal and special lightweight connections, with those that complete OK getting a green checkmark. Once the analysis completes, however, Real-Time ADDM indicates it has found two issues of note.

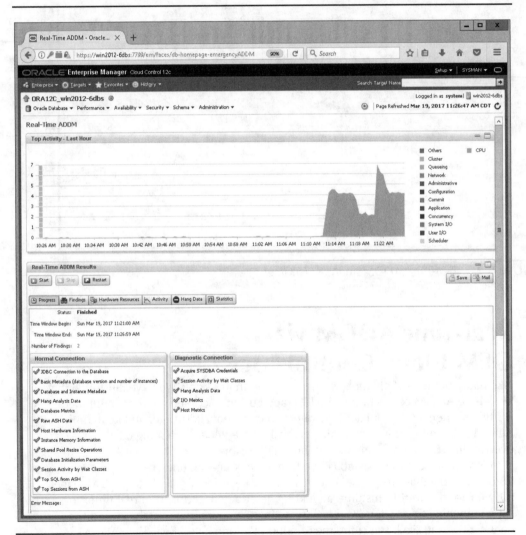

FIGURE 8-3. *Real-Time ADDM via OEM R2 Cloud Control: Progress tab*

Detailed Findings

The Findings tab shown in Figure 8-4 explains the two findings that Real-Time ADDM has isolated. Unsurprisingly, as the text-based reports generated via scripting have already illustrated, SQL statements are consuming system resources, but in this invocation Real-Time ADDM also reports that the underlying database's I/O subsystem is inadequate for the task at hand. This I/O rating is assigned based on the average expected time it should take to perform a single-block read from storage, which is set to 10 milliseconds by default.

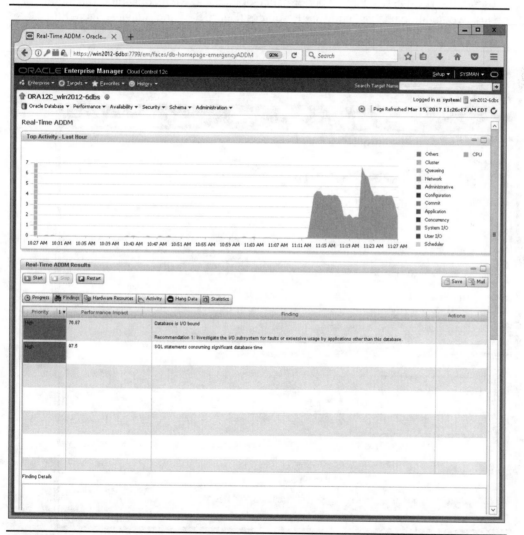

FIGURE 8-4. *Real-Time ADDM via OEM R2 Cloud Control: Findings tab*

NOTE
Because many storage systems today easily surpass an average time of 10 ms for single-block reads, this assumption can be modified by setting the value of `DBIO_EXPECTED` *to a more appropriate value via procedure* `SET_DEFAULT_TASK_PARAMETER` *that is part of package DBMS_ADVISOR.*

To complete this tuning scenario and gain some final insights into the apparent causes of the TPC-DS benchmark performance bottleneck, we'll concentrate attention on just two additional tabs: Hardware Resources (Figure 8-5) and Activity (Figure 8-6).

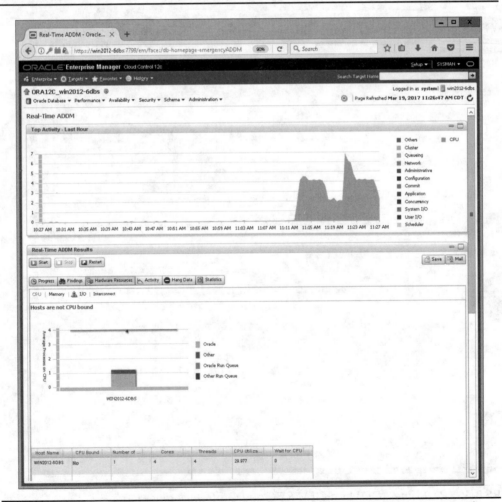

FIGURE 8-5. *Real-Time ADDM via OEM R2 Cloud Control: Hardware Resources tab*

Hardware Resources Analysis

Figure 8-5 clearly shows that the database server is not CPU bound: the various run queues are fairly short, and the workload is averaging just a little over one process per CPU in total. However, if the database instance had been running on a host with an insufficient number of CPUs, or if the application's SQL statements dramatically overused the parallel query option (PQO), then the Oracle and Other run queues would indicate that extravagance. Finally, it's important to put in perspective what appear to be relatively high spikes of CPU utilization in the top-most graph on this screen, when compared to other resources actually being used, which becomes clearer in Figure 8-6.

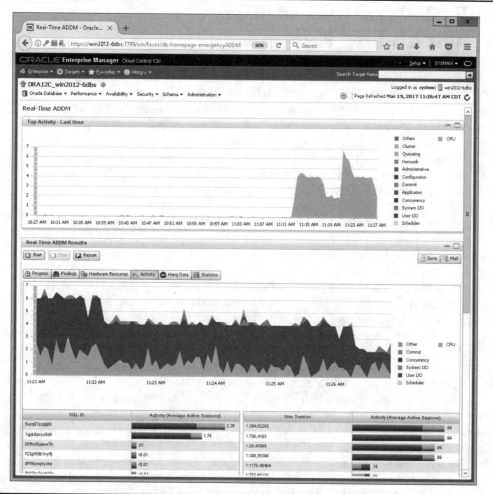

FIGURE 8-6.   *Real-Time ADDM via OEM R2 Cloud Control: Activity tab*

Activity Analysis

Figure 8-6 provides an overview of actual database activity, which provides a useful comparison to the graph at the top of Figure 8-5: the database instance is essentially doing work, so CPU utilization relative to other resources actually being used during the application workload is less of a concern—it represents only about 7 percent of activity as compared to User I/O, and that's very clearly the majority of overall activity. Thus Real-Time ADDM's analytics ring true: Many resource-hungry TPC-DS queries are executing simultaneously—CPU utilization complements that—and the only true solution to alleviate this performance issue is to consider tuning the existing I/O subsystem or obtaining a faster one.

Emergency Monitoring: When All Else Fails

For an extremely overloaded Oracle Database instance, it is possible that the instance may be so overwhelmed that it will be impossible to make a new connection via SQL*Plus or any other third-party utility. Although these situations are hopefully few and far between, an Oracle DBA might be tempted to abandon any further analysis attempt and surrender to the urge to bounce the instance. Starting with Oracle 12cR1, however, there is one final tool to reach for: Emergency Monitoring.

The Emergency Monitoring feature of OEM Cloud Control 12*c*/13*c* merges two older tools—*Memory Access Mode* and the *Hang Monitor* utility—that have been available since the introduction of OEM 10*g* Grid Control as well as the now-outmoded Oracle Database Control. Memory Access Mode enabled an Oracle DBA to gain access the barest of in-memory statistics to potentially diagnose an almost-failed database, while Hang Monitor actually provided a set of GUI hooks into the ORADEBUG hang analysis tool set. Emergency Monitoring doesn't require an explicit enablement of Memory Access Mode; it's accessed from the OEM Cloud Control Database panel by choosing Performance | Emergency Monitoring.

Once the appropriate database and host login and passwords are provided, the Emergency Performance Page (shown in Figure 8-7) will make a lightweight connection to the database instance that is performing poorly as well as its underlying host and provide just enough information to help the Oracle DBA decide whether there are any DBA-resolvable issues—for instance, a series of hanging or blocking sessions—before making the final decision to bounce the database instance.

In the scenario we've been following so far in this chapter, it's apparent from the data in the I/O section near the bottom of the screen that the pertinent metrics for Latency, IO Throughput, and IO Rate were much higher than the normally acceptable values for this system's underlying I/O components, and this correlates with what Real-Time ADDM has already confirmed: The true bottleneck for this application workload is related to an overwhelmed or malfunctioning storage system and cannot be resolved with attacking that problem as the root cause.

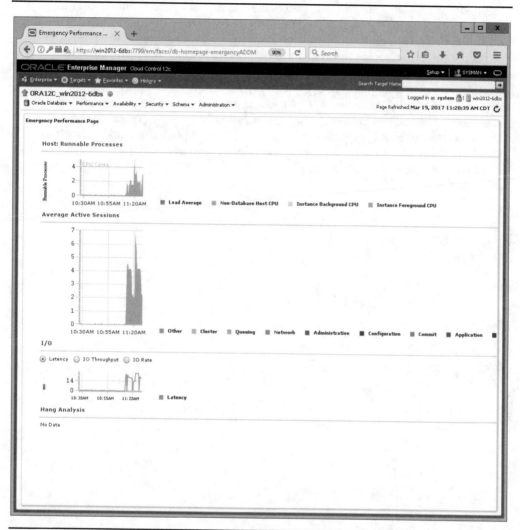

FIGURE 8-7. *Cloud Control Emergency Monitoring*

Summary

This chapter built upon the foundations we established in the prior two chapters on SQL statement and database operations monitoring and discussed how best to resolve what had been hopefully rare occurrences in many IT organizations. Oracle 12cR1's new Real-Time ADDM is one of the first tools an Oracle DBA can reach for whenever database performance suddenly degrades dramatically for no apparent reason, or even when a specific database instance appears to have "hung" so that the true root cause for the unexpected performance variance can be discovered and rectified. And if a database instance's responsiveness degrades to the point that, in the past, an Oracle DBA may have decided to bounce the instance, one more new 12*c*R1 tool—Emergency Monitoring—makes it possible to perform basic investigations for a potential root cause even when a new database connection is otherwise impossible. These two 12*c*R1 toolsets mean that an Oracle DBA may never have to bounce an instance to solve a potentially severely compromised database instance. That is especially crucial for critical application workloads when a database outage—no matter how temporary—may lead to mandatory reporting of that disruption under regulatory compliance rules.

CHAPTER
9

ASH Analytics

ctive Session History (ASH) Analytics was introduced in Oracle Enterprise Manager Cloud Control 12*c*. As the name implies, ASH Analytics is a data warehouse of sorts for Active Session History data over time. In fact, it is presented as a star schema design possessing many dimensions upon which to analyze, or "slice and dice," the data. Through its extremely effective data visualization, ASH Analytics makes it far simpler to diagnose performance problems, and you will find numerous white papers and web blogs on the subject. Moreover, once most DBAs find and use ASH Analytics, it quickly becomes one of their most indispensable tools for better understanding the true performance characteristics and bottlenecks within their database. It's also one of those rare Cloud Control features that cannot easily be replicated by simple SQL scripts, which lack charting capabilities (unless that data is imported into Excel); even hard-core command-line DBAs will give in to using a GUI tool for such a useful feature.

NOTE
*This feature requires the optional Diagnostics pack.
Furthermore, the database configuration parameter
for STATISTICS_LEVEL must be set to ALL or
TYPICAL. Finally, the configuration parameter for
CONTROL_MANAGEMENT_PACK_ACCESS is set to
DIAGNOSTIC or DIAGNOSTIC+TUNING.*

It's All a Matter of Time

To appreciate all that ASH Analytics has to offer, you must first understand some basic performance-related terms. The first and most critical idea is that of time. There are several time metrics of note:

- **Wall Clock Time**   The amount of time it takes to execute some unit of work, such as a SQL statement, as perceived from outside the database, simply measured as clock time between initial request and all results returned.

- **DB CPU Time**   Total CPU time in microseconds, as reported to the database kernel, by calls to the operating system, that were spent by database foreground and/or background processes directly servicing user-level database calls.

- **Non-Idle Wait Time**   Total time in microseconds, reported by the database kernel, where Oracle processes must pause and where that pause is considered important from a performance perspective—for example, when an Oracle process must pause to wait for a lock or a latch.

- **Idle Wait Time**   Total time in microseconds, reported by the database kernel, where Oracle processes must pause and where that pause is not considered important from a performance perspective—for example, when an Oracle process must pause to wait for a PX idle wait or SQL*Net message from client.

- **DB Time**   Total time spent by all user processes that are actively working in or actively waiting for database calls. It includes the CPU Time, Non-Idle Wait Time, and IO Wait Time (which is really a notable Non-Idle Wait).

Armed with these basic definitions, we can define a precise formula to define DB Time as *DB CPU Time + Non-Idle Wait Time*. However, some would argue that the definition is more popularly stated as *DB Time = Service Time + Non-Idle Wait Time*, where *Service Time* includes both CPU and I/O times. Thus, separating *IO Time* from *Non-Idle Wait Time*, the final and more accurate formula is *DB Time = DB CPU Time + I/O Time + Non-Idle Wait Time*. This leads to the following two important performance formulas for a given session:

- DB Time = DB CPU Time + I/O Time + Non-Idle Wait Time

- Wall Time = Elapsed Time / Effective Parallelism

Using these formulas, we can now define some nonsession-specific performance terms and formulas as well:

- Active Sessions = All sessions at a point in time in a database call and thus contributing to DB Time

- Average Activity of a Session = Active Time / Elapsed Time

- Average Active Sessions = Either of the following:

  - Total of average activity across all sessions

  - Total DB Time / Elapsed Time

ASH Data Warehouse Design

Figure 9-1 shows a diagram of how ASH Analytics collects and holds for analysis. The obvious key point is that the DB Time of active sessions that is sampled from the database is amassed and summarized for analysis along numerous performance criteria. In short, DB Time is the single most critical measure for analyzing what's happening with your database, and ASH Analytics is designed from the ground up to analyze that data.

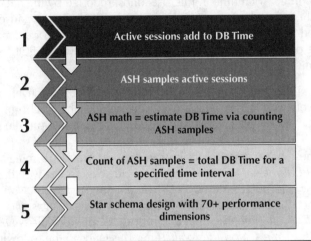

1   Active sessions add to DB Time

2   ASH samples active sessions

3   ASH math = estimate DB Time via counting ASH samples

4   Count of ASH samples = total DB Time for a specified time interval

5   Star schema design with 70+ performance dimensions

FIGURE 9-1. *ASH data collection scheme*

NOTE
Many DBAs would argue that DB Time is the one and only completely accurate and reliable performance metric.

Once all that ASH data has been collected into a star schema design, you can analyze on several dimensions comprising five key categories with numerous options, as shown in Figure 9-2. Of course, not all of these dimensions may be useful all the time, so it's quite likely that you will find a handful that generally works best for your analyses. But over time dealing with various performance problems, you will find a use case for each of these many dimensions. Just start small and work your way up.

You can perform five categories of analytic operations on the ASH data, as shown in Figure 9-3. For a typical business analyst who works daily with such analysis tools and techniques, these analytic operations may seem somewhat obvious. But for the average DBA more accustomed to raw data and/or reports summarizing raw data, these analytic operations may be somewhat new. The Enterprise Manager Cloud Control GUI is designed to make it easy. You can just begin to work on the data and choose operations naturally.

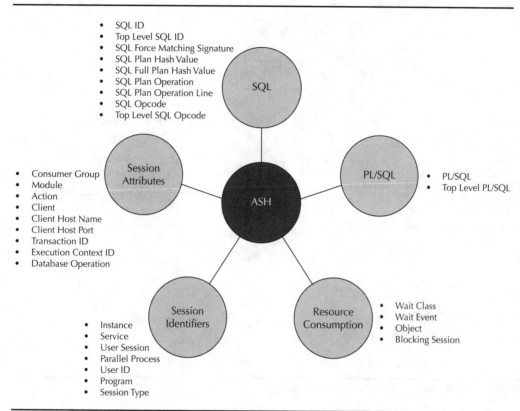

FIGURE 9-2. *ASH analytics dimensions*

ASH Analytics in Action

The complete version of ASH Analytics is fully available only with OEM Cloud Control. (OEM Express offers a more restricted version, covered later in this chapter.) Once you've navigated to a database target, ASH Analytics will be displayed in the Performance section.

The ASH Analytics home screen is shown in Figure 9-4. By default, it displays the Activity style line graph for wait class. As you can see in the figure, the number one wait class is User I/O. That makes sense, because in this example, a subset of the 99 TPC-DS queries is being run.

Suppose you're more interested in viewing the actual wait events rather than the wait classes. By opening the Wait Class drop-down list, shown in Figure 9-5, you can select and view one of the five major categories and dimensions shown in

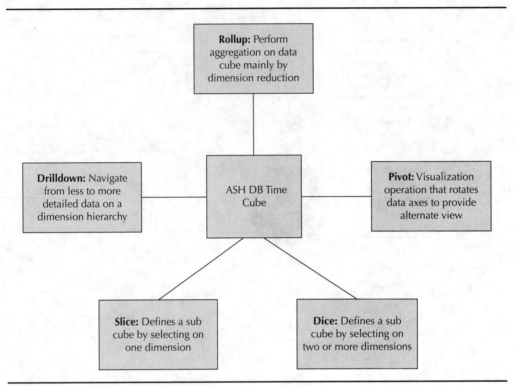

FIGURE 9-3. *Data cube analytic operations*

Figure 9-2. Moreover, by clicking Top Dimensions, you'll see a bar chart summarizing the analytics involved.

Choose the Wait Event option to open the screen shown in Figure 9-6, where you can see that the most pressing wait event is direct path read (note the cursor pointing at the right of the screenshot). Once again that makes sense, because a subset of the 99 TPC-DS queries is currently running. But why is Oracle doing direct path reads and skipping the database buffer cache? In this case, it's because the TPC-DS benchmark makes use of parallel query, which in many cases might choose to perform direct path reads. So the data makes total sense.

Although Figures 9-4 and 9-6 are easy to read and relate the information quite nicely, ASH Analytics offers another unique and powerful visual—the load map. By changing the display style from the default of Activity to Load Map, you'll see get a screen similar to Figure 9-7. The ASH Analytics Load Map is essentially a tree map–type display for whatever dimension you're working on. Some might even think this looks a lot like the Oracle 12c heat map feature; however, the coloration here is not intended to indicate amount of activity or heat. This diagram style is often easier to use, since it presents the data in a much less cluttered and confusing style.

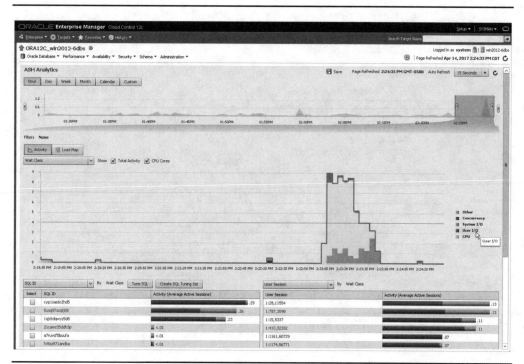

FIGURE 9-4.   *ASH Analytics – Wait Classes*

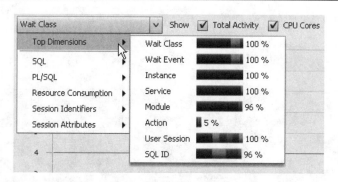

FIGURE 9-5.   *ASH Analytics dimension selection*

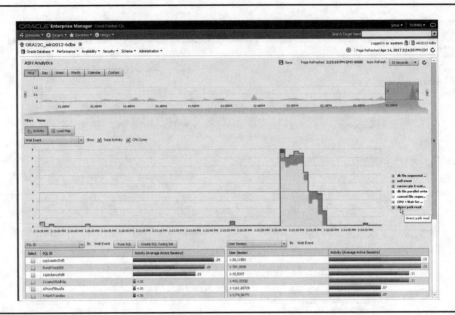

FIGURE 9-6. *ASH Analytics – Wait Events*

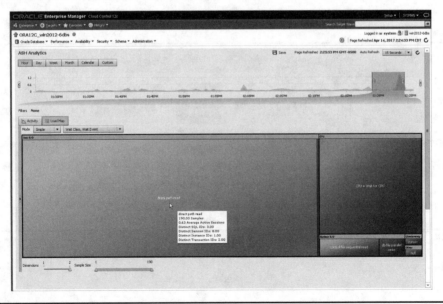

FIGURE 9-7. *ASH Analytics – Load Map*

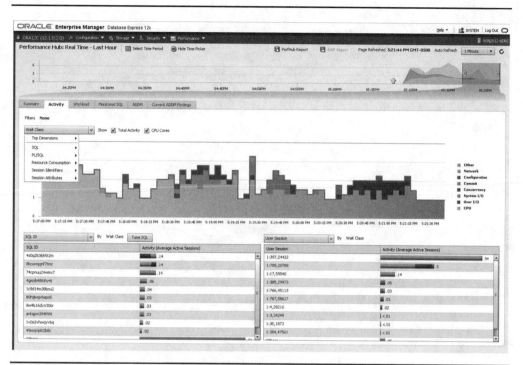

FIGURE 9-8. *OEM Express ASH Analytics*

As previously mentioned, the complete version of ASH Analytics is fully available only in OEM Cloud Control. OEM Express offers the same basic capabilities, minus the Load Map or tree map option, as shown in Figure 9-8. You reach this screen by choosing Performance Hub and navigating to the Activity. Remember, too, that OEM Express is a lightweight and free tool that many DBAs may find useful for many situations rather than the full-blown OEM Cloud Control.

Summary

Like many business analysis tools that enable you to perform data analysis using data warehouses and business intelligence or data analytics tools, OEM Cloud Control now offers DBAs ASH Analytics for dissecting and reporting on active session data, especially with regard to DB Time. Armed with this tool, DBAs can diagnose performance problems with far more ease than in days past. Visualization of ASH data through ASH Analytics compliments all the techniques we've covered in Chapters 3 through 8. ASH Analytics should become a staple addition to your DBA toolkit. You will soon wonder how you ever did without it.

PART
IV

Testing to Destruction:
Real Application Testing

CHAPTER
10

SQL Performance
Analyzer

A production database is typically modified only when necessary, and this is why most DBAs are extremely careful with every modification performed on production databases. Changes, however, are impossible to avoid—whether they be major changes, such as migrating to a new server or upgrading the database version, or minor ones, such as changing a database parameter or creating a new index. Regardless of the type change requested, thorough planning and testing is needed to verify that a change will not break applications or negatively impact their performance. Oracle offers two solutions for performing change analysis: SQL Performance Analyzer (SPA) and Database Workload Capture and Replay (DWC/R).

Before we dive into a discussion of these two tools, you'll find it helpful to have a simplistic visualization of their high-level architectures and functions, shown in Figure 10-1. SPA enables you to capture some queries as a SQL Tuning Set (STS), to copy them from the source database to the target database, and then to examine the performance of those queries on the target database. Obviously, the capture is a subset of all the activity and the focus is more on the individual SQL statements versus entirely complete transactions. DWC/R, on the other hand captures all activity, including transactions performed upon the data by DML statements. Because transactions are replayed, the data on the target system must match the initial state of the source database to avoid results that are skewed or even meaningless. Thus, these two facilities are actually quite different in both design and purpose.

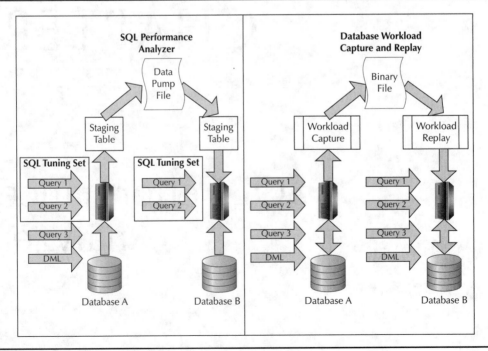

FIGURE 10-1. *High-level view of SPA versus DWC/R*

Using SQL Performance Analyzer

SQL Performance Analyzer was introduced in Oracle Database 11gR1 as an Oracle solution to analyze the impact of a change by identifying performance divergence on SQL statements to avoid SQL performance regression.

SPA needs at least two trials to perform the analysis: The first trial is created in the environment where the impending change we want to test has not yet been applied. The second trial is created in the environment where the change is implemented, so that you can measure the impact. For any trial, SPA can either execute the SQL statements or create *explain plans* without actually executing the SQL statements. An Oracle explain plan provides a good estimation of how the SQL statement might be executed; however, the Automatic Tuning Optimizer can, during execution, deviate from or modify that plan, and that's why the SQL statements must be executed by SPA if you want to use the actual metrics and execution times in the analysis.

When the SQL statements are executed by SPA, its execution consumes intensive resources. In addition, every SQL statement is executed at least twice—the first execution warms the buffer cache, and the second (and any subsequent) execution is used to calculate the runtime execution statistics. In the SPA analysis, the statistics from the first execution are not used. SPA will always try to execute the SQL statement as many times as it can until the SPA task times out, up to a maximum of ten times. The number of times the statement is executed is determined by the SQL statement elapsed time. If SPA categorizes a SQL statement as a long-running one, it will be executed twice; if SPA categorizes the SQL statement as a fast-running one, it will try to execute the SQL statement as many times as it can until the SPA times out, or up to ten times. When a SQL statement is executed by SPA more than three times, the execution statistics are averaged over these executions, and the average is used by SPA in the analysis. When the input of SPA is an STS, all the SQL statements are executed, one by one, without preserving their capture order or their concurrency.

When an STS includes SQL statements that change data, such as an update, an insert, or a delete, SPA executes the query portion of only those operations unless the task parameter `EXECUTE_FULLDML` is used to modify this behavior. In that case, after every DML, SPA executes a rollback so that the database data remains unchanged. This behavior occurs because SPA is focused on how a SQL statement is *executed*, not on actual *data changes*. A disadvantage of SPA is that it doesn't support parallel DML; the query portions of DMLs are executed only if parallel hits are removed.

SPA can be used to test the impact of a change in the following use cases (among others):

- Database version upgrade
- OS or hardware upgrades
- OS or hardware changes

- Database parameter changes
- Optimizer parameter changes
- Schema changes
- New statistics tests
- Validation of the creation or deletion of an index

SPA vs. DWC/R: What's the Difference?

DWC/R, whose features are covered extensively in Chapters 11 and 12, may at first glance seem to offer comparable features to those offered by SPA. The key difference between the tools is that SPA focuses on comparing the before-and-after results of a few specific changes as they affect a specific *set* of capture SQL statements. DWC/R focuses on comparing the before-and-after results of one or more changes to *an Oracle database*, an *entire system environment*, or *both*. Also, SPA cannot be used to analyze a workload that contains DML statements, because the DML would change the contents of the database itself; conversely, DWC/R is designed to handle both queries and DML statements to identify not just statement performance regression, but also differences in the results of applying database changes in the new environment. Finally, DWC/R maintains the concurrency of recorded activity; in other words, it ensures that the application workload is replayed in the precise order and timing that it was recorded in (though this feature can be overridden if desired—for example, during a simulated "test to destruction").

Table 10-1 lists more differences between the two.

SPA	DWC/R
Tests the impact of a change for a small set of SQL statements	Tests the impact of a change for a whole database
Doesn't change data	Can change data
Comparison report doesn't include information about database parameters changes	Comparison report includes information about database parameter changes
Works with SQL statements	Works with a workload
SQL statements to analyze cannot be altered	Captured workload can be altered

TABLE 10-1. *SPA versus DWC/R*

SPA	DWC/R
Executes the SQL statement or uses explain plan	Replays the captured workload
Executes SQL statements in a pre-change environment and then it executes the statements in a post-change environment	Captures the workload in a pre-change environment and replays it in a post-change environment
Can execute SQL statements in a remote database	Captures files must be transferred to the environment where the workload will be replayed
Doesn't generate any files	Both capture and replay processes generate files in the capture directory
Can execute SQL statements several times to analyze the execution metrics better	Replays a captured workload
Generates one simple comparison report	Generates several types of comparison reports
Can be used started with version 11gR1	Can be used with versions up to 9i by applying a patch
Analysis consumes considerable resources since every query is executed at least twice for long-running queries and several times for fast-running queries	Replays the same captured workload
Several inputs for SQL statements (cache, AWR, STS, or text)	Input is a workload
SQL statements executed with no order	Database replays the workload in the time and order in which it was captured

TABLE 10-1. *SPA versus DWC/R (continued)*

As you can see, the decision of whether to use SPA or DWC/R is not based on whether the change is big (such as a hardware upgrade) or small (such as a database parameter). The decision is mostly based on the target for which you want to test, either for small set of SQL statements (SPA) or for a whole database (DWC/R). Oracle recommends that you first execute SPA on SQL statements that have performance problems, then analyze the metric divergences and perform fixes, and then use DWC/R to get an overall report about the impact of a change.

SQL Performance Analyzer Inputs

SPA can use a SQL statement from several inputs:

- **Shared SQL area** The SQL ID of the SQL statement has to be provided.

- **Text of a SQL statement** In this case, the Automatic Tuning Optimizer executes the SQL statement provided to gather information about how the SQL tuning statement is currently being executed, such as physical reads, logical reads, CPU consumption, and so forth.

- **AWR** The starting snapshot, ending snapshot, and SQL ID must be provided to filter the problematic SQL statement.

- **A SQL Tuning Set** An existing STS is needed; because an STS can store several SQL statements, a filter can be also used to select only those SQL statements from the STS that need to be analyzed.

Figure 10-2 shows an overview of how SPA works. Basically, the SQL statement can be taken from SQL area, AWR, STS, or SQL text to create the first SQL trial before the change, then create a second SQL trial after the change, and finally create a report with metric divergence that can be used to estimate the impact of a change.

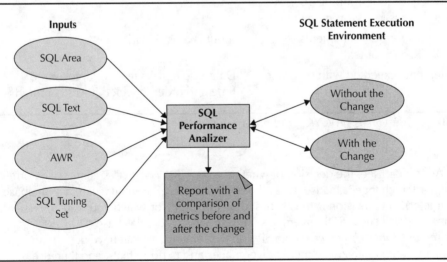

FIGURE 10-2. *SQL Performance Analyzer overview*

Testing the Impact of a Change

To test the impact of a change in a database, follow these steps:

1. Select the Input

Select the input from which you will take the SQL statement. We strongly recommend using STSs. Review Chapter 3 for more about using STSs.

2. Create an SPA Task

Use the procedure DBMS_SQLPA.CREATE_ANALYSIS_TASK. Provide the name of the task as well as the input to register the SQL statement.

3. Prepare to Execute the SPA Task

This is an optional step, but it may be required depending on how you want to create the SQL trials, either remotely or locally. If you will execute the SQL statement remotely, a database link is required. In this step, you also grant the privilege ADVISOR, which is required by SPA, as the database user who will execute the SQL statement.

4. Create the First SQL Trial

To create the first SQL trial, you can execute the SQL statement or generate an explain plan of the execution without actually executing it. This behavior is managed by the procedure DBMS_SQLPA.EXECUTE_ANALYSIS_TASK with the parameter execution_type set to the value 'TEST EXECUTE' to execute the SQL statement or to the value 'EXPLAIN PLAN' to generate the explain plan only and not execute the statement. The SQL statements should be processed in a test environment, where the change's impact can be measured. We strongly recommend building a test environment that's as similar as possible to the physical resources and software versions of the production environment. In some cases, such as a database version upgrade, the environment without the change differs from the environment with the change. The first SQL trial must be executed in the environment where the change is not implemented, and the second SQL trial is executed in the environment where the change is implemented. Both SQL trials can be executed remotely, as shown in Figure 10-3.

In some cases, such as for an index creation, the environment without the change is the same as the environment with the change. In such cases, the first and second SQL trials can be executed in the same environment, as shown in Figure 10-4.

5. Monitor the SPA Task

While the first SQL trial is being executed, you can monitor its progress using either the view DBA_ADVISOR_EXECUTIONS or the view V$ADVISOR_PROGRESS.

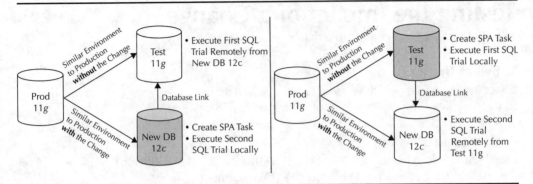

FIGURE 10-3. *Database version upgrade scenario*

6. Perform the Change

If the environment without the change and the environment with the change are one and the same, as the case of an index creation, in this step the change is implemented (to create the index). Otherwise, the change is based on a new environment that likely is already created, as in the case of a database version upgrade, and this step can be skipped.

7. Create a Second SQL Trial

As in the first SQL trial, the second SQL trial can be executed locally or remotely. What matters is that the second SQL trial is executed where the change is implemented. The procedure and its parameters are the same used to execute the first SQL trial.

8. Monitor SPA Task

The second SQL trial can also be monitored using the view DBA_ADVISOR_ EXECUTIONS or V$ADVISOR_PROGRESS.

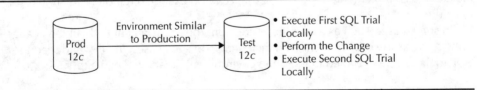

FIGURE 10-4. *Index creation scenario*

9. Execute the Comparison

Once the first SQL and second SQL trials are executed successfully, you can compare the performance metrics of both trials to review the metric divergences. To execute this comparison, use the procedure DBMS_SQLPA.EXECUTE_ ANALYSIS_TASK with the parameter execution_type set to the value 'COMPARE PERFORMANCE'.

10. Generate the Report

Once the comparison is executed, you can review the results and the performance metric divergence by creating a report with HTML, text, or XML. Create the report with the procedure DBMS_SQLPA.REPORT_ANALYSIS_TASK. This procedure receives the type of the report. The report can be also customized with the level of information displayed by using the parameter level, which can be set to ALL, BASIC, CHANGED, CHANGED_PLANS, ERRORS, IMPROVED, REGRESSED, TIMEOUT, TYPICAL (default), UNCHANGED, UNCHANGED_PLANS, or UNSUPPORTED. The sections in the report, using the parameter section, can be set to the value SUMMARY (default), which displays only the summary section, or ALL, which displays all the sections in the report. Set how to order the SQL statements in the report using the parameter order_by, which can be set to the values CHANGE_ DIFF, NULL (Default), SQL_IMPACT, WORKLOAD_IMPACT, and METRIC_DELTA.

The report has three main sections:

- **General Information**   The General Information section shows information of the SPA task, parameters used to run the SPA task, general information gathered before the change and after the change, information of the STS used, the metric used to compare both SQL trials, and the parameter values used to execute both SQL trials.

- **Report Summary**   Report Summary has information about overall impact, impact on workload and execution frequency, metric before and after the change, impact on SQL statements, and any plan change recommendations. As the report name says, it is a summary of all the information found in the Report Details section.

- **Report Details**   This section includes all the details regarding the SQL statements used in the SQL trials, such as SQL ID; SQL text; several metric results before and after the change such as elapsed time, parse time, CPU time, user IO time, buffer gets, cost, reads, and writes; impact and benefit of the change; execution plan before and after the change; and findings. This information is presented for every SQL statement included in the STSs.

11. Analyze the Results

This step is performed by the DBA, who looks at the results of the comparison report to see performance metric divergences, evaluate percentage of benefits, and decide whether the results of the change are acceptable for the set of SQL statements analyzed or whether any performance degradation must be considered and/or fixed before the change is implemented. This is where the actual impact of the change is discovered.

12. Decide Whether or Not to Perform Fixes

Based on the previous step, the DBA must decide whether or not to implement the change. Any fixes that need to be made before implementation can be documented and planned in this step. If the performance result is acceptable for the SQL statements that were analyzed, we recommend that you use DWC/R with SPA. In some cases, the performance results for the set of SQL statements are so bad that the decision not to implement the change is easily made.

Using SPA to Estimate the Impact of a Change with a CLI

SPA can be executed using commands (from the command line interface) or from Oracle Enterprise Manager (OEM). In this section, you'll learn how to use SPA with SQL*Plus. The example used here is based on the scenario shown in Figure 10-3, which is the same scenario we'll use in Chapters 11 and 12. Let's review the impact of a database version upgrade from Enterprise Edition 11.2.0.3 using Filesystem to Enterprise Edition 12.2.0.1 using Oracle Automatic Storage Management (ASM). In this chapter, we'll test the impact of a change for two TPCDS queries; in Chapters 11 and 12, you will see the impact of this change for an entire workload.

1. Select the Input

In this example, a STS named STS_QUERY_70_82 is used to create the SPA task. The STS includes the Query 70 (SQL_ID = 2hj59zh9p5npq) and Query 82 (SQL_ID = 6w097st7tjags) from the TPCDS repository, as shown here:

```
SQL> SELECT sql_id,
elapsed_time,
buffer_gets,
cpu_time,
disk_reads
FROM  table( DBMS_SQLTUNE.SELECT_SQLSET(
                          sqlset_name=>'STS_QUERY_70_82',
                          attribute_list=>'BASIC'));
```

```
SQL_ID          ELAPSED_TIME BUFFER_GETS CPU_TIME    DISK_READS
-------------   ------------ ----------- ----------  ----------
2hj59zh9p5npq   105132305     2190858     30016436    2187512
6w097st7tjags   113569678     358866      97996103    357133
```

2. Create the SPA Task

We'll create the SPA task in version 12.2.0.1, which is the scenario described on the left side of Figure 10-3. The name provided for the SPA task is SPA_TASK01.

```
SQL> var sts_name varchar2(30);
SQL> var task_name varchar2(30);
SQL> exec :sts_name := 'STS_QUERY_70_82';

PL/SQL procedure successfully completed.

SQL> exec :task_name := 'SPA_TASK01';

PL/SQL procedure successfully completed.

SQL> exec :task_name := dbms_sqlpa.create_analysis_task(
sqlset_name => :sts_name,
task_name => :task_name);

PL/SQL procedure successfully completed.
```

If the SPA task was created successfully, its state should be INITIAL, as shown in the following output:

```
SQL>  SELECT task_name, status
FROM user_advisor_tasks
WHERE task_name = 'SPA_TASK01';

TASK_NAME    STATUS
----------   -----------
SPA_TASK01 INITIAL
```

3. Prepare to Execute the SPA Task

The privilege ADVISOR will be granted to the user TPCDS, since this user will execute the SQL statements 70 and 82 in the remote environment that does not have the change (database upgrade)—in this case, the database in 11.2.0.3.

```
SQL> grant advisor to tpcds;

Grant succeeded.
```

Create the database link used to execute the first SQL trial:

```
SQL> create public database link DB_11_2_0_3 connect to tpcds
identified by tpcds using 'db11g';

Database link created.
```

4. Create the First SQL Trial

It's time to execute the SPA task; this execution will create the first SQL Trial which will be used in the comparison once the second SPA Trial is also created:

```
begin
DBMS_SQLPA.EXECUTE_ANALYSIS_TASK(
task_name => 'SPA_TASK01', -- SPA Task Name
execution_type => 'TEST EXECUTE', -- Execution type
execution_name => 'PRE_UPGRADE_11G', -- First SQL Trial name
execution_params => dbms_advisor.arglist(
'DATABASE_LINK',
'DB_11_2_0_3') -- database link name
);
end;
/

PL/SQL procedure successfully completed.
```

5. Monitor the SPA Task

In the environment where the SPA task was created, review the status of the first SQL trial using the following query:

```
SQL> select execution_name, task_id, advisor_name, status from
DBA_ADVISOR_EXECUTIONS where task_name='SPA_TASK01';

EXECUTION_NAME   TASK_ID    ADVISOR_NAME             STATUS
---------------- ---------- ------------------------ -----------
PRE_UPGRADE_11G 580         SQL Performance Analyzer EXECUTING
```

The environment where the first SQL trial is being executed (which is the environment in which the change has *not* been implemented yet) in this example is the database with the version 11.2.0.3. Query the view V$SESSION to see the SQL statement being executed:

```
SQL> select username, sql_id , event , status from v$session where
username ='TPCDS';

USERNAME   SQL_ID        EVENT                   STATUS
---------- ------------- ----------------------- --------
TPCDS      andx5g7bcaav0 db file scattered read ACTIVE
```

Once the first SQL trial executes successfully, you will see the status of that execution shown as COMPLETED:

```
SQL> select execution_name, task_id, advisor_name, status from
DBA_ADVISOR_EXECUTIONS where task_name='SPA_TASK01'

EXECUTION_NAME  TASK_ID   ADVISOR_NAME             STATUS
--------------- --------- ------------------------ -----------
PRE_UPGRADE_11G 580       SQL Performance Analyzer COMPLETED
```

6. Perform the Change

In this example, the change is a database version upgrade. As described in Figure 10-3, the database with the new version 12.2.0.1 is already created.

7. Create the Second SQL Trial

Because the SPA task was created in the environment with version 12.2.0.1, which is the scenario described on the left side of Figure 10-3, the second SQL trial is executed locally.

```
begin
DBMS_SQLPA.EXECUTE_ANALYSIS_TASK(
task_name => 'SPA_TASK01', -- SPA Task Name
execution_type => 'TEST EXECUTE',  -- Execution type
execution_name => 'POST_UPGRADE_12CR2'); -- Second SQL Trial name
end;
/

PL/SQL procedure successfully completed.
```

8. Monitor the SPA Task

While the second SQL trial is being processed, its status will be EXECUTING:

```
SQL> select execution_name, task_id, advisor_name, status from
DBA_ADVISOR_EXECUTIONS where task_name='SPA_TASK01';

EXECUTION_NAME       TASK_ID  ADVISOR_NAME             STATUS
-------------------- -------- ------------------------ -----------
POST_UPGRADE_12CR2   581      SQL Performance Analyzer EXECUTING
PRE_UPGRADE_11G      581      SQL Performance Analyzer COMPLETED
```

Once the second SQL trial is completed, you will see COMPLETED as its status:

```
SQL> select execution_name, task_id, advisor_name, status from
DBA_ADVISOR_EXECUTIONS where task_name='SPA_TASK01';
```

```
EXECUTION_NAME          TASK_ID  ADVISOR_NAME               STATUS
--------------------    -------- ----------------------     -----------
POST_UPGRADE_12CR2      581      SQL Performance Analyzer   COMPLETED
PRE_UPGRADE_11G         581      SQL Performance Analyzer   COMPLETED
```

9. Execute a Comparison

In this example, you'll compare the first SQL trial, PRE_UPGRADE_11G, with the second SQL trial, POST_UPGRADE_12CR2. The name used to identify this comparison will be COMPARISON_11GR2_12CR2:

```
SQL> begin
DBMS_SQLPA.EXECUTE_ANALYSIS_TASK(
task_name => 'SPA_TASK01', -- SPA Task Name
execution_type => 'COMPARE PERFORMANCE', -- Execution type
execution_name => 'COMPARISON_11GR2_12CR2', -- Comparison name
execution_params => dbms_advisor.arglist(
      'comparison_metric',
      'elapsed_time') -- Metric used to compare both SQL Trials
      );
end;
/

PL/SQL procedure successfully completed.
```

10. Generate the Report

We will display each report in text format as well as in HTML format. The following query can be used to generate a text report:

```
set long 100000
set longchunksize 100000
set linesize 200
set head off
set feedback off
set echo off
spool reportSPA.txt  -- File name for the output
SELECT dbms_sqlpa.report_analysis_task(
           task_name=>'SPA_TASK01', -- SPA Task name
           type=>'TEXT',   -- Format of the report
           level=>'ALL',   -- Level of details in the report
           section=>'ALL' -- Sections displayed in the report
           ) FROM dual;
spool off
```

In the General Information area (Figure 10-5), you can see that two SQL statements were processed, there are no errors presented, and the scope of the execution was comprehensive, which means a complete execution was performed. The metric used for the comparison is ELAPSED TIME.

```
General Information
--------------------------------------------------------------------------------

 Task Information:                        Workload Information:
 ----------------------------------       ----------------------------------------
  Task Name     : SPA_TASK01               SQL Tuning Set Name     : STS_QUERY_70_82
  Task Owner    : SYS                      SQL Tuning Set Owner     : SYS
  Description   :                          Total SQL statement Count  : 2

Execution Information:
--------------------------------------------------------------------------------
  Execution Name  : COMPARISON_11GR2_12CR2   Started        : 04/15/2017 08:26:45
  Execution Type  : COMPARE PERFORMANCE      Last Updated   : 04/15/2017 08:26:45

  Description     :                          Global Time Limit  : UNLIMITED
  Scope           : COMPREHENSIVE            Per-SQL Time Limit : UNUSED
  Status          : COMPLETED                Number of Errors   : 0

Analysis Information:
--------------------------------------------------------------------------------
 Before Change Execution:                 After Change Execution:
 ----------------------------------       ----------------------------------------
  Execution Name     : PRE_UPGRADE_11G      Execution Name     : POST_UPGRADE_12CR2
  Execution Type     : TEST EXECUTE REMOTE  Execution Type     : TEST EXECUTE
  Database Link      : DB_11_2_0_3          Scope              : COMPREHENSIVE
  Scope              : COMPREHENSIVE        Status             : COMPLETED
  Status             : COMPLETED            Started            : 04/15/2017 05:58:51

  Started            : 04/15/2017 05:43:02  Last Updated       : 04/15/2017 06:00:30
  Last Updated       : 04/15/2017 05:50:32  Global Time Limit  : UNLIMITED
  Global Time Limit  : UNLIMITED            Per-SQL Time Limit : UNUSED
  Per-SQL Time Limit : UNUSED               Number of Errors   : 0
  Number of Errors   : 0


 --------------------------------------------
 Comparison Metric: ELAPSED_TIME
 -----------------
 Workload Impact Threshold: 1%
 -------------------------
 SQL Impact Threshold: 1%
 -----------------------
```

General Information

Task Information:

Task Name : SPA_TASK01
Task Owner : SYS
Description :

Workload Information:

SQL Tuning Set Name : STS_QUERY_70_82
SQL Tuning Set Owner : SYS
Total SQL Statement Count : 2

Execution Information:

Execution Name : COMPARISON_11GR2_12CR2
Execution Type : COMPARE PERFORMANCE
Description :
Scope : COMPREHENSIVE
Status : COMPLETED

Started : 04/15/2017 08:26:45
Last Updated : 04/15/2017 08:26:45
Global Time Limit : UNLIMITED
Per-SQL Time Limit : UNUSED
Number of Errors : 0

Analysis Information:

Before Change Execution:

Execution Name : PRE_UPGRADE_11G
Execution Type : TEST EXECUTE REMOTE
Database Link : DB_11_2_0_3
Scope : COMPREHENSIVE
Status : COMPLETED
Started : 04/15/2017 05:43:02
Last Updated : 04/15/2017 05:50:32
Global Time Limit : UNLIMITED
Per-SQL Time Limit : UNUSED
Number of Errors : 0

After Change Execution:

Execution Name : POST_UPGRADE_12CR2
Execution Type : TEST EXECUTE
Scope : COMPREHENSIVE
Status : COMPLETED
Started : 04/15/2017 05:58:51
Last Updated : 04/15/2017 06:00:30
Global Time Limit : UNLIMITED
Per-SQL Time Limit : UNUSED
Number of Errors : 0

Comparison Metric: ELAPSED_TIME

Workload Impact Threshold: 1%

SQL Impact Threshold: 1%

FIGURE 10-5. *SPA Report – General Information*

The Report Summary (Figure 10-6) presents two SQL IDs, 6w097st7tjags, which is the SQL ID for TPCDS Query 82, and 2hj59zh9p5npq, which is the SQL ID for the TPCDS Query 70. The summary indicates that both SQL statements were improved in the 12cR2 environment and both SQL statements got new execution plans. Query 82 was improved by 93.61 percent and TPCDS Query 70 was improved by 69.95 percent.

```
Report Summary
------------------------------------------------------------------------------------------

Projected Workload Change Impact:
------------------------------------------
 Overall Impact      :  77.71%
 Improvement Impact  :  77.71%
 Regression Impact   :  0%

SQL statement Count
------------------------------------------
 SQL Category   SQL Count   Plan Change Count

 Overall            2              2
 Improved           2              2

Top 2 SQL Sorted by Absolute Value of Change Impact on the Workload
------------------------------------------------------------------------------------------

|           |              | Impact on | Execution | Metric    | Metric   | Impact | Plan   |
| object_id | sql_id       | Workload  | Frequency | Before    | After    | on SQL | Change |
------------------------------------------------------------------------------------------
|         9 | 6w097st7tjags |   48.03% |         1 | 115452276 |  7377519 | 93.61% | y      |
|         8 | 2hj59zh9p5npq |   29.68% |         1 | 109576568 | 42786777 | 60.95% | y      |
------------------------------------------------------------------------------------------
Note: time statistics are displayed in microseconds
------------------------------------------------------------------------------------------
```

Report Summary

Projected Workload Change Impact:

Overall Impact   : **77.71%**
Improvement Impact : **77.71%**
Regression Impact   : **0%**

SQL Statement Count

SQL Category	SQL Count	Plan Change Count
Overall	2	2
Improved	2	2

Top 2 SQL Sorted by Absolute Value of Change Impact on the Workload

object_id	sql_id	Impact on Workload	Execution Frequency	Metric Before	Metric After	Impact on SQL	Plan Change
9	6w097st7tjags	48.03%	1	115452276	7377519	93.61%	y
8	2hj59zh9p5npq	29.68%	1	109576568	42786777	60.95%	y

Note: time statistics are displayed in microseconds

FIGURE 10-6.   *SPA Report – Report Summary*

The Report Details (Figure 10-7) includes details for both SQL statements that were processed. The elapsed time of TPCDS Query 82 improved from 115.45 seconds to 7.37 seconds—this is a huge improvement. This query also improved its CPU time, user IO time, buffer gets, reads, and writes. The cost was dramatically reduced from 2,049,348 to 98,247. The only metric that had a worse value was the parse time; it seems Oracle spent more time parsing this SQL statement in the 12*c*R2 database, but this divergence is nothing compared to the other noted improvements.

```
------------------------------------------------------------------------------------

Report Details
------------------------------------------------------------------------------------


SQL Details:
-----------------------------
 Object ID          : 9
 Schema Name        : TPCDS
 Container Name     : Unknown (con_dbid: 1416159483)

 SQL ID             : 6w097st7tjags
 Execution Frequency : 1
 SQL Text           : select /* query82 */ i_item_id ,i_item_desc
                      ,i_current_price from item, inventory, date_dim,
                      store_sales where i_current_price between 30 and 60 and
                      inv_item_sk = i_item_sk and d_date_sk=inv_date_sk and
                      d_date between '30-MAY-95' and '30-JUL-03' and
                      i_manufact_id in (437,191,515,649,129,727,663) and
                      inv_quantity_on_hand between 10 and 50000 and ss_item_sk
                      = i_item_sk group by
                      i_item_id,i_item_desc,i_current_price order by i_item_id

Execution Statistics:

-----------------------------
----------------------------------------------------------------------------
|                      | Impact on | Value      | Value      | Impact    |
| Stat Name            | Workload  | Before     | After      | on SQL    |
----------------------------------------------------------------------------
| elapsed_time         |    48.03% | 115.452276 |   7.377519 |    93.61% |
| parse_time           | -2441.63% |    .001607 |     .07217 | -4390.98% |
| cpu_time             |    68.11% | 100.443731 |      6.413 |    93.62% |
| user_io_time         |    14.56% |  13.971046 |     .54887 |    96.07% |
| buffer_gets          |      .06% |     358672 |     357163 |      .42% |
| cost                 |    73.68% |    2049348 |      98247 |    95.21% |
| reads                |        0% |     355491 |     355408 |      .02% |
| writes               |        0% |          0 |          0 |        0% |
|                      |           |            |            |           |
| io_interconnect_bytes |       0% | 2912182272 | 2911502336 |      .02% |
| rows                 |           |        131 |        131 |           |
----------------------------------------------------------------------------
Note: time statistics are displayed in seconds
```

```
Notes:
----------------------------
Before Change:
  1. The statement was first executed to warm the buffer cache.
  2. Statistics shown were from the second execution.

After Change:
  1. The statement was first executed to warm the buffer cache.

  2. Statistics shown were from the second execution.
```

Report Details

SQL Details:

Object ID : 9
Schema Name : TPCDS
Container Name : Unknown (con_dbid: 1416159483)
SQL ID : 6w097st7tjags
Execution Frequency : 1
SQL Text : select /* query82 */ i_item_id ,i_item_desc ,i_current_price from item, inventory, store_sales where i_current_price between 30 and 60 and inv_item_sk = i_item_sk and d_date_sk=inv_date_sk and d_date between '30-MAY-95' and '30-JUL-03' and i_manufact_id in (437,191,515,649,129,727,663) and inv_quantity_on_hand between 10 and 50000 and ss_item_sk = i_item_sk group by i_item_id,i_item_desc,i_current_price order by i_item_id

Execution Statistics:

Stat Name	Impact on Workload	Value Before	Value After	Impact on SQL
elapsed_time	48.03%	115.452276	7.377519	93.61%
parse_time	-2441.63%	.001607	.07217	-4390.98%
cpu_time	68.11%	100.443731	6.413	93.62%
user_io_time	14.56%	13.971046	.54887	96.07%
buffer_gets	.06%	358672	357163	.42%
cost	73.68%	2049348	98247	95.21%
reads	0%	355491	355408	.02%
writes	0%	0	0	0%
io_interconnect_bytes	0%	2912182272	2911502336	.02%
rows		131	131	

Note: time statistics are displayed in seconds

Notes:

Before Change:
  1. The statement was first executed to warm the buffer cache.
  2. Statistics shown were from the second execution.

After Change:
  1. The statement was first executed to warm the buffer cache.
  2. Statistics shown were from the second execution.

FIGURE 10-7. *SPA Report – Report Details*

From the Findings section (Figure 10-8), you can see two important things. The first is that TPCDS Query 82 was improved, which we already know from the previous section of this report. The second important thing is that the query used a new execution plan. You read about how to obtain a good plan using SQL Plan Management in Chapter 5. The details of the execution plan before the change as well as the execution plan after the change (Figure 10-9) are also displayed:

```
Findings (2):
----------------------------
1. The performance of this SQL has improved.
2. The structure of the SQL execution plan has changed.


Execution plan Before Change:
-----------------------------
Plan Id           : 4
Plan Hash Value   : 2893236059
```

Id	Operation	Name	Rows	Bytes	Cost	Time
0	SELECT STATEMENT		2240	185920	2049348	06:49:53
1	SORT GROUP BY		2240	185920	2049348	06:49:53
* 2	FILTER		0	0	4294967295	00:00:00
* 3	HASH JOIN		284910960	23647609680	101850	00:20:23
* 4	TABLE ACCESS FULL	DATE_DIM	2985	41790	414	00:00:05
* 5	HASH JOIN		285002422	19665167118	100078	00:20:01
6	NESTED LOOPS		163387	8822898	1764	00:00:22
* 7	TABLE ACCESS FULL	ITEM	140	6860	1062	00:00:13
* 8	INDEX RANGE SCAN	STORE_SALES_PK_IDX	1168	5840	5	00:00:01
* 9	TABLE ACCESS FULL	INVENTORY	107584200	1613763000	96955	00:19:24

```
Predicate Information (identified by operation id):
------------------------------------------
* 2 - filter(TO_DATE('30-MAY-95')<=TO_DATE('30-JUL-03'))
* 3 - access("D_DATE_SK"="INV_DATE_SK")
* 4 - filter("D_DATE"<='30-JUL-03' AND "D_DATE">='30-MAY-95')
* 5 - access("INV_ITEM_SK"="I_ITEM_SK")
* 7 - filter("I_CURRENT_PRICE"<=60 AND "I_CURRENT_PRICE">=30 AND ("I_MANUFACT_ID"=129 OR "I_MANUFACT_ID"=191
  OR "I_MANUFACT_ID"=437 OR "I_MANUFACT_ID"=515 OR "I_MANUFACT_ID"=649 OR
  "I_MANUFACT_ID"=663 OR "I_MANUFACT_ID"=727))
* 8 - access("SS_ITEM_SK"="I_ITEM_SK")
* 9 - filter("INV_QUANTITY_ON_HAND">=10 AND "INV_QUANTITY_ON_HAND"<=50000)


Execution plan After Change:
-----------------------------
Plan Id           : 6
Plan Hash Value   : 770764949
```

Id	Operation	Name	Rows	Bytes	Cost	Time
0	SELECT STATEMENT		2192	164400	98247	00:00:04
1	SORT GROUP BY		2192	164400	98247	00:00:04
* 2	HASH JOIN RIGHT SEMI		244099	18307425	98241	00:00:04
3	VIEW	VW_GBF_31	2985	17910	413	00:00:01
* 4	FILTER					
* 5	TABLE ACCESS FULL	DATE_DIM	2985	41790	413	00:00:01
* 6	HASH JOIN		244099	16842831	97828	00:00:04
7	NESTED LOOPS SEMI		140	7560	1341	00:00:01
* 8	TABLE ACCESS FULL	ITEM	140	6860	1061	00:00:01
* 9	INDEX RANGE SCAN	STORE_SALES_PK_IDX	72011000	360055000	2	00:00:01
* 10	TABLE ACCESS FULL	INVENTORY	107584200	1613763000	96201	00:00:04

```
Predicate Information (identified by operation id):
-------------------------------------------
* 2 - access("ITEM_1"="INV_DATE_SK")

* 4 - filter(TO_DATE('30-MAY-95')<=TO_DATE('30-JUL-03'))
* 5 - filter("D_DATE"<='30-JUL-03' AND "D_DATE">='30-MAY-95')
* 6 - access("INV_ITEM_SK"="I_ITEM_SK")
* 8 - filter("I_CURRENT_PRICE"<=60 AND "I_CURRENT_PRICE">=30 AND ("I_MANUFACT_ID"=129 OR "I_MANUFACT_ID"=191
OR "I_MANUFACT_ID"=437 OR "I_MANUFACT_ID"=515 OR "I_MANUFACT_ID"=649 OR
  "I_MANUFACT_ID"=663 OR "I_MANUFACT_ID"=727))
* 9 - access("SS_ITEM_SK"="I_ITEM_SK")
* 10 - filter("INV_QUANTITY_ON_HAND">=10 AND "INV_QUANTITY_ON_HAND"<=50000)
-------------------------------------------------------------------------------------
```

Findings (2):

1. The performance of this SQL has improved.
2. The structure of the SQL execution plan has changed.

Execution Plan Before Change:

Plan Id   : 4
Plan Hash Value : 2893236059

Id	Operation	Name	Rows	Bytes	Cost	Time
0	SELECT STATEMENT		2240	185920	2049348	06:49:53
1	SORT GROUP BY		2240	185920	2049348	06:49:53
* 2	FILTER		0	0	4294967295	00:00:00
* 3	HASH JOIN		284910960	23647609680	101850	00:20:23
* 4	TABLE ACCESS FULL	DATE_DIM	2985	41790	414	00:00:05
* 5	HASH JOIN		285002422	19665167118	100078	00:20:01
6	NESTED LOOPS		163387	8822898	1764	00:00:22
* 7	TABLE ACCESS FULL	ITEM	140	6860	1062	00:00:13
* 8	INDEX RANGE SCAN	STORE_SALES_PK_IDX	1168	5840	5	00:00:01
* 9	TABLE ACCESS FULL	INVENTORY	107584200	1613763000	96955	00:19:24

Predicate Information (identified by operation id):

- 2 - filter(TO_DATE('30-MAY-95')<=TO_DATE('30-JUL-03'))
- 3 - access("D_DATE_SK"="INV_DATE_SK")
- 4 - filter("D_DATE"<='30-JUL-03' AND "D_DATE">='30-MAY-95')
- 5 - access("INV_ITEM_SK"="I_ITEM_SK")
- 7 - filter("I_CURRENT_PRICE"<=60 AND "I_CURRENT_PRICE">=30 AND ("I_MANUFACT_ID"=129
  OR "I_MANUFACT_ID"=191 OR "I_MANUFACT_ID"=437 OR "I_MANUFACT_ID"=515 OR
  "I_MANUFACT_ID"=649 OR "I_MANUFACT_I D"=663 OR "I_MANUFACT_ID"=727))
- 8 - access("SS_ITEM_SK"="I_ITEM_SK")
- 9 - filter("INV_QUANTITY_ON_HAND">=10 AND "INV_QUANTITY_ON_HAND"<=50000)

FIGURE 10-8.   *SPA Report – Findings and pre-execution plan*

Execution Plan After Change:

Plan Id : 6
Plan Hash Value : 770764949

Id	Operation	Name	Rows	Bytes	Cost	Time
0	SELECT STATEMENT		2192	164400	98247	00:00:04
1	SORT GROUP BY		2192	164400	98247	00:00:04
* 2	HASH JOIN RIGHT SEMI		244099	18307425	98241	00:00:04
3	VIEW	VW_GBF_31	2985	17910	413	00:00:01
* 4	FILTER					
* 5	TABLE ACCESS FULL	DATE_DIM	2985	41790	413	00:00:01
* 6	HASH JOIN		244099	16842831	97828	00:00:04
7	NESTED LOOPS SEMI		140	7560	1341	00:00:01
* 8	TABLE ACCESS FULL	ITEM	140	6860	1061	00:00:01
* 9	INDEX RANGE SCAN	STORE_SALES_PK_IDX	72011000	360055000	2	00:00:01
* 10	TABLE ACCESS FULL	INVENTORY	107584200	1613763000	96201	00:00:04

Predicate Information (identified by operation id):

- 2 - access("ITEM_1"="INV_DATE_SK")
- 4 - filter(TO_DATE('30-MAY-95')<=TO_DATE('30-JUL-03'))
- 5 - filter("D_DATE"<='30-JUL-03' AND "D_DATE">='30-MAY-95')
- 6 - access("INV_ITEM_SK"="I_ITEM_SK")
- 8 - filter("I_CURRENT_PRICE"<=60 AND "I_CURRENT_PRICE">=30 AND ("I_MANUFACT_ID"=129
  OR "I_MANUFACT_ID"=191 OR "I_MANUFACT_ID"=437 OR "I_MANUFACT_ID"=515 OR
  "I_MANUFACT_ID"=649 OR "I_MANUFACT_I D"=663 OR "I_MANUFACT_ID"=727))
- 9 - access("SS_ITEM_SK"="I_ITEM_SK")
- 10 - filter("INV_QUANTITY_ON_HAND">=10 AND "INV_QUANTITY_ON_HAND"<=50000)

FIGURE 10-9. *SPA Report – post-execution plan*

In the SQL Details section (Figure 10-10), you can see that TPCDS Query 70 had its elapsed time improved from 109.57 seconds to 42.78 seconds; this is considerable difference that represents 60.95 percent of improvement. This query had also improved its CPU time, user IO time, and buffer gets. The cost was not changed, and it seems Oracle performed more reads in the 12cR2 database than in the 11gR2 database, because the reads increased 5.88 percent. The parse time was also increased, and this is the same behavior that TPCDS Query 82 had; it seems Oracle spent more time parsing this SQL statement in the 12cR2 database, but in the end, TPCDS Query 70 was executed almost 61 percent faster, which is considerable and a great number—so we are tagging this query as an improved one.

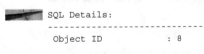

```
SQL Details:
----------------------------
Object ID           : 8

Schema Name         : TPCDS
Container Name      : Unknown (con_dbid: 1416159483)
```

```
SQL ID              : 2hj59zh9p5npq
Execution Frequency : 1
SQL Text            : select /* query70 */ sum(ss_net_profit) as total_sum
                      ,s_state ,s_county ,grouping(s_state)+grouping(s_county)
                      as lochierarchy ,rank() over ( partition by
                      grouping(s_state)+grouping(s_county), case when
                      grouping(s_county) = 0 then s_state end order by
                      sum(ss_net_profit) desc) as rank_within_parent from
                      store_sales,date_dim d1,store where d1.d_month_seq
                      between 1176 and 1240 and d1.d_date_sk = ss_sold_date_sk
                      and s_store_sk=ss_store_sk and s_state in ( select

                      s_state from (select s_state as s_state, rank() over (
                      partition by s_state order by sum(ss_net_profit) desc) as
                      ranking from store_sales, store, date_dim where
                      d_month_seq between 1176 and 1240 and d_date_sk =
                      ss_sold_date_sk and s_store_sk=ss_store_sk group by
                      s_state ) tmp1? where ranking <= 5 ) group by
                      rollup(s_state,s_county) order by lochierarchy desc ,case
                      when lochierarchy = 0 then s_state end
                      ,rank_within_parent
```

Execution Statistics:

Stat Name	Impact on Workload	Value Before	Value After	Impact on SQL
elapsed_time	29.68%	**109.576568**	**42.786777**	**60.95%**
parse_time	-352.35%	.001283	.011466	-793.69%
cpu_time	2.92%	37.607283	33.572	10.73%
user_io_time	78.53%	78.213049	5.816534	92.56%
buffer_gets	.14%	2190658	2187076	.16%
cost	.11%	598730	595850	.48%
reads	-5.02%	2062849	2184158	**-5.88%**
writes	0%	0	0	0%
io_interconnect_bytes	-5.02%	16898859008	17892622336	-5.88%
rows		3	3	

Note: time statistics are displayed in seconds

Notes:

Before Change:
 1. The statement was first executed to warm the buffer cache.
 2. Statistics shown were from the second execution.

After Change:
 1. The statement was first executed to warm the buffer cache.
 2. Statistics shown were from the second execution.

SQL Details:

Object ID : 8

Schema Name : TPCDS

Container Name : Unknown (con_dbid: 1416159483)

SQL ID : 2hj59zh9p5npq

Execution Frequency : 1

SQL Text : select /* query70 */ sum(ss_net_profit) as total_sum ,s_state ,s_county ,grouping(s_state)+grouping(s_county) as lochierarchy ,rank() over (partition by grouping(s_state)+grouping(s_county), case when grouping(s_county) = 0 then s_state end order by sum(ss_net_profit) desc) as rank_within_parent from store_sales,date_dim d1,store where d1.d_month_seq between 1176 and 1240 and d1.d_date_sk = ss_sold_date_sk and s_store_sk=ss_store_sk and s_state in (select s_state from (select s_state as s_state, rank() over (partition by s_state order by sum(ss_net_profit) desc) as ranking from store_sales, store, date_dim where d_month_seq between 1176 and 1240 and d_date_sk = ss_sold_date_sk and s_store_sk=ss_store_sk group by s_state) tmp1? where ranking <= 5) group by rollup(s_state,s_county) order by lochierarchy desc ,case when lochierarchy = 0 then s_state end ,rank_within_parent

Execution Statistics:

Stat Name	Impact on Workload	Value Before	Value After	Impact on SQL
elapsed_time	29.68%	109.576568	42.786777	60.95%
parse_time	-352.35%	.001283	.011466	-793.69%
cpu_time	2.92%	37.607283	33.572	10.73%
user_io_time	78.53%	78.213049	5.816534	92.56%
buffer_gets	.14%	2190658	2187076	.16%
cost	.11%	598730	595850	.48%
reads	-5.02%	2062849	2184158	-5.88%
writes	0%	0	0	0%
io_interconnect_bytes	-5.02%	16898859008	17892622336	-5.88%
rows		3	3	

Note: time statistics are displayed in seconds

Notes:

Before Change:
1. The statement was first executed to warm the buffer cache.
2. Statistics shown were from the second execution.

After Change:
1. The statement was first executed to warm the buffer cache.
2. Statistics shown were from the second execution.

FIGURE 10-10. *SPA Report – SQL Details*

From the Findings section, you see that SPA has marked this SQL statement as an improved one and that the execution plan used in the 12cR2 database was new. The details of the execution plan before the change as well as the execution plan after the change are displayed (Figures 10-11 and 10-12).

```
Findings (2):
----------------------------
1. The performance of this SQL has improved.
2. The structure of the SQL execution plan has changed.
```

```
Execution plan Before Change:
-----------------------------
Plan Id          : 3
Plan Hash Value  : 3517345661
```

Id	Operation	Name	Rows	Bytes	Cost	Time
0	SELECT STATEMENT		1	66	598730	01:59:45
1	SORT ORDER BY		1	66	598730	01:59:45
2	WINDOW SORT		1	66	598730	01:59:45
3	SORT GROUP BY ROLLUP		1	66	598730	01:59:45
* 4	HASH JOIN		3897438	257230908	598179	01:59:39
* 5	VIEW		1	16	299172	00:59:51
* 6	WINDOW SORT PUSHED RANK		1	32	299172	00:59:51
7	HASH GROUP BY		1	32	299172	00:59:51
* 8	HASH JOIN		3897438	124718016	298988	00:59:48
9	TABLE ACCESS FULL	STORE	110	770	18	00:00:01
* 10	HASH JOIN		3897438	97435950	298951	00:59:48
* 11	TABLE ACCESS FULL	DATE_DIM	2009	20090	413	00:00:05
12	TABLE ACCESS FULL	STORE_SALES	72011000	1080165000	298195	00:59:39
* 13	HASH JOIN		3897438	194871900	298988	00:59:48
14	TABLE ACCESS FULL	STORE	110	2750	18	00:00:01
* 15	HASH JOIN		3897438	97435950	298951	00:59:48
* 16	TABLE ACCESS FULL	DATE_DIM	2009	20090	413	00:00:05
17	TABLE ACCESS FULL	STORE_SALES	72011000	1080165000	298195	00:59:39

```
Predicate Information (identified by operation id):
---------------------------------------------------
* 4 - access("S_STATE"="S_STATE")
* 5 - filter("RANKING"<=5)

* 6 - filter(RANK() OVER ( PARTITION BY "S_STATE" ORDER BY SUM("SS_NET_PROFIT") DESC )<=5)
* 8 - access("S_STORE_SK"="SS_STORE_SK")
* 10 - access("D_DATE_SK"="SS_SOLD_DATE_SK")
* 11 - filter("D_MONTH_SEQ">=1176 AND "D_MONTH_SEQ"<=1240)
* 13 - access("S_STORE_SK"="SS_STORE_SK")
* 15 - access("D1"."D_DATE_SK"="SS_SOLD_DATE_SK")
* 16 - filter("D1"."D_MONTH_SEQ">=1176 AND "D1"."D_MONTH_SEQ"<=1240)


Execution plan After Change:
----------------------------
Plan Id          : 5
Plan Hash Value  : 3545695459
```

Id	Operation	Name	Rows	Bytes	Cost	Time
0	SELECT STATEMENT		1	50	595850	00:00:24
1	SORT ORDER BY		1	50	595850	00:00:24
2	WINDOW SORT		1	50	595850	00:00:24
3	SORT GROUP BY ROLLUP		1	50	595850	00:00:24
* 4	FILTER					
* 5	HASH JOIN		3897438	194871900	297770	00:00:12
6	TABLE ACCESS FULL	STORE	110	2750	18	00:00:01
* 7	HASH JOIN		3897438	97435950	297742	00:00:12
* 8	TABLE ACCESS FULL	DATE_DIM	2009	20090	412	00:00:01
9	TABLE ACCESS FULL	STORE_SALES	72011000	1080165000	297139	00:00:12
* 10	VIEW		1	17	297770	00:00:12
* 11	WINDOW SORT PUSHED RANK		1	32	297770	00:00:12
12	SORT GROUP BY NOSORT		1	32	297770	00:00:12
* 13	HASH JOIN		3897438	124718016	297770	00:00:12
* 14	TABLE ACCESS FULL	STORE	110	770	18	00:00:01
* 15	HASH JOIN		3897438	97435950	297742	00:00:12
* 16	TABLE ACCESS FULL	DATE_DIM	2009	20090	412	00:00:01
17	TABLE ACCESS FULL	STORE_SALES	72011000	1080165000	297139	00:00:12

```
Predicate Information (identified by operation id):
-------------------------------------------
* 4 - filter( EXISTS (SELECT 0 FROM (SELECT "S_STATE" "S_STATE",RANK() OVER ( PARTITION BY "S_STATE" ORDER
BY SUM("SS_NET_PROFIT") DESC ) "RANKING" FROM "DATE_DIM" "DATE_DIM","STORE"
  "STORE","STORE_SALES" "STORE_SALES" WHERE "D_DATE_SK"="SS_SOLD_DATE_SK" AND "S_STORE_SK"="SS_STORE_SK"
AND "S_STATE"=:B1 AND "D_MONTH_SEQ">=1176 AND "D_MONTH_SEQ"<=1240 GROUP BY "S_STATE") "TMP1?"
  WHERE "RANKING"<=5))
* 5 - access("S_STORE_SK"="SS_STORE_SK")
* 7 - access("D1"."D_DATE_SK"="SS_SOLD_DATE_SK")
* 8 - filter("D1"."D_MONTH_SEQ">=1176 AND "D1"."D_MONTH_SEQ"<=1240)
* 10 - filter("RANKING"<=5)
* 11 - filter(RANK() OVER ( PARTITION BY "S_STATE" ORDER BY SUM("SS_NET_PROFIT") DESC )<=5)
* 13 - access("S_STORE_SK"="SS_STORE_SK")
* 14 - filter("S_STATE"=:B1)
* 15 - access("D_DATE_SK"="SS_SOLD_DATE_SK")
* 16 - filter("D_MONTH_SEQ">=1176 AND "D_MONTH_SEQ"<=1240)
```

Findings (2):

1. The performance of this SQL has improved.
2. The structure of the SQL execution plan has changed.

Execution Plan Before Change:

Plan Id   : 3
Plan Hash Value : 3517345661

Id	Operation	Name	Rows	Bytes	Cost	Time
0	SELECT STATEMENT		1	66	598730	01:59:45
1	SORT ORDER BY		1	66	598730	01:59:45
2	WINDOW SORT		1	66	598730	01:59:45
3	SORT GROUP BY ROLLUP		1	66	598730	01:59:45
* 4	HASH JOIN		3897438	257230908	598179	01:59:39
* 5	VIEW		1	16	299172	00:59:51
* 6	WINDOW SORT PUSHED RANK		1	32	299172	00:59:51
7	HASH GROUP BY		1	32	299172	00:59:51
* 8	HASH JOIN		3897438	124718016	298988	00:59:48
9	TABLE ACCESS FULL	STORE	110	770	18	00:00:01
* 10	HASH JOIN		3897438	97435950	298951	00:59:48
* 11	TABLE ACCESS FULL	DATE_DIM	2009	20090	413	00:00:05
12	TABLE ACCESS FULL	STORE_SALES	72011000	1080165000	298195	00:59:39
* 13	HASH JOIN		3897438	194871900	298988	00:59:48
14	TABLE ACCESS FULL	STORE	110	2750	18	00:00:01
* 15	HASH JOIN		3897438	97435950	298951	00:59:48
* 16	TABLE ACCESS FULL	DATE_DIM	2009	20090	413	00:00:05
17	TABLE ACCESS FULL	STORE_SALES	72011000	1080165000	298195	00:59:39

Predicate Information (identified by operation id):

- 4 - access("S_STATE"="S_STATE")
- 5 - filter("RANKING"<=5)
- 6 - filter(RANK() OVER (PARTITION BY "S_STATE" ORDER BY SUM("SS_NET_PROFIT") DESC)<=5)
- 8 - access("S_STORE_SK"="SS_STORE_SK")
- 10 - access("D_DATE_SK"="SS_SOLD_DATE_SK")
- 11 - filter("D_MONTH_SEQ">=1176 AND "D_MONTH_SEQ"<=1240)
- 13 - access("S_STORE_SK"="SS_STORE_SK")
- 15 - access("D1"."D_DATE_SK"="SS_SOLD_DATE_SK")
- 16 - filter("D1"."D_MONTH_SEQ">=1176 AND "D1"."D_MONTH_SEQ"<=1240)

FIGURE 10-11. *SPA Report – Findings and pre-execution plan*

Execution Plan After Change:

Plan Id   : 5
Plan Hash Value : 3545695459

Id	Operation	Name	Rows	Bytes	Cost	Time
0	SELECT STATEMENT		1	50	595850	00:00:24
1	SORT ORDER BY		1	50	595850	00:00:24
2	WINDOW SORT		1	50	595850	00:00:24
3	SORT GROUP BY ROLLUP		1	50	595850	00:00:24
* 4	FILTER					
* 5	HASH JOIN		3897438	194871900	297770	00:00:12
6	TABLE ACCESS FULL	STORE	110	2750	18	00:00:01
* 7	HASH JOIN		3897438	97435950	297742	00:00:12
* 8	TABLE ACCESS FULL	DATE_DIM	2009	20090	412	00:00:01
9	TABLE ACCESS FULL	STORE_SALES	72011000	1080165000	297139	00:00:12
* 10	VIEW		1	17	297770	00:00:12
* 11	WINDOW SORT PUSHED RANK		1	32	297770	00:00:12
12	SORT GROUP BY NOSORT		1	32	297770	00:00:12
* 13	HASH JOIN		3897438	124718016	297770	00:00:12
* 14	TABLE ACCESS FULL	STORE	110	770	18	00:00:01
* 15	HASH JOIN		3897438	97435950	297742	00:00:12
* 16	TABLE ACCESS FULL	DATE_DIM	2009	20090	412	00:00:01
17	TABLE ACCESS FULL	STORE_SALES	72011000	1080165000	297139	00:00:12

Predicate Information (identified by operation id):

- 4 - filter(EXISTS (SELECT 0 FROM (SELECT "S_STATE" "S_STATE",RANK() OVER (PARTITION BY "S_STATE" ORDER BY SUM("SS_NET_PROFIT") DESC) "RANKING" FROM "DATE_DIM" "DATE_DIM","STORE" "STORE","STOR E_SALES" "STORE_SALES" WHERE "D_DATE_SK"="SS_SOLD_DATE_SK" AND "S_STORE_SK"="SS_STORE_SK" AND "S_STATE"=:B1 AND "D_MONTH_SEQ">=1176 AND "D_MONTH_SEQ"<=1240 GROUP BY "S_STATE") "TMP1?" WHERE "RANKIN G"<=5))
- 5 - access("S_STORE_SK"="SS_STORE_SK")
- 7 - access("D1"."D_DATE_SK"="SS_SOLD_DATE_SK")
- 8 - filter("D1"."D_MONTH_SEQ">=1176 AND "D1"."D_MONTH_SEQ"<=1240)
- 10 - filter("RANKING"<=5)
- 11 - filter(RANK() OVER (PARTITION BY "S_STATE" ORDER BY SUM("SS_NET_PROFIT") DESC)<=5)
- 13 - access("S_STORE_SK"="SS_STORE_SK")
- 14 - filter("S_STATE"=:B1)
- 15 - access("D_DATE_SK"="SS_SOLD_DATE_SK")
- 16 - filter("D_MONTH_SEQ">=1176 AND "D_MONTH_SEQ"<=1240)

FIGURE 10-12. *SPA Report – post-execution plan*

The following query can be used to generate a text report:

```
set long 100000
set longchunksize 100000
set linesize 200
set head off
set feedback off
set echo off
spool reportSPA.html  -- File name for the output
SELECT dbms_sqlpa.report_analysis_task(
        task_name=>'SPA_TASK01', -- SPA Task name
```

```
              type=>'HTML',   -- Format of the report
              level=>'ALL',   -- Level of details in the report
              section=>'ALL'  -- Sections displayed in the report
              ) FROM dual;
spool off
```

11. Analyze the Results

Based on the results in the text report, we can conclude that for these two SQL statements, TPCDS Query 70 and Query 82, the database version upgrade from 11.2.0.3 to 12.2.0.1 is a good change, since both queries were improved considerably. As per Oracle's recommendation, the next step would be to test the change not only for a few SQL statements, but for a whole workload in the database using DWC/R. And this is what we will do in the next two chapters: Chapter 11 will cover the capture and Chapter 12 will cover the replay.

12. Decide Whether or Not to Perform Fixes

In this example, no findings required fixes. However, if there were information or findings in the comparison report that made the DBA doubt about implementing the change (in this example, a database upgrade), those findings would need to be analyzed, and if there were fixes required, they would need to be implemented before accepting the change.

Using SPA to Estimate the Impact of a Change with OEM Cloud Control

OEM Cloud Control also can be used with SPA to analyze the impact of a change. We'll use OEM 13*c*R2 Cloud Control in this example to execute a first and second SQL trial and a comparison report with a few mouse clicks.

1. After accessing the OEM 13*c*R2 home page of the database for which we will create the SPA task, choose Performance | Advisors Home, as shown in Figure 10-13.

2. On the Advisors Central page (Figure 10-14), select the option SQL Performance Analyzer Home.

3. Several options are listed on the SQL Performance Analyzer Home page. As you can see in Figure 10-15, the page includes options for very common use cases such as using SPA for a parameter change, upgrading from 10.2

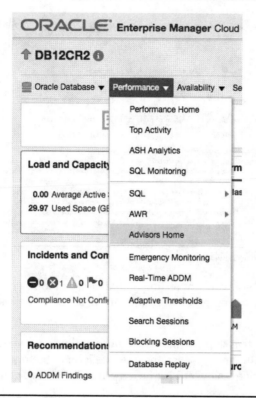

FIGURE 10-13. *Choosing Advisors Home from the Performance menu*

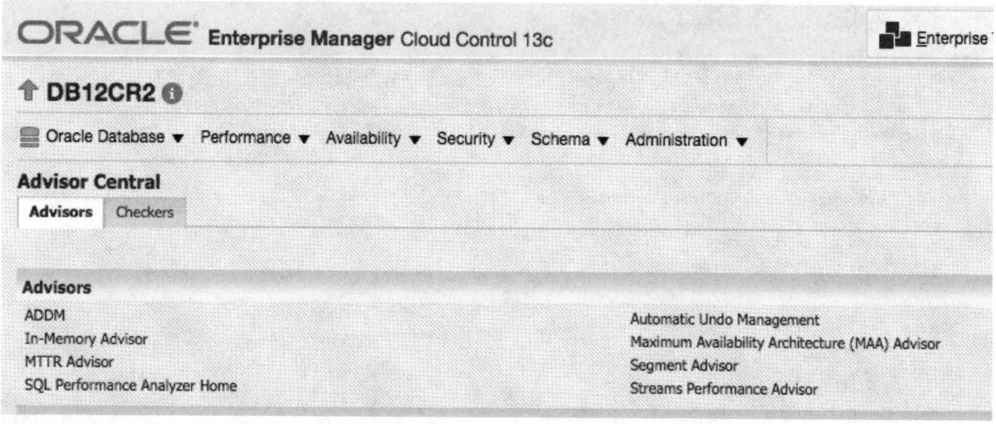

FIGURE 10-14. *Select SQL Performance Analyzer Home.*

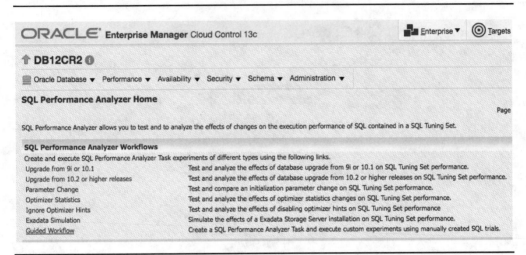

FIGURE 10-15. *Select Guided Workflow.*

to a later database version, testing a change in the optimizer statistics, and so on. For this example, select a standard procedure, Guided Workflow (Figure 10-15).

4. SPA will show five steps, which are similar to the steps we used earlier in the chapter with the CLI. Click the Execute icon to the right of step 1, Create SQL Performance Analyzer Task Based On SQL Tuning Set (Figure 10-16).

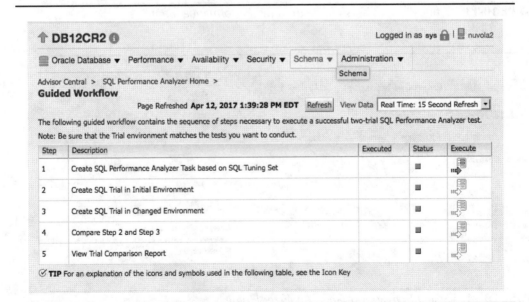

FIGURE 10-16. *Select to create an SPA task based on STS.*

5. Enter the name of the SPA task as well as the name of STS. For the SPA task name for this example, enter **SPA_TASK_01**, and for the STS name, enter **STS_QUERY_70_28** (see Figure 10-17), which is the same STS used in the previous section with CLI. (If no STS has been created, click the search button.) In this case, click the Create button to proceed.

6. Click the Execute icon to the right of step 2, Create SQL Trial In Initial Environment (Figure 10-18).

7. On the next page, you must provide section several important options, such as the name of the first SQL trial, which in this example is a system-generated name. You also must indicate whether the SQL trial should be executed locally or remotely, and a timeout per SQL statement. If the SQL trial will be executed remotely, as in this example, enter a database link name—for this example, enter **DB_11_2_0_3**. The time to execute the SQL trial is also requested: select the Immediately radio button, as shown in Figure 10-19. Once completed, click Submit to submit a job to execute the first SQL trial.

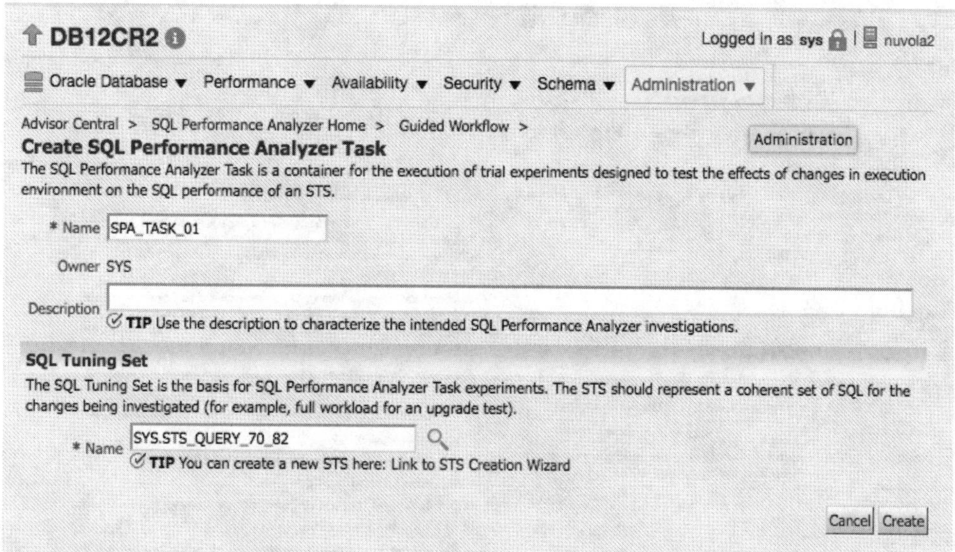

FIGURE 10-17. *Enter SPA task name and STS name.*

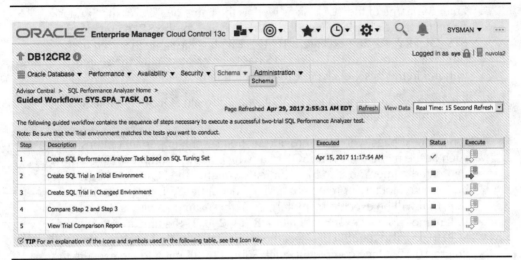

FIGURE 10-18. *Create the SPA trial in the initial environment.*

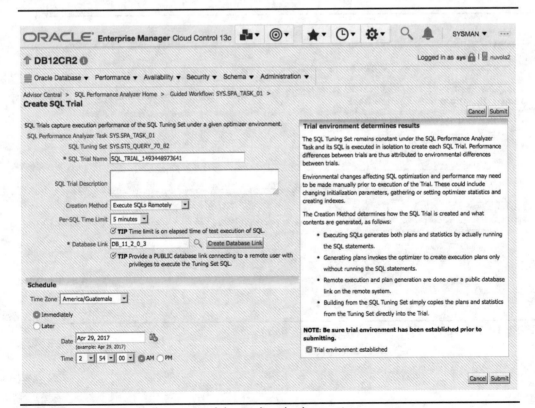

FIGURE 10-19. *Enter the name of the trial and other options.*

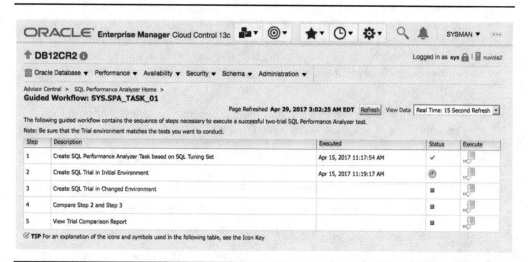

FIGURE 10-20. *A checkmark in the status column indicates that the job is completed.*

8. In the Status column, you can see that the job is being executed. You must wait until this job is completed. Once the job is completed, a check mark will appear in the Status column (Figure 10-20).

9. Click the Execute icon to the right of step 3, Create SQL Trial In Changed Environment (Figure 10-21).

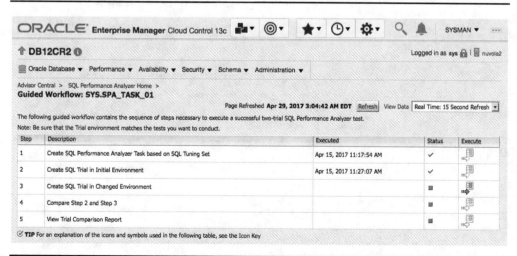

FIGURE 10-21. *Click the Execute icon for step 3.*

10. For the second SQL trial, the information requested is exactly the same as that for the first SQL trial. In this step, the environment in which the second SQL trial will be executed is the database 12cR2. Because in this database we created the SPA task, we are executing the second SQL trial locally (Figure 10-22). Provide the rest of the information and click the Submit button to start the execution of the second SQL trial.

11. In the Status column, you can see that the job is being executed. After the job is completed, a check mark is displayed in the Status column (Figure 10-23).

12. Click the Execute icon to the right of step 4, Compare Step 2 And Step 3 (Figure 10-24).

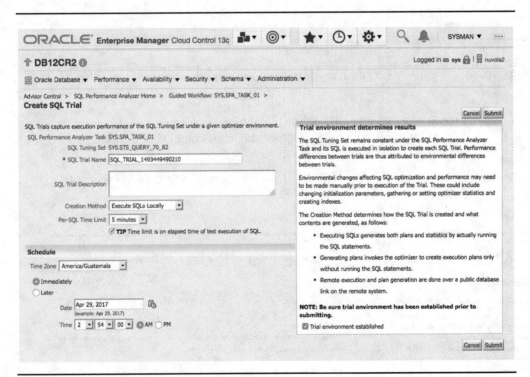

FIGURE 10-22. *Create a second SPA trial.*

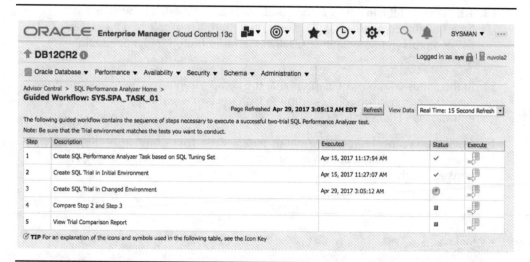

FIGURE 10-23.   *SPA trial creation completed.*

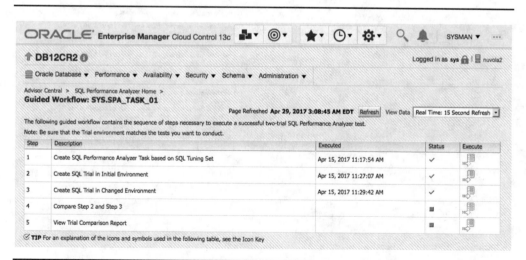

FIGURE 10-24.   *Compare steps 2 and 3.*

13. The names of the first and second SQL trials are requested as well as the time that the comparison will be executed. In this example, we'll execute the comparison Immediately, so select the radio button under Schedule (Figure 10-25).

14. In the Status column, you can see that the comparison job is being executed. After the comparison job is completed, a check mark will appear in the column (see Figure 10-26).

15. Click the Execute icon to the right of step 5, View Trial Comparison Report (Figure 10-27) to look at the result metrics and the performance divergence between both SQL trials.

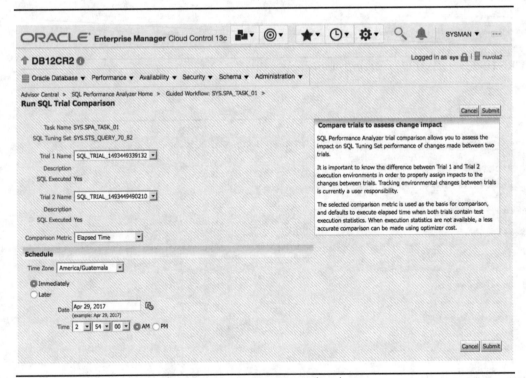

FIGURE 10-25. *Run the SQL trial comparison immediately.*

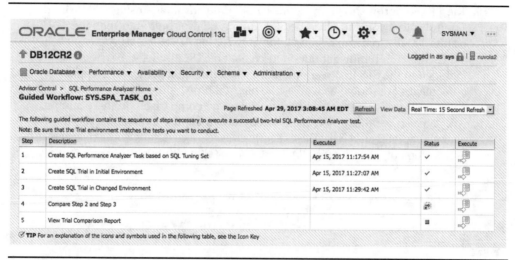

FIGURE 10-26. *Compare steps 2 and 3.*

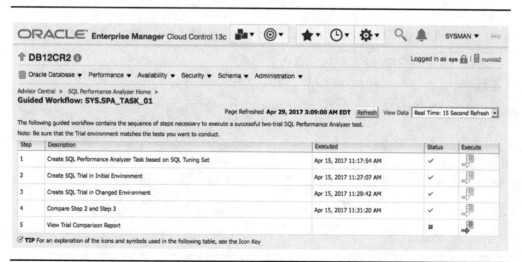

FIGURE 10-27. *View the Trial Comparison report.*

16. The Task Report is shown in Figure 10-28. One advantage using OEM Cloud Control is that you can click the SQL Tuning Advisor button to send the results directly to be analyzed by the SQL Tuning Advisor, and you can click the Create SQL Tuning Set button to create an STS. All the SQL statements included in the STS that were used are listed in a table, where the impact percentages are shown as well as the elapsed time before and after the change, since the elapsed time was used to the comparison. In this example, you can also see that a new plan was used in the environment that has the change implemented—database 12cR2. To see more details about another SQL statement, click its SQL ID. Now click SQL ID 2hj59zh9p5npq.

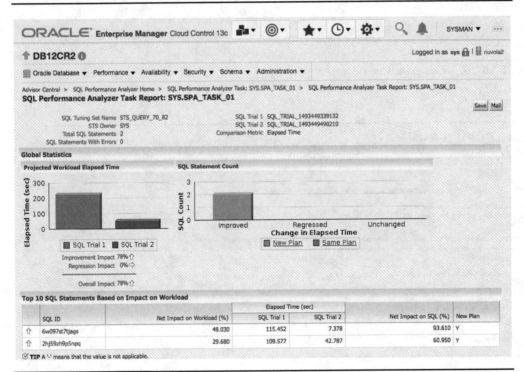

FIGURE 10-28. *SPA Task Report*

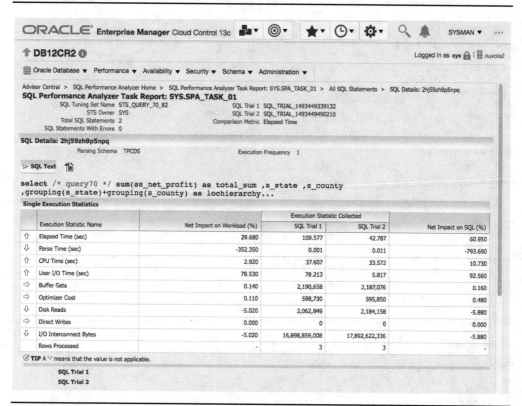

FIGURE 10-29.   *Viewing improvements to the SQL statement in SPA results*

Figure 10-29 shows the details of several metrics between the execution in the environment before the change (database 11.2.0.3) and the environment with the change implemented (database 12.2.0.1). You can use this information to review how the SQL statement was improved, where it had the most benefit, and decide whether or not the change improved this SQL statement.

Next to the metric comparison between the first and second SQL trials, the execution plan used in the environment without the change is shown (Figure 10-30). You can review all the step-by-step details of this execution plan as well as the rows returned in every step, the cost, and other information such as the predicate and the objects touched.

The execution plan used in the environment with the change is also shown (Figure 10-31). You can review all the step-by-step details of this execution plan.

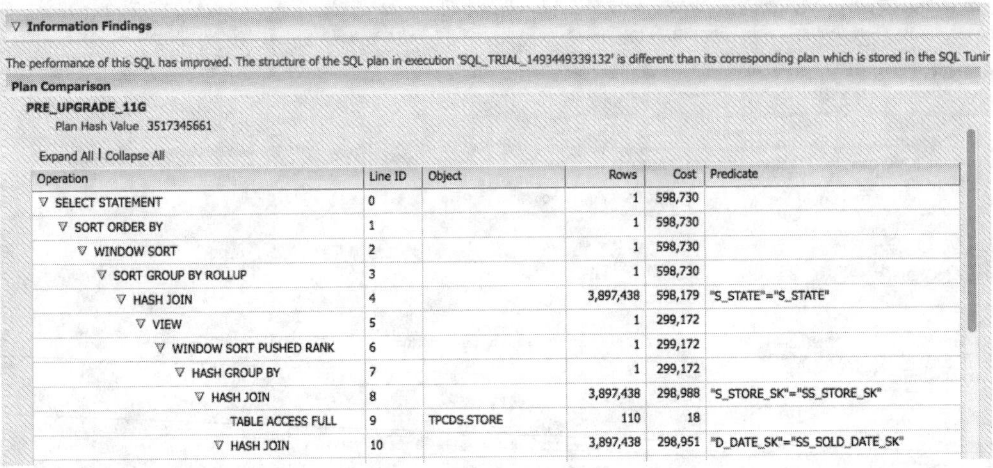

▽ **Information Findings**

The performance of this SQL has improved. The structure of the SQL plan in execution 'SQL_TRIAL_1493449339132' is different than its corresponding plan which is stored in the SQL Tunir

Plan Comparison

PRE_UPGRADE_11G
    Plan Hash Value 3517345661

Expand All | Collapse All

Operation	Line ID	Object	Rows	Cost	Predicate
▽ SELECT STATEMENT	0		1	598,730	
▽ SORT ORDER BY	1		1	598,730	
▽ WINDOW SORT	2		1	598,730	
▽ SORT GROUP BY ROLLUP	3		1	598,730	
▽ HASH JOIN	4		3,897,438	598,179	"S_STATE"="S_STATE"
▽ VIEW	5		1	299,172	
▽ WINDOW SORT PUSHED RANK	6		1	299,172	
▽ HASH GROUP BY	7		1	299,172	
▽ HASH JOIN	8		3,897,438	298,988	"S_STORE_SK"="SS_STORE_SK"
TABLE ACCESS FULL	9	TPCDS.STORE	110	18	
▽ HASH JOIN	10		3,897,438	298,951	"D_DATE_SK"="SS_SOLD_DATE_SK"

FIGURE 10-30. *Viewing details of the SQL environment without the change*

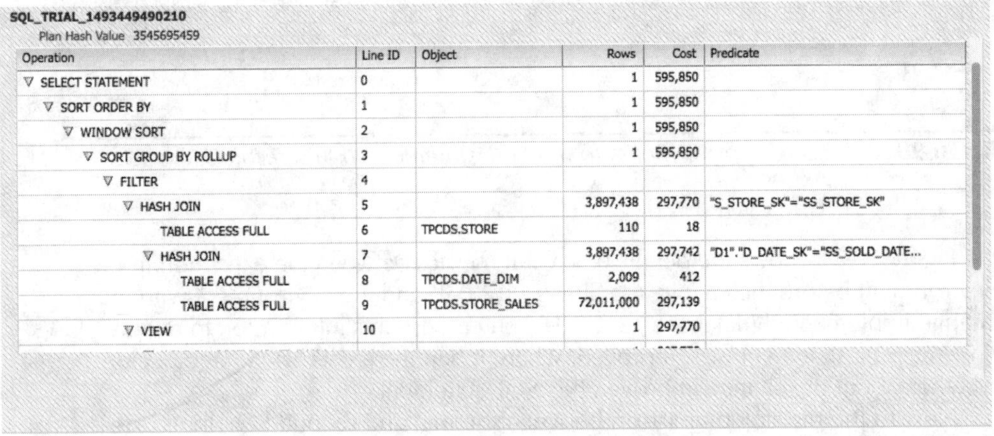

SQL_TRIAL_1493449490210
    Plan Hash Value 3545695459

Operation	Line ID	Object	Rows	Cost	Predicate
▽ SELECT STATEMENT	0		1	595,850	
▽ SORT ORDER BY	1		1	595,850	
▽ WINDOW SORT	2		1	595,850	
▽ SORT GROUP BY ROLLUP	3		1	595,850	
▽ FILTER	4				
▽ HASH JOIN	5		3,897,438	297,770	"S_STORE_SK"="SS_STORE_SK"
TABLE ACCESS FULL	6	TPCDS.STORE	110	18	
▽ HASH JOIN	7		3,897,438	297,742	"D1"."D_DATE_SK"="SS_SOLD_DATE...
TABLE ACCESS FULL	8	TPCDS.DATE_DIM	2,009	412	
TABLE ACCESS FULL	9	TPCDS.STORE_SALES	72,011,000	297,139	
▽ VIEW	10		1	297,770	

FIGURE 10-31. *Viewing details of the SQL environment with the change*

Summary

In this chapter, we showed you how to use SQL Performance Analyzer to measure the impact of a database version upgrade for two SQL statements, including the appropriate inputs, the steps required, the parameters for comparing the results, and the reports offered by SPA. DBAs can interpret these results easily from the SPA user interface. SPA is the first tool to use to measure the impact of a change in a whole environment, followed by Oracle Database Workload Capture and Replay, the main topic discussed in the next chapter.

CHAPTER
11

Database Workload Capture and Workload Intelligence

One of the most difficult questions for any Oracle DBA to answer—regardless of their years of experience or levels of certification attained—is exactly how a current production application workload will perform in a new production environment. Answering this question cogently is difficult because the scope of what *new* means may range from relatively small differences between source and target production environments to changes that are so massive that it will be virtually impossible to forecast performance accurately. For example, it should be relatively easy to predict how application workload performance will progress or regress as the result of applying a minor database patch; however, migrating an Oracle 11*g*R2 database running on a virtualized Linux server that resides on commodity hardware to Oracle 12*c*R2 on a "bare metal" SPARC SuperCluster introduces so many variables that it may be next to impossible to predict the workload's expected performance.

Database Workload Capture and Replay

Fortunately, Oracle 11*g*R1 introduced a new feature set—Database Workload Capture and Replay (DWC/R)—that made it possible for the first time to make exactly these types of predictions. As we will demonstrate in this chapter, Database Workload Capture (DWC) makes it simple to capture an actual production workload in its source environment for eventual replay through Database Workload Replay (DWR) within the eventual target environment. This makes it possible to identify precisely where performance regression is most likely to occur after migrating to that new environment; most importantly, it also enables an Oracle DBA to respond proactively to any challenges well before actual transitioning to the new production environment.

Database Workload Capture and Replay: Suggested Use Cases

DWC/R is useful in an almost dizzying array of situations, some of which a typical Oracle DBA may not have encountered yet. Because it captures actual application workloads from a source database—usually, a production environment—and can replicate that same workload, either all or in part against a completely different testing environment, it makes short work of determining whether the replayed workload will perform better or worse after transitioning to the new environment. Here are just a few use cases we believe an Oracle DBA will be able to leverage DWC/R for immediate benefit.

Upgrading to a New Database Version

Upgrading a database to a new major release—for example, from Oracle 11.2.0.3 to 12.2.0.1—will hopefully result in performance improvements because of positive enhancements to the optimizer, the availability of new optimizer parameters, the ability to leverage new kinds of histograms or optimizers statistics, improvements in internal memory structures for better application concurrency, and so forth. The bigger the difference between database versions, the more significant the optimizer changes, and although these enhancements almost always result in better performance for most SQL statements, there is always a possibility that the performance of at least some SQL statements may regress.

Migrating to a New Database Architecture

When an organization is first born, its application workload requirements may start out quite small—perhaps needing to leverage Oracle Database Standard Edition on a single server. But as the organization grows, it's not unusual for its needs to grow as well—for example, its applications may eventually require the larger feature set of Oracle Database Enterprise Edition in a RAC configuration with several nodes. In this case, DWC/R can be invaluable to simulate the new multi-node environment, experiment with modifications to the applications supported—especially when deploying application workloads across multiple nodes using database services—and meter the performance improvement to justify the investment of such architecture. Another scenario in this category includes migrating from a little-endian system such as Linux or Windows to a big-endian system such as Solaris, HP-UX, or AIX.

Migrating to Enterprise Systems

Oracle Engineered Enterprise Systems—including Oracle Database Appliance (ODA), Exadata Database Machine, and SPARC SuperCluster, to name a few—have become popular in the last decade; numerous IT organizations have migrated their databases to these solutions because they are specifically designed to improve the performance of Oracle databases as well as reduce the complexity of initial configuration. They introduce several advanced features to take advantage of every component inside the machine, including flash cards, multiple processors, storage devices (both spinning disk and solid-state devices), and ultra-high-speed network components. For example, Oracle Exadata Database Machine's exclusive features such as Smart Scan, Smart Flash Cache, and Write-Back Flash Cache predicate offloading and storage indexes are designed to increase the performance of application workloads dramatically, especially those employing extreme analytical processing. However, these enterprise systems are also expensive to license, so it's important for the Oracle DBA to ensure that those resources are leveraged at maximum capacity to wring every dime from their IT budget. DWC/R can be invaluable for ensuring that application workloads will perform optimally before a single query is migrated to a production Exadata environment; it can also help determining which SQL statements may need adjustment (for example, removal of optimizer hints) as well as which indexes can be made invisible or even eliminated.

Hardware, Firmware, and OS Upgrades

The typical refresh cycle for commodity hardware is about three years. Even if an IT organization decides to replenish aging hardware with newer models from the same vendor, it's not unusual to encounter performance differences after upgrading to the latest computing hardware, SAN storage, or networking components. Likewise, every operating system requires occasional patching for security vulnerabilities or bug fixes, improved hardware and firmware interfaces, and revised device drivers and codices. Since it's impossible to test every combination of hardware component, firmware upgrade, and OS patch against every incarnation of Oracle Database, it is not unusual to encounter an unexpected failure when an application workload is ramped up to its full production capacity. But DWC/R can replay an actual recorded production workload against a QA destination platform that's been patched and upgraded *before* deploying that workload in production to determine exactly what failures may occur.

Migrating Database Files to Different File Formats or Media

When an Oracle DBA decides to migrate an Oracle database's database files to a different storage environment—for example, from a GFS, EXT3/4, or NTFS file system to Oracle Automatic Storage Management (ASM), ASM Clustered File System (ACFS), or even Network File System (NFS)—there is a possibility of application performance regression. Likewise, moving these same files from spinning disk to solid-state drives (SSDs) or NVM Express (NVMe) will almost certainly improve physical I/O performance, but it's important to be able to measure the expected versus actual performance improvement to recognize expected return on investment. Again, DWC/R makes it simple to measure the I/O performance before and after migrating the application's database to its final storage subsystem.

Migrating to a New Virtualization Solution

Many IT organizations have decided to migrate their Oracle databases from virtual machines (via a hypervisor) either to Docker containers or Linux containers (LXCs). Because the hypervisor layer is removed from the stack, there will almost certainly be potential changes to application performance. Likewise, simply adding more memory or additional processors to a virtualized environment may likely improve application performance, but it's important to consider that, depending on the virtualization environment in use (for example, VMware versus Oracle VM), this performance improvement may come at a higher licensing cost. In these cases, DWC/R can be invaluable for proving out the performance gains relative to the costs before the new virtualized environment is officially implemented in production.

Migrating to the Cloud

Finally, IT organizations have begun in earnest to migrate their Oracle databases into one of several possible cloud environments, including Oracle public, private, hybrid cloud; Amazon Web Services (AWS); and Microsoft Azure Cloud. The driving force behind this migration is ostensibly to reduce infrastructure maintenance costs while simultaneously obtaining the ability to rescale compute, memory, and storage resources quickly as workloads demand. However, this new flexibility often masks hidden or unexpected costs, especially when data egress charges vary so widely between cloud solutions. Fortunately, DWC/R provides an excellent methodology to perform deep testing before databases are migrated to the selected cloud solution to guarantee against unexpected application performance regression.

Database Workload Capture

To provide intelligent answers to the use cases we've presented, Oracle Database 12c actually provides three separate DWC/R toolsets. To make exploration of those toolsets more manageable, we will divide our discussion across two chapters: in this chapter, we'll focus on Database Workload Capture (DWC) as well as another lesser-known tool, Workload Intelligence (WI), first introduced in Oracle 12cR1. We'll then move on to the numerous methods available to replay a workload with Database Workload Replay (DWR) in Chapter 12.

DWC: Concepts and Architecture

Before DWC became available in Oracle 11.1.0.7, Oracle DBAs struggled to capture application workloads accurately. Techniques for workload capture often involved gathering a representative sample of SQL statements executed during a specific time period—for example, during a peak workload, batch loading process, or other extreme system stress—and then simply reexecuting those SQL statements via shell scripts later against the new target nonproduction environment to duplicate the workload. Other third-party tools, such as HPE LoadRunner, could construct a sample application workload and run it against the target database environment, but several limitations didn't simulate the complexity of a real-life production environment.

Perhaps the biggest challenge with these capture methods is that they didn't take into account what most Oracle DBAs already knew through painful experience: It's not the 90 percent of the most commonly executed SQL statements that cause performance to degrade suddenly, but the 10 percent least commonly executed statements that, when run at unexpected times, cause serious application workload waits to occur. One additional problem with simply capturing just the SQL statements themselves and reexecuting those same statements was that several other important factors were not captured, such as the time sequence to execute the SQL statements, the bind variables used, optimizer and execution statistics, the actual execution plan(s) used, and whether parallelism was used—and, if so, the degrees of parallelism used.

DWC overcomes these challenges because it not only captures the text of SQL statements, but it also gathers the statements' actual execution time, database time, system change number (SCN), execution plan, concurrency, bind variables, rows returned, and other transaction characteristics of the original workload as it executed during a particular timeframe in its current production system. In addition, it also records attributes of the user session invoking the statements as well as the precise order in which statements originally occurred. That's particularly crucial when replaying DML statements with implicit or explicit dependencies—for example, creating a new entry in dimension table TPCDS.CUSTOMERS before creating a new corresponding row in fact table TPCDS.STORE_SALES—because otherwise there would be significant divergence when that workload is reproduced in the destination database.

The basic architecture of DWC is shown in Figure 11-1. In this scenario, we will be capturing a workload against an Oracle 11.2.0.4 database for later replay against its eventual new environment—an Oracle 12.2.0.1 database—in Chapter 12.

After an Oracle DBA initiates a DWC capture process against the source database, it deploys one or more extremely thin clients called *shadow workload capture processes* to gather all related information into a directory—the *capture directory*—as a series of simple OS files. DWC creates two subdirectories within the capture directory. The first one, cap, contains detailed information about the DWC execution; those files are described in Table 11-1.

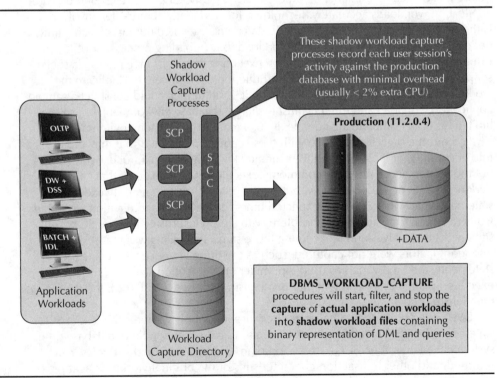

FIGURE 11-1. *Database Workload Capture architecture*

File	Format	Description
wcr_cr.txt	Text	Text version of DWC Activity Report, including details of significant workload attributes and top SQL statements that make up the workload
wcr_cr.html	HTML	An HTML version of the DWC Activity Report
wcr_cr.xml	XML	An XML version of the DWC Activity Report
wcr_scapture.wmd	Binary	Flag file generated at DWC capture start
wcr_fcapture.wmd	Binary	Flag file generated at DWC capture conclusion

TABLE 11-1. *DWC Files Retained in cap Directory*

The second directory, capfiles, also contains several subdirectories created by DWC as it gathers *shadow capture files*—a series of binary files that contain the results of all captured activity and named in a specific format (wcr_<id>.rec). Note that the work done by background processes will not be recorded within the capture files.

One of the biggest advantages of DWC/R is that all of these capture files are platform independent. This means that the workload can be captured in any environment—for instance, against an Oracle 10.2.0.4 single instance database running in a Microsoft Windows 32-bit platform on bare metal—but can replayed repeatedly against any other Oracle database environment, such as an Oracle 12.2.0.1 RAC database running in an Oracle Enterprise Linux x86-64 platform running within an Oracle Virtual Machine (OVM).

NOTE
DWC functionality is included within package DBMS_WORKLOAD_CAPTURE. It was introduced in Oracle 10gR2 (10.2.0.4) but it can be even used against Oracle 9iR2 (9.2.0.8) databases to capture workloads, though it's necessary first to apply a patch to the source database and the value for initialization parameter PRE_11G_ENABLE_ CAPTURE must be modified appropriately as well. For further information on enabling so that DWC for databases still running on releases prior to Oracle 11gR1, review MOSC Note 560977.1, Mandatory Patches for Database Testing Functionality for Current and Earlier Releases.

DWC/R vs. SQL Performance Analyzer: What's the Difference?

The other half of Real Application Testing—SQL Performance Analyzer, whose features we cover extensively in Chapter 10—at first glance may seem to offer comparable features to what DWC/R offer. The key difference between the tools is that SQL Performance Analyzer focuses on comparing the before-and-after results of a few specific changes as they affect a specific *set* of capture SQL statements. DWC/R focuses on comparing the before-and-after results of one or more changes to an Oracle database, an entire system environment, or both. Also, SQL Performance Analyzer cannot be used to analyze a workload that contains DML statements, because that DML would change the contents of the database itself; conversely, DWC/R is designed to handle *both* queries *and* DML statements to identify not just statement performance regression, but also differences in the results of applying database changes in the new environment. Finally, DWC/R maintains the concurrency of recorded activity; in other words, it ensures that the application workload is replayed in the precise order and timing that it was recorded in (though this feature can be overridden when desirable—for example, during a simulated test to destruction).

DWC: Overheads of Note

Once DWC is enabled against a database, every session writes into its own shadow capture file. While it's recording workload activity, DWC does incur a small penalty in terms of additional CPU overhead; however, this overhead is negligible—usually no more than 2 percent additional CPU is required for captures performed against 12cR1 database workloads and as little as 5 percent additional CPU resources for 11gR2 and earlier database releases. Each shadow capture session also requires only 64KB of additional PGA memory.

Additionally, the shadow capture files that DWC produces consume a relatively small footprint within its shadow capture directories. The size of each shadow capture file doesn't depend on the length of time that the session is executing SQL statements. In the sample DWC session we present later in this chapter, even though the DWC capture period spanned a full 60 minutes, the shadow capture files produced only consume 96.56 KB of disk space.

NOTE
Unfortunately, package DBMS_WORKLOAD_CAPTURE doesn't supply a function to estimate the amount of disk space required for these files; as a workaround, we recommend executing a DWC session during a representative time period, measuring the resulting disk space consumed, and then simply extrapolating those results to obtain a reasonably accurate estimate of disk space required for a complete DWC execution.

Notable DWC Improvements in Oracle 12*c*

The largest enhancement to DWC in Oracle Database Release 12.1.0.1 was the addition of WI features, which we will cover later in this chapter. Two other notable DWC features bear mentioning as well:

- **Support for Multitenant architecture** DWC now supports Oracle Multitenant databases. Capture processes can gather all workload activity across every pluggable database (PDB) within a single container database (CDB); it can also capture activity from a subset of PDBs within a CDB, or even from a single PDB.

- **Extended SQL statement capture** Starting in Oracle 12.2.0.1, a new parameter, `plsql_mode`, for the function `START_CAPTURE` in package DBMS_WORKLOAD_CAPTURE specifies the PL/SQL capture mode. It can be set to a value of either `TOP_LEVEL` (which instructs DWC to capture only top-level PL/SQL calls—essentially, the same behavior in pre-12.2.0.1 releases) or `EXTENDED` (which enables DWC to capture both top-level PL/SQL as well as any SQL or PL/SQL statements called from within PL/SQL). See My Oracle Support Note 2166850.1, 12.2: *Database Replay Enhanced PL/SQL Support*, for details.

Capturing Application Workloads with DWC

For a practical example of the value of DWC/R, we will simulate a not-uncommon scenario: the migration of an Oracle database from an earlier database release to a later release with the added complexity of switching the database's database files from non-ASM storage to ASM storage. We'll use DWC to record a query-only application workload generated via Swingbench against the TPC-DS schema on an Oracle 11.2.0.3 database running on a Linux V6U4 virtual machine; this database's files are retained within an EXT3 file system.

As we have done throughout this book, we'll look at this from two perspectives: If your IT organization has selected Oracle Enterprise Manager (OEM) Cloud Control as its tool of choice for managing its Oracle database environments, this next section provides insight on how to capture an application workload using that method with just a few mouse clicks. We also provide an example of how to accomplish the same goal using purely scripted methods immediately following this section.

NOTE
A prerequisite for using OEM for any DWC/R operation is that the database that will be the source of the desired application workload to be captured must already be registered as a database target in OEM.

DWC: Capturing an Application Workload Using OEM Cloud Control

OEM Cloud Control offers excellent visibility into ongoing as well as completed DWC activity. To demonstrate, we'll use OEM 13c Cloud Control (OEM for short) to capture the aforementioned database application workload with a series of mouse clicks.

Starting a DWC Operation

Once we have accessed the OEM home page of our source database (db11g), we select Performance | Database Replay, as shown in Figure 11-2.

Selecting the Database Replay option gives us access to the entire suite of DWR/C options; because we're interested in capturing an application workload, we select the Capture Workload option under the Capture Production Workload section to initiate a DWC operation (Figure 11-3).

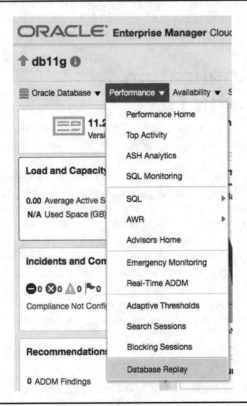

FIGURE 11-2. *Accessing DWR/C from OEM*

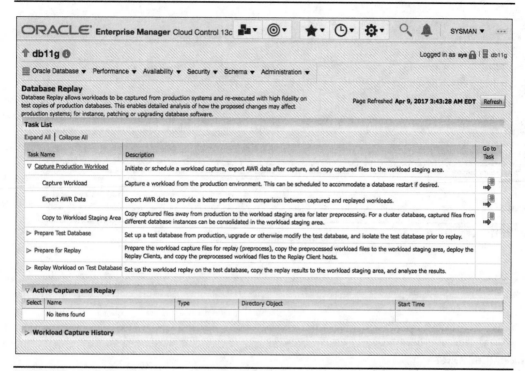

FIGURE 11-3. *DWR/C Central control panel*

DWC: Checklist

Figure 11-4 shows a particularly helpful feature of OEM: it explains exactly which steps need to be performed and—more importantly—exactly *why* each step is crucial to a successful DWC operation in the form of a detailed checklist. OEM makes sure that a DWC operation can proceed only after each step has been acknowledged by checking the appropriate checkbox before clicking the Next button to proceed.

DWC: Specifying Capture Options

Figure 11-5 shows several options for the DWC operations, including whether to gather a SQL Tuning Set (STS) during application workload generation, which filters should be applied against the gathered workload, and—probably most importantly— whether to restart the database before the DWC operation begins. (The benefits and drawbacks of restarting or not restarting the source database are discussed later in the chapter in the "Point/Counterpoint: To Restart or Not to Restart?" sidebar.)

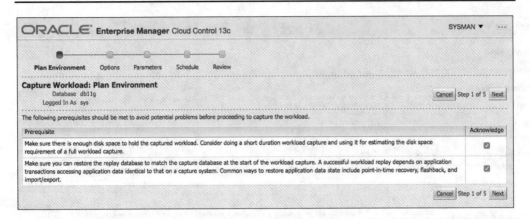

FIGURE 11-4. *Starting a DWC operation*

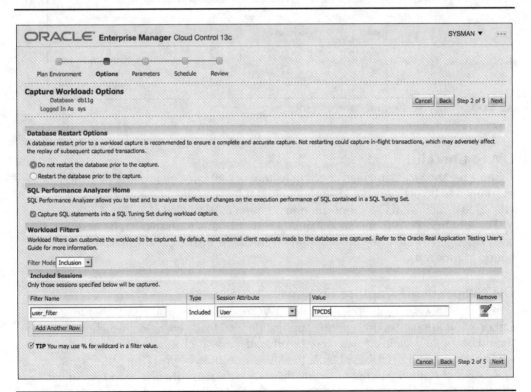

FIGURE 11-5. *Selecting DWC options*

Collecting an STS while a DWC operation executes offers an interesting benefit: Although it makes almost no difference in terms of the resources needed to capture a workload, it enables a SQL Performance Analyzer (SPA) task to be executed without having to rerun the application workload that's been captured. Also note that selecting Inclusion for the Filter Mode option means that OEM will capture only the matching workload attributes specified, while selecting the Exclusion option will explicitly ignore the workload attributes specified. We'll discuss the numerous filtering options available when we review the ADD_FILTER procedure of package DBMS_WORKLOAD_CAPTURE in the next section, as well as some subtle differences between how OEM presents these filtering options versus a DWC operation executed via PL/SQL scripts.

Point/Counterpoint: To Restart or Not to Restart?

The reason for this recommendation is to insure that DWC begins capturing application workloads from a clean starting point without any in-flight transaction activity, and that means there could be some divergence between the captured workload and the replayed workload. If the captured workload is essentially read-only—a likely possibility for decision support, analytic, or data warehouse applications—this divergence likely will not matter; on the other hand, if the captured workload includes DML statements, there will almost certainly be divergence between a previously captured workload's statistics when it is replayed against its new database environment. In the real world, of course, restarting a production database to obtain a clean starting point will not be possible because of the demands of high availability for most production environments, so at least some minor divergence during a replay operation is an acceptable trade-off.

DWC: Specifying Task Name and Directory

Next, we specify a unique name for the DWC operation and the Oracle directory object that will become the capture directory in which all capture workload files will be created (see Figure 11-6). If an Oracle directory object hasn't been created yet, we click the Create Directory Object button to create it. Once the directory has been identified, we click Next to tell OEM to verify whether the chosen directory path is actually empty, because DWC will never overwrite any capture files.

DWC: Scheduling Options

We will schedule the DWC task to start immediately before we trigger an appropriate application workload—but it's important to note an extremely valuable feature: the ability to schedule a DWC operation for some point in the future using Oracle Scheduler technology. Figure 11-7 shows the panel that's displayed next; it permits

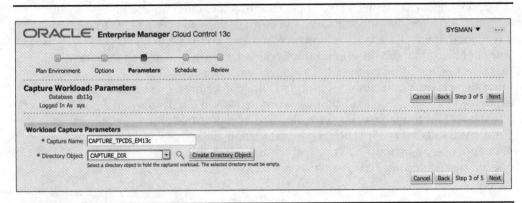

FIGURE 11-6. *Specifying DWC Capture Name and Directory Object*

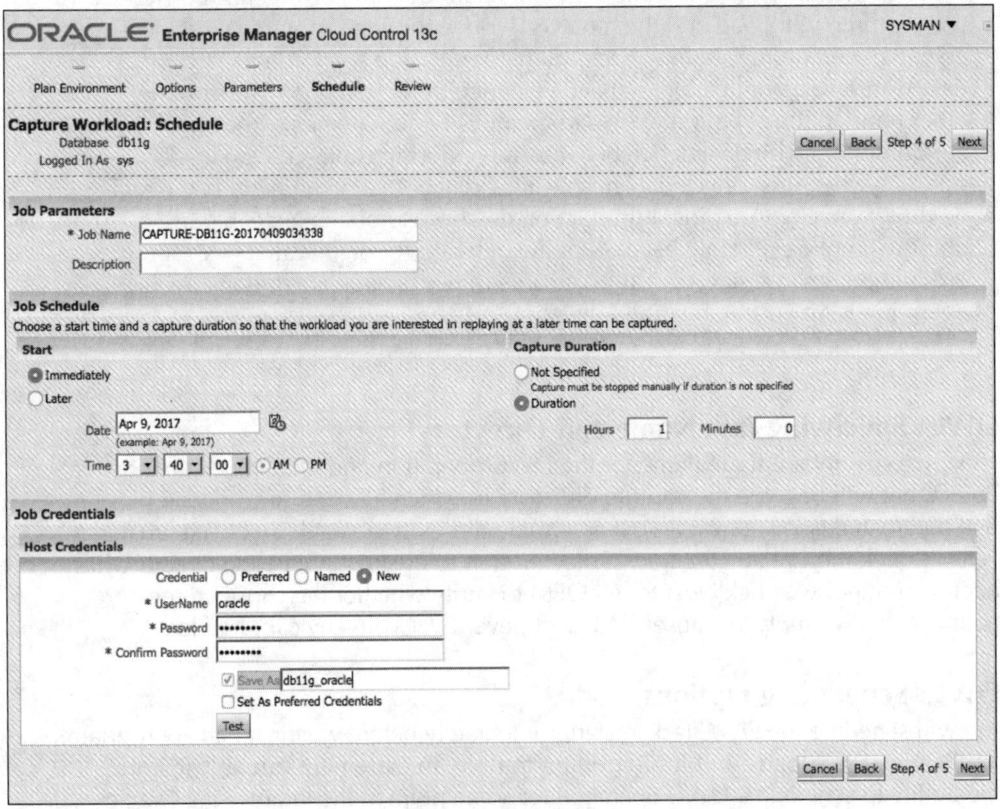

FIGURE 11-7. *Scheduling a DWC operation*

specification of a Job Name, scheduled start time, the duration of the capture period—in this case, one hour—and OS credentials needed to connect to the host on which the database resides.

The application workload is now ready for capture to commence. As Figure 11-8 shows, clicking the Submit button after a final review will initiate the DWC operation at its scheduled time.

Once the DWC task is initiated, OEM submits the scheduled task in the background (see Figure 11-9), so even if we accidentally closed the browser, the task will continue to execute at its scheduled time. We will move on to executing the application workload immediately so it can be captured.

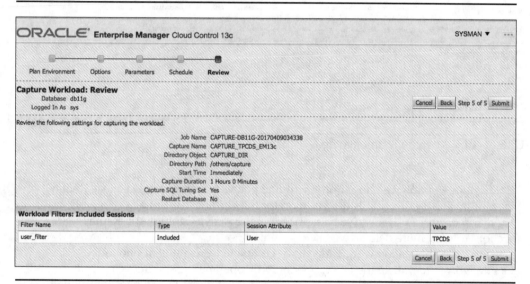

FIGURE 11-8. *DWC operation – final review*

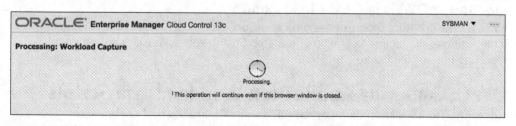

FIGURE 11-9. *DWC operation – processing*

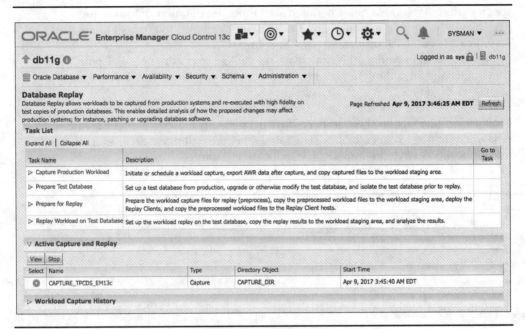

FIGURE 11-10. *Monitoring an ongoing DWC operation*

The same option we chose from the home page (Performance | Database Replay) to start the DWC operation is used to monitor the current status of an ongoing DWC operation (Figure 11-10). We see a new row in the Active Capture And Replay section; to view more details, we click the link.

Once the application workload(s) have completed executing, it's up to the Oracle DBA to terminate the DWC operation by opening the still-active task, clicking the End Capture button, and then responding to the dialog questions either to terminate the DWC operation immediately or do so after waiting the specified number of seconds.

Monitoring DWC via OEM Cloud Control

Once a DWC capture process has completed successfully, a plethora of valuable information is available; selecting a completed DWC process displays all available reporting option (see Figure 11-11).

DWC: Capturing Application Workloads via Scripts

Not every IT organization has adopted OEM as its GUI-based tool of choice to determine how their Oracle environments are performing, and some Oracle DBAs may prefer a scripted approach to capturing application workloads with DWC.

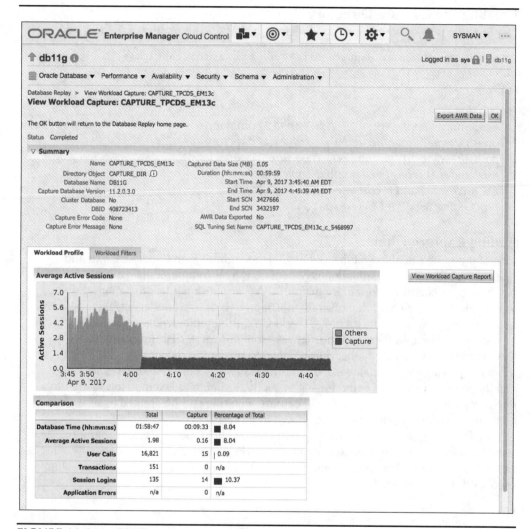

FIGURE 11-11.   *DWC operation – results summary*

Therefore, let's dive deeper into what's really going on under the hood during a DWC operation by revisiting the same application workload capture scenario: instead of leveraging OEM, we'll reproduce the identical workload capture results with some relatively simple calls to the procedures and functions of package DBMS_WORKLOAD_CAPTURE, plus a handful of SQL queries.

Creating the Capture Directory

Our first step is to create the capture directory for DWC's output files, as shown here:

```
SQL> CREATE DIRECTORY capture_dir AS '/home/oracle/capture';
Directory created.
```

> **NOTE**
> *Remember that the CREATE DIRECTORY command*
> *doesn't require that the underlying physical directory*
> *path already exists on the host, so be sure it does*
> *exist and that it has been granted appropriate*
> *OS ownership and read/write privileges before*
> *proceeding with the DWC operation.*

Adding Capture Filters

One of the most valuable features of DWC is the ability for an Oracle DBA to add one or more filters before initiating DWC sessions against a particular source database application workload. By default, DWC applies no filters to captured workloads, and as we will demonstrate in Chapter 12, it's certainly possible to filter out any undesired parts of a recorded workload during replay with DWR.

However, because there is almost always some unwanted or unnecessary extraneous database activity that doesn't need to be captured—for example, OEM agent queries against the database, or automatically executed system tasks such as nightly optimizer statistics gathering—it's usually desirable to leverage this feature to minimize the scope of what DWC will capture. Filtering can be applied against any combination of the session attributes shown in Table 11-2.

The following sample code leverages the USER filter type to restrict capture of only the application workload activity that user TPCDS generates—an especially useful feature when several users are connected and only the workload for a specific user needs to be captured.

```
BEGIN
    DBMS_WORKLOAD_CAPTURE.ADD_FILTER (
        fname => 'user_filter', -- Name for the filter
        fattribute => 'USER', -- Type of the filter
        fvalue => 'TPCDS'); -- User generating application workloads

END;
/
```

As we will discuss shortly, the actual application of these filters is tightly coupled with the default_action argument of function DBMS_WORKLOAD_CAPTURE .START_CAPTURE.

Filtering Attribute	Description
INSTANCE_NUMBER	If applicable, with a RAC database, you can filter the workload of which instance(s) you want to capture.
USER	Filters the captured workload to include statements generated by one or more Oracle database user(s).
MODULE	Filters the captured workload to include only statements tagged with one of the specified MODULE labels. The MODULE tag is typically attached to the workload component via a call to DBMS_APPLICATION_INFO.SET_MODULE.
ACTION	Filters the captured workload to include only statements tagged with one of the specified ACTION labels. The ACTION tag is typically attached to the workload component via a call to DBMS_APPLICATION_INFO.SET_MODULE.
PROGRAM	Filters the captured workload to include statements generated by one or more application executable name(s).
SERVICE	Filters the captured workload to include statements generated by one or more Oracle database service(s).
PDB_NAME	Restrains the workload to the listed PDBs. Applies only if the database from which the workload is being captured is a CDB.

TABLE 11-2. *DWC Filters Available*

Starting DWC

Before starting a DWC process, Oracle best practices suggest that the source database be restarted. However, note that this is optional and is not required for the capture process to succeed.

Calling the START_CAPTURE procedure of DBMS_WORKLOAD_CAPTURE initiates a DWC operation, as this code snippet shows:

```
SQL> BEGIN
    DBMS_WORKLOAD_CAPTURE.START_CAPTURE (
        name => 'TPCDS_CAPTURE', --Name of the Capture Process
        dir => 'CAPTURE_DIR', -- Capture Directory
        duration => 3600, -- DWC duration (in seconds)
        default_action=>'EXCLUDE',
        capture_sts => TRUE, -- Automatically create a related SQL Tuning Set (STS)
        sts_cap_interval => 60); -- Frequency (in seconds) at which to refresh STS
END;
/
```

NOTE
The default_action *parameter is somewhat counterintuitive. If set to a value of* EXCLUDE*, then only the workload defined through the filters applied through* DBMS_WORKLOAD_CAPTURE.ADD_FILTER *will be captured, and the rest of the workload in the database will be ignored. Contrariwise, if this parameter is set to* INCLUDE*, the entire workload in the database will be captured* with the exception of *the workload defined through the filters applied with* DBMS_WORKLOAD_CAPTURE.ADD_FILTER*.*

Although this example duplicates our previous OEM example for controlling the duration of a DWC operation, it's also possible to start and end a DWC operation via manual means. This may be especially desirable when you're unsure of exactly how long an application workload may execute. To start a DWC operation manually, simply supply a NULL value to the DURATION argument of START_CAPTURE. You can then invoke the FINISH_CAPTURE procedure after the desired application workload has completed. We also recommend employing a suitable time interval to allow any ongoing transactions or reporting to terminate gracefully; as shown in the next code example, the TIMEOUT parameter specifies how many seconds—in this case, 90—to wait before the DWC operation is terminated:

```
BEGIN
    DBMS_WORKLOAD_CAPTURE.FINISH_CAPTURE(
        timeout => 90,
        ,reason => 'Termination (after 90 seconds)');
END;
/
```

Starting the Application Workload
Once the DWC process has been initiated against the source production database, it's time to start the application workload or stand back and let the ongoing workload that already exists be captured. In our example use case, we unleashed a Swingbench-generated workload against the targeted database using four separate sessions to execute SELECT statements against the TPC-DS schema. We will highlight the importance of four concurrent sessions later when we examine the resulting workload statistics and information in the Workload Replay section of the related DWC reports.

Monitoring DWC via Scripted Reporting
Once the DWC process has been initiated, it can be monitored using view DBA_WORKLOAD_CAPTURES using a query similar to the one shown here:

```
SQL> SELECT id,name, status, error_message FROM DBA_WORKLOAD_CAPTURES;

        ID NAME            STATUS          ERROR_MESSAGE
---------- --------------- --------------- --------------------
        42 TPCDS_CAPTURE   IN PROGRESS
```

Once the DWC process has completed, the report will return the following output:

```
SQL> SELECT id,name, status, error_message FROM DBA_WORKLOAD_CAPTURES;

        ID NAME            STATUS          ERROR_MESSAGE
---------- --------------- --------------- --------------------
        42 TPCDS_CAPTURE   COMPLETED
```

The summary of the captured application workload can be reviewed via the following query:

```
SQL> SELECT
         id
       ,name
          ,directory
        ,duration_secs
        ,(capture_size/1024) capsize_kb
        ,filters_used
        ,user_calls
        ,user_calls_total
        ,(dbtime/1000) dbtime_ms
     FROM dba_workload_captures;
    ID NAME         DIRECTORY   DURATION_SECS CAPSIZE_KB FILTERS_USED USER_CALLS USER_CALLS_TOTAL DBTIME_MS
------ ------------ ----------- ------------- ---------- ------------ ---------- ---------------- ----------
    42 TPCDS_CAPTURE CAPTURE_DIR        3599 96.5576172            1         56              653 12514514.5
```

Exporting DWC AWR Data

Every time a DWC process begins and ends, it automatically triggers creation of a new AWR snapshot. This makes it easy for an Oracle DBA to gather valuable information about all database and application activity that occurred during the DWC timeframe, but this data will reside only in the AWR of the source Oracle database unless it is first exported so it can be imported eventually into the destination database for comparison to subsequent DWR operations.

Once the DWC operation has completed, the resulting AWR data and STSs generated during the capture process are gathered via the Oracle Data Pump export utility (expdp) through procedure EXPORT_AWR of package DBMS_WORKLOAD_CAPTURE, as the following listing shows. Note that the capture ID for the DWC operation must be supplied:

```
BEGIN
    DBMS_WORKLOAD_CAPTURE.EXPORT_AWR (capture_id => 42);
END;
/
```

The files created as a result in the capture directory are listed in Table 11-3.

File	Format	Description
wcr_ca.dmp	Binary	AWR Data Pump export dump file
wcr_ca.log	Text	Data Pump export log
wcr_cap_us_graph.extb	Binary	User calls graph
wcr_ca_sts.dmp	Binary	"Packed" STS

TABLE 11-3. *Files Created via EXPORT_AWR*

DWC: Workload Reporting

Even though we have yet to prepare the captured workload for its eventual replay against its new destination environment, these DWC reports provide some excellent insights into exactly what happened during the application workload's execution.

DWC Report Contents

Once a DWC operation has completed successfully (or even if it has been aborted), Oracle saves a report in the Workload Capture directory in HTML format that summarizes all activity captured. Though there is minimal diagnostic or tuning information at this point in the DWC/R process, this report nevertheless summarizes key information about the DWC operation itself, including the timeframe and duration of the workload captured, several key metrics, top activity dimensions, and even information on the SQL statements that were captured. Figures 11-12 and 11-13

DB Name	DB Id	Release	RAC	Capture Name	Status
DB11G	408723413	11.2.0.3.0	NO	TPCDS_CAPTURE	COMPLETED

Information	Capture
Start time:	20-Mar-17 23:01:30 (SCN = 3186127)
End time:	21-Mar-17 00:01:29 (SCN = 3193068)
Duration:	59 minutes 59 seconds
Capture size:	96.56 KB
Directory object:	CAPTURE_DIR
Directory path:	/others/capture
Directory shared in RAC:	TRUE
Filters used:	1 INCLUSION filter

FIGURE 11-12. *DWC operation – captured workload summary*

Captured Workload Statistics

- 'Value' represents the corresponding statistic aggregated across the entire captured database workload.
- '% Total' is the percentage of 'Value' over the corresponding system-wide aggregated total.

Statistic Name	Value	% Total
DB time (secs)	12514.51	77.86
Average Active Sessions	3.48	
User calls captured	56	8.58
User calls captured with Errors	0	
Session logins	5	3.36
Transactions	0	0.00

FIGURE 11-13. *DWC operation – Captured Workload Statistics*

show a summary of the overall DWC operation and the resulting workload statistics for the operation.

Figure 11-14 lists the most active system events, the most active database services, and most active SQL statements collected during the DWC operation, respectively. Finally, Figure 11-15 shows which sessions were most active during the DWC operation.

Generating a DWC Workload Report in Text Format

It's also possible to generate a DWC workload report in a purely text format using the REPORT function of DBMS_WORKLOAD_CAPTURE, as the following PL/SQL script shows. Note that as with calls to most other DBMS_WORKLOAD_CAPTURE procedures and functions, it is necessary to supply the DWC capture ID (in this case, 42) as well as the destination directory and filename of the resulting report. See the code in Example 11-1 in Appendix B.

The corresponding output from this report is included in Example 11-2 of Appendix B.

NOTE
It's also possible to regenerate an HTML version of a DWC report using the DBMS_WORKLOAD_CAPTURE.REPORT function as well. See Example 11-3 in Appendix B.

Top Events Captured

Event	Event Class	% Event	Avg Active Sessions
CPU + Wait for CPU	CPU	27.36	1.22
direct path read	User I/O	21.14	0.94
direct path write temp	User I/O	20.71	0.93
direct path read temp	User I/O	8.46	0.38
db file scattered read	User I/O	6.22	0.28

Back to Workload Captured
Back to Top

Top Service/Module Captured

Service	Module	% Activity	Action	% Action
db11g	Swingbench User Thread	84.14	UNNAMED	84.14

Back to Workload Captured
Back to Top

Top SQL Captured

SQL ID	% Activity	Event	% Event	SQL Text
7bvd762nt0t3z	61.19	CPU + Wait for CPU	23.01	with year_total as (select c_...
		direct path write temp	20.15	
		direct path read temp	8.27	
ck52qcn50mj6s	7.52	direct path read	5.53	WITH ssr as (SELECT s_store_id...
		CPU + Wait for CPU	1.31	
b9y8rw5dsr00z	6.59	direct path read	6.03	SELECT /*query9*/ CASE WHEN (S...
cdwvbk03ku8sd	2.55	CPU + Wait for CPU	1.74	WITH wscs AS (SELECT sold_dat...
458uvnydxrb18	2.18	direct path read	1.93	select /*query7*/ i_item_id, a...

FIGURE 11-14.   *DWC operation – Top Events, Top Service/Module, Top SQL Captured*

Top Sessions Captured

- '# Samples Active' shows the number of ASH samples in which the session was found waiting for that particular event. The percentage shown in this column is calculated with respect to wall clock time and not total database activity.
- 'XIDs' shows the number of distinct transaction IDs sampled in ASH when the session was waiting for that particular event
- For sessions running Parallel Queries, this section will NOT aggregate the PQ slave activity into the session issuing the PQ. Refer to the 'Top Sessions running PQs' section for such statistics.

Sid, Serial#	% Activity	Event	% Event	User	Program	# Samples Active	XIDs
56, 173	22.20	CPU + Wait for CPU	7.71	TPCDS	JDBC Thin Client	124/360 [34%]	2
		direct path read	5.66			91/360 [25%]	2
		direct path write temp	5.10			82/360 [23%]	1
76, 215	20.96	CPU + Wait for CPU	6.53	TPCDS	JDBC Thin Client	105/360 [29%]	1
		direct path read	5.22			84/360 [23%]	1
		direct path write temp	5.22			84/360 [23%]	1
109, 87	20.71	CPU + Wait for CPU	6.09	TPCDS	JDBC Thin Client	98/360 [27%]	1
		direct path write temp	5.53			89/360 [25%]	1
		direct path read	5.10			82/360 [23%]	1
68, 109	20.27	CPU + Wait for CPU	6.90	TPCDS	JDBC Thin Client	111/360 [31%]	1
		direct path read	5.10			82/360 [23%]	1
		direct path write temp	4.79			77/360 [21%]	1

FIGURE 11-15. *DWC operation – Top Sessions Captured*

Workload Intelligence: Making the Invisible Visible

A particularly thorny predicament for any Oracle DBA to encounter is an application workload that is essentially hidden within a "black box"—perhaps as a part of commercial off-the-shelf (COTS) software. In this situation, the Oracle DBA typically has little to no insight into the actual SQL statements that make up the application until its workload is actually executed. To make matters worse, the actual patterns of the SQL statements' execution—for example, which statements are primarily reporting functions versus which statements are responsible for generating transactions—are likely to be invisible until users start using the application in production.

Fortunately, the Real Application Testing suite offers an elegant solution to the predicament just described: introduced in Oracle Database Release 12cR1 (12.1.0.2), WI enables any Oracle DBA to perform in-depth analysis of any application workloads recorded through a prior DWC operation to identify, classify and analyze intra-workload execution patterns. Although this is immensely valuable for COTS-generated SQL statements, the ability to identity patterns within application workloads is also eminently useful to validate assumptions about what a completely visible application is actually executing against a particular database.

> ## Workload Intelligence: Underlying Methods
>
> The key concepts behind WI were originally described in an elegant white paper aptly titled *Oracle Workload Intelligence* authored by Quoc Trung Tran, Konstantinos Morfonis, and Neoklis Polyzotis and presented at SIGMOD15 in June 2015. As of this writing, Tran and Morfonis still work for Oracle, and Morfonis kindly collaborated with the authors as we expanded our understanding of their paper's various mathematical models that underpin the features of WI in Oracle Database 12*c*R1. See Appendix C for references to the scholarly work of these authors; it provides interesting insights into the enormous research that goes into creating a complex product like WI.

Workload Intelligence: Concepts

As shown in Figure 11-16, each WI analysis involves four simple steps; the basic concepts behind this feature set are explained in more detail next.

1. **Workload scoping and definition**   First, WI gathers all pertinent data from a defined application workload that DWC has previously captured, including all SQL statements as well as the objects that the workload interacted with.

2. **Model construction**   WI creates a model of the application workload's SQL statements, including the order in which they were processed and the amount of database time each statement consumed during workload capture.

3. **Pattern matching**   Once the application execution model has been constructed, WI will isolate and identify patterns within the recorded workload. It also attempts to group execution patterns together based on complex mathematic algorithms.

4. **Reporting**   WI produces a detailed report of its pattern matching results. The resulting report is produced in HTML format by default, but results can also be reported in plain-text or XML format as well.

The complete WI feature set is accessed through calls to a set of Java classes. The main Java class, `workload.intelligence`, is part of the dbrintelligence.jar Java Archive (JAR) file that is located within the $ORACLE_HOME/rdbms/jlib directory of the Oracle database home. In addition, the various WI metadata that's produced during a WI task's execution is exposed through simple SQL queries against data dictionary views, as we'll demonstrate in the next section.

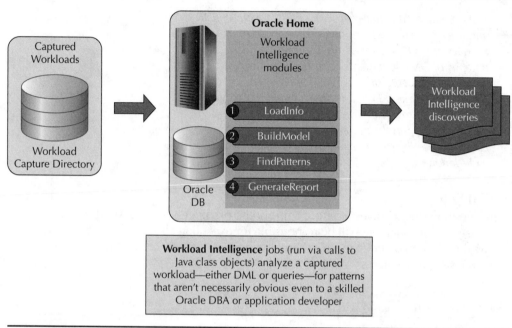

FIGURE 11-16. *How Workload Intelligence analyzes information*

NOTE
*As of Oracle 12.2.0.1, the interface to WI
functionality is admittedly not particularly
sophisticated, and there is no corresponding
GUI execution method available; however, this
may change in later database releases as the power
of the WI feature set becomes more popular.*

WI: A Practical Example

For a practical demonstration of the features of WI, we will generate a somewhat less-than-random workload against the TPC-DS schema, capture the workload via DWC, and then leverage WI to analyze the workload to classify any meaningful patterns. We will leverage a custom-built package, PKG_DML_GENERATOR, that leverages a framework that's extremely similar to the same one that the Swingbench application workload generator uses to generate DML statements against the TPCDS schema.

NOTE
The only difference between PKG_DML_GENERATOR and the one that Swingbench uses for single-row transactions is that it generates a series of random batches of DML statements against six fact tables and the CUSTOMER dimension. This simulated batch-processing workload is somewhat simpler to analyze using WI features. The source code for PKG_DML_GENERATOR and the additional database objects required to leverage it to simulate these workloads is included in Example 12-5 of Appendix B.

Initial Setup

This one-time step involves granting appropriate privileges to the desired Oracle database user account that will be responsible for executing all WI tasks. Listing 11-1 shows the creation of an Oracle database user account named wrc that we will use to demonstrate WI features.

Listing 11-1 *Creating the wrc user*

```
DROP USER wrc CASCADE;
CREATE USER wrc
    IDENTIFIED BY wrc
    DEFAULT TABLESPACE tpcds_data
    TEMPORARY TABLESPACE temp
    PROFILE DEFAULT
    QUOTA UNLIMITED ON tpcds_data;

GRANT CREATE SESSION TO wrc;
GRANT SELECT,INSERT,ALTER ON wi$_job TO wrc;
GRANT INSERT,ALTER ON wi$_template TO wrc;
GRANT INSERT,ALTER ON wi$_statement TO wrc;
GRANT INSERT,ALTER ON wi$_object TO wrc;
GRANT INSERT,ALTER ON wi$_capture_file TO wrc;
GRANT SELECT,INSERT,ALTER ON wi$_execution_order TO wrc;
GRANT SELECT,INSERT,UPDATE,DELETE,ALTER
    ON wi$_frequent_pattern TO wrc;
GRANT SELECT,INSERT,DELETE,ALTER
    ON wi$_frequent_pattern_item TO wrc;
GRANT SELECT,INSERT,DELETE,ALTER
    ON wi$_frequent_pattern_metadata TO wrc;
GRANT SELECT ON wi$_job_id TO wrc;
GRANT EXECUTE ON dbms_workload_replay TO wrc;
```

NOTE
We will use this same Oracle database user account during DWR operations that we will demonstrate in Chapter 12.

Constructing a WI Task

Our first task is to create a WI task that will be referenced throughout the WI process as each analysis proceeds toward its conclusion. Regardless of its successful completion, each WI task is assigned a unique job ID that is used to relate all metadata throughout the process.

The LoadInfo Java program module that is part of the `workload.intelligence` Java class creates the WI task. LoadInfo connects to the specified Oracle database, performs some initial intelligence gathering, and then registers all pertinent SQL statements and database objects within that database's data dictionary. Listing 11-2 shows an invocation of the LoadInfo module to create a new WI task named `wi_oltp_100` against the DWC workload that currently resides in the specified directory path (/home/oracle/DBRControl). Table 11-4 defines the common and unique parameters for all WI modules.

Listing 11-2 *Constructing a new WI task*

```
# Export Java CLASSPATH variable to enable simpler execution
    $> export  CLASSPATH=$ORACLE_HOME/rdbms/jlib/dbrintelligence.jar: \
    $ORACLE_HOME/rdbms/jlib/dbrparser.jar: \
    $ORACLE_HOME/jdbc/lib/ojdbc8.jar
# Execute LoadInfo for specific DWC capture files
$> java oracle.dbreplay.workload.intelligence.LoadInfo \
-job wi_oltp_100 -cdir /home/oracle/DBRControl \
-cstr jdbc:oracle:thin:@192.168.1.1.121:1539:NCDB122 -user wrc
$> Enter password: ***
```

Note that we exported the Java `CLASSPATH` environment variable to make it simpler to execute all WI tasks, and that the Java module does request a valid database password for the wrc account whenever we request an execution of the WI modules.

Once WI has completed analyzing the DWC workload, any resulting WI files will be retained within a separate workload intelligence subdirectory within the same path as the Workload capture files.

Constructing a WI Model

Next, the BuildModel module is invoked to create a model of the application workload's SQL statements, including the order in which they were processed and

WI Parameter	Description
-job	Name assigned to WI task.
-cstr	Connection string for Oracle database that will retain all WI metadata.
-user	Oracle database user account name for Oracle database that will retain all WI metadata.
-cdir	Directory containing DWC workload capture files. LoadInfo module uses this to process all workload capture files prior to building a WI model.
-t	Threshold value that FindPatterns module uses to determine how aggressively it should search for patterns. The default value (0.5) should be sufficient for most analyses; a lower value forces FindPatterns to search more aggressively for matching patterns and generally returns more data, while a higher value searches less aggressively for apparent patterns.
-out	Output path and filename that the GenerateReport module uses to store generated WI results.

TABLE 11-4. *Workload Intelligence Modules – Input Parameter Definitions*

the amount of database time each statement consumed during workload capture, as shown in Listing 11-3:

Listing 11-3 *Constructing a WI model*

```
$> java oracle.dbreplay.workload.intelligence.BuildModel \
-cstr jdbc:oracle:thin:@192.168.1.121:1539:NCDB122 \
-user wrc -job wi_oltp_100
```

Finding WI Patterns

Once the application execution model has been constructed, it's time to invoke the FindPatterns module to isolate and identify patterns within the recorded workload. This step can take quite a bit longer than just about any other step, because the FindPatterns module identifies execution patterns and groups statements together based on complex mathematic algorithms (see Listing 11-4).

Listing 11-4 *Searching for WI patterns*

```
$> java oracle.dbreplay.workload.intelligence.BuildModel \
-cstr jdbc:oracle:thin:@192.168.1.121:1539:NCDB122 \
-user wrc -job wi_oltp_100 -t 0.1
```

Generating a WI Report

Finally, the results of the WI pattern matching are formatted into a concise HTML-formatted report via the GenerateReport module (Listing 11-5). A sample of the WI report output is shown in Listing 11-6.

Listing 11-5 *Generating a WI report*

```
$> java oracle.dbreplay.workload.intelligence.GenerateReport \
-job wi_oltp_140 -cstr jdbc:oracle:thin:@192.168.1.121:1539:NCDB122 \
-user wrc -out /home/oracle/wi_oltp_140.html
```

NOTE
Though it's not recorded in the official documentation for the package itself, this report can also be generated by passing the appropriate arguments to and then executing procedure WORKLOAD_INTELLIGENCE_REPORT of the package DBMS_WORKLOAD_REPOSITORY in Oracle 12cR1 and 12cR2.

Listing 11-6 *Generating a WI report in non-HTML format*

```
SQL> ALTER SESSION
        SET EVENTS '31151 TRACE NAME CONTEXT FOREVER, LEVEL 0x40000';
SET SERVEROUTPUT ON
SET LINESIZE 132
SET PAGESIZE 0
SET LONGCHUNKSIZE 1000000
SET LONG 1000000
VARIABLE creport CLOB;
BEGIN
    :creport :=
            DBMS_WORKLOAD_REPLAY.WORKLOAD_INTELLIGENCE_REPORT(
                wi_job_name => 'wi_oltp_100'
                ,top_results => 20
                ,format =>'html'
            );
END;
/
SQL> SPOOL /home/oracle/wi_oltp_100.html
SQL> PRINT :creport
SQL> SPOOL OFF
```

Workload Intelligence: Findings

The findings reported via WI bear a closer look. The report is broken down into two major sections. The General Information section includes general attributes of the WI task, including the capture directory encompassing the DWC files used as a source for the analysis as well as the threshold that was applied for the WI analyses. As its name implies, the Discovered Patterns section uncovers the various patterns that WI identified during its analyses. The HTML format of the report makes it simple to drill down into each set of patterns that were discovered.

Top Patterns by DB Time

This report section identifies groupings of SQL statements based on the observed database time that each statement expended. This analysis is therefore valuable when ascertaining where the captured workload spent most of its effort executing a collection of SQL statements.

Top Patterns by Number of Executions

This report section categorizes SQL statements based on another valuable dimension: how often a collection of statements were executed as a group within all captured statements. This analysis can be valuable in determining the relative frequency of SQL statement execution within a captured workload and can be helpful in determining where an Oracle DBA would need to spend the majority of time when deciding to tune one group of SQL statements over another group.

Top Patterns by Length

Finally, this report section gathers SQL statements together based on the observed character length of the SQL statements themselves—a relative measure of their possible complexity, based on the simple assumption that longer statements will generally be more convoluted and therefore require additional tuning.

Figure 11-17 shows an example of the first report section, including a detailed drill down into some of the statements that made up the first few WI groupings. Note that statement C was identified as one of the key performance participants—it's the actual call to the package procedure that generates all random DML—but that it was preceded by statement B, which called the DBMS_APPLICATION_INFO package to activate appropriate values for the corresponding MODULE and ACTION tags.

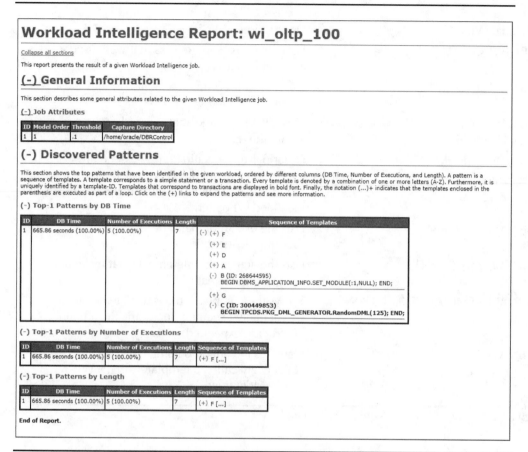

FIGURE 11-17.   *WI: Top patterns By DB time*

Workload Intelligence: Metadata

Although its interfaces aren't necessarily extremely sophisticated, WI does provide extensive visibility into its job tasks, the models it has constructed, and the application workload execution patterns it has found. The corresponding metadata for WI jobs, models, and patterns is shown in Table 11-5.

Metadata View	Description
DBA_WI_CAPTURE_FILES	Lists the DWC capture files that were used as input into a WI job task.
DBA_WI_JOBS	Describes all WI job tasks that currently exist within the database.
DBA_WI_OBJECTS	Lists all WI job tasks that currently exist within the database.
DBA_WI_PATTERN_ITEMS	Describes the specific items—essentially, a template that encompasses a set of one or more SQL statements—that make up an identified WI pattern.
DBA_WI_PATTERNS	Lists the execution patterns that WI has successfully identified.
DBA_WI_STATEMENTS	Lists the actual SQL statements that make up a significant WI pattern.
DBA_WI_TEMPLATE_EXECUTIONS	Shows the number of times a WI template was actually executed, including the amount of DB time expended.
DBA_WI_TEMPLATES	Identifies the encompassing patterns—collectively called a template—that a WI task has identified.

TABLE 11-5.   *Workload Intelligence Metadata Views*

An example of how to leverage this metadata to produce a custom, in-depth WI analysis from these WI data dictionary views is shown in the resulting output in Figure 11-18. The SQL*Plus query used to produce this custom report is captured in Example 11-4 of Appendix B.

Pattern: 3 Length: 20 DB Time: 226622151

Trans-Action	SQL Statement	Stmt Count
Y	BEGIN TPCDS.PKG_DML_GENERATOR.RandomDML(125); END;	1
	COMMIT	10,456
	INSERT INTO CATALOG_SALES(CS_SOLD_DATE_SK ,CS_SOLD_TIME_SK	65
	INSERT INTO CUSTOMER (C_CUSTOMER_SK ,C_CUSTOMER_ID ,C_CURRE	249
	INSERT INTO STORE_SALES(SS_SOLD_DATE_SK ,SS_SOLD_TIME_SK ,S	99
	INSERT INTO WEB_SALES(WS_SOLD_DATE_SK ,WS_SOLD_TIME_SK ,WS_	200
	SELECT SEQ_CATALOG_SALES.NEXTVAL FROM "SYS"."DUAL"	65
	SELECT SEQ_STORE_SALES.NEXTVAL FROM "SYS"."DUAL"	99
	SELECT SEQ_WEB_SALES.NEXTVAL FROM "SYS"."DUAL"	9,067

Pattern: 5 Length: 21 DB Time: 332479493

Trans-Action	SQL Statement	Stmt Count
Y	BEGIN TPCDS.PKG_DML_GENERATOR.RandomDML(250); END;	1
	COMMIT	21,369
	INSERT INTO CATALOG_SALES(CS_SOLD_DATE_SK ,CS_SOLD_TIME_SK	106
	INSERT INTO CUSTOMER (C_CUSTOMER_SK ,C_CUSTOMER_ID ,C_CURRE	1
	INSERT INTO STORE_SALES(SS_SOLD_DATE_SK ,SS_SOLD_TIME_SK ,S	428
	INSERT INTO WEB_SALES(WS_SOLD_DATE_SK ,WS_SOLD_TIME_SK ,WS_	332
	SELECT SEQ_CATALOG_SALES.NEXTVAL FROM "SYS"."DUAL"	104
	SELECT SEQ_STORE_SALES.NEXTVAL FROM "SYS"."DUAL"	406
	SELECT SEQ_WEB_SALES.NEXTVAL FROM "SYS"."DUAL"	18,528

FIGURE 11-18. *Example of custom WI report output*

Summary

Oracle Database 11.1.0.7 was the first release to offer Database Workload Capture and Replay (DWC/R) features, and Oracle 12cR1 expanded that original rich feature set to include several new abilities. This chapter first discussed several scenarios in which these features can be invaluable for determining exactly how a production application workload will perform in its new environment by capturing the precise details of the workload including all SQL statements, execution statistics, and system resource utilization information so that the identical workload can be replayed over and over again. We also illustrated exactly how to capture a production workload against a source database using either OEM Cloud Control or a scripted approach.

Finally, we demonstrated how Oracle 12cR1's new Workload Intelligence features make it easy to identify potentially unnoticed application workload execution patterns, a particularly useful set of findings when an Oracle DBA is facing an unknown "black box" application workload generated from a third-party application without any visibility into the actual SQL statements contained within.

CHAPTER
12

Database
Workload Replay

The previous chapter discussed the various methods that any Oracle DBA can leverage to capture an application workload with Database Workload Capture (DWC). Now that we've explained that process in sufficient detail, it's time to turn our attention to the whole reason for capturing a workload from a production source: leveraging the power of Database Workload Replay (DWR) to play back the captured workload against a new database environment to satisfy one or more of the scenarios identified in the introduction to Chapter 11.

DWR Concepts and Architecture

In its most elemental form, DWR consumes the files captured during a DWC operation to replay the identical application workload against a different Oracle database environment—usually one that has been enhanced, upgraded, or otherwise modified—so that the impact of those changes on the application workload can be ascertained with a significant degree of accuracy. A DWR operation therefore dramatically increases the probability that when the changes are applied against the next iteration of the production environment, any potential vectors for application performance variance will have already been identified and either corrected ahead of time or at least anticipated well in advance. We Figure 12-1 presents a basic overview of how a DWR operation unwinds.

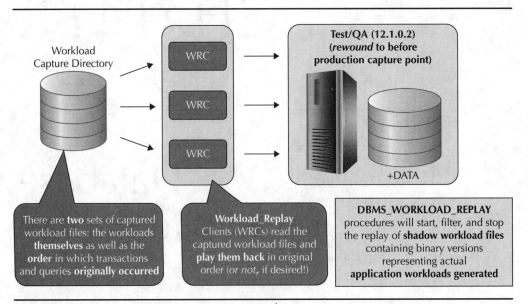

FIGURE 12-1. *How a DWR operation unwinds*

DWR Operations: A Checklist

The myriad complex capabilities of DWR can seem daunting to master at first, especially when compared to the relative simplicity of recording database workloads with DWC. To help you leverage DWR, we've provided a simple checklist (see Figure 12-2) of the six basic steps that you'll typically need to perform for just about every DWR operation. You will soon find, however, that the ways you can leverage DWR within your IT organization will be limited only by your cleverness, creativity, and flexibility.

1. Acquire DWC Files

The binary nature of the files captured during a DWC operation makes it extremely simple to transport them to the DWR destination database's environment. Workload Capture files can simply be copied via a utility such as SCP or any other method that's appropriate to your IT organization's security standards.

2. Preprocess DWC Files

Because it's possible that DWC operations have taken place against an Oracle database of an entirely different release, operating system, platform, and/or endianness than the eventual DWR destination database, the DWC files must be preprocessed to enable them to be replayed at the destination.

3. Prepare the Destination Database

Deciding which method is most appropriate for preparing the database that's the target of a DWR operation can be confusing, because the method will depend on several factors. The most important of these is the need to avoid any divergence

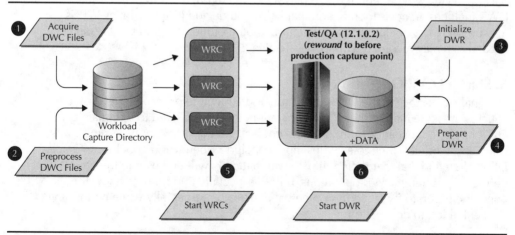

FIGURE 12-2. *DWR operations flowchart*

between recorded and replayed results. Since DWR essentially unwinds a DWC workload against the destination database, there will be less divergence if the starting point of the replay is as nearly identical as the starting point during which the workload(s) were originally captured. Obviously, this will be nearly impossible in some cases, but as long as you understand the implications of divergence, all will be well. (See the sidebar titled "Preparing the Database for DWR: Choose Wisely" for an in-depth discussion of possible methods for resetting the destination database before replaying workload[s].)

4. Initiate a DWR Operation

Perhaps the trickiest part of any successful DWR operation is deciding exactly how you'd like to see the captured workload replayed. This phase involves several crucial decisions, including application of filters against the captured workload and the remapping of database activity originally recorded against one database service or user account against a totally different service or account during replay. This step also permits an Oracle DBA to decide whether the timing and order of originally recorded statements will be strictly maintained or will be adjusted for faster or slower replay. In the case of a true test to destruction, it's even possible to execute all of the application workload's SQL statements without regard to their original concurrency to simulate an overwhelming workload that probes the limits of the new database environment. We'll illustrate these concepts in the upcoming scenarios in this chapter.

5. Start a Workload Replay Client

Much as its name implies, a workload replay client (WRC) is an application that consumes the various files produced during a DWC operation and replays the workload based on how the DWR operation has been initialized. In most cases, only one WRC will be required to replay a workload, but as we'll demonstrate, DWR includes an advisory function that helps you decide just how many WRCs may be necessary, including the minimum amount of memory and CPU resources needed to replay recorded workloads effectively.

6. Start a DWR Operation

The final step is to start the DWR operation and allow it to proceed to its eventual conclusion. Note that unlike a DWC operation, there is no need to terminate a DWR operation, because (presuming, of course, that the destination system has sufficient resources) the replay will simply conclude whenever it concludes. Oracle DBAs often find that that their ability to wait patiently will be taxed to the utmost during long-running DWR operations, but it's especially important to allow the operation to run to its (hopefully) eventual conclusion, especially while performing a potential test to destruction.

Preparing the Database for DWR: Choose Wisely

Deciding how to configure the target database environment for a DWR operation is an important consideration for a successful analysis, especially since there is always a chance that a captured workload may encompass not only SELECT statements, but DML statements as well.

We therefore strongly recommend that you consider the following rules of thumb:

- Understand the potential impact of data divergence for your post-DWR analyses. This is extremely important when you're trying to narrow down any potential divergence between application code versions, especially if you're keenly interested in identifying any unexpected results—for example, an exception that's been raised during application workload replay. It's obviously important to make sure the target database is as nearly transactionally consistent with the corresponding production system when the workload was originally recorded; ideally, it should be reset to the same system change number (SCN) used by the source database before the application workload capture commenced. In these situations, it may be advantageous to leverage a tool such as Oracle GoldenGate to replicate data between the production and test environments so that data divergence is minimized or eliminated.

- If only application code changes or modified initialization parameters are being tested, use a test database that matches the current production environment as closely as possible. For this case, a snapshot clone of the production database—perhaps built via Recovery Manager backups, or (even better) a Data Guard physical standby database that's been temporarily placed in snapshot standby mode—will work best. We recommend leveraging the powerful features of Flashback Database to enable the ability to rewind the target database back to its initial state before each restart of a DWR operation. Note that opening a physical standby in snapshot standby mode automatically creates a guaranteed restore point to enable Flashback Database features.

- For more extreme changes—for example, a complete restructuring of entities, implementing partitioning for tables, changing indexing strategies—the DataPump Export/Import utility may be an excellent alternative choice. Although it does require additional disk space to store the export dump sets, DataPump offers myriad methods to filter, rearrange, and reload data within the target database, and it can leverage parallelism effectively to speed the reinitialization process.

(continued)

■ For a complete makeover of the production database environment—
say, shifting from a big-endian to a little-endian OS, or completely
different hardware platforms, or even moving from a non-RAC
to a RAC database—consider leveraging the power of Recovery
Manager's transportable tablespace features, including cross-platform
transportable tablespaces (XTTS), for faster initialization of the target
environment.

■ There may be no single best way to synchronize your production
initially and test environments before starting a new DWR operation,
so consider using a combination of all of these methods when it makes
the most sense to do so. The authors have written PL/SQL code to
reinitialize and resynchronize the test environment when the scale of
the resynchronization permitted that alternative.

Analyzing DWR Results

Once the captured workload has been replayed, DWR provides several reports to
measure the resulting performance variance. This is really useful for diagnosing
performance problems after modifications to the database, environment, or
application code have been applied so that the impact can be accurately
ascertained and any potential issues or errors resolved before applying those
changes to a production environment.

Every successful DWR operation automatically generates a DWR summary
report that includes metrics for the captured workload that are compared directly
against the replayed workload. This provides detailed information identifying a
plethora of potential factors—database initialization parameters, memory sizes,
CPUs available, and other hardware components—and whether they have diverged
between capture and replay. This report also provides details of any significant
divergence between capture and replay in terms of execution times, wait events,
errors, DML failures, and even the number rows returned from queries. Finally, this
report looks at these metrics from the perspective of the entire workload and several
different workload dimensions (for example, services, modules, and actions), and it
even covers whether individual SQL statements performed better or worse.

For in-depth analysis, Oracle DBAs can leverage several of their most powerful
diagnostic and tuning tools already on their tool belts. AWR reports are extremely
useful for comparing prior DWC or DWR operations to the one just completed,
while Active Session History (ASH) reports run against the various WRC sessions can
also be instrumental in helping to discern any bottlenecks at the statement or session
level that need to be investigated and/or resolved.

DWR Improvements in Oracle 12*c*

Oracle Database 12*c* enhanced DWR significantly by introducing several functionalities.

Support for Multitenant Databases

Oracle 12.1.0.1 introduced the concept of multitenant databases. Simply put, a multitenant database employs a central container database (CDB) that comprises one or more pluggable databases (PDBs) that share memory, storage, and I/O resources more effectively. DWC can record a workload from either a single PDB or a non-CDB, and then DWR can replay that workload against a single CDB (12.1.0.1), a single PDB (12.1.0.2), or even a selected subset of PDBs within the same CDB (12.2.0.1). Database Workload Capture and Replay (DWC/R) is therefore extremely useful for determining exactly how an existing application workload from a non-CDB will perform after it's been successfully migrated into a multitenant environment.

Support for Database Consolidation

Released in Oracle 12cR1, this functionality enables an Oracle DBA to use DWR to replay completely different application workloads that were previously captured via DWC from completely different databases. The captured workloads may have been captured from different database releases, completely different platforms, and even at different times, but all can be replayed simultaneously against a destination database. This is an extremely useful feature when you're consolidating multiple different application workloads—perhaps with utterly different workload characteristics—into a single database environment, because it provides an excellent picture of just how well that new environment will be able to cope with a complex, combined workload.

For example, an Oracle 10gR2 database that's hosting an OLTP workload may be targeted for consolidation into an existing Oracle 12cR2 CDB as a new PDB, but that new CDB may already be hosting two other PDBs, one with a primarily batch-oriented workload and another with a heavy read-only data warehousing workload; it's crucial to determine exactly how the new PDB's workload will collide with the demands of the existing PDBs. Another useful consolidation example occurs when an IT organization decides to move several smaller databases running analytical application workloads to a single Exadata Database Machine or SPARC SuperCluster platform, because those engineered systems are designed to provide superior performance for analytic queries, especially when paired with Oracle 12cR2 and its Database In-Memory (DBIM) features that we discuss in Chapters 13 and 14. DWR's database consolidation techniques enable the replay of all three databases' activity simultaneously to see how well the new environment will cope with that increased demand, as well as which database workloads might need to be restrained via Database Resource Manager and I/O Resource Manager.

Database Replay Workload Scale-Up and Characterization

Starting with Oracle 12.1.0.1, DWR is now able to scale up a previously captured DWC workload to stress test a database environment to discover its maximum capacity to handle a known workload. This capability is especially useful for capacity planning by ramping up simulated levels of application user activity to many times beyond the current level. This also means that DWR essentially offers the ability to test an environment to its utter destruction by scaling the workload well beyond any expected current level of database throughput.

We will we demonstrate and fully explore the methods that DWR employs to ramp up application workload activity and the limitations of workload scale-up in the section "DWR: Employing Workload Scale-Up."

Scheduling for Database Workload Replay

Released in Oracle 12.1, Consolidated Database Replay supports scheduling of the individual replays, enabling investigations of various scenarios (for example, what if all my individual workloads hit their peak utilizations at the same time?).

Enhanced Database Replay Reporting

After DWR has completed replaying workloads, it's crucial that you find out exactly which aspects of which replayed activity have shown performance degradation or improvement, as well as ascertaining all possible root causes for any unexpected performance variance. As of Oracle 12.1.0.2, DWR reporting has been enhanced to provide detailed analyses using the Active Session History (ASH) analytics framework to deliver a report with several details comparing the captured workload with the replayed workload. This significantly reduces the time an Oracle DBA will need to spend comparing the originally captured workloads to any replayed workload, and any replayed workload can be compared with any other replayed workload. Further, multiple individually replayed workloads can be compared against a single consolidated replayed workload to ascertain differences in results.

PLSQL_MODE Parameter

As part of Oracle 12.1.0.2, this parameter was introduced in package DBMS_WORKLOAD_REPLAY for the functions `INITIALIZE_CONSOLIDATED_REPLAY`, `INITIALIZE_REPLAY`, and `PROCESS_CAPTURE`. It controls how PL/SQL statements will be replayed during a DWR operation. If `TOP_LEVEL` (the default) is specified, only top-level PL/SQL calls are replayed; however, specifying `EXTENDED` tells DWR to replay both top-level PL/SQL as well as all SQL called from within PL/SQL statements.

NOTE
Specifying a value of EXTENDED *for any of these DWR procedures has no meaning if the workloads captured with DWC were not also captured using a value of* EXTENDED *for* DBMS_WORKLOAD_CAPTURE.

Leveraging Oracle Enterprise Manager Cloud Control

Based on the rich complexity of DWR options, it is obvious that replaying an application workload using DWR requires quite a bit of preparation and forethought for even an experienced DBA. Fortunately, as we'll demonstrate in this section, Oracle Enterprise Manager (OEM) greatly simplifies the DWR process—in fact, in most cases, it will reduce the necessary interaction to a few mouse clicks to prepare a previously recorded workload for eventual replay.

In this first scenario, we'll simply replay the workload exactly as it was originally recorded so that we can accurately ascertain the potential impact of proposed changes to our current database's production environment. We'll leverage OEM Cloud Control to replay the workload captured in Chapter 11 against a test database that has been upgraded to Oracle Database 12.2.0.1. This new test environment also includes another wrinkle: we've deployed the database's files within Automatic Storage Management (ASM) instead of the non-ASM storage that the production database source used.

Preprocessing DWC Capture Files

Our first step is to preprocess the DWC workload so that it can be replayed against our 12.2.0.1 destination database. Just as with a DWC operation, an Oracle directory object must already exist, or it can be created during this phase.

Accessing DWR

Just as with DWC, DWR is accessed from the Home page of our target 12.2.0.1 database, which is aptly named DB12CR2. Choosing the Performance | Database Replay menu option opens the same panel, but this time we will use the DWR-related options (Figure 12-3).

Because we have already copied all required DWC files to the appropriate host, we'll specify a directory object that already exists, named REPLAY_DIR, on the destination database's host, and then click Next to continue, as Figure 12-4 shows.

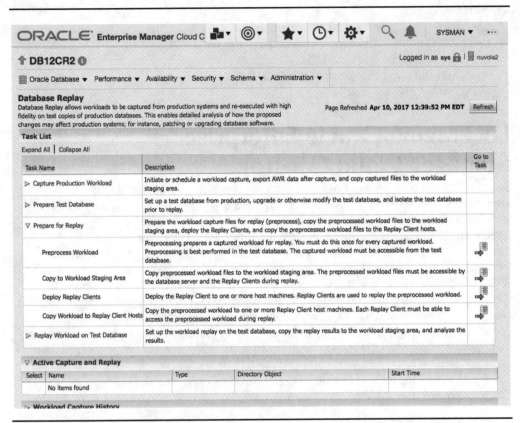

FIGURE 12-3. *Database Replay options*

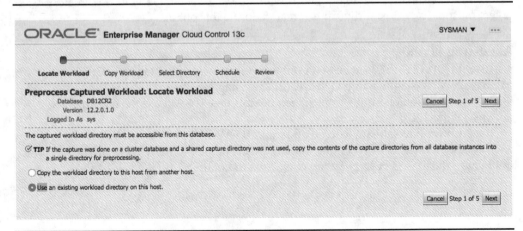

FIGURE 12-4. *DWR workload preprocessing, locating the workload*

Once a valid set of DWC application workload files have been located, OEM shows information identifying the captured workload. Clicking the Next button completes the selection process, as shown in Figure 12-5.

Our next step is to schedule the corresponding DWR preprocessing task. Depending on the size of the DWC capture files to be preprocessed, it may make sense to schedule this task for a later time; in our situation, however, we'll schedule the task to execute immediately, as shown in Figure 12-6. After a final review (see Figure 12-7), we'll complete submitting the task.

Oracle Enterprise Manager Cloud Control will present you a review of the inputs that were provided by the DBA. If everything is fine, click the Submit button to proceed to preprocess the captured workload.

This scheduled task usually runs for just a few seconds as it analyzes the DWC files, prepares them for DWR execution, and saves the results, including estimates of how many DWR replay clients will be required (Figure 12-8).

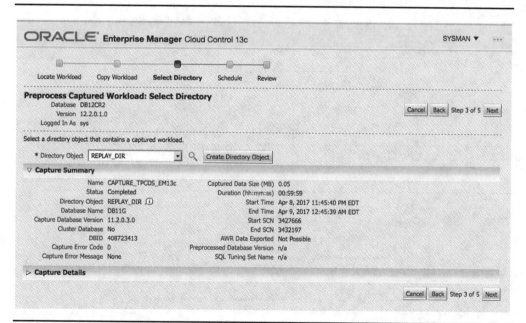

FIGURE 12-5. *Choosing a capture directory*

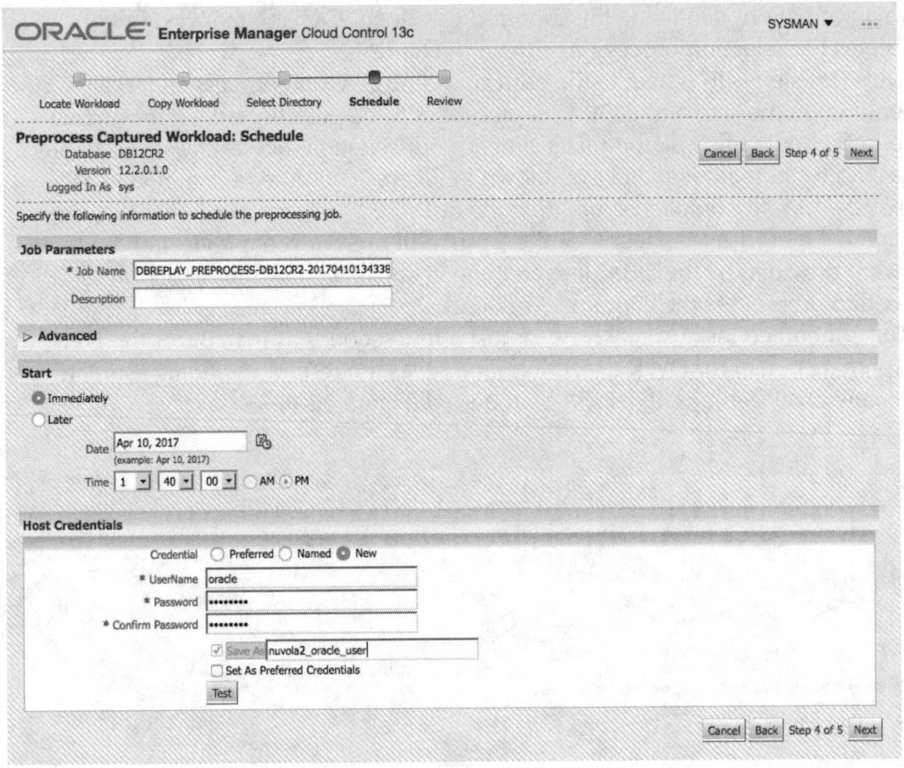

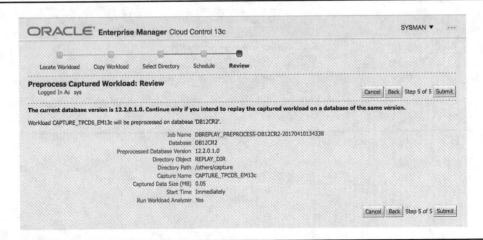

FIGURE 12-6. *Scheduling the task*

FIGURE 12-7. *Reviewing the task*

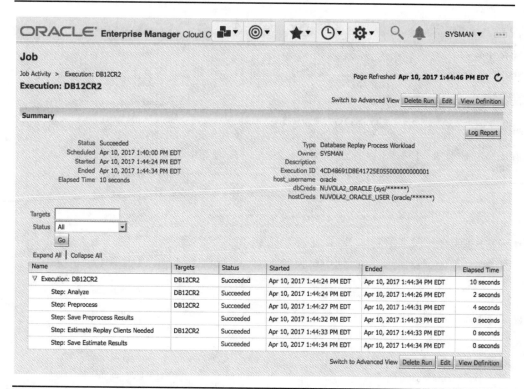

FIGURE 12-8. *Monitoring the job*

Replaying the Preprocessed Workload

After the DWC workload capture files have been successfully preprocessed, we move on to the next step: scheduling a DWR operation.

We choose Performance | Database Replay option to access DWR, but this time, we'll choose the Replay Workload On Test Database option to proceed (see Figure 12-9). Note that OEM provides a nifty checklist that reminds us precisely what steps we'll need to follow to begin replaying the preprocessed workload.

Our first step is to tell DWR where the preprocessed workload resides. In our case, we'll choose the directory object we just used for the previous preprocessing step, but as Figure 12-10 shows, it's also possible to copy another preprocessed workload from another directory on the same host or even another host.

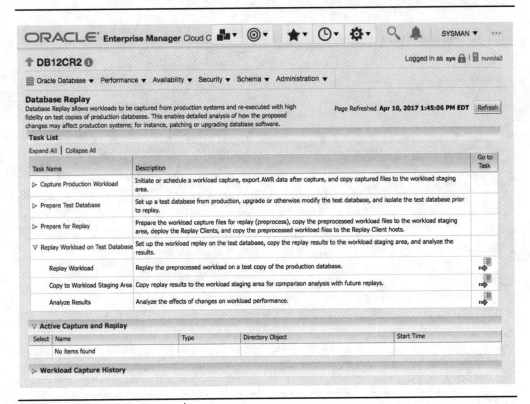

FIGURE 12-9. *Starting a replay process*

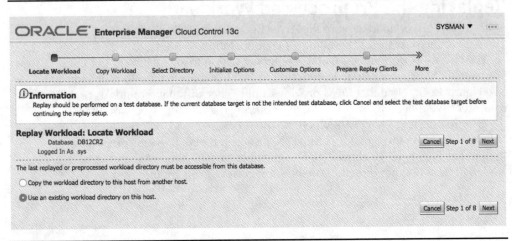

FIGURE 12-10. *Choosing a preprocessed workload location*

After we select the workload directory, OEM displays a confirmation panel describing the contents of the workload that DWC had originally captured (Figure 12-11).

Now that we've confirmed this is indeed the desired workload to replay, our next step is to confirm the initialization options for the DWR task (Figure 12-12). Note that OEM suggests a task name, but we recommend choosing something that makes the most sense for DWR tracking. OEM also provides the option to capture all replayed statements and their corresponding execution statistics and metrics into a SQL Tuning Set for later analysis through SQL Performance Analyzer.

OEM reads the contents of the preprocessed workload directory and then initializes the test database for replay operations, as shown in Figure 12-13.

OEM offers us a chance to alter how the workload will be replayed. We can decide to reroute application activity to completely different database services

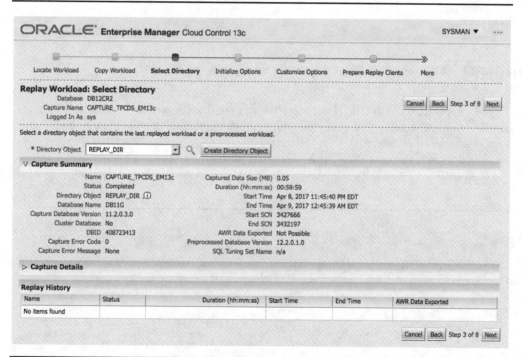

FIGURE 12-11. *Confirming the selected workload*

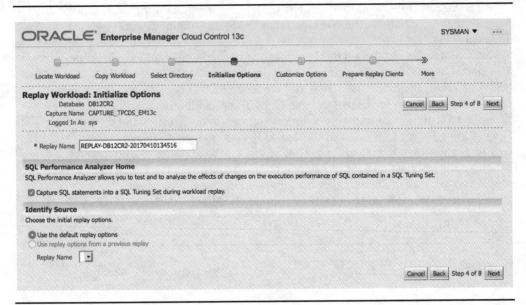

FIGURE 12-12. *Choosing initialization options*

(Figure 12-14) than the default database service; note, however, that it's also possible to route activity that occurred on the production database's service to a completely different service.

This option is extremely valuable when exploring the impact of isolating application activity to a database service that's been configured differently—for

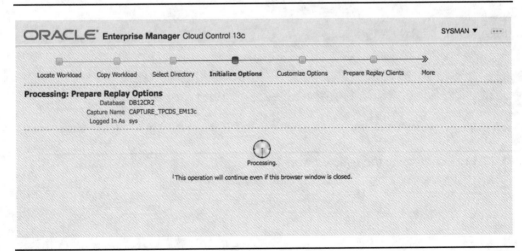

FIGURE 12-13. *Preparing replay options*

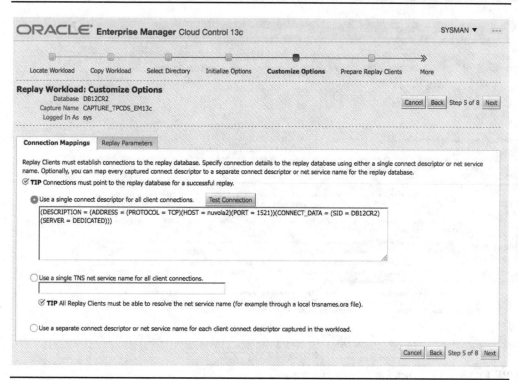

FIGURE 12-14. *Specifying connection remapping*

example, different failover characteristics, or performance limitations enforced through Database Resource Manager (DBRM) resource plan directives. It's also valuable for determining how a single-instance production workload will now perform against a RAC database, especially when a transactional workload may now be propagated to multiple instances of a RAC database through database services, or when data warehouse reports are potentially executed in parallel through the RAC In-Memory Parallel Execution capabilities

As Figure 12-15 shows, we also can decide to modify precisely how quickly the captured application workload will be replayed against our test database. We break down what each of these parameters actually control in Table 12-1.

For this particular scenario, we've chosen simply to accept the default options, so the workload's recorded statements will be replayed using the default database service in the precise order that they originally occurred with identical time intervals between each statement's execution. (We'll delve into a situation for which it might make sense to modify these replay options in an upcoming scenario.)

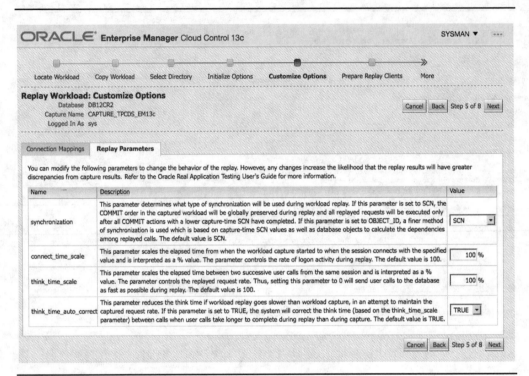

FIGURE 12-15. *Customizing replay options*

Parameter	What It Controls
`synchronization`	Controls which method DWR will use to keep the workload synchronized during its replay. The default value (**SCN**) means that DWR will use the SCNs used to commit transactions to determine the order in which transactions will be replayed. If set to a value of **TIME**, DWR uses the wall time in which the action took place to synchronize the transactions.
`connect_time_scale`	Tells DWR either to increase or decrease the time between the start of the DWC operation and the session's connection. The default value (100) means that the original connection time interval should be used; a lower value allows for more sessions to connect, while a higher value delays the number of connections that can occur.

TABLE 12-1. *DBMS_WORKLOAD_REPLAY.PREPARE_REPLAY Parameters*

Parameter	What It Controls
`think_time_scale`	Affects the intra-session time between two successive user calls within the same session. The default value (`100`) means that the original intra-session time should be maintained; a lower value effectively decreases the time between intra-session activity, while a higher value increases intra-session activity time.
`think_time_auto_correct`	Tells DWR to adjust the replay execution speed so that the workload finishes within the same wall time of the original captured workload by adjusting the value of `think_time_scale`. The default value (`TRUE`) means that DWR will attempt to reduce think time automatically when it detects that the replay is proceeding more slowly than the original capture.

TABLE 12-1. *DBMS_WORKLOAD_REPLAY.PREPARE_REPLAY Parameters (continued)*

Now it's time to start up at least one WRC that will consume the recorded production workload and replay it against the test system (Figure 12-16). Fortunately, OEM provides a method to estimate how many replay clients should be needed to replay the workload; simply click the Estimate button and OEM will estimate the total number of WRCs as well as the amount of CPU cores necessary to replay the workload. For the workload in this scenario, OEM estimated a single WRC would be satisfactory.

Once OEM has finished its WRC estimations, click Add Replay Client Hosts to tell OEM to offer a list of potential hosts on which a WRC can be started. In this scenario, we will start a single WRC on the same host as the test database, nuvola2 (Figure 12-17).

After we select the WRC host, OEM offers the option to start the recommended number of WRCs (Figure 12-18) and then configure connectivity between the WRC application on that host and the test database platform (Figure 12-19). Note that while we are constructing the DWR operation connected as the SYS user, the SYS database account cannot be used for the WRC application to connect to the test database; rather, Oracle recommends creating a completely separate user account (in this scenario, a user account aptly named wrc) for any WRC activity. We will discuss the requirements for this separate user account in the next scenario.

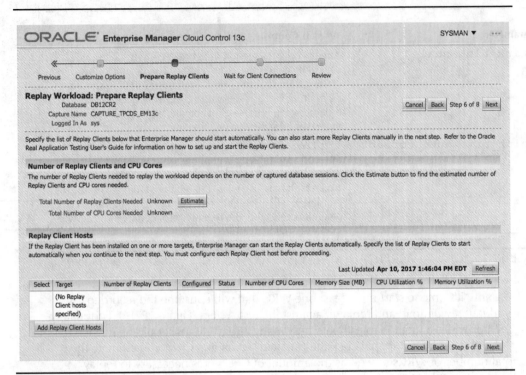

FIGURE 12-16. *Workload replay, preparing WRCs*

Search and Select: Replay Client Host

☑ **TIP** A Replay Client host is a Host target on which one or more Replay Clients should be started to replay the selected workload.   Cancel   Select

     Click 'Go' to find eligible client hosts.

Search

     Target Type   Host

     Target Name   [nuvola2]   Go

- -

Select All | Select None

Select	Target	Status	Number of CPU Cores	CPU Utilization %
☑	nuvola2	⬆	1	1.62

     Cancel   Select

FIGURE 12-17. *Selecting WRC host*

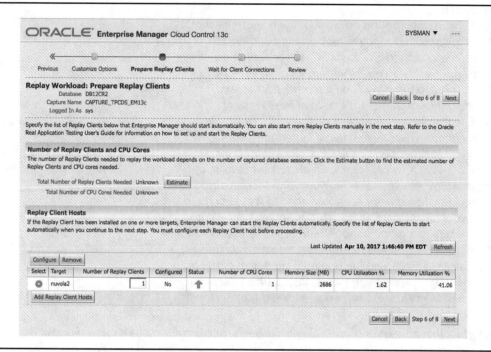

FIGURE 12-18. *Preparing WRC connections*

Configure: Replay Client Host

Close | Apply

Target nuvola2
Operating System Linux

Name	Value
* Host User Name	oracle
* Host Password	••••••
* Database User Name	wrc
* Database Password	•••
* Server Connection Identifier	(DESCRIPTION = (ADDRESS = (PROTOCOL = TCP)(HOST = nuvola2)(PORT = 152
* Number of Replay Clients	1
* Client Oracle Home	/u01/app/oracle/product/12.2.0/dbhome_1
* Client Replay Directory	/others/capture
Client TNS_ADMIN Directory	
Client Work Directory	
Additional Parameters	

Close | Apply

FIGURE 12-19. *Configuring WRC connectivity*

NOTE
Because the application workload we are replaying in this scenario requires only one WRC, there is no reason not to run the WRC on the same host as our test database. However, it's also perfectly possible to run a WRC on a remote host as well; the only requirement is that the Oracle Instant Client software is installed on the WRC's host. This technique is valuable when a larger number of WRCs are recommended or the CPU requirements for those WRCs would steal valuable resources from the database server; it also provides for a more realistic replay when the application workload was generated through calls from an application server layer—not unlikely in a modern, non–client-server application system. And using a remote host is also a valuable way to demonstrate the potential latency of network round trips, something that is not possible to simulate when the WRCs are run from the test database server.

Now that at least one WRC client has been successfully started, OEM reports that it's establishing connectivity between the WRC sessions and the DWR operation (Figure 12-20). Once connectivity is successfully established (Figure 12-21), it's time to start the DWR operation after one last review (Figure 12-22).

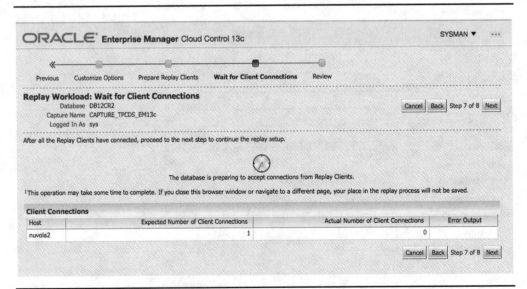

FIGURE 12-20. *Waiting for WRC handshake*

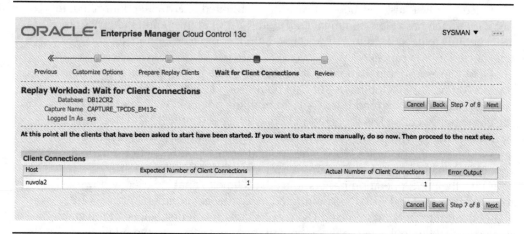

FIGURE 12-21. *Successful WRC connectivity*

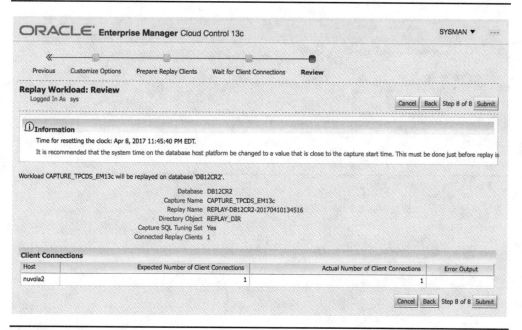

FIGURE 12-22. *Final review*

Once the DWR task has been successfully submitted, OEM will confirm that the DWR operation has at last commenced (Figure 12-23); at this point, the DWR task will continue to execute in the background until it completes, terminates unexpectedly, or is cancelled.

OEM makes it simple to monitor the progress of the DWR operation as it runs toward completion, including useful data points such as Duration, Database Time, Average Active Sessions, and User Calls for both the original DWC operation versus the currently executing DWR operation Replay Process (Figure 12-24). The progress of DWC versus DWR operations is also conveniently charted, yielding a birds-eye view of how much better (or worse) the application workload is performing in its new environment.

Once the DWR operation has completed, it's time to analyze exactly how well (or poorly) the original workload performed in its new environment. Figure 12-25 shows the results of our completed DWR operation, and at first glance of the graph, it appears that the replay completed about 40 percent faster than the original workload. Although this may initially appear to be a fantastically desirable outcome, there are several ways to analyze these results, as we will cover in the next section.

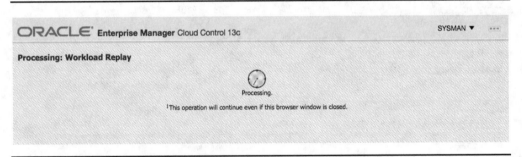

FIGURE 12-23. *Replay confirmation*

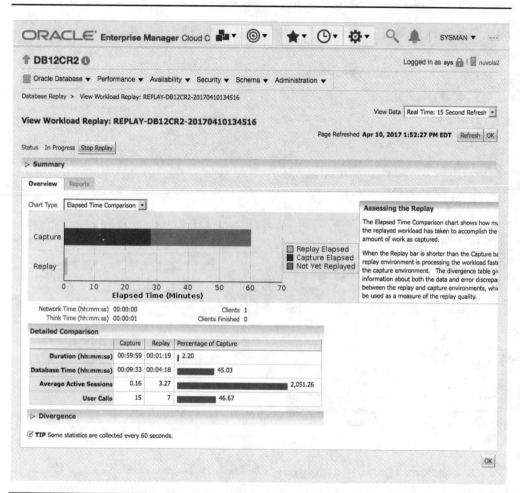

FIGURE 12-24.   *Monitoring an ongoing operation*

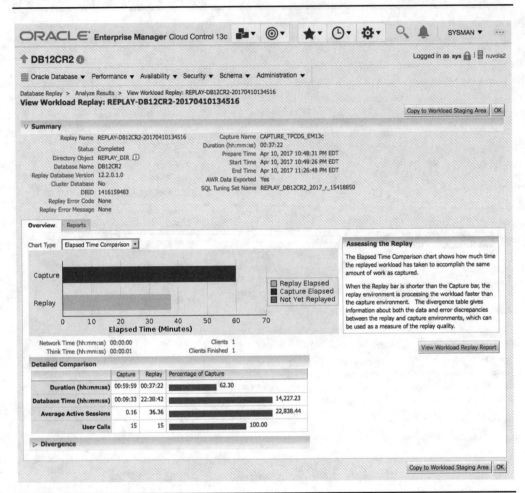

FIGURE 12-25. *Results from a completed task*

Analyzing Performance Impacts

The whole point of DWC/R is to help you make intelligent decisions about how an existing production application workload will perform once it has been transitioned to its new environment. Now the real work of our process begins: analyzing the true impact of the new environment's configuration upon the previously captured workload and determining the hopefully positive impact on overall application performance.

DWR Workload Replay Report

Thankfully, DWR automatically creates a workload replay report that provides immediate and useful insight into the differences between captured versus replayed workloads. The report is created automatically in the Replay directory, and it's subdivided into several sections that highlight those differences.

NOTE
A text-only version of a DWR replay report can be generated using the function DBMS_WORKLOAD_ REPLAY.REPORT. See Example 12-1 in Appendix B for an example of how to accomplish this; the text-only version of the report is also provided as Example 12-3. It's also possible to re-create the HTML version of the DWR replay report using the function DBMS_WORKLOAD_REPLAY.REPORT; for an example, see Example 12-2 in Appendix B.

Replay Information and Statistics

The Replay Information section (Figure 12-26) displays basic information about the DWR operation itself, including the different database versions, database names, and even the wall clock times of the replay operation versus its initial capture duration, while the Replay Statistics section (Figure 12-27) compares them based on database time—essentially, the amount of time the database itself expended while executing the replay operation—as well as average session activity.

Replay Divergence Summary

It's crucial to review the Replay Divergence Summary report section (Figure 12-28) because it detects any observed divergence between captured and replay operations. In our opinion, this is one of the most often overlooked benefits of DWC/R, because any divergence recorded here is worth investigating, especially since it may indicate one or more reasons for application performance divergence. This report section may also indicate some unexpectedly different performance divergences— perhaps because an incorrect version of application code had been deployed, or even an unexpected set of exceptions raised—that may prevent the deployment of an application workload's code base in its current state to production.

Because this particular captured workload replayed only queries against the TPC-DS schema, we wouldn't expect there to be any serious divergence, because no data changed as a result of DML statements and we were careful to verify that the test database's contents matched those of the production database before starting the DWR operation. However, if we had been replaying a workload that comprised a mixed workload (such as DML plus SELECT statements), or if we had unwittingly

DB Name	DB Id	Release	RAC	Replay Name	Replay Status
DB12CR2	1416159483	12.2.0.1.0	NO	TPCDS_REPLAY	COMPLETED

Replay Information

Information	Replay	Capture
Name	TPCDS_REPLAY	TPCDS_CAPTURE
Status	COMPLETED	COMPLETED
Database Name	DB12CR2	DB11G
Database Version	12.2.0.1.0	11.2.0.3.0
Start Time	21-03-17 15:42:19	20-03-17 23:01:30
End Time	21-03-17 16:24:52	21-03-17 00:01:29
Duration	42 minutes 33 seconds	59 minutes 59 seconds
Directory Object	REPLAY_DIR	REPLAY_DIR
Directory Path	/others/capture	/others/capture
AWR DB Id	1416159483	
AWR Begin Snap Id	15	
AWR End Snap Id	16	
PL/SQL Capture Mode	TOP_LEVEL	TOP_LEVEL
Replay Directory Number	458314925	
Replay Schedule Name		

FIGURE 12-26. *Replay Information*

Replay Statistics

Statistic	Replay	Capture
DB Time	10698.461 seconds	12514.515 seconds
PL/SQL DB Time	0.000 seconds	0.000 seconds
Average Active Sessions	4.19	3.48
User calls	56	56
PL/SQL user calls	0	0
PL/SQL subcalls	0	0

FIGURE 12-27. *Capture versus replay statistics*

Replay Divergence Summary

Divergence Type	Count	% Total
Session Failures During Replay	0	0.00
Errors No Longer Seen During Replay	0	0.00
New Errors Seen During Replay	0	0.00
Errors Mutated During Replay	0	0.00
DMLs with Different Number of Rows Modified	0	0.00
SELECTs with Different Number of Rows Fetched	0	0.00

FIGURE 12-28. *Replay Divergence Summary section*

run a query-only workload against an unsynchronized test database, this report section would record the fact that at least some queries might have returned different row counts.

Finally, if we had been testing changes to recently modified application code, this section is invaluable for pointing out that different exceptions had been raised during replay processing—something that might normally be apparent only during quality assurance unit testing of the application or (even worse) immediately after production deployment.

Top Events, SQL, and Sessions

The next report sections—Top Events (Figure 12-29), Top SQL with Top Events (Figure 12-30) and Top Sessions with Top Events (Figure 12-31)—begin to delve deeper into the lower levels of the DWR operation. Unfortunately, these sections don't compare capture versus replay performance at this level, so we'll need to generate some better reportage to determine whether performance improvement or regression occurred.

Top Events
(-) Hide

Event	Event Class	% Activity
CPU + Wait for CPU	CPU	73.28
direct path write temp	User I/O	11.83
direct path read temp	User I/O	11.07
direct path read	User I/O	0.10

FIGURE 12-29. *Top Events*

Top SQL with Top Events
(-) Hide

SQL ID	Planhash	Sampled Number of Executions	% Activity	Event Drilldown	
7bvd762nt0t3z	3019389580	4	71.47	**Event**	**% Activity**
				CPU + Wait for CPU	49.05
				direct path write temp	11.83
				direct path read temp	10.59
ck52qcn50mj6s	1743075189	4	9.45	**Event**	**% Activity**
				CPU + Wait for CPU	8.87
				direct path read temp	0.48
				direct path read	0.10
cdwvbk03ku8sd	2166267056	4	6.49	**Event**	**% Activity**
				CPU + Wait for CPU	6.49
f9f17bjar4ru2	154212656	4	3.91	**Event**	**% Activity**
				CPU + Wait for CPU	3.91
2uw47w3cyzwbj	2898011891	4	2.29	**Event**	**% Activity**
				CPU + Wait for CPU	2.29

FIGURE 12-30. *Top SQL with Top Events*

Top Sessions with Top Events
(-) Hide

Session ID	Session Serial	Username	Program	% Activity	Event Drilldown	
52	12536	TPCDS	wrc@localhost.localdomain (TNS V1-V3)	24.14	**Event**	**% Activity**
					CPU + Wait for CPU	18.32
					direct path read temp	3.44
					direct path write temp	2.39
55	31059	TPCDS	wrc@localhost.localdomain (TNS V1-V3)	24.05	**Event**	**% Activity**
					CPU + Wait for CPU	18.80
					direct path write temp	2.77
					direct path read temp	2.39
					direct path read	0.10
74	9193	TPCDS	wrc@localhost.localdomain (TNS V1-V3)	24.05	**Event**	**% Activity**
					CPU + Wait for CPU	17.94
					direct path write temp	3.63
					direct path read temp	2.48
80	42056	TPCDS	wrc@localhost.localdomain (TNS V1-V3)	24.05	**Event**	**% Activity**
					CPU + Wait for CPU	18.23
					direct path write temp	3.05
					direct path read temp	2.77

FIGURE 12-31. *Top Sessions with Top Events*

DWR Comparison Reporting

The most useful report that Oracle DWR provides is the comparison report, which diagnoses the root cause either of performance improvement or performance regression.

Importing the AWR Data for the Captured Workload

We showed you how to export the corresponding AWR snapshots data once the Workload Capture process completes in Chapter 11, and for good reason: to create the DWR comparison report, we will first have to import the corresponding AWR snapshots from the originally captured DWC workload into our test database, as shown here:

```
DECLARE
   cap_id    NUMBER;
   awr_id    NUMBER;
BEGIN
      cap_id  := DBMS_WORKLOAD_CAPTURE.GET_CAPTURE_INFO(
dir => 'REPLAY_DIR'); -- Directory Name
awr_id :=DBMS_WORKLOAD_CAPTURE.IMPORT_AWR (
      capture_id => cap_id, --Capture ID
      staging_schema => 'WRC'); -- Schema to store the AWR Data
END;
/
```

Generating a DWR HTML Workload Comparison Report

This report is one of the most useful reports for diagnosing the root cause of either performance improvement or performance regression. The following PL/SQL can be used to generate an HTML comparison report. The workload replay task ID must be provided (in this case, it is 131). The directory in which the HTML report will be created also must be specified; in this example, the Replay Directory is used.

```
DECLARE
   rep_id           NUMBER;
   out_File         UTL_FILE.FILE_TYPE;
   buffer           VARCHAR2(32767);
   offset           NUMBER(38);
   buffer_size      CONSTANT BINARY_INTEGER := 32767;
   amount BINARY_INTEGER;
   rep_rpt          CLOB;

BEGIN
   DBMS_WORKLOAD_REPLAY.COMPARE_PERIOD_REPORT (
      replay_id1 => 131,
      replay_id2 => null, --Null uses the capture data
      format => DBMS_WORKLOAD_REPLAY.TYPE_HTML,
      result => rep_rpt);
```

```
out_File := UTL_FILE.FOPEN(
    'REPLAY_DIR', -- Directory Name
'ReplayCompareReport.html', -- File Name
'W',max_linesize => buffer_size);
  amount := buffer_size;
  offset := 1;

  WHILE
amount >= buffer_size
  LOOP
    DBMS_LOB.READ(lob_loc => rep_rpt,
amount => amount,
offset => offset,
buffer => buffer);
OFFSET := OFFSET + AMOUNT;
UTL_FILE.PUT(file => out_File,
buffer => buffer);
UTL_FILE.FFLUSH(file => out_File);
  END LOOP;
  UTL_FILE.FCLOSE(out_File);

END;
/
```

Comparison: Parameter Changes

Several report sections (Figure 12-32) highlight potential vectors for differences
between the original captured workload and the replayed workload.

- **Changes to Important Parameters** This section shows some key parameters
  and their values that tend to impact application performance, especially
  the values for PROCESSES, SESSIONS, and COMPATIBLE. Because these
  values can have a dramatic impact in terms of the database resources that
  are available to execute an application workload, they're isolated here to
  help eliminate or confirm this.

- **Changes to Optimizer-Relevant Parameters** As its name implies, this section
  focuses on the database parameters that directly impact optimizer behavior.

- **Changes to Memory Configuration Parameters** Because memory size
  can often have dramatic impacts on application performance, this section
  focuses on the size of the PGA and SGA.

Just from these three short report sections, it's obvious that the test database
environment is quite different from the one against which the replayed workload
was originally captured. This may explain why some differences between capture

(-) Changes to Important Parameters

	Capture	Replay
processes	150	300
sessions	247	472
compatible	11.2.0.0.0	12.2.0

(-) Changes to Optimizer-Relevant Parameters

	Capture	Replay
pga_aggregate_target	491 M	414 M
optimizer_features_enable	11.2.0.3	12.2.0.1

(-) Changes to Memory Configuration Parameters

	Capture	Replay
sga_target	1.45 G	1.22 G
sga_max_size	1.45 G	1.22 G
pga_aggregate_target	491 M	414 M

FIGURE 12-32. *Parameter changes*

and replay performances are observed—for example, more processes and sessions are permitted within a smaller memory footprint on the test system.

■ **Changes to Underscore Parameters** This section, shown in Figure 12-33, lists all of the "undocumented" parameters with different values between captured and replayed workloads. This information is extremely useful to know, since it's not unusual to encounter a performance deviance that is ultimately caused by a nonstandard parameter that's still set on the source database of the captured workload, but not set identically on the test database environment.

NOTE
We have observed what we like to call "parameter inertia" in many systems we've tuned, especially when the initial release of the Oracle database hosting the current application workload was created in the previous millennium. The current Oracle DBA is often completely unaware of the original reason for activating the parameter and has been told never to change it, but also lacks an understanding of what that particular undocumented parameter actually does.

(-) Changes to Underscore Parameters

	Capture	Replay
_adaptive_window_consolidator_enabled	NULL	TRUE
_aggregation_optimization_settings	NULL	0
_always_anti_join	NULL	CHOOSE
_always_semi_join	NULL	CHOOSE
_and_pruning_enabled	NULL	TRUE
_b_tree_bitmap_plans	NULL	TRUE
_bloom_filter_enabled	NULL	TRUE
_bloom_filter_ratio	NULL	35
_bloom_folding_enabled	NULL	TRUE
_bloom_pruning_enabled	NULL	TRUE
_bloom_serial_filter	NULL	ON
_complex_view_merging	NULL	TRUE
_compression_compatibility	NULL	12.2.0
_connect_by_use_union_all	NULL	TRUE
_convert_set_to_join	NULL	FALSE
_cost_equality_semi_join	NULL	TRUE
_cpu_to_io	NULL	0
_db_block_numa	NULL	1
_diag_adr_trace_dest	NULL	/u01/app/oracle/diag/rdbms/db12cr2/DB12CR2/trace
_dimension_skip_null	NULL	TRUE
_distinct_agg_optimization_gsets	NULL	CHOOSE
_ds_enable_view_sampling	NULL	TRUE
_ds_sampling_method	NULL	PROGRESSIVE
_ds_xt_split_count	NULL	1
_eliminate_common_subexpr	NULL	TRUE
_enable_type_dep_selectivity	NULL	TRUE
_fast_full_scan_enabled	NULL	TRUE
_first_k_rows_dynamic_proration	NULL	TRUE

FIGURE 12-33. *Changes to Underscore Parameters*

Comparison: Performance Statistics

Another nifty part of this comparison report is the Main Performance Statistics section (Figure 12-34), which shows the timing differences for database events, especially the Change In DB Time column. As this example shows, the negative values for Database Time, CPU Time, and User I/O Wait Time indicate that on an overall basis, the replayed workload executed more efficiently, performing dramatically better in all three cases. Contrariwise, any positive values in that column indicate that the replayed workload exhibited performance regression.

(-) Main Performance Statistics

This section does a high-level performance comparison of the two periods. Start by looking for a change in Database Time. If there is no significant change in Database Time, you can assume performance as a whole is similar. You can look for a change in the Database Time pieces that follow (CPU, User I/O, and Cluster) to see how the different ingredients of Database Time changed from one period to the next, either to explain a change in Database Time or to see if some pieces regressed and others improved.

	Change in DB time	Capture total time	Replay total time	Capture % of DB time	Replay % of DB time
Database Time	-37%	16076.58 seconds	10127.66 seconds	100	100
CPU Time	-17.38%	2716.94 seconds	2244.77 seconds	16.9	22.16
User I/O Wait Time	-75.38%	9814.02 seconds	2416.6 seconds	61.05	23.86

FIGURE 12-34. *Main Performance Statistics*

Comparison: SQL Statements

Diving deeper into our performance comparison, we can observe some deflections in the execution performance of individual SQL statements:

- **Top SQL/Call**   This section shows which individual SQL statements have seen the most dramatic change in performance (see Figure 12-35).

- **Top Call by Change in DB Time**   Similar to Top SQL/Call, this section shows which calls to individual SQL statements have demonstrated a performance impact (see Figure 12-36). (Remember that the same SQL statement— for example, a query that uses bind variables—could have dramatically different results depending on the bind variable values passed.) The Change in Average Response Time column highlights which SQL statements and calls exhibited the biggest performance difference; again, a negative number here indicates performance improvement, while a positive value indicates an opportunity for additional SQL tuning because of regression.

(-) Top SQL/Call

(-) Top SQL by Change in DB Time

This section compares the performance change of individual SQL statements from one period to the next. SQL statements are identified by their force matching signature to account for literal usage. They are ordered by the total change in DB Time, as the most relevant changes are those that impact total throughput the most. Any SQL tuning you do should begin with the statement that regressed by the most DB Time.

Force Matching Signature	example SQL_ID	Change in DB Time	Change in Average Response Time	Capture DB time	Replay DB time	example sql text
4177016511511125167	7bvd762nt0t3z	-2373.53 seconds	-24.01%	9884.04 seconds	7510.51 seconds	(+) with year_total as (select c_customer_id custom [...]
1664167327479740393	cdwvbk03ku8sd	-1719.12 seconds	-71.6%	2400.98 seconds	681.86 seconds	(+) WITH wscs AS (SELECT so [...]
16220816690003995489	b9y8rw5dsr00z	-1140.47 seconds	-100%	1140.47 seconds	0 seconds	(+) SELECT /*query9*/ CASE WHEN (SELECT COUNT(*) [...]

FIGURE 12-35. *Top SQL/Call section*

(-) Top Call by Change in DB Time

This section compares the performance change of individual database calls from one period to the next. A call is identified by File ID and Call Counter. They are ordered by the change in DB Time, as the most relevant changes are those that impact total throughput the most. SQL_ID and SQL text are displayed for information purpose about the call. Any SQL tuning you do should begin with the statement that regressed by the most DB Time.

File ID	Call Counter	SQL_ID	Change in DB Time	Change in Average Response Time	Capture DB time	Replay DB time	SQL text
15030646658360672263	10	7bvd762nt0t3z	-635.95 seconds	-25.53%	2491.02 seconds	1855.07 seconds	(+) with year_total as (select c_customer_id custom [...]
15030646658360672261	10	7bvd762nt0t3z	-615.92 seconds	-24.83%	2481.02 seconds	1865.09 seconds	(+) with year_total as (select c_customer_id custom [...]
15030646658360672262	10	7bvd762nt0t3z	-565.9 seconds	-23.28%	2430.99 seconds	1865.09 seconds	(+) with year_total as (select c_customer_id custom [...]
15030646658360672264	10	7bvd762nt0t3z	-555.76 seconds	-22.4%	2481.02 seconds	1925.26 seconds	(+) with year_total as (select c_customer_id custom [...]

FIGURE 12-36. *Top Call by Change in DB Time section*

Comparison: Common SQL

Finally, the report Common SQL section isolates the SQL statements that appeared in both the captured and replayed workloads and that consumed a significant amount of database time:

■ **Common SQL by Total DB Time** This section, shown in Figure 12-37, makes it easy to identify statements exhibiting performance progression or regression. Note that one particular SQL statement (query6) actually shows performance regression: it took only 290 seconds to complete when executed during its original capture, but it took 410 seconds during replay, so this statement should be analyzed with SQL Performance Analyzer or SQL Tuning Advisor to determine the reasons for its regression.

(-) Common SQL

This section reports the common sql in both the time periods. Note that this only reports sqls with significant db time (not all common sql).

(-) Common SQL By Total DB Time

SQL Text	Total DB Time(1)	Total DB Time(2)	DIFF(Total DB Time)
(+) with year_total as (select c_customer_id custom [...]	9880	7490	+2390
(+) WITH wscs AS (SELECT so [...]	2400	680	+1720
(+) WITH customer_total_return AS (SELECT sr_custom [...]	330	40	+290
(+) WITH ssr as (SELECT s_store_id, SUM([...]	1210	990	+220
(+) select /*query6*/ a.ca_state state, count(*) cnt [...]	290	410	-120
(+) select /*query7*/ i_item_id, avg(ss_quantity) ag [...]	350	240	+110
(+) SELECT /*query8*/ s_store_name ,sum([...]	280	260	+20

FIGURE 12-37. *Common SQL section*

(-) Common Long Running SQL

SQL Text	Avg Res Time(1)	Max Res Time(1)	Min Res. Time(1)	Median Res Time(1)	Avg Res Time(2)	Max Res Time(2)	Min Res Time(2)	Median Res Time(2)	DIFF(Avg Res Time)
(+) WITH customer_total_return AS (SELECT sr_custom [...]	59.071	66.573	36.563	66.573	24.323	24.323	24.323	24.323	+34.748
(+) SELECT /*query8*/ s_store_name ,sum([...]	124.445	129.89	117.121	125.385	98.053	108.551	69.576	107.042	+26.392
(+) with year_total as (select c_customer_id custom [...]	133.235	141.903	126.066	132.486	124.243	126.017	123.652	123.652	+8.992
(+) WITH ssr as (SELECT s_store_id, SUM([...]	131.014	141.73	120.383	130.971	124.662	141.154	114.149	121.6725	+6.352
(+) select /*query7*/ i_item_id, avg(ss_quantity) ag [...]	104.815	105.75	102.041	105.735	110.762	126.498	102.492	107.0295	-5.947
(+) WITH wscs AS (SELECT so [...]	120.676	138.11	114.746	114.923	124.954	126.454	123.454	124.954	-4.278
(+) select /*query6*/ a.ca_state state, count(*) cnt [...]	118.465	123.601	114.66	117.8	120.273	123.196	114.219	121.8385	-1.808

FIGURE 12-38. *Common Long Running SQL section*

- **Common Long Running SQL**   As its name implies, this section isolates the longest running SQL statements (see Figure 12-38). Again, a few of these statements showed modest regression during replay and would probably benefit from additional analysis via SQL Performance Advisor or SQL Tuning Advisor.

Comparison: Observations

After reviewing these comparisons, you'll see that it's safe to conclude that the performance of most of the SQL statements were improved in the new test environment; this conclusion is confirmed after a further review of the key database wait events and waits. However, some SQL statements will most likely benefit from additional, separate analysis, either via SQL Performance Analyzer or other SQL tuning advisors.

Consolidated Database Replay

One of the most powerful new features of DWR in Oracle 12cR1 is the ability to combine two completely different workloads—perhaps recorded at different times of the day or during a different part of an organization's business cycle—to determine in advance whether those workloads could peacefully coexist at the same time within the same database. Since Oracle 12c has been specially positioned for simpler database consolidation efforts, this feature is an excellent addition to any Oracle DBA's tool belt.

In the following scenario, we will leverage DWR's Consolidated Database Replay features to combine two completely different simulated workloads—the previous read-only reporting workload we've already replayed, plus a new OLTP application workload—to demonstrate the advantages of this new feature. The two application workloads were executed against the same Oracle 11.2.0.3 database environment we've described previously; we used DWC to capture the workloads during two completely different timeframes. We'll then demonstrate how to use Consolidated Replay to replay both workloads simultaneously against the new 12.2.0.1 database environment we used previously. We'll then analyze the results to ascertain whether both workloads could be satisfied through the new test system's environment. Finally, since we used OEM to perform DWR operations, this scenario will illustrate how to leverage DWR functionality using a purely scripted approach.

Gathering the New Workload

Our first step is to generate, capture, and verify an additional workload that is significantly different from the query-centric workload we generated in the earlier DWR scenario.

DWC: Capturing the OLTP Workload

First, we used DWC to capture a new simulated OLTP workload against our production source database using the same techniques we engaged in Chapter 11. We generated the workload using the same PL/SQL module, PKG_DML_ GENERATOR, that we used to generate the sample workload for analysis by Workload Intelligence in Chapter 11. The source code for that package is included in Example 12-5 of Appendix B.

DWR: Replaying the OLTP Workload

Next, we confirmed the "replayability" of the captured OLTP workload using the same techniques we described earlier in this chapter. Figure 12-39 shows the result of replaying the OLTP workload against our test database environment; note that this new workload consisted of 15 concurrent sessions invoking DML statements. Figures 12-40 and 12-41 show the resulting activity against our testing environment from the perspective of OEM as the OLTP-centric workload was replayed.

DWR: Replaying a Consolidated Workload

To consolidate the OLTP and query workloads before they can be replayed simultaneously, we'll first need to make some additional preparations in our test environment. A minor but crucial detail involves the appropriate placement of the DWC workload capture files.

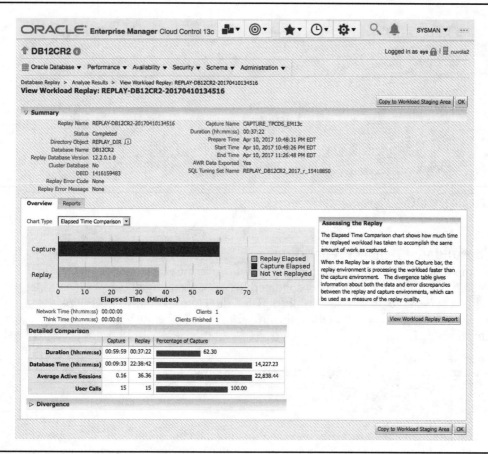

FIGURE 12-39.   *DWR: Replaying OLTP Workload*

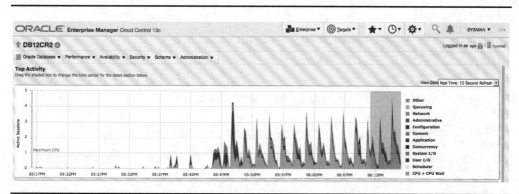

FIGURE 12-40.   *OEM: Replaying OLTP workload*

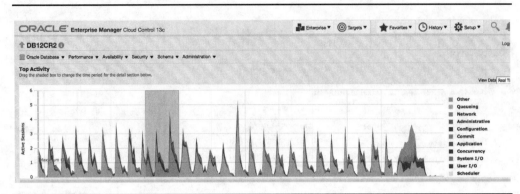

FIGURE 12-41. *OEM: Replaying OLTP workload*

Consolidated Replay Preparations

It's important that you recognize one small wrinkle in the placement of the workload capture directories for a DWR Consolidated Replay operation: all capture directories must be *subdirectories* of a single consolidated directory. Should you overlook this requirement, you'll encounter the following error as you attempt your first Consolidated Replay:

```
ERROR at line 1:
ORA-20223: Error: Invalid Input. The directory path "/others/capture_readonly"
of "TPCDS_READONLY" is not a sub-directory of "/others/capture_consolidated"
ORA-06512: at "SYS.DBMS_WORKLOAD_REPLAY", line 5673
ORA-06512: at line 16
```

Creating separate directories and then moving the corresponding DWC captured workload files into them satisfies this requirement, as the following code snippets show:

```
$> pwd
/others
$> mkdir -p capture_consolidated
$> mv capture_readonly capture_consolidated/
$> mv capture_oltp capture_consolidated/

$> ls -l capture_consolidated/
total 8
drwxr-xr-x 6 oracle oinstall 4096 May  2 12:37 capture_oltp
drwxr-xr-x 5 oracle oinstall 4096 May  2 13:21 capture_readonly


SQL> create directory TPCDS_OLTP as '/others/capture_consolidated/capture_oltp';
Directory created.
SQL> create directory TPCDS_READONLY as '/others/capture_consolidated/capture_readonly';
Directory created.
```

```
SQL> create directory TPCDS_CONSOLIDATED as '/others/capture_consolidated';
Directory created.
SQL> grant read, write on directory TPCDS_READONLY to wrc;
Grant succeeded.
SQL> grant read, write on directory TPCDS_OLTP to wrc;
Grant succeeded.
SQL> grant read, write on directory TPCDS_CONSOLIDATED to wrc;
Grant succeeded.
```

Creating a Schedule

Next, we'll combine our two captured workloads with appropriate calls to DBMS_
WORKLOAD_REPLAY procedures and functions, as shown in the following code
listing. Essentially, this code enables DWR to schedule both workloads so they can
be replayed simultaneously even though they were recorded at completely different
times against our source production database.

```
SQL> DECLARE
    cpt_id NUMBER;
BEGIN
    DBMS_WORKLOAD_REPLAY.PROCESS_CAPTURE(
        capture_dir => 'TPCDS_READONLY');
    DBMS_WORKLOAD_REPLAY.PROCESS_CAPTURE(
        capture_dir => 'TPCDS_OLTP');
    DBMS_WORKLOAD_REPLAY.SET_REPLAY_DIRECTORY(
        replay_dir => 'TPCDS_CONSOLIDATED');
    DBMS_WORKLOAD_REPLAY.BEGIN_REPLAY_SCHEDULE (
    schedule_name => 'SCHEDULE_CONSOLIDATED_WORKLOAD');

    cpt_id :=
        DBMS_WORKLOAD_REPLAY.ADD_CAPTURE(
            capture_dir_name => 'TPCDS_READONLY'
            ,start_delay_seconds => 0
            ,stop_replay => FALSE
            ,take_begin_snapshot => TRUE
            ,take_end_snapshot => TRUE
            ,query_only => FALSE
        );
    cpt_id :=
        DBMS_WORKLOAD_REPLAY.ADD_CAPTURE(
            capture_dir_name => 'TPCDS_OLTP'
            ,start_delay_seconds => 0
            ,stop_replay => FALSE
            ,take_begin_snapshot => TRUE
            ,take_end_snapshot => TRUE
            ,query_only => FALSE
        );
    DBMS_WORKLOAD_REPLAY.END_REPLAY_SCHEDULE;
END;
/
```

NOTE
Although we didn't do it here, it's possible to schedule separate sections of a consolidated workload to execute at different times within the scheduled timeframe.

Initialization Phase

Now we'll initialize the DWR operation against our test database environment. For a Consolidated Replay operation, the initialization process is a bit different from the regular DWR operation. As the following code shows, we're essentially initializing the DWR *schedule* we just created rather than a singular DWC *operation* as we'd typically do. Note that we also remapped several of the database services that were used during the generation of the DWC for the OLTP workloads so that they could be replayed using appropriate database services on the test database environment.

```
SQL> BEGIN
    DBMS_WORKLOAD_REPLAY.INITIALIZE_CONSOLIDATED_REPLAY(
        replay_name => 'REPLAY_CONSOLIDATED_WORKLOAD'
        ,schedule_name => 'SCHEDULE_CONSOLIDATED_WORKLOAD');
    DBMS_WORKLOAD_REPLAY.REMAP_CONNECTION(
        connection_id => 1
        ,replay_connection =>
            '(DESCRIPTION=(ADDRESS=(PROTOCOL=TCP)(HOST=nuvola2)
(PORT=1521))(CONNECT_DATA=(SERVER=DEDICATED)(SERVICE_NAME=ADHOC)))');
    DBMS_WORKLOAD_REPLAY.REMAP_CONNECTION(
        connection_id => 2
        ,replay_connection =>
            '(DESCRIPTION=(ADDRESS=(PROTOCOL=TCP)(HOST=nuvola2)
(PORT=1521))(CONNECT_DATA=(SERVER=DEDICATED)(SERVICE_NAME=BATCH)))');
    DBMS_WORKLOAD_REPLAY.REMAP_CONNECTION(
        connection_id => 3
        ,replay_connection =>
            '(DESCRIPTION=(ADDRESS=(PROTOCOL=TCP)(HOST=nuvola2)
(PORT=1521))(CONNECT_DATA=(SERVER=DEDICATED)(SERVICE_NAME=OLTP)))');

END;
/
```

To confirm the status of the initialized Consolidated Replay, we'll query several data dictionary views that capture information about DWR operations. These queries will work for any DWR operation and provide a perfect alternative when OEM isn't available or more customized output is desired.

```
SQL> select id, name, status
    from dba_workload_replays
    where id = (select max(id) from dba_workload_replays);
```

```
      ID NAME                                STATUS
---------- ------------------------------- --------------------
     182 REPLAY_CONSOLIDATED_WORKLOAD   INITIALIZED

SQL> select conn_id, replay_conn
       from dba_workload_connection_map
     where replay_id = (select max(id) from dba_workload_replays);

  CONN_ID REPLAY_CONN
---------- -----------------------------------------------------------
       1 (DESCRIPTION=(ADDRESS=(PROTOCOL=TCP)(HOST=nuvola2)(PORT=1521))
               (CONNECT_DATA=(SERVER=DEDICATED)(SERVICE_NAME=ADHOC)))

       2 (DESCRIPTION=(ADDRESS=(PROTOCOL=TCP)(HOST=nuvola2)(PORT=1521))
               (CONNECT_DATA=(SERVER=DEDICATED)(SERVICE_NAME=BATCH)))

       3 (DESCRIPTION=(ADDRESS=(PROTOCOL=TCP)(HOST=nuvola2)(PORT=1521))
               (CONNECT_DATA=(SERVER=DEDICATED)(SERVICE_NAME=OLTP)))
```

Preparing for Replay

Our next step is to prepare the test database for replaying the consolidated workload. The call to the PREPARE_REPLAY procedure of DBMS_WORKLOAD_REPLAY sets up our test database to receive connection requests from WRC clients just as it would have if we'd used OEM to prepare for the replay process.

```
SQL> BEGIN
       DBMS_WORKLOAD_REPLAY.PREPARE_REPLAY(
       synchronization => 'SCN',
       scale_up_multiplier =>1,
       capture_sts => TRUE,
       connect_time_scale=>100,
       think_time_scale=>100,
       think_time_auto_correct=>TRUE,
       sts_cap_interval => 60,
       query_only => FALSE);
END;
/
```

Note that we're going to allow the Consolidated Replay to unwind at the same pace as it would have if our two captured workloads had actually occurred simultaneously. We'll confirm the status of the ongoing DWR operation via the same simple query against the view DBA_WORKLOAD_REPLAY; note that its state has now changed its status to PREPARE:

```
SQL> select id, name, status
       from dba_workload_replays
     where id = (select max(id) from dba_workload_replays);

      ID NAME                                STATUS
---------- ------------------------------- --------------------
     161 REPLAY_CONSOLIDATED_WORKLOAD   PREPARE
```

Starting WRCs

Our test environment is ready to receive WRC connection requests. Invoking the WRC clients on the same host on which the test database resides involves just two quick invocations of the wrc application; note that we connect to the test database using the same wrc database user account we set up previously when we invoked DWR through OEM. (While we could have probably used just one WRC, we're using two to guarantee that a single WRC won't be overwhelmed by application workload replay demands and become a potential bottleneck to a successfully replay.)

```
$> nohup wrc wrc/wrc mode=replay replaydir=/others/capture_consolidated &
$> nohup wrc wrc/wrc mode=replay replaydir=/others/capture_consolidated &
```

Starting the Replay

At last, it's time to initiate the Consolidated Replay via a call to procedure START_CONSOLIDATED_REPLAY (instead of the START_REPLAY procedure we'd normally use if this were a standard DWR operation). Note that we called procedure SET_REPLAY_TIMEOUT to insure that the DWR operation wouldn't terminate until every last captured workload component was replayed:

```
SQL> BEGIN
    DBMS_WORKLOAD_REPLAY.SET_REPLAY_TIMEOUT(FALSE);
    DBMS_WORKLOAD_REPLAY.START_CONSOLIDATED_REPLAY;
END;
/


SQL> select id, name, status
    from dba_workload_replays
    where id = (select max(id) from dba_workload_replays);

     ID NAME                             STATUS
---------- ------------------------------   ------------------------------
    182 REPLAY_CONSOLIDATED_WORKLOAD     IN PROGRESS
```

Note that V$SESSION also reflects the fact that the Consolidated Replay operation has indeed commenced and that SQL statements are being replayed:

```
SQL> select username, sql_id, status
    from v$session
    where username='TPCDS';

USERNAME                        SQL_ID        STATUS
------------------------------   -------------  --------
TPCDS                           asq3p6y4jku9u ACTIVE
TPCDS                           asq3p6y4jku9u ACTIVE
. . . <rows eliminated for brevity>
```

```
TPCDS                           asq3p6y4jku9u ACTIVE
TPCDS                           asq3p6y4jku9u ACTIVE

17 rows selected.
```

Conclusion

Once the consolidated workload replay completes, we can review the results of the DWR operation via the Database Replay option from OEM (Figure 12-42).

Also, the Average Active Sessions graph on the database's Performance page (Figure 12-43) gives us an interesting indication of just how much more intense the consolidated workload was as compared to the original OLTP workload we recorded in Figure 12-41, shown earlier.

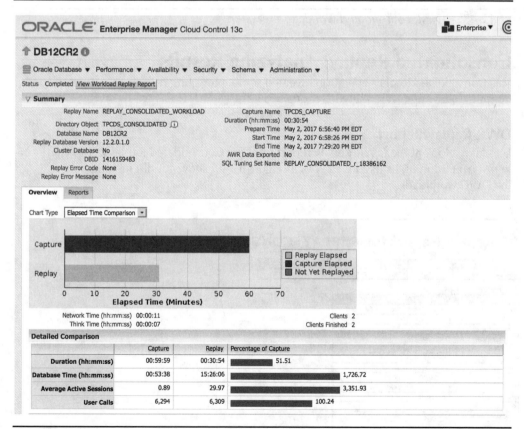

FIGURE 12-42. *DWR, consolidated workload execution*

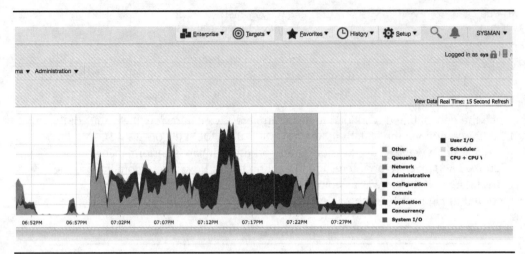

FIGURE 12-43. *OEM, consolidated workload execution*

Consolidated Replay: Analyzing Results

This Consolidated Replay operation revealed some interesting results, as excerpts from the following DWR analytic reports show.

DWR Replay Report

Let's take a look at the DWR Replay report first. The Consolidated Replay completed in just over 30 minutes (Figure 12-44); as Figure 12-45 shows, it did include both of the DWC workloads.

DB Replay Report for REPLAY_CONSOLIDATED_WORKLOAD

DB Name	DB Id	Release	RAC	Replay Name	Replay Status
DB12CR2	1416159483	12.2.0.1.0	NO	REPLAY_CONSOLIDATED_WORKLOAD	COMPLETED

Replay Information

Information	Replay
Name	REPLAY_CONSOLIDATED_WORKLOAD
Status	COMPLETED
Database Name	DB12CR2
Database Version	12.2.0.1.0
Start Time	02-05-17 22:58:26
End Time	02-05-17 23:29:20
Duration	30 minutes 54 seconds
Directory Object	TPCDS_CONSOLIDATED
Directory Path	/others/capture_consolidated
AWR DB Id	1416159483
AWR Begin Snap Id	229
AWR End Snap Id	234
PL/SQL Capture Mode	TOP_LEVEL
Replay Directory Number	603959449
Replay Schedule Name	SCHEDULE_CONSOLIDATED_WORKLOAD2

FIGURE 12-44. *DBR Replay Report, consolidated workload timing*

Replay Schedule Information
Schedule SCHEDULE_CONSOLIDATED_WORKLOAD2 contains 2 captures:

Information	Capture 1
Name	CAPTURE_TPCDS_EM13c
Status	COMPLETED
Database Name	DB11G
Database Version	11.2.0.3.0
Start Time	09-04-17 03:45:40
End Time	09-04-17 04:45:39
Duration	59 minutes 59 seconds
DB Time	572.780 seconds
User Calls	15
Average Active Sessions	.16
Directory Object	TPCDS_READONLY
Directory Path	/others/capture_consolidated/capture_readonly
Start Delay	0 second
Query Only	N

Information	Capture 2
Name	TPCDS_CAPTURE
Status	COMPLETED
Database Name	DB11G
Database Version	11.2.0.3.0
Start Time	02-05-17 09:26:45
End Time	02-05-17 10:26:44
Duration	59 minutes 59 seconds
DB Time	3218.290 seconds
User Calls	6294
Average Active Sessions	.89
Directory Object	TPCDS_OLTP
Directory Path	/others/capture_consolidated/capture_oltp
Start Delay	0 second
Query Only	N

FIGURE 12-45. *DBR replay report, consolidated workload components*

The workload profile shows that our test database was actually quite busy, with almost 45 percent of DB activity spent on CPU executing SQL statements; a little more surprising is the `direct path read temp` and `direct path write temp` events (Figure 12-46). Note that all database services were used during the Consolidated Replay, with the Swingbench-generated application workload leading the pack for activity.

Workload Profile
Top Events
(-) Hide

Event	Event Class	% Activity
CPU + Wait for CPU	CPU	44.79
direct path read temp	User I/O	29.24
direct path write temp	User I/O	11.70
direct path read	User I/O	4.71
db file sequential read	User I/O	1.71

Top Service/Module/Action
(-) Hide

Service Name	Module Name	% Activity	Action Drilldown	
ADHOC	Swingbench User Thread	83.02	**Action Name**	**% Activity**
			UNNAMED	83.02
OLTP	SQL*Plus	4.56	**Action Name**	**% Activity**
			UNNAMED	4.56
SYS$USERS	SQL*Plus	1.85	**Action Name**	**% Activity**
			UNNAMED	1.85
BATCH	SQL*Plus	1.57	**Action Name**	**% Activity**
			UNNAMED	1.57
OLTP	wrc@nuvola2 (TNS V1-V3)	1.28	**Action Name**	**% Activity**
			UNNAMED	1.28

FIGURE 12-46. *Workload Profile*

AWR Report: Consolidated Workload Components

As we might expect, the AWR report generated for the snapshots that make up the Consolidated Replay offers some additional details. The Top 10 Foreground Events report section (Figure 12-47) correlates with other reports' findings that there was an inordinately high amount of database time was expended for the `direct path read temp` wait event. (Because the replayed workload took advantage of several degrees of parallelism, it may appear that wait event is somewhat inflated, but the key takeaway here is that wait event usually indicates an undersized PGA, as later sections of the report identify and clarify.)

Meanwhile, the Time Model Statistics section (Figure 12-48) shows that even despite the unexpectedly high rate of temporary tablespace read and write activity, the database itself still performed relatively well, spending the majority of its time (almost 98 percent) executing SQL statements without any extraneous parsing.

Top 10 Foreground Events by Total Wait Time

Event	Waits	Total Wait Time (sec)	Avg Wait	% DB time	Wait Class
direct path read temp	647,158	1883.4	2.91ms	26.0	User I/O
DB CPU		1215.6		16.8	
direct path write temp	180,957	701.1	3.87ms	9.7	User I/O
direct path read	54,386	248.7	4.57ms	3.4	User I/O
db file sequential read	30,441	79.9	2.62ms	1.1	User I/O
PX qref latch	1,170	47.1	40.22ms	.6	Other
CRS call completion	21	34.4	1639.57ms	.5	Other
db file scattered read	8,108	19.8	2.44ms	.3	User I/O
db file parallel read	1,573	14.9	9.46ms	.2	User I/O
control file sequential read	5,231	14.4	2.74ms	.2	System I/O

FIGURE 12-47. *AWR report Top 10 Events section*

And the SQL Ordered by Elapsed Time section (Figure 12-49) highlights one particular SQL statement—SQL ID 3xvs5gxdq53pq—that is the longest-running SQL statement of the entire workload, which would bear investigating for performance improvement because it took up nearly 71 percent of the database time of the total consolidated workload. Again, because we did leverage several degrees of parallelism

Time Model Statistics

- DB Time represents total time in user calls
- DB CPU represents CPU time of foreground processes
- Total CPU Time represents foreground and background processes
- Statistics including the word "background" measure background process time, therefore do not contribute to the DB time statistic
- Ordered by % of DB time in descending order, followed by Statistic Name

Statistic Name	Time (s)	% of DB Time	% of Total CPU Time
sql execute elapsed time	7,084.44	97.71	
DB CPU	1,215.64	16.77	97.58
parse time elapsed	202.95	2.80	
hard parse elapsed time	184.23	2.54	
connection management call elapsed time	78.41	1.08	
PL/SQL execution elapsed time	50.86	0.70	
PL/SQL compilation elapsed time	8.57	0.12	
hard parse (sharing criteria) elapsed time	3.64	0.05	
hard parse (bind mismatch) elapsed time	0.38	0.01	
sequence load elapsed time	0.36	0.01	
failed parse elapsed time	0.17	0.00	
repeated bind elapsed time	0.02	0.00	
DB time	7,250.27		
background elapsed time	329.14		
background cpu time	30.17		2.42
total CPU time	1,245.81		

FIGURE 12-48. *Time Model Statistics section*

SQL ordered by Elapsed Time

- Resources reported for PL/SQL code includes the resources used by all SQL statements called by the code.
- % Total DB Time is the Elapsed Time of the SQL statement divided into the Total Database Time multiplied by 100
- %Total - Elapsed Time as a percentage of Total DB time
- %CPU - CPU Time as a percentage of Elapsed Time
- %IO - User I/O Time as a percentage of Elapsed Time
- Captured SQL account for 98.0% of Total DB Time (s): 7,250
- Captured PL/SQL account for 12.5% of Total DB Time (s): 7,250

Elapsed Time (s)	Executions	Elapsed Time per Exec (s)	%Total	%CPU	%IO	SQL Id	SQL Module	SQL Text
5,120.85	1	5,120.85	70.63	17.10	50.17	3xvs5gxdq53pq	Swingbench User Thread	with year_total as (select c_...
494.06	298	1.66	6.81	7.50	0.04	9cmf0v8a3hy7f	SQL*Plus	SELECT MIN(CD_DEMO_SK) , MAX(C...
309.58	1	309.58	4.27	20.47	17.56	ck52qcn50mj6s	Swingbench User Thread	WITH ssr as (SELECT s_store_id...
290.68	120	2.42	4.01	7.09	0.53	c2ur80rwga0ht	SQL*Plus	BEGIN TPCDS.PKG_DML_GENERATOR....
281.66	1	281.66	3.88	18.48	9.55	asq3p6y4jku9u	Swingbench User Thread	WITH wscs AS (SELECT sold_dat...
219.97	1	219.97	3.03	31.31	66.55	axq9hvrz2h25a	Swingbench User Thread	SELECT /*query9*/ CASE WHEN (S...
146.55	60	2.44	2.02	6.93	0.38	99s4w29h4b94y	SQL*Plus	BEGIN TPCDS.PKG_DML_GENERATOR....
128.61	58	2.22	1.77	7.64	0.43	9tv1hqpz869bc	SQL*Plus	BEGIN TPCDS.PKG_DML_GENERATOR....
124.26	60	2.07	1.71	8.01	0.55	87d1bww4hkchm	SQL*Plus	BEGIN TPCDS.PKG_DML_GENERATOR....
78.64	300	0.26	1.08	4.64	3.28	60zzqsnvxuk1y	DMLGenerator	BEGIN dbms_wrr_internal.save_r...

FIGURE 12-49.   *SQL Ordered by Elapsed Time section*

as we executed the workload, it may appear that single SQL statement ran for nearly 90 minutes (5120 seconds) of DB time. (We've noticed this apparently aberrant execution time reported when using DWR to scale up a workload as well.) The key takeaway here is that this specific SQL statement needs to be analyzed for possible performance improvement.

ASH Report

For an even lower level of detail, the corresponding ASH report for the Consolidated Replay (Figure 12-50) shows that the same SQL statement—SQL ID **3xvs5gxdq53pq**—that was previously identified by AWR as the longest-running SQL statement is a likely candidate for investigation and SQL Tuning, especially since it appears to have consumed an excessive amount of temporary file I/O.

ADDM Report

Finally, the corresponding ADDM report for this Consolidated Replay operation has a few interesting recommendations beyond tuning individual SQL statements: It recommends resizing the Program Global Area (PGA) from 416MB to 745MB to eliminate at least some of the I/O to temporary tablespaces (Figure 12-51).

Consolidated Replay: Final Takeaways

The key takeaways from all of these reports is encouraging: There doesn't appear to be any reason that these two disparate workloads couldn't be combined to run at the same time against the new test database environment. Therefore, their source

Active Session History (ASH) Report

- **Top SQL with Top Events**
- **Top SQL with Top Row Sources**
- **Top Sessions**
- **Top Blocking Sessions**
- **Top PL/SQL Procedures**
- **Top Events**
- **Top Event P1/P2/P3 Values**
- **Top DB Objects**
- **Activity Over Time**

Back to Top

Top SQL with Top Events

- Top SQL statements by DB Time along with the top events by DB Time for those SQLs.
- % Activity is the percentage of DB Time due to the SQL.
- % Event is the percentage of DB Time due to the event that the SQL is waiting on.
- % Row Source is the percentage of DB Time due to the row source for the SQL waiting on the event.
- Executions is the number of executions of the SQL that were sampled in ASH.

SQL ID	Plan Hash	Executions	% Activity	Event	% Event	Top Row Source	% Row Source	SQL Text
3xvs5gxdq53pq	1473485598	1	69.66	direct path read temp	29.20	HASH - GROUP BY	12.82	with year_total as (select c_...
				CPU + Wait for CPU	28.06	HASH - GROUP BY	6.27	
				direct path write temp	11.54	HASH - GROUP BY	7.41	
9cmf0v8a3hy7f	4114719769	43	6.13	CPU + Wait for CPU	6.13	SORT - AGGREGATE	3.99	SELECT MIN(CD_DEMO_SK) , MAX(C...
ck52qcn50mj6s	2905840545	1	4.27	CPU + Wait for CPU	3.13	UNION-ALL	0.71	WITH ssr as (SELECT s_store_id...
asq3p6y4jku9u	2998380289	1	3.56	CPU + Wait for CPU	2.99	HASH - GROUP BY	1.85	WITH wscs AS (SELECT sold_dat...
axq9hvrz2h25a	762459664	1	2.99	direct path read	2.85	TABLE ACCESS - FULL	0.43	SELECT /*query9*/ CASE WHEN (S...

FIGURE 12-50. *ASH Report, SQL statements detail*

databases are good candidates for consolidation, and we can confidently proceed to construct our plan to consolidate them into a single database. However, a few SQL statements should definitely be analyzed with SQL Tuning Advisor to see if there are any additional recommendations for performance improvement once their workloads are transitioned to the new database environment.

```
Finding 2: Undersized PGA
Impact is 1.49 active sessions, 30.48% of total activity.
-------------------------------------------------------------
The PGA was inadequately sized, causing additional I/O to temporary
tablespaces to consume significant database time.
The value of parameter "pga_aggregate_target" was "416 M" during the analysis
period.

   Recommendation 1: Database Configuration
   Estimated benefit is 1.05 active sessions, 21.34% of total activity.
   ----------------------------------------------------------------
   Action
      Increase the size of the PGA by setting the value of parameter
      "pga_aggregate_target" to 745 M.

   Symptoms That Led to the Finding:
   ---------------------------------
      Wait class "User I/O" was consuming significant database time.
      Impact is 1.63 active sessions, 33.23% of total activity.
```

FIGURE 12-51. *ADDM Report Findings*

DWR: Employing Workload Scale-Up

One other extremely useful feature that is part of Oracle 12c DWC/R is the capability to scale up a captured workload when it is replayed against its test environment. This feature is invaluable when attempting to determine the outer boundaries of performance for the database that's servicing a particular application workload.

For example, how much would the overall database performance suffer when the number of database sessions increased unexpectedly by an order of magnitude—perhaps because our IT organization is suddenly tasked with adding an entirely new group of application users as a result of corporate merger and acquisition activity? Or what would happen if the "think time" between transactions suddenly decreased dramatically, perhaps because transactions were being generated by faster robotic application services, or from a network of Internet of Things (IoT) devices?

In these situations, an Oracle DBA could truly ride to the rescue of her CIO or CTO simply by replaying a scaled-up workload using DWR. We illustrate an example of how to scale up an application workload in Example 12-4 in Appendix B. This example leverages a few simple modifications to parameter settings for the INITIALIZE_REPLAY procedure of package DBMS_WORKLOAD_REPLAY that we summarized in Table 12-1 earlier in the chapter.

For example, we can decrease the think time—literally, the amount of time recorded between transactions as a user pondered what to do next—to increase the rate at which transactions will impact the test database. For SELECT statements, it's also possible to ramp up the number of times that a statement is executed during replay to simulate a dramatic increase in the number of user queries against the test database. It's even possible for an Oracle DBA to simulate a "nightmare" scenario—when an entire workload is executed simultaneously without any pauses between execution of SQL statements—by eliminating any think time between captured activity as well as ramping up the number of simulated user sessions well beyond any observed application workload activity in an attempt to discover the outer boundaries of the test system's possible performance capabilities as part of a true test to destruction.

Summary

Database Workload Replay (DWR) makes it eminently possible for any Oracle DBA to reproduce a production application workload accurately in an entirely new testing environment. This means that the impact of multiple potential factors, including different storage components, new memory configurations, and computational resources, can be evaluated, as well as changes to the database itself, including different releases, changes to initialization parameters, and even newer features like 12c Database In-Memory.

This chapter also explored how disparate application workloads captured via Database Workload Capture (DWC) can be replayed simultaneously or even ramped up beyond normally expected levels of application user activity to perform true testing to destruction and thus discover precisely when a test environment's capacity to handle those workloads will be exceeded. Finally, we demonstrated how to leverage and interpret the various analytical reports that DWR produces to determine exactly how well an application workload has performed after a successful DWR operation.

PART
V

A Brave New World:
Database In-Memory

CHAPTER
13

Database
In-Memory Advisor

Oracle introduced *Database In-Memory* (DBIM) features in Oracle Database Release 12*c*R1 (12.1.0.2) to dramatically increase the speed of complex analytic queries. One of the significant issues that Oracle DBAs have often encountered while leveraging DBIM features is figuring out which database objects would most benefit from being placed within the In-Memory Column Store (IMCS). After a brief review of the key concepts behind DBIM, we will shift our attention to the numerous features of the latest version of the Oracle Database 12*c In-Memory Advisor* (IMADV) in extensive detail.

Database In-Memory Concepts: A Quick Review

Prior to Oracle Database Release 12.1.0.2, a SQL statement typically accessed data from a database table or table partition once it was captured as a memory-resident database buffer in the buffer cache of the database instance's System Global Area (SGA) or from the Program Global Area (PGA) during direct-path reads. Just as with the actual physical database block retained on storage media, this data was represented in *row-major* format.

Row-major format tends to provide excellent response when using data manipulation language (DML)—for example, when adding new rows into an existing table via an `INSERT` statement, modifying column values in a small subset of existing rows with an `UPDATE` statement, or removing rows from a table through a `DELETE` statement. But row-major format can also severely limit the performance of a `SELECT` statement when performing analytic queries against extremely large tables that are either *deep* (containing many millions of rows) or *wide* comprising dozens or even hundreds of columns), and sometimes both *deep* and *wide*.

Query performance tends to degrade because of the nature of analytic queries themselves, often regardless of the underlying I/O storage system, CPU processing power, or available compute node memory. That's because analytic operations often need to filter out a significant proportion of data from extremely large tables, either through complex joins or selection criteria. And wide tables often cause considerable grief for analytic processing because the majority of the table's columns are often unnecessary to answer the query, yet row-major format requires retrieval of the entire row, regardless of how few of the table's columns are needed to retrieve the necessary data.

Oracle's line of enterprise hardware—including Exadata Database Machine and SPARC SuperCluster—are often able to offload much of this join processing and filtering to those platforms' storage cells, and queries run against those platforms can leverage their *columnar projection* features to return only the result set that a query has requested. But there is actually a much simpler way to overcome these issues, and it's one of the key concepts behind Database In-Memory (DBIM).

DBIM: In-Memory Column Store

Oracle Database 12c Release 1 (12.1.0.2) was the first release to offer an additional format for retaining data within an instance's memory: in a columnar format stored within the new In-Memory Column Store (IMCS). Data from database tables, table partitions, and materialized views can be populated within the IMCS. If you visualize data stored within a database object in row-major format as a gigantic spreadsheet, with column headings at the top of each column and corresponding ROWIDs running down the left side, then data retained in columnar format simply involves rotating that spreadsheet counter-clockwise by 90 degrees to the left; column IDs become row headers, and vice versa.

There are several advantages to this columnar format. It's extremely easy to identify common values within each column, and it's also simpler to discard columns that are unnecessary to answer a query. The new format also makes it possible to apply in-memory compression to nondistinct values within the structure, and that means data can be handled much more efficiently during analytic processing, especially when filtering, joining, or aggregating values.

Just like the database buffer is the memory structure for the database buffer cache, an object's data is retained within the IMCS as part of at least one or more *In-Memory Compression Unit* (IMCU). Figure 13-1 shows the IMCU architecture as implemented in Oracle 12.1.0.2; in Chapter 14, we will discuss how this architecture was significantly enhanced as part of Oracle 12.2.0.1.

NOTE
Be aware that the features of Database In-Memory are offered only with Oracle Enterprise Edition; further, these features do require additional Oracle licensing, which can be somewhat costly depending upon the environment in which it's implemented. The authors strongly recommend checking your IT organization's existing Oracle licensing agreement before implementing any DBIM features.

DBIM: How Objects Get Populated

Once an object has been chosen as a candidate for the IMCS, the following logic is used to populate that object's data into the IMCS, as shown in Figure 13-2.

1.   If a query requests data that is part of an existing table or partition that is an IMCS candidate, then Oracle checks to see if any of its data is already present in columnar format within the IMCS, and it will return that columnar-formatted data to the requesting session.

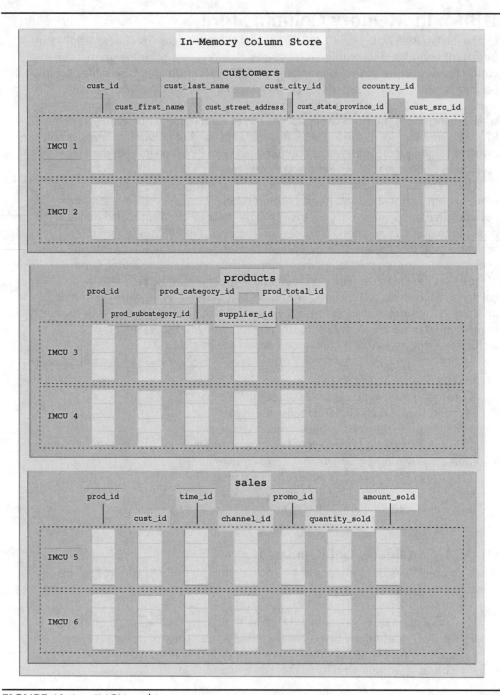

FIGURE 13-1. *IMCU architecture*

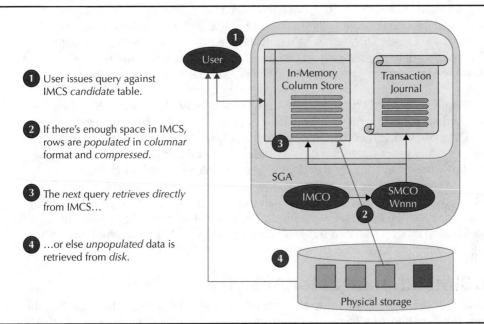

1 User issues query against IMCS *candidate* table.

2 If there's enough space in IMCS, rows are *populated* in *columnar* format and *compressed*.

3 The *next* query *retrieves directly* from IMCS...

4 ...or else *unpopulated* data is retrieved from *disk*.

FIGURE 13-2.   *IMCS: Basic architecture and population concepts*

2. If no data for the object is yet present in the IMCS, and if there is sufficient space within the IMCS, then data is retrieved via physical reads from storage, transformed into columnar format, and populated within the IMCS, as well as returned to the requesting session. During population, the requested level of In-Memory compression is also applied. There are five different compression levels available, with the lowest compression level, MEMCOMPRESS FOR DML, most effective for objects that still encounter frequent updates, and the highest compression level, MEMCOMPRESS FOR CAPACITY HIGH, most effective for objects that may be occasionally accessed but still desirable to remain within the IMCS.

3. The next query will use the data stored within the IMCS in columnar format, decompressing it only as necessary to answer the query.

4. If an object is not fully populated in the IMCS, or if there's insufficient space to populate the entire object, the database still uses whatever data is formatted within the IMCS for fastest access and will retrieve the remaining data via physical reads. This means that a query can leverage IMCS-resident data immediately even while the remaining data is still being populated.

Note that in Oracle 12.1.0.2, once any portion of a database object has been populated into the IMCS, it will remain there until either the database instance is shut down or the Oracle DBA forces its removal by setting its status to NO INMEMORY. This changes quite dramatically in Oracle 12.2.0.1 with the availability of *Information Lifecycle Management* (ILM) *Automatic Data Optimization* (ADO) policies for objects within the IMCS, which we will cover in detail in Chapter 14.

Finally, note that DML statements aren't processed within the IMCS; rather, the standard life cycle of dirtied buffers that are eventually written back to physical storage via Database Writer (DBW0) processes still applies. The obvious benefit is that this isolates query processing from data maintenance, while simultaneously leveraging what row-major storage is best at doing. When a table's data values change, the deltas of those changed values are written to a separate journal within the IMCS, and Oracle 12*c* is smart enough to access the journaled entries instead of the original values still retained within the IMCUs. On a periodic basis, the In-Memory Coordinator (IMCO) background process signals a series of worker processes (W00n) to refresh the affected IMCUs from the journaled entries.

DBIM: Advantages for Analytics

Isolating query processing from data maintenance is not the only advantage that the new IMCS architecture offers; there are several additional special features of DBIM that benefit heavy analytic processing, especially in data warehousing environments.

In-Memory Joins and Filtering

It's not unusual to encounter fact tables in a modern data warehouse that consist of hundreds of millions, or even billions, of rows. Even when tables are partitioned, the Oracle optimizer often selects the hash join method when an extremely large fact table must be joined to smaller fact tables and/or other smaller dimensions. But when objects reside within the IMCS, the 12*c* optimizer can often make more intelligent choices about hash joins and employ a Bloom filter to augment hash join operations with a more efficient scan and filter operation. Because these scan and filter operations occur within memory, they are often significantly more efficient than standard hash join processing.

In addition, IMCS can leverage a storage index—an in-memory index that identifies precisely which IMCUs do not contain particular values for a column—to limit scans of IMCUs to a bare minimum, especially when applying selection criteria.

NOTE
If the IMCS concept of storage indexes seem vaguely familiar, they should be! This is the same strategy that Oracle Exadata Smart Scan employs to limit unnecessary Smart Scans on that platform.

In-Memory Aggregation

Many modern data warehouses employ a star schema architecture—a set of fact tables that are surrounded by numerous dimensions. Improving the performance of queries against a star schema can be particularly thorny to resolve, and prior to 12c, efficient star schema query processing often relied heavily upon creating bitmap join indexes to assist in identifying the matching dimension-fact table values. In concert with DBIM, the Oracle 12c optimizer offers the ability to leverage vector transformation—a completely new set of optimizer methods designed to capture matching dimension keys, and then apply those dimensions' limiting filters against the query's fact tables. This offers significant performance advantages for queries, especially when they are performing aggregation, sorting, and grouping.

NOTE
An in-depth discussion of vector transformation methods, including VECTOR GROUP BY *operations, is beyond the scope of this chapter. See Sections 4.5.4 and 20.8.6 of the* Oracle Database 12cR2 Data Warehousing Guide *for a detailed explanation of these unique features.*

Analytical queries also often employ complex analytic functions that require at least some level of aggregation—for example, AVERAGE(), MIN(), MAX(), SUM(), and COUNT(). The good news is that vector transformation methods can take advantage of single-instruction processing multiple data values (SIMD) processing so that it's essentially possible to capture and process all possible values in one or more dimensional row sets simultaneously.

Introducing the In-Memory Advisor (IMADV)

Not long after the release of Oracle Database 12.1.0.2, Oracle DBAs realized that the new Database In-Memory features would most likely present some excellent opportunities to increase the efficiency and speed of analytical query workloads. However, even the most enthusiastic supporters of these new DBIM features soon realized that simple trial-and-error experimentation wouldn't necessarily provide answers to some pressing questions:

■ Which database objects should be included within the IMCS to obtain the greatest benefit for a representative analytic workload?

- What should be the corresponding size of the IMCS to accommodate those objects? This is quite important in Oracle 12.1.0.2, because the IMCS cannot be dynamically resized, and any adjustment to its size required a bounce of the database instance—something that's quite undesirable for any heavily loaded production database instance. (This is remedied in Oracle 12.2.0.1, as we will demonstrate in Chapter 14.)

- Is there any way to predict which SQL statements within an analytic workload are most likely to benefit from placing their underlying objects within the IMCS?

- Perhaps most importantly, what is the estimated cumulative effect of leveraging the IMCS for analytical workloads so that the cost of licensing the DBIM option could be weighed realistically against its projected benefits?

The good news is that the In-Memory Advisor (IMADV) offers Oracle DBAs some practical answers to these questions by providing detailed advice and practical justifications on placing database objects intelligently within the IMCS, including cost-benefit factors at both the object and SQL statement level.

NOTE
Please be aware that using the IMADV does require licensing the SQL Tuning Pack. The authors strongly recommend checking your IT organization's existing Oracle licensing agreement before implementing IMADV features.

IMADV: A Brief History

The original version of IMADV (version 1.0) was available in February 2015. It supported execution against any Oracle Database release 11.2.0.3 or later. Of course, executing IMADV against any database prior to 12.1.0.2 didn't mean that DBIM could be leveraged against that database, but it did provide guidance for which database objects should offer the best performance benefit once the application workload's tables were migrated to a release 12.1.0.2 database.

IMADV 1.0 could be executed against a live Oracle database to obtain its required input metadata, but it was also possible to leverage existing SQL Tuning Sets or even Automatic Workload Repository (AWR) data as input. If the target database's release was at least 12cR1, it supported execution against both a non-CDB as well as any online container within the target CDB, either an individual PDB as well as CDB$ROOT. Finally, it transferred the generated recommendations to the specified directory within the target database.

The latest version of IMADV (version 2.0) was released in December 2016 and offers several new features as well as some welcome enhancements:

- **In-Memory Area Sizing**   The In-Memory Area must fit within the target database's SGA. An Oracle DBA usually knows the size of the targeted database's SGA ahead of time and may even already know just how much of the SGA can be realistically dedicated to the In-Memory Area. IMADV 2.0 now enables the DBA to specify a desired INMEMORY_SIZE so that IMADV can take that target value into account during its analysis. Otherwise, the DBA can just allow IMADV determine the optimal INMEMORY_SIZE regardless of SGA memory available.

- **Faster In-Memory Advisor Execution**   In earlier releases of IMADV 1.0, an evaluation task typically consumed significant system resources, and it wasn't unusual for the task to take quite a long time to execute. The good news here is that IMADV 2.0 is significantly more efficient and returns meaningful results quickly. In addition, once an IMADV task has been executed, its metadata is retained within the target database, so when an Oracle DBA just wants to re-evaluate the results by rerunning an already-existing task—perhaps choosing a different size for the In-Memory Area—IMADV now returns a list of those tasks so that they can be rerun and includes a list of INMEMORY_SIZE estimates to choose from.

- **RAC Support**   If IMADV is executed against a Real Applications Cluster (RAC) database, that's automatically detected and the Oracle DBA is then prompted for which instance IMADV should be run against.

- **Augmented AWR Workloads**   The concept of an augmented AWR workload was introduced in a primitive form in Oracle Release 10gR2. Put simply, an augmented AWR is simply AWR data that has been imported from a database other than the current local database—for example, the results of a Database Workload Capture session that was performed against a different database, but retained within the local database for later comparison against AWR data captured during a Database Workload Replay session on that same local database. Augmented AWR data is still retained within the AWR but is identified by a different DBID than that of the local database.

  If an augmented AWR workload is indeed present for the targeted database, IMADV automatically detects this and presents a list of augmented workloads for selection as well as normal, nonaugmented AWR workloads as targets for IMADV evaluation.

- **Simpler Invocation**   An IMADV task executed via the interactive script imadvisor_recommendations.sql—which replaces the original interactive script, `imadvisor_analyze_and_report.sql`—offers default values during execution. And just as with most Oracle-defined scripted tasks, it's now also possible to presupply settings prior to IMADV task invocation via SQL*Plus `DEFINE` commands for the appropriate values.

- **Improved Metadata** IMADV now offers several views that explain its recommendations for object placement into the IMCS, including the cost-benefit factors it used to make those decisions. See Table 13-1 for a list of these views.

Metadata View	Description
DBA_IMA_TASK_INFORMATION	Yields details about any existing IMADV tasks, including which input sources were fed into the Advisor.
DBA_IMA_BENEFIT_COST	Retains the summary recommendations for sizing the IMCS, including the estimated performance improvement factor for each size.
DBA_IMA_RECOMMENDATIONS	Provides extremely detailed information about every database object that was analyzed to determine an appropriate cost–benefit ratio, including the rationale for placing or not placing the object within the IMCS.
DBA_IMA_RECOMMENDATION_FILES	Retains the information used to generate all IMADV evaluation reports within character large objects (CLOBs) for faster report regeneration.
DBA_IMA_RECOMMENDATION_LINES	Retains the information used to generate all IMADV evaluation reports on a line-by-line basis.
DBA_IMA_AWR_AUGMENTS	If any augmented AWR data is present, this view lists information about those AWRs, including the source database, its release, and other pertinent details that factored into determining which database objects should be resident in the IMCS.

TABLE 13-1. *IMADV 2.0 Metadata Views*

IMADV 2.0: Installation

As of this writing, it is still necessary to obtain the source code for IMADV installation from the My Oracle Support Center (MOSC) via MOS Note 1965343.1. This note does include some valuable links to other documents as well, including detailed IMADV installation notes, IMADV release notes, and a technical overview of Oracle Database In-Memory features available in 12cR2.

Installation Preparations

Once the source code has been downloaded, it's a simple matter to unzip the compressed file to a staging directory and then execute the script named instimadv.sql from that directory to configure IMADV within the selected database. In a standalone non-CDB database, the installer will simply build a new user named IMADVISOR that owns all database objects related to IMADV. In a multitenant database, things get a little trickier, so it's therefore important to choose wisely when implementing IMADV in a multitenant 12c environment:

- If you choose to install it within the root container (CDB$ROOT), the IMADV installer will create a new common user named C#IMA_ADMIN in that container.

- If you decide to install IMADV within a separate PDB, then the IMADV installer creates a local user named IMADVISOR only within that PDB.

Installing IMADV: An Example

An Oracle DBA needs to make only a few decisions during the IMADV installation process. Because IMADV creates some relatively small (less than 10MB) additional database objects for retention of its tasks' recommendations, a permanent tablespace needs to be identified; additionally, because it also generates some temporary segments, a temporary tablespace needs to be identified. The default permanent and temporary tablespaces are presumed to be SYSTEM and TEMP, respectively; if these tablespaces already exist, there's no need to override them during installation.

```
SQL> @instimadv
Welcome to the Oracle Database In-Memory Advisor (DBMS_INMEMORY_ADVISOR)
installation.

DBMS_INMEMORY_ADVISOR uses Active Session History (ASH), Automatic
Workload Repository (AWR) and optionally SQL Tuning Sets (STS) to
determine which tables, partitions and subpartitions to place In Memory
for optimized analytics processing performance. DBMS_INMEMORY_ADVISOR
produces a recommendation report and a SQLPlus script to implement its
recommendations.
```

```
DBMS_INMEMORY_ADVISOR users require the ADVISOR privilege.

This installation script will create user C##IMADVISOR and add object
definitions to the schema. This user is created using the IDENTIFIED BY
password method with a random-generated password. If you prefer to use
either the IDENTIFIED EXTERNALLY or IDENTIFIED GLOBALLY method, abort this
installation by pressing ^C. Then create user C##IMADVISOR using your
preferred method. Add no objects or grants to the C##IMADVISOR schema. Then
run this installation script again.

User C##IMADVISOR requires both a permanent and temporary tablespace.
Available tablespaces:
TABLESPACE_NAME
------------------------------
SYSAUX
SYSTEM (default permanent tablespace)
TEMP (default temporary tablespace)
UNDOTBS1
USERS

Enter value for permanent_tablespace:
Permanent tablespace to be used with C##IMADVISOR: SYSTEM

Enter value for temporary_tablespace:
Temporary tablespace to be used with C##IMADVISOR: TEMP

No errors.
. . .
No errors.

All done!
DBMS_INMEMORY_ADVISOR installation successful.
Users who will use the DBMS_INMEMORY_ADVISOR package must be granted the
ADVISOR privilege.
DBMS_INMEMORY_ADVISOR installation and setup complete.
To uninstall:
SQL> @catnoimadv.sql
```

IMADV: Deinstallation

The good news is that if any unexpected issues should arise during installation,
it's a simple matter to deinstall IMADV by connecting as a database user with
administrative privileges and then executing the catnoimadv.sql script, which will
completely remove all IMADV components from the selected non-CDB, root
container, or pluggable database. Note that version 1.0 of IMADV offered no
such deinstallation script; it was necessary to drop the corresponding IMADV

schema (`DROP USER C##IMADVISOR CASCADE;`), but this process was notorious for leaving behind several synonyms during its cleanup process. No such issues arose during our experiments when removing this version of IMADV.

> **IMADV and Security**
> The latest version of IMADV also offers improved security features. During creation, the IMADVISOR schema is assigned a random and secure password. Also, it's no longer necessary to grant execute privileges to the DBMS_INMEMORY_ADVISOR package that's at the heart of the advisory services it provides, because IMADV has been formally integrated into the standard Oracle Advisor Framework security. If a user account should need access to IMADV, all that is required is granting the ADVISOR privilege to that account.

Leveraging IMADV: A Practical Example

Now that IMADV has been installed successfully, let's immediately put it to good use against a sample application workload comprising several of the most resource-intensive queries from among the 99 standard TPC-queries.

Capturing an Application Workload for Analysis

The application workload will be generated using Swingbench against a sample database containing approximately 3GB of TPC-DS data loaded into the standard TPC-DS schema as described in Chapter 2. During workload generation, the In-Memory Area will be disabled by setting initialization parameter `INMEMORY_SIZE` to a value of zero (0). The sample workload will run for 30 minutes to give Swingbench a chance to execute each query at least once during the evaluation period.

We can capture the generated workload live by leveraging procedure `DBMS_SQLTUNE.SELECT_CURSOR_CACHE` to locate all SQL statements executed through Swingbench as the TPC-DS schema owner, as shown next. The resulting SQL Tuning Set can then be fed directly into IMADV for later analysis to reduce contention for database resources while other workloads are being executed.

```
SET SERVEROUTPUT ON;
DECLARE
    cur DBMS_SQLTUNE.SQLSET_CURSOR;
BEGIN
    BEGIN
        DBMS_SQLTUNE.DROP_SQLSET('STS_IMADV_100');
    END;
```

```
DBMS_SQLTUNE.CREATE_SQLSET('STS_IMADV_100','TPC-DS Pre-InMemory');
OPEN cur FOR
    SELECT VALUE(P)
      FROM table(
        DBMS_SQLTUNE.SELECT_CURSOR_CACHE(
        'parsing_schema_name = ''TPCDS'' \
         and module = ''Swingbench User Thread'''
         ,NULL,NULL,NULL,NULL,1,NULL,ALL')) P;
DBMS_SQLTUNE.LOAD_SQLSET(
    sqlset_name => 'STS_IMADV_100'
   ,populate_cursor => cur);
CLOSE cur;
END;
/
```

Another way to capture the application workload into a SQL Tuning Set is shown next. This method leverages procedure DBMS_SQLTUNE.CAPTURE_CURSOR_ CACHE_SQLSET to query the database instance's library cache every 5 seconds for 1800 seconds (that is, 30 minutes) while the workload is executing; it also filters out any SQL statement that isn't being executed by user TPCDS through the Swingbench application workload generator.

```
SET SERVEROUTPUT ON;
DECLARE
    cur DBMS_SQLTUNE.SQLSET_CURSOR;
BEGIN
    BEGIN
        DBMS_SQLTUNE.DROP_SQLSET('STS_IMADV_100');
    END;

    DBMS_SQLTUNE.CREATE_SQLSET('STS_IMADV_100','TPC-DS Pre-InMemory');
    DBMS_SQLTUNE.CAPTURE_CURSOR_CACHE_SQLSET(
        sqlset_name => 'STS_IMADV_100'
       ,time_limit => 1800
       ,repeat_interval => 5
       ,capture_option => 'UPDATE'
       ,capture_mode => DBMS_SQLTUNE.MODE_REPLACE_OLD_STATS
       ,basic_filter => 'parsing_schema_name = ''TPCDS'' \
                  and module = ''Swingbench User Thread'''
       ,sqlset_owner => 'SYS'
       ,recursive_sql => DBMS_SQLTUNE.NO_RECURSIVE_SQL
    );
END;
/
```

Yet another alternative is to capture the SQL Tuning Set from the AWR repository itself using procedure `DBMS_SQLTUNE.SELECT_WORKLOAD_REPOSITORY`, as demonstrated in Chapter 3. This approach to SQL statement capture is recommended when capturing longer duration workloads, with one caveat: Because an AWR snapshot by default retains only the top 30 SQL statements consuming database resources, it's not unlikely that at least some SQL statements that were truly part of the application workload may be excluded from capture. To override this default behavior, an Oracle DBA can generate a custom AWR snapshot specific to the timeframe during which the application workload is running. The following code will capture all SQL statements in the library cache as well as detailed execution statistics:

```
EXEC DBMS_WORKLOAD_REPOSITORY.CREATE_SNAPSHOT('ALL');
```

NOTE
Depending on how long these original application workload performance statistics may need to be retained for analysis, it is probably worth considering the creation of an AWR baseline that comprises these two snapshot periods via procedure `DBMS_WORKLOAD_REPOSITORY.CREATE_BASELINE`.

Generating IMADV Advice: Constructing an IMADV Task
Our next step is to pass the captured SQL Tuning Set to IMADV and render advice on the size of the In-Memory Area as well as exactly which database objects would most benefit from placement within the IMCS. The following script implements the creation and execution of an IMADV task named `IMADV_TPCDS`:

```
SET SERVEROUTPUT ON;
DECLARE
    sql_coverage_pct NUMBER;
BEGIN
    BEGIN
        DBMS_INMEMORY_ADVISOR.DROP_TASK (
            task_name =>'IMADV_TPCDS'
            ,force=>TRUE);
    END;
    -- Create IMA task
    DBMS_INMEMORY_ADVISOR.CREATE_TASK (
        task_name =>'IMADV_TPCDS'
        ,task_desc  => 'In-Memory Advisor Analysis - TPC-DS Simulated Workload ');
    -- Add SQL statements into IMA task from SQL Tuning Set:
```

```
        DBMS_INMEMORY_ADVISOR.ADD_SQLSET(
            task_name =>'IMADV_TPCDS'
            ,sqlset_name => 'STS_IMADV_100'
            ,sqlset_owner => 'SYS');
        -- Add AWR statistics into IMA task:
        DBMS_INMEMORY_ADVISOR.ADD_STATISTICS (
            task_name =>'IMADV_TPCDS'
            ,capture_window_start => SYSTIMESTAMP - 60
            ,capture_window_end => SYSTIMESTAMP);
        -- Capture ASH coverage percentage:
        sql_coverage_pct := DBMS_INMEMORY_ADVISOR.ASH_SQL_COVERAGE_PCT(
            task_name =>'IMADV_TPCDS');
        DBMS_OUTPUT.PUT_LINE (
            'ASH SQL Coverage Percentage: ' || sql_coverage_pct);
        -- Execute IMA task
        DBMS_INMEMORY_ADVISOR.EXECUTE_TASK(task_name =>'IMADV_TPCDS');
        -- Generate IMA recommendations
        DBMS_INMEMORY_ADVISOR.GENERATE_RECOMMENDATIONS(
            task_name =>'IMADV_TPCDS'
            ,single_page_report => TRUE);
END;
/
```

Let's step through this script to understand exactly what it accomplishes through calls to the `DBMS_INMEMORY_ADVISOR` package's functions and procedures:

1. Should an IMADV task named `IMADV_TPCDS` already exist, it is deleted by calling the `DROP_TASK` procedure.

2. Procedure `CREATE_TASK` creates a new IMADV task named `IMADV_TPCDS`.

3. A SQL Tuning Set named `STS_IMADV_100` is added to task `IMADV_TPCDS` via the `ADD_SQLSET` procedure.

4. Any available ASH statistics from the AWR repository are also added to `IMADV_TPCDS` via the `ADD_STATISTICS` procedure, and the percentage of those statistics' availability versus the SQL statements captured from the SQL Tuning Set are calculated and captured via function `ASH_SQL_COVERAGE_PCT`.

5. Finally, procedure `EXECUTE_TASK` executes the IMADV task, and procedure `GENERATE_RECOMMENDATIONS` generates both the HTML version of the IMADV report as well as a SQL script to implement IMADV recommendations for object placement.

IMADV: Adjusting Performance and Fine-Tuning Recommendations

The latest version of IMADV offers several parameters that can modify the way recommendations are performed, as well as adjust its impact on the targeted database's performance. These parameters are summarized in Table 13-2.

Factor	Description
MIN_OVERALL_BENEFIT_FACTOR	A threshold that determines whether any useful recommendations will be produced. The default value of 1.05 means that the total performance benefit for both analytic and nonanalytic processing must exceed 105 percent; otherwise, no recommendations are created.
MIN_INMEMORY_OBJECT_SIZE	Sets the minimum size of a database object for consideration for placement within the IMCS. The default value is 65536 (64KB).
FAVOR_HIGH_COMPRESSION	When set to its default value (0), IMADV tends to favor reduction in analytic workload execution time over increased In-Memory compression; setting this parameter to 1 favors higher compression instead.
LOB_BENEFIT_REDUCTION	Controls how IMADV treats large objects (LOBs) as candidates for the IMCS. The default value (1.0) tells IMADV to favor LOBs stored completely inline within their tables.
INMEMORY_READ_PERF_FACTOR	Adjusts the expected benefit of DBIM so that the database's read activity for an object will be at least n times faster by implementing DBIM. The default value is 10 (that is, 10X improvement).
INMEMORY_WRITE_PERF_FACTOR	Adjusts the expected benefit of DBIM so that the database's write activity for an object will be no more than n times slower by implementing DBIM. The default value is 0.9 (no more than 10 percent degradation, or 90 percent of the original performance observed).
INMEMORY_CPU_PERF_FACTOR	Adjusts the expected benefit of DBIM so that the CPU activity spent processing a given object will be at least n times faster by implementing DBIM. The default value is 2 (2X improvement).

TABLE 13-2.   *IMADV Performance Factors*

Factor	Description
SUPPRESS_LIVE_STATISTICS	Controls the scope of data gathered during IMADV task execution against a live workload: ■ If set to F (false, the default), IMADV will gather both live data from the active workload as well as execution statistics already stored within the AWR. ■ If set to T (true), IMADV will capture data only from the AWR-resident execution statistics, thus significantly reducing the volume of data analyzed and speeding IMADV analysis at the cost of more accurate results.

TABLE 13-2. *IMADV Performance Factors (continued)*

Reviewing IMADV Recommendations

Once the IMADV task has completed execution, it's time to turn attention to its results. IMADV produces two key artifacts, both of which will be written to whichever directory you specified when installing IMADV:

■ An HTML-based report that highlights the recommended size for the IMCS, a list of which database objects are most likely to benefit from placement within the IMCS, and the rationale behind IMADV's recommendations for object placement

■ A ready-to-run SQL script that implements the placement of those objects into the IMCS

NOTE
If no directory path was specified during IMADV installation, the default directory is the path assigned to the DATA_PUMP_DIR directory object for the target database.

Exploring and Interpreting the IMADV HTML Report

The following sections describe a sample In-Memory Advisor report that was generated from the supplied application workload, including actual report content.

Workload Database Usage   The first section of the HTML report (shown in Figure 13-3) summarizes some basic statistics, including the target database's database time spent processing analytical workloads versus the total database time for the analyzed time period. This metric provides a reasonably fair gauge of whether there will be any positive impact on the selected application workload; obviously, the more analytic the workload, the larger the benefit that should be attainable by placing at least some database objects within the IMCS.

In-Memory Sizes   The report section shown in Figure 13-4 offers recommendations for INMEMORY_SIZE in decreasing magnitude and provides estimates of how much more efficient analytical processing will be if the estimated IMCS size should be chosen. While a mere 1.9X performance improvement may seem minimal, recall

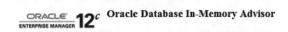

ORACLE ENTERPRISE MANAGER **12**^{c} **Oracle Database In-Memory Advisor**

Advisor Objectives

The In-Memory database feature can be employed to improve the performance of a variety of database operations, the greatest of which is analytics processing.

The objective of the In-Memory Advisor is to produce recommendations to optimize analytics processing. As with SQL optimizer cost estimates, estimates for In-Memory sizes and performance benefits need not be precise in order to produce optimal In-Memory configurations.

Workload Database Usage

Total Database Time (Seconds)	Analytics Processing Time (Seconds)	Analytics Processing Percentage
1206830	400840	33%

FIGURE 13-3.   *Workload Database Usage*

In-Memory Sizes

Up to an application-specific limit, larger In-Memory sizes will result in greater analytics processing performance improvements.

The In-Memory Advisor first produces a list of In-Memory sizes and estimated analytics processing performance improvement factors. These estimates are based on statistics captured from your database while your application was running.

For this report, the default In-Memory size (the largest In-Memory recommendation size) is 619.1MB.

In-Memory Size	Percentage of Maximum SGA Size (12.00GB)	Estimated Analytics Processing Time Reduction (Seconds)	Estimated Analytics Processing Performance Improvement Factor
619.1MB	5%	186094	1.9X
588.2MB	5%	185686	1.9X
557.2MB	5%	185307	1.9X
526.3MB	4%	172434	1.8X
495.3MB	4%	167543	1.7X
464.4MB	4%	167543	1.7X
433.4MB	4%	152849	1.6X
402.4MB	3%	152849	1.6X
371.5MB	3%	152012	1.6X
340.5MB	3%	149629	1.6X
309.6MB	3%	136508	1.5X
278.6MB	2%	111303	1.4X
247.7MB	2%	111303	1.4X
216.7MB	2%	111303	1.4X
185.7MB	2%	109303	1.4X
154.8MB	1%	86270	1.3X
123.8MB	1%	86270	1.3X
92.87MB	1%	83272	1.3X
61.91MB	1%	65998	1.2X
30.96MB	0%	43020	1.1X

FIGURE 13-4. *In-Memory sizing recommendations*

that the TPCDS schema we used to produce this example is quite small, so the majority of the data would easily fit into the 2GB allocated for the IMCS once it's been compressed for In-Memory usage.

Top 10 SQL Statements   A typical analytic workload could potentially encompass hundreds of different SQL statements, so the next report section (see Figure 13-5) focuses on the top ten statements that would most benefit if the recommended database objects were placed within the IMCS, in descending order of improved performance.

The following recommendations are designed to optimize your database application's analytics processing with the default 619.1MB In-Memory size which is the largest In-Memory recommendation size.

With 619.1MB, Top 10 SQL Statements With Analytics Processing Benefit

SQL Id	SQL Text	Analytics Processing Time Used (Seconds)	Estimated Analytics Processing Time Reduction (Seconds) With Unlimited Memory	Estimated Analytics Processing Performance Improvement Factor With Unlimited Memory	Estimated Analytics Processing Time Reduction (Seconds) With 619.1MB	Estimated Analytics Processing Performance Improvement Factor With 619.1MB
0ytvuzcgakgm2	/*QUERY22*/ select /*query22*/ i_product_name ,i_brand ,i...	5900	4940	6.1X	4940	6.1X
68h05n473pjxw	/*QUERY21*/ select /*query21*/ * from (select w_warehouse_name ,i_item_id ...	6330	4958	4.6X	4958	4.6X
bzhn573du0pju	/*QUERY77*/ with ss as (select s_store_sk, sum(ss_ext_sales_price) as sales, s...	8270	5845	3.4X	5845	3.4X
g0czub2fum2zu	/*QUERY49*/ select /*query49*/ 'web' as channel ,web.item ,web.return_ratio ,web.return_rank ...	7170	4910	3.2X	4910	3.2X
66ky9kdg6z2h2	/*QUERY80*/ with ssr as (select s_store_id as store_id, sum(ss_ext_sales_price) as sa...	5190	3504	3.1X	3504	3.1X
7hf33494g4agu	/*QUERY05*/ WITH ssr as (SELECT s_store_id, SUM(sales_price) AS sales, ...	13940	7762	2.3X	7762	2.3X
fvh06x3abxc1b	/*QUERY75*/ WITH all_sales AS (SELECT d_year ,i_brand_id ,i_class_id ,i_ca...	12780	6237	2.0X	6237	2.0X
g73kh0v5021q1	/*QUERY39.1*/ with inv as (select w_warehouse_name,w_warehouse_sk,i_item _sk,d_moy ...	10440	4344	1.7X	4344	1.7X
3jupx9x1y69qp	/*QUERY37*/ select /*query37*/ i_item_id ,i_item_desc ,i_current_price from ...	210	88	1.7X	88	1.7X
016cx8hddypga	/*QUERY39.2*/ with inv as (select w_warehouse_name,w_warehouse_sk,i_item _sk,d_moy ,stdev,...	10240	3966	1.6X	3966	1.6X

Click here to view all 19 SQL Statements that are estimated to have a performance improvement factor with In-Memory size = 619.1MB.

FIGURE 13-5.   *Top 10 benefactor SQL statements*

NOTE
One nice feature of IMADV 2.0 is that each section of the report contains useful help information that's available just by mousing over the corresponding heading of each section. If a report section wasn't generated, mousing over the section heading provides some useful advice for regenerating the IMADV task to capture additional data that's desired.

Top 10 Objects Complementing the prior report section, this part of the report (see Figure 13-6) lists the database objects that should be placed within the IMCS in descending order of a computed cost-to-benefit ratio for analytic workload

With 619.1MB, Top 10 Objects Recommended To Place In-Memory For Analytics Processing

Object Type	Object	Compression Type	Estimated In-Memory Size	Analytics Processing Seconds	Estimated Reduced Analytics Processing Seconds	Estimated Analytics Processing Performance Improvement Factor	Benefit / Cost Ratio (Reduced Analytics Processing / In-Memory Size)
TABLE	TPCDS.DATE_DIM	Memory compress for query low	2.229MB	63239	42169	3.0X	1127 : 1
TABLE	TPCDS.HOUSEHOLD_DEMOGRAPHICS	Memory compress for query low	1.063MB	1231	851	3.2X	764 : 1
TABLE	TPCDS.WEB_SALES	Memory compress for query low	55.57MB	28080	20778	3.8X	357 : 1
TABLE	TPCDS.CUSTOMER_ADDRESS	Memory compress for query low	2.174MB	16539	11026	3.0X	302 : 1
TABLE	TPCDS.INVENTORY	Memory compress for query low	93.81MB	28844	25310	8.2X	257 : 1
TABLE	TPCDS.CATALOG_SALES	Memory compress for query low	111.3MB	34903	26820	4.3X	230 : 1
TABLE	TPCDS.CUSTOMER	Memory compress for query low	3.920MB	19436	13001	3.0X	198 : 1
TABLE	TPCDS.STORE_SALES	Memory compress for query low	142.9MB	38596	29489	4.2X	197 : 1
TABLE	TPCDS.ITEM	Memory compress for query low	1.987MB	4484	2989	3.0X	90 : 1
TABLE	TPCDS.CUSTOMER_DEMOGRAPHICS	Memory compress for query low	24.73MB	18139	12225	3.1X	29 : 1

Click here to view all 15 objects that are estimated to have a performance improvement factor with In-Memory size = 619.1MB.

FIGURE 13-6. *Top 10 objects recommended for IMCS*

improvement. Interestingly, this example shows that placing two TPC-DS dimension tables into the IMCS—DATE_DIM and HOUSEHOLD_DEMOGRAPHICS—offered the best cost–benefit ratio. That's not too surprising, because these two dimensions are used in almost every query in the generated application workload; of course, for most data warehousing application workloads, a date/time dimension is used heavily for filtering purposes.

Database Details At this point, the IMADV report shifts its focus from advice to information. The report section in Figure 13-7 shows pertinent details of the database environment and the scope of the application workload used to produce the IMADV analysis.

Database For Which The In-Memory Advisor Optimized

Oracle Database Name	NCDB1
Oracle Database Identifier	3983841919
Oracle Database Creation Date	30-JAN-17
Oracle Database Instance Name	NCDB1
Oracle Database Instance Number	1
Oracle Database Instance Version	Oracle Database 12c Enterprise Edition Release 12.2.0.1.0 - 64bit Production
SGA Maximum Size	12.00GB
In-Memory Size	0.000B
Unused In-Memory Space	0.000B
Oracle Database In-Memory Advisor	Version 2.0.0.1.0 Build #1064.1 Build date 2016-JUN-08 13:41:40 Installation date 2017-FEB-06 08:41:52
Capture Start Time	2017-JAN-30 08:49:05
Capture End Time	2017-FEB-06 14:31:51
Report Date	2017-FEB-06 14:38:10

Click here to view the DDL script that implements the above described recommendations.

FIGURE 13-7. *Database details*

All SQL Statements   Any SQL statement that would receive at least some benefit from implementing all object placement recommendations is listed in Figure 13-8.

All Recommended Objects   Likewise, all database objects that would fit within the recommended size of the IMCS are shown in the next report section (Figure 13-9).

With 619.1MB, All 19 SQL Statements With Analytics Processing Benefit

SQL Id	SQL Text	Analytics Processing Time Used (Seconds)	Estimated Analytics Processing Time Reduction (Seconds) With Unlimited Memory	Estimated Analytics Processing Performance Improvement Factor With Unlimited Memory	Estimated Analytics Processing Time Reduction (Seconds) With 619.1MB	Estimated Analytics Processing Performance Improvement Factor With 619.1MB
0ytvuzcgakgm2	/*QUERY22*/ select /*query22*/ i_product_name ,i_brand ,i...	5900	4940	6.1X	4940	6.1X
68h05n473pjxw	/*QUERY21*/ select /*query21*/ * from (select w_warehouse_name ,i_item_id ...	6330	4958	4.6X	4958	4.6X
bzhn573du0pju	/*QUERY77*/ with ss as (select s_store_sk, sum(ss_ext_sales_price) as sales, s...	8270	5845	3.4X	5845	3.4X
g0czub2fum2zu	/*QUERY49*/ select /*query49*/ 'web' as channel ,web.item ,web.return_ratio ,web.return_rank ...	7170	4910	3.2X	4910	3.2X
66ky9kdg6z2h2	/*QUERY80*/ with ssr as (select s_store_id as store_id, sum(ss_ext_sales_price) as sa...	5190	3504	3.1X	3504	3.1X
7hf33494g4agu	/*QUERY05*/ WITH ssr as (SELECT s_store_id, SUM(sales_price) AS sales, ...	13940	7762	2.3X	7762	2.3X
fvh06x3abxc1b	/*QUERY75*/ WITH all_sales AS (SELECT d_year ,i_brand_id ,i_class_id ,i_ca...	12780	6237	2.0X	6237	2.0X
g73kh0v5021q1	/*QUERY39.1*/ with inv as (select w_warehouse_name,w_warehouse_sk,i_item_sk,d_moy ...	10440	4344	1.7X	4344	1.7X
3jupx9x1y69qp	/*QUERY37*/ select /*query37*/ i_item_id ,i_item_desc ,i_current_price from ...	210	88	1.7X	88	1.7X
016cx8hddypga	/*QUERY39.2*/ with inv as (select w_warehouse_name,w_warehouse_sk,i_item_sk,d_moy ,stdev,...	10240	3966	1.6X	3966	1.6X
8sbq8cw24d68x	/*QUERY72*/ select /*query72*/ i_item_desc ,w_warehouse_name ,d1.d_week_seq ,su...	30530	6948	1.3X	6948	1.3X
2947rd02bkfb2	/*QUERY13*/ select /*query13*/ avg(ss_quantity) ,avg(ss_ext_sales_price) ,a...	50	7	1.2X	7	1.2X
gg6xmcpdxmhx0	/*QUERY04*/ with year_total as (select c_customer_id customer_id ,c_firs...	10030	540	1.1X	540	1.1X
	/*QUERY14.1*/ WITH cross_items AS					

FIGURE 13-8.   *All SQL statements yielding analytics processing benefits*

With 619.1MB, All 15 Objects Recommended To Place In-Memory For Analytics Processing

Object Type	Object	Compression Type	Estimated In-Memory Size	Analytics Processing Seconds	Estimated Reduced Analytics Processing Seconds	Estimated Analytics Processing Performance Improvement Factor	Benefit / Cost Ratio (Reduced Analytics Processing / In-Memory Size)
TABLE	TPCDS.DATE_DIM	Memory compress for query low	2.229MB	63239	42169	3.0X	1127:1
TABLE	TPCDS.HOUSEHOLD_DEMOGRAPHICS	Memory compress for query low	1.063MB	1231	851	3.2X	764:1
TABLE	TPCDS.WEB_SALES	Memory compress for query low	55.57MB	28080	20778	3.8X	357:1
TABLE	TPCDS.CUSTOMER_ADDRESS	Memory compress for query low	2.174MB	16539	11026	3.0X	302:1
TABLE	TPCDS.INVENTORY	Memory compress for query low	93.81MB	28844	25310	8.2X	257:1
TABLE	TPCDS.CATALOG_SALES	Memory compress for query low	111.3MB	34903	26820	4.3X	230:1
TABLE	TPCDS.CUSTOMER	Memory compress for query low	3.920MB	19436	13001	3.0X	198:1
TABLE	TPCDS.STORE_SALES	Memory compress for query low	142.9MB	38596	29489	4.2X	197:1
TABLE	TPCDS.ITEM	Memory compress for query low	1.987MB	4484	2989	3.0X	90:1
TABLE	TPCDS.CUSTOMER_DEMOGRAPHICS	Memory compress for query low	24.73MB	18139	12225	3.1X	29:1
TABLE	TPCDS.CATALOG_PAGE	Memory compress for query low	1.063MB	204	136	3.0X	22:1
TABLE	TPCDS.STORE_RETURNS	Memory compress for query low	23.38MB	717	511	3.5X	21:1
TABLE	TPCDS.CATALOG_RETURNS	Memory compress for query low	24.44MB	568	379	3.0X	15:1
TABLE	TPCDS.WEB_RETURNS	Memory compress for query low	25.50MB	557	372	3.0X	14:1
TABLE	TPCDS.TIME_DIM	Memory compress for query low	1.854MB	56	37	3.0X	1:1

FIGURE 13-9. *All objects yielding analytics processing benefits*

Recommended Rationales IMADV shows a bit more of what it's doing under the covers to perform its analysis in the next report section, shown in Figure 13-10. These rationales offer some insight into why IMADV intelligently discarded some database objects from consideration because they offered little analytic processing benefit. It is interesting to note that IMADV has determined that six database objects are considered ineligible for placement within the IMCS because they're simply not large enough for Database In-Memory features to take advantage of, as this query against DBA_IMA_RECOMMENDATIONS shows:

```
COL table_name   FORMAT A14      HEADING "Table Name"
COL uncmpr_mb    FORMAT 99.999   HEADING "Uncomp-|ressed|Size|(MB)"
```

```
COL rationale    FORMAT A54      HEADING "Rationale" WRAP
SELECT
     table_name
    ,(uncompressed_bytes / (1024*1024)) uncmpr_mb
    ,rationale
  FROM dba_ima_recommendations
 WHERE rationale LIKE '%too small%'
 ORDER BY 1;

            Uncomp-
            ressed
            Size
Table Name  (MB) Rationale
----------- ----- ---------------------------------------------------------
CALL_CENTER .002 Size is too small to be eligible for In-Memory placement
PROMOTION   .051 Size is too small to be eligible for In-Memory placement
SHIP_MODE   .002 Size is too small to be eligible for In-Memory placement
STORE       .004 Size is too small to be eligible for In-Memory placement
WAREHOUSE   .001 Size is too small to be eligible for In-Memory placement
WEB_SITE    .018 Size is too small to be eligible for In-Memory placement
```

Recommendation Rationale Summary

Rationale	Candidate Count
Fits along with any other objects recommended to be placed into in-memory storage with the inmemory_size used in this report and resulting in an estimated additional DB time reduction	15
Would fit along with any other objects recommended to be placed into in-memory storage with an even smaller inmemory_size than the one used in this report and resulting in an estimated additional DB time reduction; but with the larger inmemory_size used in this report, a related recommendation provides greater benefit	11
Object is either owned by a system user or its type is not eligible for in-memory placement	128
Size is too small to be eligible for In-Memory placement	6
All partitions within this table are estimated to have a similar benefit; therefore, only the entire table will be considered as a candidate	356
The estimated benefit of placing this object in the in-memory store shows no reduction in DB time	114
The estimated benefit of placing this object with this compression type into the in-memory store does not exceed the estimated benefits of other recommendations related to this object	476

FIGURE 13-10. *Recommendation rationales*

> ### *Recommendation Implementation SQL Script*
>
> *The following shows the recommended DDL statements for In-Memory placement.*
>
> ALTER TABLE "TPCDS"."DATE_DIM" INMEMORY MEMCOMPRESS FOR QUERY LOW;
>
> ALTER TABLE "TPCDS"."STORE_SALES" INMEMORY MEMCOMPRESS FOR QUERY LOW;
>
> ALTER TABLE "TPCDS"."CATALOG_SALES" INMEMORY MEMCOMPRESS FOR QUERY LOW;
>
> ALTER TABLE "TPCDS"."INVENTORY" INMEMORY MEMCOMPRESS FOR QUERY LOW;
>
> ALTER TABLE "TPCDS"."WEB_SALES" INMEMORY MEMCOMPRESS FOR QUERY LOW;
>
> ALTER TABLE "TPCDS"."CUSTOMER" INMEMORY MEMCOMPRESS FOR QUERY LOW;
>
> ALTER TABLE "TPCDS"."CUSTOMER_DEMOGRAPHICS" INMEMORY MEMCOMPRESS FOR QUERY LOW;
>
> ALTER TABLE "TPCDS"."CUSTOMER_ADDRESS" INMEMORY MEMCOMPRESS FOR QUERY LOW;
>
> ALTER TABLE "TPCDS"."ITEM" INMEMORY MEMCOMPRESS FOR QUERY LOW;
>
> ALTER TABLE "TPCDS"."HOUSEHOLD_DEMOGRAPHICS" INMEMORY MEMCOMPRESS FOR QUERY LOW;
>
> ALTER TABLE "TPCDS"."STORE_RETURNS" INMEMORY MEMCOMPRESS FOR QUERY LOW;
>
> ALTER TABLE "TPCDS"."CATALOG_RETURNS" INMEMORY MEMCOMPRESS FOR QUERY LOW;
>
> ALTER TABLE "TPCDS"."WEB_RETURNS" INMEMORY MEMCOMPRESS FOR QUERY LOW;
>
> ALTER TABLE "TPCDS"."CATALOG_PAGE" INMEMORY MEMCOMPRESS FOR QUERY LOW;
>
> ALTER TABLE "TPCDS"."TIME_DIM" INMEMORY MEMCOMPRESS FOR QUERY LOW;

FIGURE 13-11. *Script to implement recommendations*

Implementation of Recommendations　At last, the report section in Figure 13-11 provides an Oracle DBA with something truly actionable: a complete list of SQL commands that implement the recommendations. Note that these same SQL statements are also provided in a ready-to-run script that will be named the same as the IMADV task (imadvisor_IMADV_TPCDS.sql).

Summary

Oracle Database 12.1.0.2 was the first release to offer the revolutionary features of the In-Memory Column Store (IMCS) that enables an Oracle DBA to lace selected database objects frequently used as targets of analytical queries into a special area of the SGA. This enables the capabilities of the Database In-Memory option to act upon data stored in columnar format with extreme efficiency, especially when filtering, joining, or performing aggregations against the typically huge volumes of data in a modern data warehouse.

This chapter first summarized the key concepts behind Oracle 12*c* Database In-Memory concepts, including a brief review of the latest improvements available in Oracle 12.2.0.1, and then explored the latest features of In-Memory Advisor (IMADV) 2.0 to help any Oracle DBA to eliminate guesswork when sizing the IMCS. It also offered an example of how IMADV can help an Oracle DBA determine with a high degree of confidence which database objects should be placed within the IMCS so that an application workload receives the most benefit from this optionally licensed feature set.

CHAPTER
14

In-Memory Central

As Chapter 13 has shown, the Oracle Database In-Memory Advisor (IMADV) makes short work of determining which database objects would most benefit from being placed within the In-Memory Column Store (IMCS). However, it's equally important for Oracle DBAs to be able to monitor the status of objects that have been placed within the IMCS. The good news is that Oracle 12*c*R2 introduced an extremely valuable tool called *In-Memory Central* as part of Oracle Enterprise Manager 13*c* Cloud Control that makes it extremely simple for an Oracle DBA to monitor the state of all objects within the IMCS as well as determine how effectively a database object is able to take advantage of IMCS.

Oracle Database 12*c*R2: Database In-Memory Enhancements

Before we discuss the power and features of In-Memory Central, let's take a brief look at some of the newest features of Database In-Memory (DBIM) in Oracle 12*c*R2 and how In-Memory Central becomes even more useful once those features are understood.

DBIM: Architectural Enhancements

Oracle Database 12*c* Release 2 has improved DBIM significantly; in fact, there are so many new features that Oracle has created a separate *In-Memory Guide* of more than 200 pages in length to encompass them. We will therefore concentrate on the features most likely to be important to Oracle DBAs who are already familiar with the DBIM features introduced in Oracle Release 12*c*R1.

IMCS: Architecture Enhancements

Oracle 12*c*R2 introduced significant improvements to the IMCS that dramatically expand its capabilities. The enhanced memory architecture of the IMCS is shown in Figure 14-1. The most significant improvement is the new *In-Memory Expression Unit* (IMEU) because it dramatically expands the efficiency of queries that employ expressions and functions for analytic processing as well as for complex filtering criteria.

In-Memory Expressions

Each IMEU is linked to an existing *In-Memory Compression Unit* (IMCU) that contains data for the corresponding database object. An IMEU contains something quite different, however: one or more expressions related to the database object. IMEUs were implemented to enable Oracle 12*c*R2 to capture frequently used expressions in queries—for example, the result of a complex analytic function that returns a deterministic result. These In-Memory Expressions (IMEs) also permit

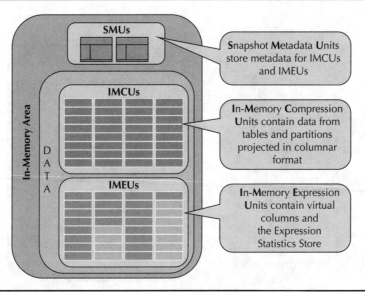

FIGURE 14-1. *IMCS: enhanced architecture in Oracle 12cR2*

capturing and storing the resulting expression that is mapped when a table employs a virtual column—for example, the difference between the values stored within columns SS_LIST_PRICE and SS_SALES_PRICE in table TPCDS.STORE_SALES.

These IMEs are retained within the *Expression Statistics Store* (ESS), a collection of metadata as well as statistics on how often an IME has been accessed. The Oracle optimizer leverages the ESS as it decides the optimal path to accessing data for a SQL statement; if an expression has already been populated into IMEUs within the IMCS, the optimizer will definitely consider leveraging it instead of building the expression from scratch, thus saving valuable CPU cycles during statement execution.

As Figure 14-1 shows, Oracle 12cR2 also added one other new structure to the IMCS—*Snapshot Metadata Units* (SMUs)—that contains all the metadata for and are used to keep track of the corresponding contents and status of both IMCUs and IMEUs.

In-Memory Join Improvements: Join Groups
Every IMCU has a local dictionary that contains references to the data values actually stored within it. Consider a table containing sales data that references a geographical region, for example, with one column of that table named COUNTRY that describes where the sale occurred. Each value for COUNTRY is retained within a separate column unit within the IMCU, but each distinct value is assigned a code within that IMCU's local dictionary, as shown in Figure 14-2. Because the local

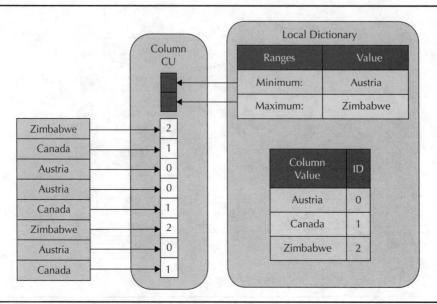

FIGURE 14-2. *IMCU column unit and local dictionary*

dictionary identifies the minimum and maximum values within each IMCU, it is extremely efficient for a query that is searching only for sales made in Austria first to interrogate the IMCU's local dictionary for that value; if nothing is found, the IMCU can be ignored.

Of course, not every IMCU will contain every possible value for COUNTRY as all other IMCUs, so the IMCU's local dictionary becomes much less valuable when performing In-Memory Joins between tables, especially hash joins. For example, invoking a hash join on COUNTRY between two or more tables involves first decompressing the actual values for COUNTRY within each IMCU, then adding those values to a separate hash table for each data source, and then probing that hash table for matches between the data sources. Unfortunately, performing a hash join using a hash join table is significantly less efficient than applying a Bloom filter to determine whether two sets have elements in common.

Oracle 12cR2 overcomes this issue through a new object called a *join group* that essentially stores all values for columns most typically used in join operations between tables in a common directory constructed within the PGA. A join group between two tables stores a common code for each value for all IMCUs, so in the aforementioned scenario, the join group itself is probed for the matching values, and this avoids the considerable overhead of building a hash table to accomplish the hash join. In some ways, therefore, a join group is similar in function to a bitmap join index—except, of course, a join group doesn't require any physical storage or costly processing to create and maintain it.

An Oracle DBA can create a join group using the new `CREATE INMEMORY JOIN GROUP` command. For example, here's a join group created between two tables in the TPC-DS schema, `STORE_SALES` and `CUSTOMER_DEMOGRAPHICS`, using the columns commonly used to join them together:

```
CREATE INMEMORY JOIN GROUP tpcds.jg_ss_cdemo (
    tpcds.store_sales (ss_cdemo_sk)
    ,tpcds.customer_demographics (cd_demo_sk)
);
```

NOTE
There are some additional restrictions on join groups, and detecting whether a query has definitely used a join group is a bit tricky. For more in-depth information, consult the Oracle 12cR2 In-Memory Guide.

Information Lifecycle Management Policies for In-Memory Objects

Oracle 12.1.0.1 introduced the concept of *Information Lifecycle Management* (ILM) *Automatic Data Optimization* (ADO) policies for database objects. ADO makes it simple to compress tables and table partitions, or even move those objects to lower cost storage tiers, as the data within them grows colder over time—not an unusual occurrence in a heavily partitioned data warehouse environment.

The good news for Oracle 12cR2 is that ADO policies can now be constructed for objects targeted for initial retention in the In-Memory Area; even better, they can now be retained with greater intelligence, thus enabling an Oracle DBA to at last use the IMCS as the true Tier 0 in tiered storage:

- Objects can be populated immediately upon creation, or delayed for population until a later date, with an appropriate compression level—for example, `MEMCOMPRESS FOR QUERY LOW`—when used frequently.

- Objects already populated within the IMCS can change their priority—say, from `HIGH` to `MEDIUM`—as their usage is diminished. This permits other segments with a higher priority to remain in the IMCS or have more of their partitions retained if those partitions are actually used more frequently.

- The In-Memory compression ratio of currently populated objects can be adjusted as their usage diminishes. For example, the older data stored a table that's partitioned historically based on a timestamp may not be used as frequently as recently added partitions, so as the data in the older partitions becomes "colder," those less frequently used partitions can still be retained in the IMCS, but with a higher in-memory *compression ratio*—for example, `MEMCOMPRESS FOR CAPACITY LOW`—as they are used less frequently, or even *evicted* from the IMCS if it makes more sense to free up memory for more actively used objects.

We'll delve much more deeply into ADO policies for the IMCS a bit later in this chapter as we demonstrate how to get the best use of In-Memory Central's numerous panels and sections for analysis of activity within the IMCS.

DBIM: Faster Population, Wider Availability

Oracle 12*c*R2 has certainly improved the elegant architecture of DBIM for even faster analytic query processing, but it also addresses the need to repopulate objects as quickly as possible into the IMCS as well as extending IMCS features into the wider arena of today's complex, multi-server systems.

Dynamically Resizable IMCS

When DBIM was originally released in Oracle 12.1.0.2, changing the size of the IMCS required setting a new value for `INMEMORY_SIZE` within the database instance's SPFILE and then restarting the database instance to enforce the new size, which definitely detracted from a highly available database system. In Oracle 12*c*R2, this is finally remedied: `INMEMORY_SIZE` can be increased (but never decreased) dynamically without resorting to "bouncing" the database instance. We'll demonstrate this a bit later in this chapter in the section "Activating Database In-Memory."

Faster IMCS Repopulation: The FastStart Tablespace

Most early adopters of DBIM saw immediate value in populating their heaviest used datasets into the In-Memory Area as soon as possible after an instance first started or needed to be restarted—for example, after an inadvertent RAC node reboot—but were often dissatisfied with how long it took for repopulation to occur.

Oracle 12*c*R2 added the ability to store data that has already been transformed into columnar format within the IMCS to be simultaneously retained in that same format within a new database construct: the *FastStart tablespace* dramatically decreases the time it takes to repopulate data back into the IMCS. Once provisioned and enabled, a FastStart tablespace will retain a copy of any object that is newly populated or repopulated into the IMCS. Upon instance restart, if the database instance detects that a FastStart tablespace has been configured, it will repopulate data back into the IMCS directly from that tablespace, thus bypassing the time-consuming reconstruction of database objects from row-major storage.

This feature will be most beneficial when the database instance is mainly responsible for data warehousing or analytical reporting application workloads instead of transactional workloads, because IMCU column units (CUs) that are most frequently updated may not be refreshed as frequently as their colder cohorts. Its effectiveness will also depend upon how much of the IMCS had actually been populated into the FastStart tablespace when the instance was restarted.

Activating the capabilities of FastStart is simple and involves just two steps: creating the tablespace itself, and then enabling that tablespace as the FastStart tablespace via procedure `DBMS_INMEMORY_ADMIN.FASTSTART_ENABLE`, as shown here:

```
CREATE TABLESPACE faststart
    DATAFILE '+DATA'
    SIZE 1G REUSE
    AUTOEXTEND ON
    NEXT 500K
    MAXSIZE 4G;

BEGIN
    DBMS_INMEMORY_ADMIN.FASTSTART_ENABLE('FASTSTART');
END;
/
```

DBIM and Active Data Guard

One of the most exciting new features in Oracle 12cR2 is that it's now possible to activate DBIM against a separate physical standby database when Active Data Guard has been deployed at the standby site. Since Active Data Guard enables a physical standby database to be open in read-only mode for queries—even while it's still being updated with live data from its primary database—this offers some intriguing possibilities:

- The standby database's IMCS could be populated with the identical objects already present in the IMCS of the primary database, effectively doubling the database connections possible for systems that are primarily focused on intense analytics processing.

- For hybrid systems that combine both online transaction processing (OLTP) and analytic reporting, the reporting workload could be completely offloaded only to the standby's IMCS, thus freeing the primary database to focus on satisfying the transactional demands of OLTP application workloads.

- Finally, because Oracle 12cR2 enables population of completely different sets of objects within the IMCS of the primary and standby databases, the primary database's IMCS could be populated with tables and partitions that were most recently loaded and/or updated, while the standby database's IMCS could retain mainly historical data for in-depth analytical processing.

Overview: In-Memory Central

As this chapter has already illustrated, Oracle 12cR2 Database In-Memory provides an almost dizzying array of features for even the most seasoned Oracle DBA to keep track of. Analytic query effectiveness can certainly be tracked using the scripted solutions or Oracle Enterprise Manager's numerous SQL Advisors that were covered

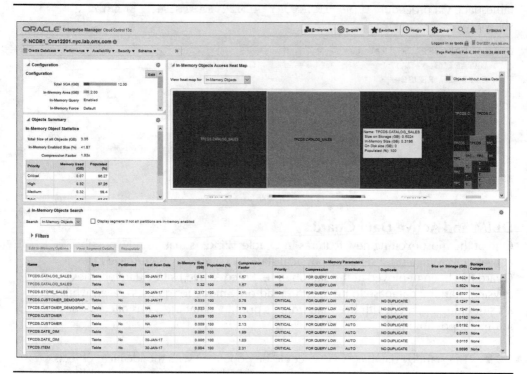

FIGURE 14-3. *In-Memory Central: main page*

in earlier chapters, but what has been missing is a centralized monitoring and governance solution for the In-Memory Area itself as well as the objects populated within it. Fortunately, the new In-Memory Central interface included with Oracle Enterprise Manager 13c Cloud Control fills this gap nicely.

In-Memory Central is accessed by choosing Administration | In-Memory Central. The main page of In-Memory Central is shown in Figure 14-3.

Activating Database In-Memory

Activating Database In-Memory is extremely simple, because it requires setting only one database initialization parameter—INMEMORY_SIZE—to a nonzero value that's larger than 128MB, as shown next. However, this will require a bounce of the database instance, so first we'll have to issue the appropriate ALTER SYSTEM command with a scope of SPFILE; otherwise, the command will fail:

```
SQL> CONN / as sysdba
Connected.
SQL> ALTER SYSTEM SET INMEMORY_SIZE = 1024M;
ALTER SYSTEM SET INMEMORY_SIZE = 1024M
*
```

```
ERROR at line 1:
ORA-02097: parameter cannot be modified because specified value is invalid
ORA-02095: specified initialization parameter cannot be modified

SQL> ALTER SYSTEM SET INMEMORY_SIZE = 1024M SCOPE=SPFILE;

System altered.

SQL> show sga

Total System Global Area 2.5770E+10 bytes
Fixed Size                  8802296 bytes
Variable Size            1.2012E+10 bytes
Database Buffers         1.3690E+10 bytes
Redo Buffers               58306560 bytes
SQL> show parameter inmemory;

NAME                                     TYPE        VALUE
---------------------------------------- ----------- ----------------
inmemory_clause_default                  string
inmemory_expressions_usage               string      ENABLE
inmemory_force                           string      DEFAULT
inmemory_max_populate_servers            integer     0
inmemory_query                           string      ENABLE
inmemory_size                            big integer 0
inmemory_trickle_repopulate_servers_     integer     1
percent
inmemory_virtual_columns                 string      MANUAL
optimizer_inmemory_aware                 boolean     TRUE

SQL> shutdown immediate;
Database closed.
Database dismounted.
ORACLE instance shut down.
SQL> startup;
ORACLE instance started.

Total System Global Area 2.5770E+10 bytes
Fixed Size                  8802296 bytes
Variable Size            1.1878E+10 bytes
Database Buffers         1.0536E+10 bytes
Redo Buffers               58306560 bytes
In-Memory Area           1073741824 bytes
Database mounted.
Database opened.
```

New in 12cR2: Resizing IMCS Dynamically

In 12.1.0.2 it was impossible to resize the IMCS without first changing INMEMORY_SIZE to a new value and then bouncing the database instance. The good news is that in 12.2.0.1, the IMCS is dynamically resizable with one small restriction. For example, attempting to resize an instance's IMCS from its current size of

1024MB to 1100MB by setting `INMEMORY_SIZE` to that new value will fail because the new size increase must be at least 128MB larger than the current size:

```
SQL> ALTER SYSTEM SET INMEMORY_SIZE = 1100M;
ALTER SYSTEM SET INMEMORY_SIZE = 1100M
*
ERROR at line 1:
ORA-02097: parameter cannot be modified because specified value is invalid
ORA-02095: specified initialization parameter cannot be modified
```

Once we've specified a size that is greater than or equal to the current memory allocation plus 128MB, however, the command is accepted:

```
SQL> ALTER SYSTEM SET INMEMORY_SIZE = 2048M;

System altered.

SQL> show sga

Total System Global Area 2.5770E+10 bytes
Fixed Size                  8802296 bytes
Variable Size             1.1610E+10 bytes
Database Buffers          9797894144 bytes
Redo Buffers                58306560 bytes
In-Memory Area            2147483648 bytes
```

One other wrinkle: Resizing the In-Memory Area dynamically to a smaller size is definitely not permitted—which makes sense, because then the database instance would have to start evicting objects from IMCS to accommodate the shrinkage. To illustrate, we'll change `INMEMORY_SIZE` to 888MB and attempt to shrink the IMCS; not unexpectedly, this command fails:

```
SQL> alter system set inmemory_size=888M;
alter system set inmemory_size=888M
*
ERROR at line 1:
ORA-02097: parameter cannot be modified because specified value is invalid
ORA-02095: specified initialization parameter cannot be modified
```

Now that that the IMCS is sized appropriately for demonstration, we'll investigate In-Memory Central as we introduce new objects into the IMCS for the first time as well as run a representative workload against the database instance.

Leveraging In-Memory Central

We're now ready to see the power of In-Memory Central for active monitoring of the IMCS and all objects within it as well as for governance of the IMCS itself. We'll start by adding objects to the IMCS based on the recommendations from the IMADV tasks we ran in Chapter 13, with some minor modifications to make this example a bit more interesting.

Adding Objects to IMCS

Even though the IMCS has been sized to 2GB and is ready to accept new objects, you'll remember that nothing really happens until an application workload requests an object that's targeted for DBIM and then that object's data is populated in columnar format within the IMCS. The following commands add all of the TPCDS schema's dimension tables and all but four of the fact tables to the IMCS; we're reserving some of the fact tables—specifically, INVENTORY, CATALOG_RETURNS, STORE_RETURNS, and WEB_RETURNS—for later population so the impact of not placing those tables into the IMCS will be readily apparent in terms of poorer performance of queries accessing those tables.

```
ALTER TABLE tpcds.call_center
    INMEMORY MEMCOMPRESS FOR QUERY LOW
    PRIORITY CRITICAL;
ALTER TABLE tpcds.catalog_page
    INMEMORY MEMCOMPRESS FOR QUERY LOW
    PRIORITY CRITICAL;
ALTER TABLE tpcds.customer
    INMEMORY MEMCOMPRESS FOR QUERY LOW
    PRIORITY CRITICAL;
. . .
<< remaining dimension tables omitted for sake of brevity >>
. . .
ALTER TABLE tpcds.catalog_sales
    INMEMORY MEMCOMPRESS FOR QUERY LOW
    PRIORITY HIGH;
ALTER TABLE tpcds.store_sales
    INMEMORY MEMCOMPRESS FOR QUERY LOW
    PRIORITY HIGH;
ALTER TABLE tpcds.web_sales
    INMEMORY MEMCOMPRESS FOR QUERY LOW
    PRIORITY HIGH;
```

Once these commands complete, we'll generate a brief workload comprising 13 TPCDS queries that access tables INVENTORY, CATALOG_RETURNS, STORE_RETURNS, and WEB_RETURNS using Swingbench and monitor the results of that workload via OEM Cloud Control 13cR2.

Figure 14-4 shows the status of application workload from the Top Activity screen, accessed via the database's Performance tab. As the Average Active Sessions graph shows, this workload is generating quite a bit of User I/O at the outset because none of the objects were present within IMCS and thus had to be populated first through physical reads from storage.

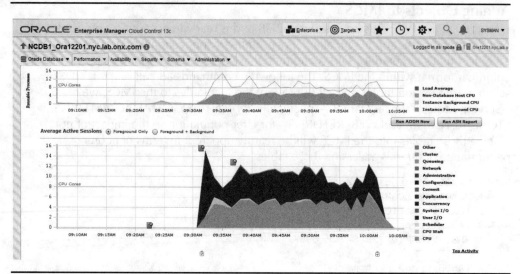

FIGURE 14-4. *Top Activity Page during initial IMCS population*

Once population of the IMCS begins, however, we can take a look at its contents and the status of each object populated within it through In-Memory Central, shown in Figure 14-5. This page is packed full of excellent information about the status of the IMCS, so let's unpack it section by section.

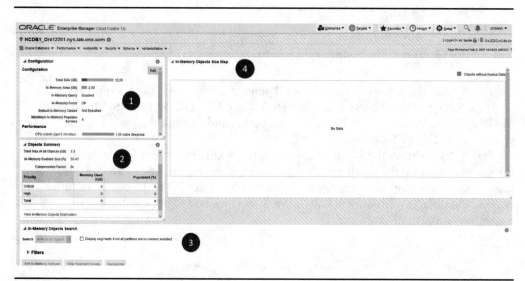

FIGURE 14-5. *In-Memory Central main page, section by section*

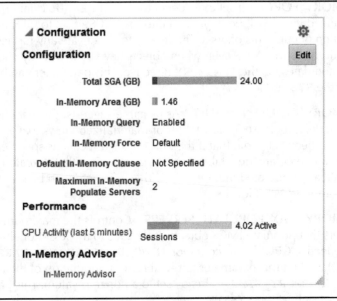

FIGURE 14-6.   *In-Memory Central: Configuration section*

Section 1: Configuration

The Configuration section, shown in Figure 14-6, displays several pertinent configuration specifics for the IMCS, including the current amount of memory allocated to the database instance's SGA, the current size of the IMCS, and other information about initialization parameters that affect how SQL statements can leverage the IMCS.

Clicking the Edit button in this section redirects to the Initialization Parameters screen, where you can change the pertinent parameters controlling how the IMCS will be populated, including the following:

- **INMEMORY_SIZE**   Determines the size of the IMCS (subject to the rules in the examples earlier in this chapter). It can be set only at the SYSTEM level.

- **INMEMORY_QUERY**   Determines whether the database instance will use objects specified for In-Memory population, regardless of whether the object hasn't been populated yet or has been populated only partially within the IMCS. It's set to ENABLE by default, but it can be set to DISABLE at either the session or system level to disable use of the IMCS temporarily, even if the object has been populated.

- **INMEMORY_FORCE**   If set to its default value of DEFAULT, tables and materialized views will be populated into the IMCS; if set to OFF, no population occurs. This offers a simple way to deactivate any further population into the IMCS even when objects have been already chosen as IMCS candidates via the INMEMORY directive. This parameter can be set only at the SYSTEM level.

- **INMEMORY_CLAUSE_DEFAULT**   As its name suggests, this parameter defines a default clause for any tables or materialized views that are created after it has been set. Note that if the INMEMORY directive is specified as part of this parameter, any new table or materialized view that's created will be automatically populated into the IMCS. This parameter can be set at either SESSION or SYSTEM level.

- **INMEMORY_MAX_POPULATE_SERVERS**   Controls the maximum number of servers that populate IMCS objects. It defaults to the *lesser* of either half of the effective CPU thread count, or INT((PGA_AGGREGATE_TARGET / 512MB)). Setting this parameter to 0 will restrict population of the IMCS (as long as INMEMORY_SIZE is already set to a nonzero value). This parameter can be set only at the SYSTEM level.

There are also two links that offer additional assistance for understanding what's happening currently within the database instance as well as determining whether there might be additional candidates for population into the IMCS:

- **CPU Activity**   Click this link to see the new ASH Analytics panel that provides detailed, multidimensional, real-time analysis of application workloads that were covered in depth in Chapter 9.

- **In-Memory Advisor**   Click this link to route control directly to IMADV, which was demonstrated and discussed at length in Chapter 13.

Section 2: Objects Summary

This section shows precisely how the IMCS is being leveraged. It shows the total size of all database objects that are resident in the IMCS in terms of their actual size in storage, their resulting compressed size within the IMCS, and the resulting overall compression factor. As Figure 14-7 illustrates, this section also captures exactly how much memory is currently allocated to IMCS objects within their assigned priority, from Critical to Low, as well as how much of each class of object has been populated into the IMCS so far.

Objects Summary

In-Memory Object Statistics

Total Size of all Objects (GB) 2.07

In-Memory Enabled Size (%) 87.43

Compression Factor 1.65x

Priority	Memory Used (GB)	Populated (%)
Critical	0.07	95.8
High	0.61	61.9
Medium	0.11	98.34
Total	0.79	71.75

FIGURE 14-7. *In-Memory Central: Objects Summary*

In-Memory Objects Distribution Chart Clicking the View In-Memory Objects Distribution link within the Objects Summary section (shown in Figure 14-5) displays a pie chart (see Figure 14-8) that shows at a glance exactly how the IMCS has been apportioned between nonpartitioned and partitioned tables, including subpartitions as well as nonpartitioned materialized views.

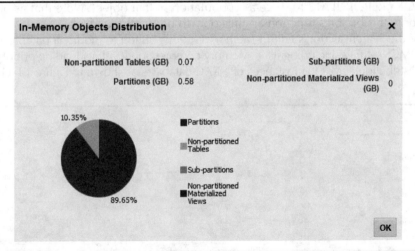

In-Memory Objects Distribution

Non-partitioned Tables (GB) 0.07   Sub-partitions (GB) 0

Partitions (GB) 0.58   Non-partitioned Materialized Views (GB) 0

10.35%

89.65%

Partitions
Non-partitioned Tables
Sub-partitions
Non-partitioned Materialized Views

OK

FIGURE 14-8. *In-Memory Central – In-Memory Objects Distribution chart*

Section 3: In-Memory Objects Search

The lower section of In-Memory Central is dedicated to a detailed list of all database objects at the table level currently populated within the IMCS. It also enables an Oracle DBA to dive deeply into details about any partitioned tables' subobjects, as well as modify the attributes of all objects within the IMCS that affect their population, level of In-Memory compression, population priority, and even how they are distributed across instances in a RAC database.

Because there could possibly be hundreds of populated objects within the IMCS, this section makes it simple to locate and appraise the state of each object, as shown in Figure 14-9.

From this section, it's also possible to filter out the "noise" in the IMCS by clicking Filters to concentrate on objects that

- have been accessed most recently

- have not yet been populated but are enabled for IMCS

- haven't been enabled at all for IMCS access

If the IMCS-resident object is partitioned, it's also possible to drill down to a complete list of all IMCS-resident partitions as well. For example, Figure 14-10 shows a view of the TPCDS.STORE_SALES partitions in greater detail, including a heat map of that object's partition segments.

If an Oracle DBA wants to force immediate population of an object within the IMCS—presuming there is any free space, of course—that can be accomplished by clicking the Repopulate button. Under the covers, this simply calls DBMS_INMEMORY.REPOPULATE to force a repopulation of that object. Note that as of this writing, this button's function applies only to nonpartitioned tables.

Click the Search section's Edit In-Memory Options button to modify a database object's IMCS settings, including its In-Memory compression level, its loading priority, and its distribution across the instances of a RAC database, as shown in Figure 14-11.

Name	Type	Partitioned	Last Scan Date	In-Memory Size (GB)	Populated (%)	Compression Factor	Priority	Compression	Distribution	Duplicate	Size on Storage (GB)	Storage Compression
TPCDS.STORE_SALES	Table	Yes	30-JAN-17	0.346	100	1.94	HIGH	FOR QUERY LOW			0.6707	None
TPCDS.CATALOG_SALES	Table	Yes	30-JAN-17	0.32	100	1.57	HIGH	FOR QUERY LOW			0.5024	None
TPCDS.CATALOG_SALES	Table	Yes	NA	0.32	100	1.57	HIGH	FOR QUERY LOW			0.5024	None
TPCDS.WEB_SALES	Table	Yes	NA	0.183	100	1.37	HIGH	FOR QUERY LOW			0.2506	None
TPCDS.WEB_SALES	Table	Yes	30-JAN-17	0.183	100	1.37	HIGH	FOR QUERY LOW			0.2506	None
TPCDS.INVENTORY	Table	Yes	30-JAN-17	0.165	100	2.42	MEDIUM	FOR QUERY LOW			0.3965	None
TPCDS.INVENTORY	Table	Yes	NA	0.165	100	2.42	MEDIUM	FOR QUERY LOW			0.3965	None
TPCDS.CUSTOMER_DEMOGRAPHICS	Table	No	30-JAN-17	0.033	100	3.76	CRITICAL	FOR QUERY LOW	AUTO	NO DUPLICATE	0.1247	None
TPCDS.CUSTOMER_DEMOGRAPHICS	Table	No	NA	0.033	100	3.78	CRITICAL	FOR QUERY LOW	AUTO	NO DUPLICATE	0.1247	None
TPCDS.CUSTOMER	Table	No	30-JAN-17	0.009	100	2.13	CRITICAL	FOR QUERY LOW	AUTO	NO DUPLICATE	0.0192	None
Total				1.828							3.3673	

FIGURE 14-9. *In-Memory Central – In-Memory Objects Search section*

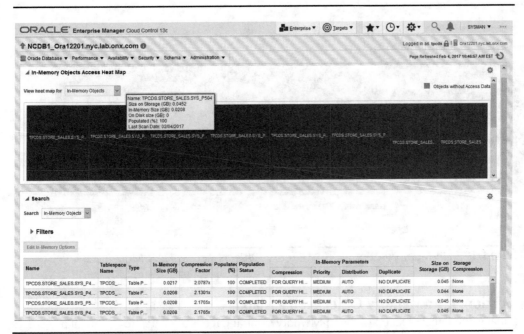

FIGURE 14-10.   *In-Memory Central – filters applied*

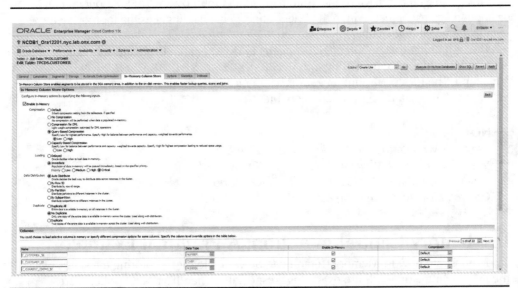

FIGURE 14-11.   *In-Memory Central – In-Memory Column Store attributes*

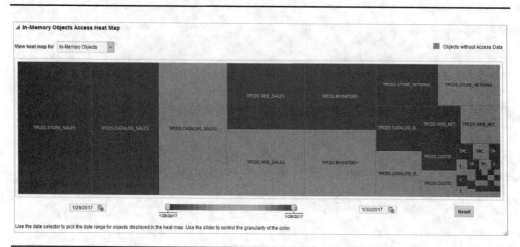

FIGURE 14-12. *In-Memory Central – In-Memory Objects Access Heat Map*

Section 4: In-Memory Objects Size Map

Finally, the largest section of the In-Memory Central page is allocated to a view of a heat map of exactly how frequently which IMCS objects are being used by application workloads, as shown in Figure 14-12. We'll explore this in much greater detail in the next section when we discuss how to leverage 12cR2's enhancements to Information Lifecycle Management (ILM) so that Automatic Data Optimization (ADO) policies can be applied against objects within the IMCS, effectively enabling it as the topmost tier of multi-tiered storage management.

The only thing that an Oracle DBA needs to do to enable this feature is to activate Heat Mapping by issuing the `ALTER SYSTEM SET HEAT_MAP=ON;` command. The `HEAT_MAP` initialization parameter is dynamic, so there's no need to "bounce" the database instance to enable it.

NOTE
As of this writing, the In-Memory Objects Size Map does not work with pluggable databases (PDBs) and container databases (CDBs) in OEM 13cR2 Cloud Control. However, it may be patched at a later date.

In-Memory Central in Action: A Practical Example

To demonstrate how In-Memory Central can be valuable for monitoring the status of the IMCS while workloads are executing—especially when ILM ADO policies are employed—we'll use the following scenario:

- All dimension tables will be given a priority of CRITICAL, which means they'll automatically be loaded first within the IMCS.

- All fact tables except for CATALOG_SALES and INVENTORY will be initially assigned a priority of HIGH so that those tables will be loaded next into the IMCS after a query first accesses those tables.

- Via an ADO policy, any partitions that are part of the CATALOG_SALES table will be added into IMCS two days after its creation with a priority of HIGH and In-Memory compression of QUERY HIGH.

- Another ADO policy will change any STORE_SALES partitions' In-Memory compression level to QUERY HIGH as well as lower their priority to MEDIUM after 15 days have elapsed since a segment was created.

- Finally, ADO policies will evict any related segments from the INVENTORY, CATALOG_RETURNS, STORE_RETURNS, and WEB_RETURNS partitioned tables after 180 days have passed without any access via SQL statement.

The PL/SQL code to establish these ILM policies is shown here:

```
ALTER TABLE tpcds.catalog_sales
    ILM ADD POLICY
        SET INMEMORY MEMCOMPRESS FOR QUERY LOW PRIORITY HIGH SEGMENT
        AFTER 2 DAYS OF CREATION;
ALTER TABLE tpcds.store_sales
    ILM ADD POLICY
        MODIFY INMEMORY MEMCOMPRESS FOR QUERY HIGH PRIORITY MEDIUM SEGMENT
        AFTER 15 DAYS OF CREATION;
ALTER TABLE tpcds.inventory
    ILM ADD POLICY
        NO INMEMORY AFTER 180 DAYS OF NO ACCESS;
ALTER TABLE tpcds.catalog_returns
    ILM ADD POLICY
        NO INMEMORY AFTER 180 DAYS OF NO ACCESS;
ALTER TABLE tpcds.store_returns
    ILM ADD POLICY
        NO INMEMORY AFTER 180 DAYS OF NO ACCESS;
ALTER TABLE tpcds.web_returns
    ILM ADD POLICY
        NO INMEMORY AFTER 180 DAYS OF NO ACCESS;
ALTER TABLE tpcds.web_sales
    ILM ADD POLICY
        NO INMEMORY AFTER 180 DAYS OF NO ACCESS;
```

In addition, we'll tweak the current ILM environment just a bit for testing purposes so that the amount of time that has elapsed since an ILM policy was checked for relevance is reduced significantly by invoking procedure `DBMS_ILM_ADMIN.CUSTOMIZE_ILM`, as shown next:

```
BEGIN
    DBMS_ILM_ADMIN.CUSTOMIZE_ILM(
        parameter => DBMS_ILM_ADMIN.POLICY_TIME
        ,value => DBMS_ILM_ADMIN.ILM_POLICY_IN_SECONDS
    );
END;
/
```

NOTE
It's not necessary to wait days to evaluate any ILM policy. Procedure `CUSTOMIZE_ILM` *of the provided package DBMS_ILM_ADMIN allows setting the* `POLICY_TIME` `ILM` *attribute to an enumerated constant—* `ILM_POLICY_IN_SECONDS` *—to treat the number of days specified in an ILM policy as seconds instead. The authors suggest changing this setting only in a test environment. It can be reverted to its proper state by setting* `POLICY_TIME` *back to its default value,* `ILM_POLICY_IN_DAYS`. *Query view DBA_ILM_PARAMETERS to display the current settings for* `POLICY_TIME` *as well as several other adjustable parameters that control evaluation of ILM policies.*

Once these ILM ADO policies have been created, we can track their statuses by querying the DBA_ILMOBJECTS and DBA_ILMDATAMOVEMENTPOLICIES data dictionary views via the following query, with corresponding output shown:

```
COL policy_name FORMAT A06 HEADING "ILM|Policy"
COL object_name FORMAT A24 HEADING "Table Name"
COL action_type FORMAT A11 HEADING "Action|Type"
COL condition_type FORMAT A20 HEADING "Condition Type"
COL condition_days FORMAT 99999 HEADING "Cndtn|Days"
COL ilm_action FORMAT A20 HEADING "Custom Function" WRAP
TTITLE "ILM Data Movement Policies|(from DBA_ILMOBJECTS and DBA_ILMDATAMOVEMENTPOLICIES)"
SELECT
    IO.policy_name
    ,IO.object_name
    ,IP.action_type
    ,IP.condition_type
    ,IP.condition_days
    ,TO_CHAR(SUBSTR(IP.actionc_clob,1,120)) ilm_action
  FROM
    dba_ilmobjects IO
    ,dba_ilmdatamovementpolicies IP
 WHERE IO.policy_name = IP.policy_name
   AND IO.object_type = 'TABLE'
```

```
   ORDER BY IO.policy_name, IO.object_name, IO.subobject_name, IO.object_type
;
TTITLE OFF
                               ILM Data Movement Policies
                       (from DBA_ILMOBJECTS and DBA_ILMDATAMOVEMENTPOLICIES)

ILM                         Action                      Cndtn
Policy  Table Name          Type       Condition Type   Days Custom Function
------  ----------------    ---------- ---------------- ------ ----------------------
P28     CATALOG_SALES       ANNOTATE   CREATION TIME      2 INMEMORY MEMCOMPRESS
                                                                    FOR QUERY LOW
                                                                    PRIORITY HIGH

P29     STORE_SALES         COMPRESSION CREATION TIME    15 INMEMORY MEMCOMPRESS
                                                                    FOR QUERY HIGH
                                                                    PRIORITY MEDIUM

P30     INVENTORY           EVICT      LAST ACCESS TIME  180
P31     CATALOG_RETURNS     EVICT      LAST ACCESS TIME  180
P32     STORE_RETURNS       EVICT      LAST ACCESS TIME  180
P33     WEB_RETURNS         EVICT      LAST ACCESS TIME  180
P34     WEB_SALES           EVICT      LAST ACCESS TIME  180

7 rows selected.
```

As the query shows, even though these ILM policies are currently enabled, none of them has been evaluated yet for possible execution. That's because ILM evaluation normally occurs as an automatic task that runs during the database's regularly scheduled maintenance window. However, we can force their evaluation with a call to procedure DBMS_ILM.EXECUTE_ILM for the desired tables, as shown next:

```
SQL> DECLARE
     tid NUMBER;
BEGIN
    DBMS_ILM.EXECUTE_ILM(owner => 'TPCDS', object_name => 'CATALOG_SALES', task_id => tid);
    DBMS_ILM.EXECUTE_ILM(owner => 'TPCDS', object_name => 'STORE_SALES', task_id => tid);
    DBMS_ILM.EXECUTE_ILM(owner => 'TPCDS', object_name => 'WEB_SALES', task_id => tid);
    DBMS_ILM.EXECUTE_ILM(owner => 'TPCDS', object_name => 'INVENTORY', task_id => tid);
    DBMS_ILM.EXECUTE_ILM(owner => 'TPCDS', object_name => 'CATALOG_RETURNS', task_id => tid);
    DBMS_ILM.EXECUTE_ILM(owner => 'TPCDS', object_name => 'STORE_RETURNS', task_id => tid);
    DBMS_ILM.EXECUTE_ILM(owner => 'TPCDS', object_name => 'WEB_RETURNS', task_id => tid);
END;
/
PL/SQL procedure successfully completed.
```

Since we enabled ILM to treat a single day's elapsed time as a single second instead, and since sufficient time has elapsed—in this case, more than 180 seconds—all of the ILM policies for the specific tables have been successfully evaluated and executed. And here's where In-Memory Central makes it simple to see the results of ILM policy execution: By changing the Search criteria to Accessed Objects and then selecting the Not Enabled radio button, we can now see that the tables for which we enabled ILM policies are no longer present within the IMCS, as reflected in the two boxed areas of Figure 14-13.

To confirm that the ILM ADO policy has actually affected the state of an object in the IMCS—for example, the recently evicted STORE_RETURNS table—we can

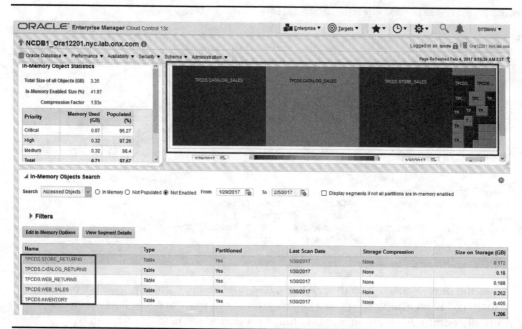

FIGURE 14-13. *In-Memory Central – post-ILM policy execution*

simply select that object in the In-Memory Objects Search section, click the Edit In-Memory Options button, and view its ILM policy status, as Figure 14-14 shows. Interestingly, note that the STORE_RETURNS table's other In-Memory attributes are essentially unchanged—it's been evicted only from the IMCS (see Figure 14-15).

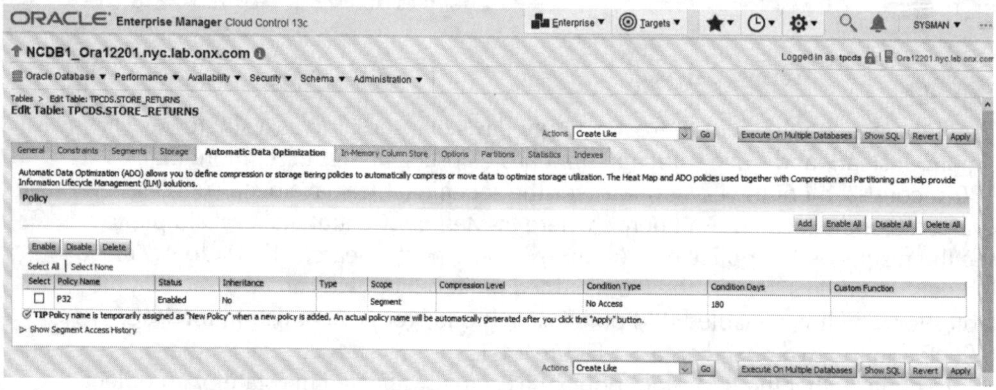

FIGURE 14-14. *Post-ILM policy execution – ILM policy status*

FIGURE 14-15. *Post-ILM policy execution – In-Memory object status*

Summary

Oracle 12*c*R2 vastly expanded the capabilities of Database In-Memory, and for an Oracle DBA this means there are more features than ever to monitor closely when evaluating the performance of DBIM, especially when analytical workloads are competing for attention within a database. We showed how an Oracle DBA can easily leverage Oracle Enterprise Manager 13*c* Cloud Control's new In-Memory Central features to keep a close watch on the contents of the IMCS as well as manage those contents with a few clicks of a mouse.

We also demonstrated how In-Memory Central provides excellent insight into the progress of ILM ADO policies as they manage the IMCS as a truly intelligent top tier within a storage hierarchy, so that only the most appropriate data remains as time progresses and older data is accessed less frequently.

PART
VI

Appendixes

APPENDIX
A

Other Performance Tuning
and Testing Tools

We have detailed a cornucopia of database performance tuning and application workload testing tools that are included within the boundaries of Oracle Database 12cR2, but a few other tool don't quite fit into those neat compartments. We wanted to make you aware of some of these tools—some included with Oracle Database itself and some home-grown by avid Oracle performance tuning experts—that you might consider adding to your Oracle DBA tool belt.

Tools Intrinsic to Oracle Database

Let's take a look at a few tools that are not only part and parcel of Oracle Database technology, but are also tools that any Oracle DBA can leverage in some unique and particular circumstances alongside (and in one case instead of) the tools we've already described in detail throughout this book.

STATSPACK

The venerable precursor to Automatic Workload Repository (AWR), STATSPACK does require installation but doesn't incur additional licensing costs. It may be an acceptable alternative to AWR in limited circumstances—primarily when in-depth performance tuning isn't likely to be required or the additional licensing costs for the AWR infrastructure are prohibitive.

STATSPACK works similarly to AWR in that it captures performance data within snapshots. A series of STATSPACK snapshots can be leveraged to generate either an HTML or a text-only report that appears quite similar to an AWR report, including sections for top SQL statements, the top events, top waits, and so forth. In addition, STATSPACK offers two levels of detailed reporting—one for the entire database, another for a specific SQL ID. However, be aware that STATSPACK captures significantly less detail than an AWR report, it offers no real in-depth analysis capability like Automatic Database Diagnostic Monitor (ADDM), and it doesn't use the in-depth features of Active Session History (ASH) statistics, as AWR does.

Optimizer Statistics Advisor (OSA)

Added in Oracle Database 12.2.0.1, the new Optimizer Statistics Advisor (OSA) provides advice on how best to gather optimizer statistics, when to gather those statistics, and even how to improve the efficiency of statistics gathering. OSA normally runs as part of the regularly scheduled AUTOTASK maintenance tasks, but an OSA task can also be created and executed manually using the DBMS_STATS package.

OSA doesn't gather new statistics; rather, it analyzes how the statistics are being gathered currently and then provides a report with findings, recommendations, and rationales for optimal statistics gathering. These rationales are particularly useful because they explain the reason behind every recommendation, and that greatly helps when you're deciding whether to implement a recommendation. The resulting OSA report can be produced as text, HTML, or XML via function REPORT_STATS_ ADVISOR_TASK of DBMS_STATS. All findings, recommendations, and rationales are also retained within the database's data dictionary for later review or customized querying.

Segment Advisor

Although it's not directly focused on improving database or SQL statement performance, the Oracle Segment Advisor can identify segments with space available for reclamation that would benefit from online segment shrink or other potential physical reorganization. A segment that could benefit from being rebuilt or reorganized to reclaim space can reduce the amount of time needed to perform physical I/O during a full scan of its contents. Segment Advisor therefore uses data from the latest AWR snapshots to focus only on those segments in tablespaces for which a critical or warning space threshold has been exceeded, segments that dominate top statement activity, and segments with the highest growth rate.

Segment Advisor normally runs as part of the regularly scheduled AUTOTASK maintenance tasks, but it can be run manually as well by scheduling a task with DBMS_ADVISOR or via Oracle Enterprise Manager. If online segment shrinking is not possible, Segment Advisor will recommend online table redefinition; it also analyzes tables for which row chaining has exceeded a threshold (usually 20 percent).

Other Home-Grown Toolsets

This book has focused predominantly on the tools that are intrinsically available within an Oracle 12cR2 database, but as we've noted, many of these toolsets do incur additional licensing costs after their initial 30-day evaluation period has expired. The good news is that the Oracle DBA community offers a panoply of additional performance-tuning tools and application-workload generators that often require no additional outlay for licensing costs. We present a few of them for your consideration.

TUNAs360

Developed by Mauro Pagano, TUNAs360 monitors an entire Oracle database (RAC or single instance) during a specific time period. TUNAs360 identifies the top five sessions and the top five SQL statements. For the five top sessions, it generates related information such as the top 15 waits, top 15 SQL_IDs, top 15 modules, and related sessions' statistics. For the top five SQL statements, it generates information about cursor statistics, execution plans information, and statistics in general. Presented in an intuitive HTML format, its results can quickly help to locate and isolate potential root causes of performance problems. TUNAs360 is free, requires no additional installation, and is ready for immediate use. It can be downloaded from https://github.com/mauropagano/tunas360/archive/master.zip.

eDB360

Carlos Sierra, the author of the well-known SQLTXPLAIN utility, developed eDB360 as the eventual successor of SQLTXPLAIN. Unlike SQLTXPLAIN—which must be downloaded from My Oracle Support and requires installation and configuration—eDB360 doesn't require any installation. As its name implies, eDB360 is most useful when several dimensions of an Oracle database's activity must be analyzed to solve a particularly thorny issue, especially when it's beyond a simple performance-tuning exercise. A typical eDB360 report has several sections, such as Database Configuration, Security, Auditing, Memory, Database Administration, Plan Stability, Cost-based Optimizer Statistics, Storage, ASM, Backup and Recovery, Sessions, Parallel Execution, Interconnect Performance (for RAC databases), and much more. eDB360 supports all Oracle databases starting with Oracle Release 10g and is free of charge. It can be downloaded from https://github.com/carlos-sierra/edb360/archive/master.zip.

SQLd360

As its name implies, SQLd360 provides a 360-degree overview around a specific SQL statement. It leverages several data dictionary views to extract information related to the whole database that impacts the provided SQL statement; it also extracts information related to that specific SQL statement itself, such as parsing times, execution plans, and so forth. SQLd360 generates a formatted HTML report that can be used to diagnose the statement's performance problems. Designed and developed by Mauro Pagano, it is included as part of eDB360 starting in that product's version #1504. SQLd360 is free, doesn't require installation within an Oracle database, and can also be adapted to run without licensing the standard Oracle Diagnostic or Tuning Pack licensing. SQLd360 supports all Oracle databases starting with Oracle Release 10g. It can be downloaded from https://github.com/mauropagano/sqld360/archive/master.zip.

Pathfinder

Also developed by Mauro Pagano, Pathfinder is a free tool designed to accept a SQL statement and then test it under multiple optimizer environments to generate different execution plans so that any Oracle DBA can easily discover whether a better plan is available when a specific optimizer environment is used. During its multiple executions of a statement, Pathfinder also takes into consideration the aspect of *cardinality feedback* as it evaluates and produces new execution plans. Pathfinder will automatically stop executing the SQL statement when the execution plan stops changing, and it reports its results in an easy-to-navigate HTML format with useful, detailed analyses for every new plan discovered. Pathfinder doesn't require installation of additional database objects, so it's ready to use out of the box. It can be downloaded from https://github.com/mauropagano/pathfinder/archive/master.zip.

MOATS

Developed by Adrian Billington and Tanel Poder, the Mother Of All The Scripts (MOATS) is another free-to-download utility worth investigating. Owned by Adrian and Tanel, MOATS is an interesting tool that quickly provides a closer look at the top activity in a database that is currently experiencing performance problems. MOATS output shows the top events, the top sessions, and the top SQL IDs along with portion of its statement text. MOATS output automatically refreshes this information every 10 seconds by default, but a neat feature is that it can be customized for faster refreshes to present the most recent information—in fact, almost in real time. MOATS, therefore, provides a good starting point for investigating an unexpected performance problem that is currently impacting an Oracle database. It does require installation, but it's particularly simple to execute via a single SELECT statement. MOATS supports all Oracle databases starting with Oracle Release 10*g*. The original version of MOATS can be downloaded from github.com/oracle-developer/moats.

SLOB

Created by Kevin Closson, Silly Little Oracle Benchmark (SLOB) is a free and unique tool, because its primary goal is to generate random physical reads and writes against an Oracle database to uncover potential I/O performance issues. To generate these workloads, SLOB first requires the creation of one or more schemas within your database. Once installation is complete, an Oracle DBA can generate a customized SLOB workload that includes the ability to impact multiple schemas simultaneously, use different degrees of parallelism, vary the percentage of reads versus percentage of writes, increase or decrease the number of user sessions, and so forth. While the simulated workload executes, SLOB automatically captures various OS statistics directly using vmstat, iostat, mpstat, and other OS utilities so that I/O performance metrics can be analyzed, both from the perspective of the Oracle database and its corresponding environment. SLOB supports all Oracle databases starting with Oracle Release 10*g*. SLOB can be downloaded from kevinclosson.net/slob/.

HammerDB

Created by Steve Shaw, HammerDB (formerly HammerORA) is a fantastic free database benchmarking tool that can perform TPC-C and TPC-H benchmarks against numerous databases, including Oracle, MySQL, PostgreSQL, IBM DB2, Microsoft SQL Server, Amazon Redis, and Apache Trafodion. HammerDB's database object creation wizards offer various advanced features such as partitioning, compression, column stores, degree of parallelism, and storage engines. Furthermore, HammerDB offers an autopilot facility to automate successively running incrementally larger concurrent user workloads. Although HammerDB makes short work of running these two database benchmarks, the GUI takes a little getting used to.

HammerDB also supports running a centralized instance that coordinates and controls multiple other instances running on remote nodes for scalability (that is, larger concurrent user workloads). HammerDB also offers an Oracle trace file replay mode so that you can perform workload capture and replays. All in all, HammerDB is a handy tool for stress testing database performance.

APPENDIX
B

Code Examples
and Listings

Whe have provided the following SQL and PL/SQL snippets, sample output listings, and other relevant code examples in one spot for you to leverage immediately as you begin to explore the use cases, scenarios, and techniques we've presented in our book. We hope these examples help clarify your understanding of the powerful tools built into every Oracle 12cR2 database to help you intelligently analyze and confidently tune your database's performance.

To save you the time of having to retype them and to help avoid mistakes during transcription, we have created a set of code files that will allow you to quickly try out any of these SQL and PL/SQL code examples. A ZIP file containing these examples is available from the McGraw-Hill Professional website at www.mhprofessional.com; simply enter this book's title or ISBN in the search box and then click the Downloads & Resources tab on the book's home page.

Chapter 11: Database Workload Capture and Workload Intelligence

Example 11-1: Generating a Text Version of a DWC Report

```
DECLARE
    cap_rpt          CLOB;
    out_File         UTL_FILE.FILE_TYPE;
    buffer           VARCHAR2(32767);
    offset           NUMBER(38);
    buffer_size      CONSTANT BINARY_INTEGER := 32767;
    amount           BINARY_INTEGER;

BEGIN
    cap_rpt := DBMS_WORKLOAD_CAPTURE.REPORT(
        capture_id =>  42 , -- Capture ID
        format => DBMS_WORKLOAD_CAPTURE.TYPE_TEXT);
    out_File := UTL_FILE.FOPEN(
'CAPTURE_DIR', -- Directory Name
'CaptureReport.txt' , -- File Name
'W',max_linesize => buffer_size);
    amount := buffer_size;
    offset := 1;

    WHILE
        amount >= buffer_size
    LOOP
      DBMS_LOB.READ(lob_loc => cap_rpt,
      amount => amount,
      offset => offset,
      buffer => buffer);
      OFFSET := OFFSET + AMOUNT;
```

```
   UTL_FILE.PUT(file => out_File,
    buffer => buffer);
   UTL_FILE.FFLUSH(file => out_File);
  END LOOP;
  UTL_FILE.FCLOSE(out_File);

END;
/
```

Example 11-2: Database Workload Capture Report in Text Format

Database Capture Report For DB11G

DB Name	DB Id	Release	RAC	Capture Name	Status
DB11G	408723413	11.2.0.3.0	NO	TPCDS_CAPTURE	COMPLETED

```
                  Start time: 20-Mar-17 23:01:30 (SCN = 3186127)
                    End time: 21-Mar-17 00:01:29 (SCN = 3193068)
                    Duration: 59 minutes 59 seconds
                Capture size: 96.56 KB
            Directory object: CAPTURE_DIR
              Directory path: /home/oracle/capture
     Directory shared in RAC: TRUE
                Filters used: 1 INCLUSION filter
```

Captured Workload Statistics   DB: DB11G Snaps: 157-164
-> 'Value' represents the corresponding statistic aggregated
     across the entire captured database workload.
-> '% Total' is the percentage of 'Value' over the corresponding
     system-wide aggregated total.

Statistic Name	Value	% Total
DB time (secs)	12514.51	77.86
Average Active Sessions	3.48	
User calls captured	56	8.58
User calls captured with Errors	0	
Session logins	5	3.36
Transactions	0	0.00

Top Events Captured   DB: DB11G Snaps: 157-164

Event	Event Class	% Event	Avg Active Sessions
CPU + Wait for CPU	CPU	27.36	1.22
direct path read	User I/O	21.14	0.94
direct path write temp	User I/O	20.71	0.93
direct path read temp	User I/O	8.46	0.38
db file scattered read	User I/O	6.22	0.28

```
Top Service/Module Captured                    DB: DB11G  Snaps: 157-164

Service        Module                  % Activity Action              % Action
-------------  ----------------------  ---------- ------------------  ----------
db11g          Swingbench User Thread      84.39 UNNAMED                  84.39
               ----------------------------------------------------------------

Top SQL Captured                               DB: DB11G  Snaps: 157-164

          SQL ID       % Activity Event                              % Event
-----------------------  -------------  ---------------------------  -------
         7bvd762nt0t3z        61.44 CPU + Wait for CPU                 23.13
with year_total as ( select c_customer_id customer_id ,c
_first_name customer_first_name ,c_last_name customer_last_name
,c_preferred_cust_flag customer_preferred_cust_flag ,c_birth
_country customer_birth_country ,c_login customer_login

                                    direct path write temp             20.21

                                    direct path read temp               8.27

         ck52qcn50mj6s         7.52 direct path read                    5.53
WITH ssr as (SELECT s_store_id, SUM(sales_price) AS sale
s, SUM(profit) AS profit, SUM(return_amt) AS returns,
 SUM(net_loss) AS profit_loss FROM ( SELECT ss_
store_sk AS store_sk, ss_sold_date_sk AS date_sk, ss_ext

                                    CPU + Wait for CPU                   1.31

         b9y8rw5dsr00z         6.59 direct path read                    6.03
SELECT /*query9*/ CASE WHEN (SELECT COUNT(*) FROM store_
sales WHERE ss_quantity BETWEEN 1 AND 20) > 107083 THEN
(SELECT AVG(ss_ext_sales_price) FROM store_sales WHERE s
s_quantity BETWEEN 1 AND 20) ELSE (SELECT AVG(ss_net_paid)

         cdwvbk03ku8sd         2.55 CPU + Wait for CPU                   1.74
WITH wscs AS ( SELECT sold_date_sk
 ,sales_price FROM (SELECT ws_sold_date_sk sold_date_s
k ,ws_ext_sales_price sales_price FROM web_sales
 UNION ALL SELECT cs_sold_date_sk sold_date_sk

         458uvnydxrb18         2.18 direct path read                    1.93
select /*query7*/ i_item_id, avg(ss_quantity) agg1, avg(
ss_list_price) agg2, avg(ss_coupon_amt) agg3, avg(ss_sal
es_price) agg4 from store_sales ,customer_demographics
 ,date_dim ,item ,promotion where

               ----------------------------------------------------------------

Top Sessions Captured                          DB: DB11G  Snaps: 157-164
-> '# Samples Active' shows the number of ASH samples in which the session
      was found waiting for that particular event. The percentage shown
      in this column is calculated with respect to wall clock time
      and not total database activity.
```

```
-> 'XIDs' shows the number of distinct transaction IDs sampled in ASH
       when the session was waiting for that particular event
-> For sessions running Parallel Queries, this section will NOT aggregate
       the PQ slave activity into the session issuing the PQ. Refer to
       the 'Top Sessions running PQs' section for such statistics.

     Sid, Serial# % Activity Event                                 % Event
---------------- ---------- ------------------------------- ----------
User                        Program                         # Samples Active    XIDs
------------------          ------------------------------- ------------------ --------
      56,   173     22.26 CPU + Wait for CPU                         7.71
TPCDS                       JDBC Thin Client                124/360 [ 34%]         2

                            direct path read                        5.72
                                                             92/360 [ 26%]         2

                            direct path write temp                  5.10
                                                             82/360 [ 23%]         1

      76,   215     21.02 CPU + Wait for CPU                         6.59
TPCDS                       JDBC Thin Client                106/360 [ 29%]         1

                            direct path read                        5.22
                                                             84/360 [ 23%]         1

                            direct path write temp                  5.22
                                                             84/360 [ 23%]         1

     109,    87     20.77 CPU + Wait for CPU                         6.09
TPCDS                       JDBC Thin Client                 98/360 [ 27%]         1

                            direct path write temp                  5.60
                                                             90/360 [ 25%]         1

                            direct path read                        5.10
                                                             82/360 [ 23%]         1

      68,   109     20.34 CPU + Wait for CPU                         6.97
TPCDS                       JDBC Thin Client                112/360 [ 31%]         1

                            direct path read                        5.10
                                                             82/360 [ 23%]         1

                            direct path write temp                  4.79
                                                             77/360 [ 21%]         1


       ------------------------------------------------------------

Top Events containing Unreplayable Calls          DB: DB11G  Snaps: 157-164

              No data exists for this section of the report.
       ------------------------------------------------------------

Top Service/Module containing Unreplayable Calls   DB: DB11G  Snaps: 157-164

              No data exists for this section of the report.
       ------------------------------------------------------------
```

```
Top SQL containing Unreplayable Calls              DB: DB11G   Snaps: 157-164

                No data exists for this section of the report.
          ----------------------------------------------------------------

Top Sessions containing Unreplayable Calls         DB: DB11G   Snaps: 157-164

                No data exists for this section of the report.
          ----------------------------------------------------------------

Top Events Filtered Out                            DB: DB11G   Snaps: 157-164

                                                             Avg Active
Event                              Event Class      % Event   Sessions
--------------------------------   --------------   -------   ----------
CPU + Wait for CPU                 CPU                10.20       0.46
direct path read                   User I/O            3.23       0.14
          ----------------------------------------------------------------

Top Service/Module Filtered Out                    DB: DB11G   Snaps: 157-164

Service        Module                   % Activity Action          % Action
-------------- ------------------------ ---------- --------------- ----------
db11g          Swingbench User Thread       14.24 UNNAMED             14.24
          ----------------------------------------------------------------

Top SQL Filtered Out                               DB: DB11G   Snaps: 157-164

              SQL ID      % Activity Event                          % Event
---------------------- --------------- ------------------------     -------
       cdwvbk03ku8sd        12.38 CPU + Wait for CPU                   8.89
WITH wscs AS ( SELECT sold_date_sk
 ,sales_price FROM (SELECT ws_sold_date_sk sold_date_s
k ,ws_ext_sales_price sales_price FROM web_sales
 UNION ALL SELECT cs_sold_date_sk sold_date_sk

                             direct path read                        3.11

       51fzx15gnqpak         1.87 CPU + Wait for CPU                   1.31
WITH customer_total_return AS ( SELECT sr_customer_sk AS ctr_custome
r_sk ,sr_store_sk AS ctr_store_sk ,sum(SR_FEE) AS ctr_to
tal_return FROM store_returns ,date_dim WHER
E sr_returned_date_sk = d_date_sk AND d_year = 1999 GROU


          ----------------------------------------------------------------

Top Sessions Filtered Out                          DB: DB11G   Snaps: 157-164
-> '# Samples Active' shows the number of ASH samples in which the session
      was found waiting for that particular event. The percentage shown
      in this column is calculated with respect to wall clock time
      and not total database activity.
-> 'XIDs' shows the number of distinct transaction IDs sampled in ASH
      when the session was waiting for that particular event
-> For sessions running Parallel Queries, this section will NOT aggregate
      the PQ slave activity into the session issuing the PQ. Refer to
      the 'Top Sessions running PQs' section for such statistics.
```

```
      Sid, Serial# % Activity Event                          % Event
--------------- ---------- ------------------------------- ----------
User                       Program                 # Samples Active    XIDs
------------------- ------ ----------------------------- ----------------- --------
        95,   21    1.80 CPU + Wait for CPU                   1.12
TPCDS                      oracle@nuvola1 (P038)      18/360 [  5%]          0

        98,   17    1.80 CPU + Wait for CPU                   1.24
TPCDS                      oracle@nuvola1 (P037)      20/360 [  6%]          0

        30,   43    1.43 CPU + Wait for CPU                   1.18
TPCDS                      oracle@nuvola1 (P039)      19/360 [  5%]          0

        39,   17    1.43 CPU + Wait for CPU                   1.18
TPCDS                      oracle@nuvola1 (P035)      19/360 [  5%]          0

        85,   17    1.43 CPU + Wait for CPU                   1.18
TPCDS                      oracle@nuvola1 (P034)      19/360 [  5%]          0

              -----------------------------------------------------------

Top Events (Jobs and Background Activity)        DB: DB11G  Snaps: 157-164

              No data exists for this section of the report.
              -----------------------------------------------------------

Top Service/Module (Jobs and Background Activity)   DB: DB11G  Snaps: 157-164

              No data exists for this section of the report.
              -----------------------------------------------------------

Top SQL (Jobs and Background Activity)           DB: DB11G  Snaps: 157-164

              No data exists for this section of the report.
              -----------------------------------------------------------

Top Sessions (Jobs and Background Activity)      DB: DB11G  Snaps: 157-164

              No data exists for this section of the report.
              -----------------------------------------------------------

Workload Filters                                 DB: DB11G  Snaps: 157-164

  # Filter Name            Type    Attribute    Value
--- ----------------------- ------- ------------ -------------------------
  1 USER_FILTER            INCLUDE USER         TPCDS
              -----------------------------------------------------------

End of Report
```

Example 11-3: Generating an HTML Version of a DWC Report

```
DECLARE
  cap_rpt          CLOB;
  out_File         UTL_FILE.FILE_TYPE;
  buffer           VARCHAR2(32767);
  offset           NUMBER(38);
  buffer_size      CONSTANT BINARY_INTEGER := 32767;
  amount           BINARY_INTEGER;
BEGIN
  cap_rpt := DBMS_WORKLOAD_CAPTURE.REPORT(
                   capture_id =>  42 , -- Capture ID
                   format => DBMS_WORKLOAD_REPLAY.TYPE_HTML);
  out_File := UTL_FILE.FOPEN(
'CAPTURE_DIR', -- Directory Name
'CaptureReport.html', -- File Name
'W',max_linesize => buffer_size);
  amount := buffer_size;
  offset := 1;

  WHILE
    amount >= buffer_size
  LOOP
    DBMS_LOB.READ(lob_loc => cap_rpt,
    amount => amount,
    offset => offset,
    buffer => buffer);
    OFFSET := OFFSET + AMOUNT;
    UTL_FILE.PUT(file => out_File,
    buffer => buffer);
    UTL_FILE.FFLUSH(file => out_File);
  END LOOP;
  UTL_FILE.FCLOSE(out_File);

END;
/
```

Example 11-4: Sample Query to Generate Workload Intelligence Reporting from WI Metadata

```
SET PAGESIZE 500
SET LINESIZE 80
SET FEEDBACK OFF
SET TERMOUT OFF
SET ECHO OFF
SET VERIFY OFF
```

```
SET MARKUP HTML ON SPOOL ON HEAD "<title>Workload Intelligence Patterns and
Templates</title><style TYPE='text/css'><!--BODY {background: ffffff} --></style>"

CLEAR BREAK
TTITLE OFF
SPOOL wirpt.html

COL pattern_id          FORMAT 99999              NEW_VALUE ptnid          NOPRINT
COL pattern_length      FORMAT 9999               NEW_VALUE ptnlen         NOPRINT
COL db_time             FORMAT 9999999999         NEW_VALUE dbtme          NOPRINT
COL is_transaction      FORMAT A06                HEADING "Trans-|Action?"
COL template_id         HEADING "Template ID"     FORMAT 99999999999999999999 NOPRINT
COL short_stmt          FORMAT A60                HEADING "SQL Statement"
COL tplt_cnt            FORMAT 999,999            HEADING "Stmt|Count"
BREAK ON pattern_id ON pattern_length ON db_time ON is_transaction SKIP PAGE
TTITLE LEFT 'Pattern: ' ptnid ' Length: ' ptnlen ' DB Time: ' dbtme

SELECT
    P.pattern_id
    ,P.length pattern_length
    ,P.db_time
    ,T.is_transaction
    ,ST.template_id
    ,SUBSTR(TO_CHAR(ST.sql_text),1,60) short_stmt
    ,COUNT(ST.template_id) tplt_cnt
  FROM
    dba_wi_templates T
    ,dba_wi_patterns P
    ,dba_wi_pattern_items PI
    ,dba_wi_statements ST
WHERE P.job_id = PI.job_id
  AND P.pattern_id =  PI.pattern_id
  AND PI.job_id = ST.job_id
  AND PI.template_id = ST.template_id
  AND T.job_id = ST.job_id
  AND T.template_id = ST.template_id
  AND ST.job_id = 5
GROUP BY
    P.pattern_id
    ,P.length
    ,P.db_time
    ,T.is_transaction
    ,ST.template_id
    ,SUBSTR(TO_CHAR(ST.sql_text),1,60)
ORDER BY
    P.pattern_id
    ,P.length
    ,P.db_time
    ,T.is_transaction
    ,ST.template_id
    ,SUBSTR(TO_CHAR(ST.sql_text),1,60)
;
SPOOL OFF
SET MARKUP HTML OFF SPOOL OFF
```

Chapter 12: Database Workload Replay

Example 12-1: Regenerating a Text-only Version of a DWR Replay Report

Note that the ID of the workload replay process must be provided, which in this example is Replay ID=131. The replay directory's name and the report's filename must be also provided.

```
DECLARE
    rep_id              NUMBER;
    out_File            UTL_FILE.FILE_TYPE;
    buffer              VARCHAR2(32767);
    offset              NUMBER(38);
    buffer_size         CONSTANT BINARY_INTEGER := 32767;
    amount              BINARY_INTEGER;
    rep_rpt             CLOB;

BEGIN
    rep_rpt:=DBMS_WORKLOAD_REPLAY.REPORT (
        replay_id   => 131, -- Replay ID
        format => DBMS_WORKLOAD_REPLAY.TYPE_TEXT);

    out_File := UTL_FILE.FOPEN(
'REPLAY_DIR', -- Directory Name
'ReplayReport.txt', -- File Name
'W',max_linesize => buffer_size);
    amount := buffer_size;
    offset := 1;

    WHILE
        amount >= buffer_size
    LOOP
        DBMS_LOB.READ(lob_loc => rep_rpt,
        amount => amount,
        offset => offset,
        buffer => buffer);
        OFFSET := OFFSET + AMOUNT;
        UTL_FILE.PUT(file => out_File,
        buffer => buffer);
        UTL_FILE.FFLUSH(file => out_File);
    END LOOP;
    UTL_FILE.FCLOSE(out_File);

END;
/
```

Example 12-2: Regenerating an HTML Version of a DWR Replay Report

Note that the ID of the workload replay process must be provided, which in this example is Replay ID=131. The replay directory's name and the report's filename must be also provided.

```
DECLARE
   rep_id              NUMBER;
   out_File            UTL_FILE.FILE_TYPE;
   buffer              VARCHAR2(32767);
   offset              NUMBER(38);
   buffer_size         CONSTANT BINARY_INTEGER := 32767;
   amount              BINARY_INTEGER;
   rep_rpt             CLOB;

BEGIN

   rep_rpt:=DBMS_WORKLOAD_REPLAY.REPORT (
            replay_id   => 131, -- Replay ID
            format => DBMS_WORKLOAD_REPLAY.TYPE_HTML);

   out_File := UTL_FILE.FOPEN(
'REPLAY_DIR', -- Directory Name
'ReplayReport.html', -- File Name
'W',max_linesize => buffer_size);
   amount := buffer_size;
   offset := 1;

   WHILE
      amount >= buffer_size
   LOOP
      DBMS_LOB.READ(lob_loc => rep_rpt,
      amount => amount,
      offset => offset,
      buffer => buffer);
      OFFSET := OFFSET + AMOUNT;
      UTL_FILE.PUT(file => out_File,
      buffer => buffer);
      UTL_FILE.FFLUSH(file => out_File);
   END LOOP;
   UTL_FILE.FCLOSE(out_File);

END;
/
```

Example 12-3: DWR Replay Report – Text-only Version

```
DB Replay Report for TPCDS_REPLAY
-----------------------------------------------------------------------------------------


-------------------------------------------------------------------------
| DB Name | DB Id       | Release     | RAC | Replay Name   | Replay Status |
-------------------------------------------------------------------------
| DB12CR2 | 1416159483  | 12.2.0.1.0  | NO  | TPCDS_REPLAY  | COMPLETED     |
-------------------------------------------------------------------------


Replay Information
-------------------------------------------------------------------------
|     Information     | Replay            | Capture            |
-------------------------------------------------------------------------
| Name                | TPCDS_REPLAY      | TPCDS_CAPTURE      |
-------------------------------------------------------------------------
| Status              | COMPLETED         | COMPLETED          |
-------------------------------------------------------------------------
| Database Name       | DB12CR2           | DB11G              |
-------------------------------------------------------------------------
| Database Version    | 12.2.0.1.0        | 11.2.0.3.0         |
-------------------------------------------------------------------------
| Start Time          | 21-03-17 15:42:19 | 20-03-17 23:01:30  |
-------------------------------------------------------------------------
| End Time            | 21-03-17 16:24:52 | 21-03-17 00:01:29  |
-------------------------------------------------------------------------
| Duration            | 42 minutes 33 seconds | 59 minutes 59 seconds |
-------------------------------------------------------------------------
| Directory Object    | REPLAY_DIR        | REPLAY_DIR         |
-------------------------------------------------------------------------
| Directory Path      | /home/oracle/capture | /home/oracle/capture |
-------------------------------------------------------------------------
| AWR DB Id           | 1416159483        |                    |
-------------------------------------------------------------------------
| AWR Begin Snap Id   | 15                |                    |
-------------------------------------------------------------------------
| AWR End Snap Id     | 16                |                    |
-------------------------------------------------------------------------
| PL/SQL Capture Mode | TOP_LEVEL         | TOP_LEVEL          |
-------------------------------------------------------------------------
| Replay Directory Number | 458314925     |                    |
-------------------------------------------------------------------------
| Replay Schedule Name |                  |                    |
-------------------------------------------------------------------------


Replay Options
--------------------------------------------------------------
|     Option Name      | Value                    |
--------------------------------------------------------------
| Synchronization      | SCN                      |
--------------------------------------------------------------
| Connect Time         | 100%                     |
--------------------------------------------------------------
| Think Time           | 100%                     |
--------------------------------------------------------------
| Think Time Auto Correct | TRUE                  |
--------------------------------------------------------------
| Number of WRC Clients | 1 (1 Completed, 0 Running ) |
--------------------------------------------------------------
```

Replay Statistics

```
-----------------------------------------------------------------------
|        Statistic      | Replay            | Capture            |
-----------------------------------------------------------------------
| DB Time               | 10698.461 seconds | 12514.515 seconds  |
-----------------------------------------------------------------------
| PL/SQL DB Time        |     0.000 seconds |     0.000 seconds  |
-----------------------------------------------------------------------
| Average Active Sessions |           4.19  |             3.48   |
-----------------------------------------------------------------------
| User calls            |              56   |               56   |
-----------------------------------------------------------------------
| PL/SQL user calls     |               0   |                0   |
-----------------------------------------------------------------------
| PL/SQL subcalls       |               0   |                0   |
-----------------------------------------------------------------------
```

Replay Divergence Summary

```
---------------------------------------------------------------------
|                  Divergence Type           | Count | % Total |
---------------------------------------------------------------------
| Session Failures During Replay             |     0 |    0.00 |
---------------------------------------------------------------------
| Errors No Longer Seen During Replay        |     0 |    0.00 |
---------------------------------------------------------------------
| New Errors Seen During Replay              |     0 |    0.00 |
---------------------------------------------------------------------
| Errors Mutated During Replay               |     0 |    0.00 |
---------------------------------------------------------------------
| DMLs with Different Number of Rows Modified |     0 |    0.00 |
---------------------------------------------------------------------
| SELECTs with Different Number of Rows Fetched |   0 |    0.00 |
---------------------------------------------------------------------
```

```
---------------------------------------------------------------------
Workload Profile Top Events
---------------------------------------------------------------------
| Event              | Event Class | % Activity |
---------------------------------------------------------------------
| CPU + Wait for CPU | CPU         |      73.28 |
---------------------------------------------------------------------
| direct path write temp | User I/O |     11.83 |
---------------------------------------------------------------------
| direct path read temp | User I/O  |     11.07 |
---------------------------------------------------------------------
| direct path read   | User I/O    |       0.10 |
---------------------------------------------------------------------
```

Top Service/Module/Action

```
-------------------------------------------------------------------------------
| Service Name | Module Name          | % Activity | Action Drilldown        |
-------------------------------------------------------------------------------
| SYS$USERS    | Swingbench User Thread |    96.28 | ----------------------- |
|              |                      |            | | Action Name | % Activity | |
|              |                      |            | ----------------------- |
|              |                      |            | | UNNAMED      |    96.28 | |
|              |                      |            | ----------------------- |
-------------------------------------------------------------------------------
```

Top SQL with Top Events

SQL ID	Planhash	Sampled Number of Executions	% Activity	Event Drilldown		
7bvd762nt0t3z	3019389580	4	71.47	Event	% Activity	
				CPU + Wait for CPU	49.05	
				direct path write temp	11.83	
				direct path read temp	10.59	
ck52qcn50mj6s	1743075189	4	9.45	Event	% Activity	
				CPU + Wait for CPU	8.87	
				direct path read temp	0.48	
				direct path read	0.10	
cdwvbk03ku8sd	2166267056	4	6.49	Event	% Activity	
				CPU + Wait for CPU	6.49	
f9f17bjar4ru2	154212656	4	3.91	Event	% Activity	
				CPU + Wait for CPU	3.91	

```
-------------------------------------------------------------------------------
| 2uw47w3cyzwbj | 2898011891 | 4          |             | 2.29 | ---------------------- |
|               |            |            |             |      | | Event    | %         | |
|               |            |            |             |      | |          | Activity  | |
|               |            |            |             |      | ---------------------- |
|               |            |            |             |      | | CPU +    |      2.29 | |
|               |            |            |             |      | | Wait for |           | |
|               |            |            |             |      | | CPU      |           | |
|               |            |            |             |      | ---------------------- |
-------------------------------------------------------------------------------

Top Sessions with Top Events
-------------------------------------------------------------------------------
| Session ID | Session Serial | Username | Program        | % Activity | Event Drilldown  |
-------------------------------------------------------------------------------
| 52         | 12536          | TPCDS    | wrc@localhost.loc |     24.14 | ----------------  |
|            |                |          | aldomain (TNS     |           | | Event | % Act | |
|            |                |          | V1-V3)            |           | |       | ivity | |
|            |                |          |                   |           | ----------------  |
|            |                |          |                   |           | | CPU + | 18.32 | |
|            |                |          |                   |           | | Wait  |       | |
|            |                |          |                   |           | | for   |       | |
|            |                |          |                   |           | | CPU   |       | |
|            |                |          |                   |           | ----------------  |
|            |                |          |                   |           | | direc |  3.44 | |
|            |                |          |                   |           | | t     |       | |
|            |                |          |                   |           | | path  |       | |
|            |                |          |                   |           | | read  |       | |
|            |                |          |                   |           | | temp  |       | |
|            |                |          |                   |           | ----------------  |
|            |                |          |                   |           | | direc |  2.39 | |
|            |                |          |                   |           | | t     |       | |
|            |                |          |                   |           | | path  |       | |
|            |                |          |                   |           | | write |       | |
|            |                |          |                   |           | | temp  |       | |
|            |                |          |                   |           | ----------------  |
-------------------------------------------------------------------------------
| 55         | 31059          | TPCDS    | wrc@localhost.loc |     24.05 | ----------------  |
|            |                |          | aldomain (TNS     |           | | Event | % Act | |
|            |                |          | V1-V3)            |           | |       | ivity | |
|            |                |          |                   |           | ----------------  |
|            |                |          |                   |           | | CPU + | 18.80 | |
|            |                |          |                   |           | | Wait  |       | |
|            |                |          |                   |           | | for   |       | |
|            |                |          |                   |           | | CPU   |       | |
|            |                |          |                   |           | ----------------  |
|            |                |          |                   |           | | direc |  2.77 | |
|            |                |          |                   |           | | t     |       | |
|            |                |          |                   |           | | path  |       | |
|            |                |          |                   |           | | write |       | |
|            |                |          |                   |           | | temp  |       | |
|            |                |          |                   |           | ----------------  |
|            |                |          |                   |           | | direc |  2.39 | |
|            |                |          |                   |           | | t     |       | |
|            |                |          |                   |           | | path  |       | |
|            |                |          |                   |           | | read  |       | |
|            |                |          |                   |           | | temp  |       | |
|            |                |          |                   |           | ----------------  |
|            |                |          |                   |           | | direc |  0.10 | |
|            |                |          |                   |           | | t     |       | |
|            |                |          |                   |           | | path  |       | |
|            |                |          |                   |           | | read  |       | |
|            |                |          |                   |           | ----------------  |
```

74	9193	TPCDS	wrc@localhost.loc aldomain (TNS V1-V3)	24.05			
						Event	% Act ivity
						CPU + Wait for CPU	17.94
						direc t path write temp	3.63
						direc t path read temp	2.48
80	42056	TPCDS	wrc@localhost.loc aldomain (TNS V1-V3)	24.05			
						Event	% Act ivity
						CPU + Wait for CPU	18.23
						direc t path write temp	3.05
						direc t path read temp	2.77

Replay Divergence Session Failures By Application

| No data exists for this section of the report. |

Error Divergence By Application

| No data exists for this section of the report. |

By SQL

| No data exists for this section of the report. |

DML Data Divergence By Application

| No data exists for this section of the report. |

```
By SQL
-------------------------------------------------
| No data exists for this section of the report. |
-------------------------------------------------
By Divergence Magnitude
-------------------------------------------------
| No data exists for this section of the report. |
-------------------------------------------------
SELECT Data Divergence By Application
-------------------------------------------------
| No data exists for this section of the report. |
-------------------------------------------------
By Divergence Magnitude
-------------------------------------------------
| No data exists for this section of the report. |
-------------------------------------------------
-------------------------------------------------------------------------------------
Replay Clients Alerts
-------------------------------------------------
| No data exists for this section of the report. |
-------------------------------------------------
Replay Filters
-------------------------------------------------
| No data exists for this section of the report. |
-------------------------------------------------

End of Report.
```

Example 12-4: DWR Scale-up

```
BEGIN
        DBMS_WORKLOAD_REPLAY.PREPARE_REPLAY (
                synchronization => 'SCN',
                scale_up_multiplier =>2,-- duplicating the workload
                capture_sts => TRUE,
                connect_time_scale=>100,
                think_time_scale=>50,-- 50% faster
                think_time_auto_correct=>TRUE,
                sts_cap_interval => 60,
                query_only => TRUE);
    END;
    /
```

Example 12-5: PKG_DML_GENERATOR

```
CREATE OR REPLACE PACKAGE tpcds.pkg_dml_generator
/*
|| Package:        TPCDS.PKG_DML_GENERATOR
|| Version:        12.2.0.1.0
|| Description:    Simulates batch loading routines against an Oracle database
||                 containing the standard Swingbench TPCDS schema for
||                 evaluation of various advanced SQL tuning tools and strategies
|| Author:         Jim Czuprynski
*/
IS
    PROCEDURE RandomDML(Iteration NUMBER);
```

```
END pkg_dml_generator;

CREATE OR REPLACE PACKAGE BODY tpcds.pkg_dml_generator
/*
|| Package Body:   TPCDS.PKG_DML_GENERATOR
|| Version:        12.2.0.1.0
|| Description:    Simulates batch loading routines against an Oracle database
||                 containing the standard Swingbench TPCDS schema for
||                 evaluation of various advanced SQL tuning tools and strategies
|| Author:         Jim Czuprynski
*/
IS
        -- Processing variables:
        SQLERRNUM         INTEGER := 0;
        SQLERRMSG         VARCHAR2(255);
        RTNVALUE          INTEGER := 0;
        MIN_ADDR_SK       INTEGER := 0;
        MAX_ADDR_SK       INTEGER := 0;
        MIN_CCTR_SK       INTEGER := 0;
        MAX_CCTR_SK       INTEGER := 0;
        MIN_CDEMO_SK      INTEGER := 0;
        MAX_CDEMO_SK      INTEGER := 0;
        MIN_CPGE_SK       INTEGER := 0;
        MAX_CPGE_SK       INTEGER := 0;
        MIN_DATE_SK       INTEGER := 0;
        MAX_DATE_SK       INTEGER := 0;
        MIN_HDEMO_SK      INTEGER := 0;
        MAX_HDEMO_SK      INTEGER := 0;
        MIN_MODE_SK       INTEGER := 0;
        MAX_MODE_SK       INTEGER := 0;
        MIN_PROMO_SK      INTEGER := 0;
        MAX_PROMO_SK      INTEGER := 0;
        MIN_STORE_SK      INTEGER := 0;
        MAX_STORE_SK      INTEGER := 0;
        MIN_TIME_SK       INTEGER := 0;
        MAX_TIME_SK       INTEGER := 0;
        MIN_WHSE_SK       INTEGER := 0;
        MAX_WHSE_SK       INTEGER := 0;
        MIN_WPGE_SK       INTEGER := 0;
        MAX_WPGE_SK       INTEGER := 0;
        MIN_WSIT_SK       INTEGER := 0;
        MAX_WSIT_SK       INTEGER := 0;

/*
|| TYPEs and RECORDS
*/

    -----
    -- WEB_SALES
    -----
    TYPE web_sales_rec IS
        RECORD (
            ws_sold_date_sk            web_sales.ws_sold_date_sk%TYPE
            ,ws_sold_time_sk           web_sales.ws_sold_time_sk%TYPE
            ,ws_ship_date_sk           web_sales.ws_ship_date_sk%TYPE
            ,ws_item_sk                web_sales.ws_item_sk%TYPE
            ,ws_bill_customer_sk       web_sales.ws_bill_customer_sk%TYPE
            ,ws_bill_cdemo_sk          web_sales.ws_bill_cdemo_sk%TYPE
            ,ws_bill_hdemo_sk          web_sales.ws_bill_hdemo_sk%TYPE
            ,ws_bill_addr_sk           web_sales.ws_bill_addr_sk%TYPE
            ,ws_ship_customer_sk       web_sales.ws_ship_customer_sk%TYPE
            ,ws_ship_cdemo_sk          web_sales.ws_ship_cdemo_sk%TYPE
            ,ws_ship_hdemo_sk          web_sales.ws_ship_hdemo_sk%TYPE
            ,ws_ship_addr_sk           web_sales.ws_ship_addr_sk%TYPE
            ,ws_web_page_sk            web_sales.ws_web_page_sk%TYPE
```

```
              ,ws_web_site_sk           web_sales.ws_web_site_sk%TYPE
              ,ws_ship_mode_sk          web_sales.ws_ship_mode_sk%TYPE
              ,ws_warehouse_sk          web_sales.ws_warehouse_sk%TYPE
              ,ws_promo_sk              web_sales.ws_promo_sk%TYPE
              ,ws_order_number          web_sales.ws_order_number%TYPE
              ,ws_quantity              web_sales.ws_quantity%TYPE
              ,ws_wholesale_cost        web_sales.ws_wholesale_cost%TYPE
              ,ws_list_price            web_sales.ws_list_price%TYPE
              ,ws_sales_price           web_sales.ws_sales_price%TYPE
              ,ws_ext_discount_amt      web_sales.ws_ext_discount_amt%TYPE
              ,ws_ext_sales_price       web_sales.ws_ext_sales_price%TYPE
              ,ws_ext_wholesale_cost    web_sales.ws_ext_wholesale_cost%TYPE
              ,ws_ext_list_price        web_sales.ws_ext_list_price%TYPE
              ,ws_ext_tax               web_sales.ws_ext_tax%TYPE
              ,ws_coupon_amt            web_sales.ws_coupon_amt%TYPE
              ,ws_ext_ship_cost         web_sales.ws_ext_ship_cost%TYPE
              ,ws_net_paid              web_sales.ws_net_paid%TYPE
              ,ws_net_paid_inc_tax      web_sales.ws_net_paid_inc_tax%TYPE
              ,ws_net_paid_inc_ship     web_sales.ws_net_paid_inc_ship%TYPE
              ,ws_net_paid_inc_ship_tax web_sales.ws_net_paid_inc_ship_tax%TYPE
              ,ws_net_profit            web_sales.ws_net_profit%TYPE
    );
TYPE web_sales_tab IS
    TABLE OF web_sales_rec
    INDEX BY PLS_INTEGER;


-----
-- Local Functions and Procedures
-----

FUNCTION Randomizer (seed NUMBER)
RETURN NUMBER
/*
|| Function:    Randomizer
|| Purpose:     Returns a randomized number from 1 to 100
||              based on the seed value supplied
|| Scope:       Private
|| Arguments:   seed - Input from calling routine
|| Returns:     Iteration - Randomized number
*/
IS
    Iteration NUMBER := 0;
BEGIN
    SYS.DBMS_RANDOM.SEED(seed);
    Iteration := ROUND(SYS.DBMS_RANDOM.VALUE(1,100));
    SYS.DBMS_RANDOM.TERMINATE;
    RETURN Iteration;
EXCEPTION
    WHEN OTHERS THEN
        RETURN 0;
END Randomizer;

FUNCTION from_mills_to_tens(value INTEGER)
    RETURN float
IS
    real_value float := 0;
BEGIN
    real_value := value/1000;
RETURN real_value;
EXCEPTION
    WHEN zero_divide THEN
        real_value := 0;
        RETURN real_value;
END from_mills_to_tens;
```

```
FUNCTION from_mills_to_secs(value INTEGER)
    RETURN float
IS
    real_value float := 0;
BEGIN
    real_value := value/1000;
RETURN real_value;
EXCEPTION
    WHEN zero_divide THEN
        real_value := 0;
        RETURN real_value;
END from_mills_to_secs;

PROCEDURE sleep(
    min_sleep INTEGER
   ,max_sleep INTEGER
)
IS
    sleeptime NUMBER := 0;
BEGIN
    IF (max_sleep = min_sleep) THEN
        sleeptime := from_mills_to_secs(max_sleep);
        DBMS_LOCK.SLEEP(sleeptime);
    ELSIF (((max_sleep - min_sleep) > 0) AND (min_sleep < max_sleep)) THEN
        sleeptime := DBMS_RANDOM.VALUE(from_mills_to_secs(min_sleep), from_mills_to_secs(max_sleep));
        DBMS_LOCK.SLEEP(sleeptime);
    END IF;
-- info_array(SLEEP_TIME) := (sleeptime * 1000) + info_array(SLEEP_TIME);
END sleep;

/*
|| Transaction Workload Generation Procedures and Functions
*/

PROCEDURE InitializeAttributeArrays
IS
BEGIN

    SELECT
        MIN(ca_address_sk)
       ,MAX(ca_address_sk)
      INTO
        MIN_ADDR_SK
       ,MAX_ADDR_SK
      FROM customer_address;

    SELECT
        MIN(cd_demo_sk)
       ,MAX(cd_demo_sk)
      INTO
        MIN_CDEMO_SK
       ,MAX_CDEMO_SK
      FROM customer_demographics;

    SELECT
        MIN(cc_call_center_sk)
       ,MAX(cc_call_center_sk)
      INTO
        MIN_CCTR_SK
       ,MAX_CCTR_SK
      FROM call_center;

    SELECT
        MIN(cp_catalog_page_sk)
       ,MAX(cp_catalog_page_sk)
```

```
   INTO
     MIN_CPGE_SK
    ,MAX_CPGE_SK
   FROM catalog_page;

SELECT
     MIN(d_date_sk)
    ,MAX(d_date_sk)
   INTO
     MIN_DATE_SK
    ,MAX_DATE_SK
   FROM date_dim
 WHERE d_date BETWEEN TO_DATE('2004-01-01','yyyy-mm-dd')
                  AND TO_DATE('2004-12-31','yyyy-mm-dd');

SELECT
     MIN(hd_demo_sk)
    ,MAX(hd_demo_sk)
   INTO
     MIN_HDEMO_SK
    ,MAX_HDEMO_SK
   FROM household_demographics;

SELECT
     MIN(sm_ship_mode_sk)
    ,MAX(sm_ship_mode_sk)
   INTO
     MIN_MODE_SK
    ,MAX_MODE_SK
   FROM ship_mode;

SELECT
     MIN(p_promo_sk)
    ,MAX(p_promo_sk)
   INTO
     MIN_PROMO_SK
    ,MAX_PROMO_SK
   FROM promotion;

SELECT
     MIN(s_store_sk)
    ,MAX(s_store_sk)
   INTO
     MIN_STORE_SK
    ,MAX_STORE_SK
   FROM store;

SELECT
     MIN(t_time_sk)
    ,MAX(t_time_sk)
   INTO
     MIN_TIME_SK
    ,MAX_TIME_SK
   FROM time_dim;

SELECT
     MIN(w_warehouse_sk)
    ,MAX(w_warehouse_sk)
   INTO
     MIN_WHSE_SK
    ,MAX_WHSE_SK
   FROM warehouse;
```

```
    SELECT
        MIN(wp_web_page_sk)
        ,MAX(wp_web_page_sk)
    INTO
        MIN_WPGE_SK
        ,MAX_WPGE_SK
    FROM web_page;

    SELECT
        MIN(web_site_sk)
        ,MAX(web_site_sk)
    INTO
        MIN_WSIT_SK
        ,MAX_WSIT_SK
    FROM web_site;

EXCEPTION
    WHEN OTHERS THEN
        SQLERRNUM := SQLCODE;
        SQLERRMSG := SQLERRM;

END InitializeAttributeArrays;

-----
-- Function:    NewCatalogSale
-- Purpose:     Inserts new CATALOG_SALES rows individually
-----
FUNCTION NewCatalogSale(
    nCustID     INTEGER
    ,min_sleep  INTEGER
    ,max_sleep  INTEGER
)
    RETURN INTEGER
IS
    nOrderNbr   NUMBER  := 0;

BEGIN

    sleep(min_sleep, max_sleep);

    nOrderNbr := seq_catalog_sales.NEXTVAL;

    INSERT INTO catalog_sales(
        cs_sold_date_sk
        ,cs_sold_time_sk
        ,cs_ship_date_sk
        ,cs_bill_customer_sk
        ,cs_bill_cdemo_sk
        ,cs_bill_hdemo_sk
        ,cs_bill_addr_sk
        ,cs_ship_customer_sk
        ,cs_ship_cdemo_sk
        ,cs_ship_hdemo_sk
        ,cs_ship_addr_sk
        ,cs_call_center_sk
        ,cs_catalog_page_sk
        ,cs_ship_mode_sk
        ,cs_warehouse_sk
        ,cs_item_sk
        ,cs_promo_sk
        ,cs_order_number
        ,cs_quantity
        ,cs_wholesale_cost
```

```
        ,cs_list_price
        ,cs_sales_price
        ,cs_ext_discount_amt
        ,cs_ext_sales_price
        ,cs_ext_wholesale_cost
        ,cs_ext_list_price
        ,cs_ext_tax
        ,cs_coupon_amt
        ,cs_ext_ship_cost
        ,cs_net_paid
        ,cs_net_paid_inc_tax
        ,cs_net_paid_inc_ship
        ,cs_net_paid_inc_ship_tax
        ,cs_net_profit
    )
    VALUES (
         ROUND(DBMS_RANDOM.VALUE(MIN_DATE_SK, MAX_DATE_SK))
        ,ROUND(DBMS_RANDOM.VALUE(MIN_TIME_SK, MAX_TIME_SK))
        ,ROUND(DBMS_RANDOM.VALUE(MIN_DATE_SK, MAX_DATE_SK))
        ,nCustID
        ,ROUND(DBMS_RANDOM.VALUE(MIN_CDEMO_SK, MAX_CDEMO_SK))
        ,ROUND(DBMS_RANDOM.VALUE(MIN_HDEMO_SK, MAX_HDEMO_SK))
        ,ROUND(DBMS_RANDOM.VALUE(MIN_ADDR_SK, MAX_ADDR_SK))
        ,nCustID
        ,ROUND(DBMS_RANDOM.VALUE(MIN_CDEMO_SK, MAX_CDEMO_SK))
        ,ROUND(DBMS_RANDOM.VALUE(MIN_HDEMO_SK, MAX_HDEMO_SK))
        ,ROUND(DBMS_RANDOM.VALUE(MIN_ADDR_SK, MAX_ADDR_SK))
        ,ROUND(DBMS_RANDOM.VALUE(MIN_CCTR_SK, MAX_CCTR_SK))
        ,ROUND(DBMS_RANDOM.VALUE(MIN_CPGE_SK, MAX_CPGE_SK))
        ,ROUND(DBMS_RANDOM.VALUE(MIN_MODE_SK, MAX_MODE_SK))
        ,ROUND(DBMS_RANDOM.VALUE(MIN_WHSE_SK, MAX_WHSE_SK))
        ,ROUND(DBMS_RANDOM.VALUE(1650,16400))
        ,ROUND(DBMS_RANDOM.VALUE(MIN_PROMO_SK ,MAX_PROMO_SK))
        ,nOrderNbr
        ,ROUND(DBMS_RANDOM.VALUE(1,100))
        ,ROUND(DBMS_RANDOM.VALUE(1,100))
        ,ROUND(DBMS_RANDOM.VALUE(1,100))
        ,ROUND(DBMS_RANDOM.VALUE(1,100))
        ,ROUND(DBMS_RANDOM.VALUE(1,100))
        ,ROUND(DBMS_RANDOM.VALUE(1,100))
        ,ROUND(DBMS_RANDOM.VALUE(1,100))
        ,ROUND(DBMS_RANDOM.VALUE(1,100))
        ,ROUND(DBMS_RANDOM.VALUE(1,100))
        ,ROUND(DBMS_RANDOM.VALUE(1,100))
        ,ROUND(DBMS_RANDOM.VALUE(1,100))
        ,ROUND(DBMS_RANDOM.VALUE(1,100))
        ,ROUND(DBMS_RANDOM.VALUE(1,100))
        ,ROUND(DBMS_RANDOM.VALUE(1,100))
        ,ROUND(DBMS_RANDOM.VALUE(1,100))
    );

    sleep(min_sleep, max_sleep);

    RETURN 0;

EXCEPTION
    WHEN OTHERS THEN
        SQLERRNUM := SQLCODE;
        SQLERRMSG := SQLERRM;
        ROLLBACK;
        RETURN SQLERRNUM;

END NewCatalogSale;
```

```
-----
-- Function:    NewStoreSale
-- Purpose:     Inserts new STORE_SALES rows individually
-----
FUNCTION NewStoreSale(
     nCustID    INTEGER
    ,min_sleep  INTEGER
    ,max_sleep  INTEGER
)
  RETURN INTEGER
IS
    nTicketNbr      NUMBER   := 0;


BEGIN
    sleep(min_sleep, max_sleep);

    nTicketNbr := seq_store_sales.NEXTVAL;

    INSERT INTO store_sales(
        ss_sold_date_sk
       ,ss_sold_time_sk
       ,ss_item_sk
       ,ss_customer_sk
       ,ss_cdemo_sk
       ,ss_hdemo_sk
       ,ss_addr_sk
       ,ss_store_sk
       ,ss_promo_sk
       ,ss_ticket_number
       ,ss_quantity
       ,ss_wholesale_cost
       ,ss_list_price
       ,ss_sales_price
       ,ss_ext_discount_amt
       ,ss_ext_sales_price
       ,ss_ext_wholesale_cost
       ,ss_ext_list_price
       ,ss_ext_tax
       ,ss_coupon_amt
       ,ss_net_paid
       ,ss_net_paid_inc_tax
       ,ss_net_profit
    )
    VALUES (
        ROUND(DBMS_RANDOM.VALUE(MIN_DATE_SK, MAX_DATE_SK))
       ,ROUND(DBMS_RANDOM.VALUE(MIN_TIME_SK, MAX_TIME_SK))
       ,ROUND(DBMS_RANDOM.VALUE(1650,16400))
       ,nCustID
       ,ROUND(DBMS_RANDOM.VALUE(MIN_CDEMO_SK, MAX_CDEMO_SK))
       ,ROUND(DBMS_RANDOM.VALUE(MIN_HDEMO_SK, MAX_HDEMO_SK))
       ,ROUND(DBMS_RANDOM.VALUE(MIN_ADDR_SK, MAX_ADDR_SK))
       ,ROUND(DBMS_RANDOM.VALUE(MIN_STORE_SK ,MAX_STORE_SK))
       ,ROUND(DBMS_RANDOM.VALUE(MIN_PROMO_SK ,MAX_PROMO_SK))
       ,nTicketNbr
       ,ROUND(DBMS_RANDOM.VALUE(1,100))
       ,ROUND(DBMS_RANDOM.VALUE(1,100))
       ,ROUND(DBMS_RANDOM.VALUE(1,100))
       ,ROUND(DBMS_RANDOM.VALUE(1,100))
       ,ROUND(DBMS_RANDOM.VALUE(1,100))
       ,ROUND(DBMS_RANDOM.VALUE(1,100))
       ,ROUND(DBMS_RANDOM.VALUE(1,100))
       ,ROUND(DBMS_RANDOM.VALUE(1,100))
       ,ROUND(DBMS_RANDOM.VALUE(1,100))
       ,ROUND(DBMS_RANDOM.VALUE(1,100))
       ,ROUND(DBMS_RANDOM.VALUE(1,100))
```

```
            ,ROUND(DBMS_RANDOM.VALUE(1,100))
            ,ROUND(DBMS_RANDOM.VALUE(1,100))
    );

    sleep(min_sleep, max_sleep);

    RETURN 0;

EXCEPTION
    WHEN OTHERS THEN
        SQLERRNUM := SQLCODE;
        SQLERRMSG := SQLERRM;
        ROLLBACK;
        RETURN SQLERRNUM;

END NewStoreSale;


-----
-- Function:    NewWebSale
-- Purpose:     Inserts new WEB_SALES rows individually
-----
FUNCTION NewWebSale(
     nCustID    INTEGER
    ,min_sleep  INTEGER
    ,max_sleep  INTEGER
)
  RETURN INTEGER
IS

BEGIN
    sleep(min_sleep, max_sleep);

    INSERT INTO web_sales(
        ws_sold_date_sk
        ,ws_sold_time_sk
        ,ws_ship_date_sk
        ,ws_item_sk
        ,ws_bill_customer_sk
        ,ws_bill_cdemo_sk
        ,ws_bill_hdemo_sk
        ,ws_bill_addr_sk
        ,ws_ship_customer_sk
        ,ws_ship_cdemo_sk
        ,ws_ship_hdemo_sk
        ,ws_ship_addr_sk
        ,ws_web_page_sk
        ,ws_web_site_sk
        ,ws_ship_mode_sk
        ,ws_warehouse_sk
        ,ws_promo_sk
        ,ws_order_number
        ,ws_quantity
        ,ws_wholesale_cost
        ,ws_list_price
        ,ws_sales_price
        ,ws_ext_discount_amt
        ,ws_ext_sales_price
        ,ws_ext_wholesale_cost
        ,ws_ext_list_price
        ,ws_ext_tax
        ,ws_coupon_amt
        ,ws_ext_ship_cost
        ,ws_net_paid
        ,ws_net_paid_inc_tax
        ,ws_net_paid_inc_ship
        ,ws_net_paid_inc_ship_tax
```

```
        ,ws_net_profit
    )
    VALUES (
        ROUND(DBMS_RANDOM.VALUE(MIN_DATE_SK, MAX_DATE_SK))
        ,ROUND(DBMS_RANDOM.VALUE(MIN_TIME_SK, MAX_TIME_SK))
        ,ROUND(DBMS_RANDOM.VALUE(MIN_DATE_SK, MAX_DATE_SK))
        ,ROUND(DBMS_RANDOM.VALUE(1650,16400))
        ,nCustID
        ,ROUND(DBMS_RANDOM.VALUE(MIN_CDEMO_SK, MAX_CDEMO_SK))
        ,ROUND(DBMS_RANDOM.VALUE(MIN_HDEMO_SK, MAX_HDEMO_SK))
        ,ROUND(DBMS_RANDOM.VALUE(MIN_ADDR_SK, MAX_ADDR_SK))
        ,nCustID
        ,ROUND(DBMS_RANDOM.VALUE(MIN_CDEMO_SK, MAX_CDEMO_SK))
        ,ROUND(DBMS_RANDOM.VALUE(MIN_HDEMO_SK, MAX_HDEMO_SK))
        ,ROUND(DBMS_RANDOM.VALUE(MIN_ADDR_SK, MAX_ADDR_SK))
        ,ROUND(DBMS_RANDOM.VALUE(MIN_WPGE_SK, MAX_WPGE_SK))
        ,ROUND(DBMS_RANDOM.VALUE(MIN_WSIT_SK, MAX_WSIT_SK))
        ,ROUND(DBMS_RANDOM.VALUE(MIN_MODE_SK, MAX_MODE_SK))
        ,ROUND(DBMS_RANDOM.VALUE(MIN_WHSE_SK, MAX_WHSE_SK))
        ,ROUND(DBMS_RANDOM.VALUE(MIN_PROMO_SK ,MAX_PROMO_SK))
        ,seq_web_sales.NEXTVAL
        ,ROUND(DBMS_RANDOM.VALUE(1,100))
        ,ROUND(DBMS_RANDOM.VALUE(1,100))
        ,ROUND(DBMS_RANDOM.VALUE(1,100))
        ,ROUND(DBMS_RANDOM.VALUE(1,100))
        ,ROUND(DBMS_RANDOM.VALUE(1,100))
        ,ROUND(DBMS_RANDOM.VALUE(1,100))
        ,ROUND(DBMS_RANDOM.VALUE(1,100))
        ,ROUND(DBMS_RANDOM.VALUE(1,100))
        ,ROUND(DBMS_RANDOM.VALUE(1,100))
        ,ROUND(DBMS_RANDOM.VALUE(1,100))
        ,ROUND(DBMS_RANDOM.VALUE(1,100))
        ,ROUND(DBMS_RANDOM.VALUE(1,100))
        ,ROUND(DBMS_RANDOM.VALUE(1,100))
        ,ROUND(DBMS_RANDOM.VALUE(1,100))
    );

    sleep(min_sleep, max_sleep);

    RETURN 0;

EXCEPTION
    WHEN OTHERS THEN
        SQLERRNUM := SQLCODE;
        SQLERRMSG := SQLERRM;
        ROLLBACK;
        RETURN SQLERRNUM;

END NewWebSale;

FUNCTION nwsBulkinsert(
    nCustID    INTEGER
    ,Iteration NUMBER
)
  RETURN INTEGER
/*
|| Function:    nwsBulkInsert
|| Purpose:     Loads a random number of WEB_SALES items using BULK INSERT
||              to simulate batch processing
|| Scope:       Private
|| Arguments:   Iteration - Maximum number of Invoices to create
```

```
*/
IS
    nws       web_sales_tab;
BEGIN
    -- Next, populate associative array ...
    FOR n IN 1..Iteration
        LOOP
            nws(n).ws_sold_date_sk              := ROUND(DBMS_RANDOM.VALUE(MIN_DATE_SK, MAX_DATE_SK));
            nws(n).ws_sold_time_sk              := ROUND(DBMS_RANDOM.VALUE(MIN_TIME_SK, MAX_TIME_SK));
            nws(n).ws_ship_date_sk              := ROUND(DBMS_RANDOM.VALUE(MIN_DATE_SK, MAX_DATE_SK));
            nws(n).ws_item_sk                   := ROUND(DBMS_RANDOM.VALUE(1650,16400));
            nws(n).ws_bill_customer_sk          := nCustID;
            nws(n).ws_bill_cdemo_sk             := ROUND(DBMS_RANDOM.VALUE(MIN_CDEMO_SK, MAX_CDEMO_SK));
            nws(n).ws_bill_hdemo_sk             := ROUND(DBMS_RANDOM.VALUE(MIN_HDEMO_SK, MAX_HDEMO_SK));
            nws(n).ws_bill_addr_sk              := ROUND(DBMS_RANDOM.VALUE(MIN_ADDR_SK, MAX_ADDR_SK));
            nws(n).ws_ship_customer_sk          := nCustID;
            nws(n).ws_ship_cdemo_sk             := ROUND(DBMS_RANDOM.VALUE(MIN_CDEMO_SK, MAX_CDEMO_SK));
            nws(n).ws_ship_hdemo_sk             := ROUND(DBMS_RANDOM.VALUE(MIN_HDEMO_SK, MAX_HDEMO_SK));
            nws(n).ws_ship_addr_sk              := ROUND(DBMS_RANDOM.VALUE(MIN_ADDR_SK, MAX_ADDR_SK));
            nws(n).ws_web_page_sk               := ROUND(DBMS_RANDOM.VALUE(MIN_WPGE_SK, MAX_WPGE_SK));
            nws(n).ws_web_site_sk               := ROUND(DBMS_RANDOM.VALUE(MIN_WSIT_SK, MAX_WSIT_SK));
            nws(n).ws_ship_mode_sk              := ROUND(DBMS_RANDOM.VALUE(MIN_MODE_SK, MAX_MODE_SK));
            nws(n).ws_warehouse_sk              := ROUND(DBMS_RANDOM.VALUE(MIN_WHSE_SK, MAX_WHSE_SK));
            nws(n).ws_promo_sk                  := ROUND(DBMS_RANDOM.VALUE(MIN_PROMO_SK ,MAX_PROMO_SK));
            nws(n).ws_order_number              := seq_web_sales.NEXTVAL;
            nws(n).ws_quantity                  := ROUND(DBMS_RANDOM.VALUE(1,100));
            nws(n).ws_wholesale_cost            := ROUND(DBMS_RANDOM.VALUE(1,100));
            nws(n).ws_list_price                := ROUND(DBMS_RANDOM.VALUE(1,100));
            nws(n).ws_sales_price               := ROUND(DBMS_RANDOM.VALUE(1,100));
            nws(n).ws_ext_discount_amt          := ROUND(DBMS_RANDOM.VALUE(1,100));
            nws(n).ws_ext_sales_price           := ROUND(DBMS_RANDOM.VALUE(1,100));
            nws(n).ws_ext_wholesale_cost        := ROUND(DBMS_RANDOM.VALUE(1,100));
            nws(n).ws_ext_list_price            := ROUND(DBMS_RANDOM.VALUE(1,100));
            nws(n).ws_ext_tax                   := ROUND(DBMS_RANDOM.VALUE(1,100));
            nws(n).ws_coupon_amt                := ROUND(DBMS_RANDOM.VALUE(1,100));
            nws(n).ws_ext_ship_cost             := ROUND(DBMS_RANDOM.VALUE(1,100));
            nws(n).ws_net_paid                  := ROUND(DBMS_RANDOM.VALUE(1,100));
            nws(n).ws_net_paid_inc_tax          := ROUND(DBMS_RANDOM.VALUE(1,100));
            nws(n).ws_net_paid_inc_ship         := ROUND(DBMS_RANDOM.VALUE(1,100));
            nws(n).ws_net_paid_inc_ship_tax     := ROUND(DBMS_RANDOM.VALUE(1,100));
            nws(n).ws_net_profit                := ROUND(DBMS_RANDOM.VALUE(1,100));
        END LOOP;

    FORALL n IN INDICES OF nws
        INSERT INTO web_sales(
             ws_sold_date_sk
            ,ws_sold_time_sk
            ,ws_ship_date_sk
            ,ws_item_sk
            ,ws_bill_customer_sk
            ,ws_bill_cdemo_sk
            ,ws_bill_hdemo_sk
            ,ws_bill_addr_sk
            ,ws_ship_customer_sk
            ,ws_ship_cdemo_sk
            ,ws_ship_hdemo_sk
            ,ws_ship_addr_sk
            ,ws_web_page_sk
            ,ws_web_site_sk
            ,ws_ship_mode_sk
            ,ws_warehouse_sk
            ,ws_promo_sk
            ,ws_order_number
            ,ws_quantity
            ,ws_wholesale_cost
            ,ws_list_price
            ,ws_sales_price
```

```
                ,ws_ext_discount_amt
                ,ws_ext_sales_price
                ,ws_ext_wholesale_cost
                ,ws_ext_list_price
                ,ws_ext_tax
                ,ws_coupon_amt
                ,ws_ext_ship_cost
                ,ws_net_paid
                ,ws_net_paid_inc_tax
                ,ws_net_paid_inc_ship
                ,ws_net_paid_inc_ship_tax
                ,ws_net_profit
            )
        VALUES(
            nws(n).ws_sold_date_sk
            ,nws(n).ws_sold_time_sk
            ,nws(n).ws_ship_date_sk
            ,nws(n).ws_item_sk
            ,nws(n).ws_bill_customer_sk
            ,nws(n).ws_bill_cdemo_sk
            ,nws(n).ws_bill_hdemo_sk
            ,nws(n).ws_bill_addr_sk
            ,nws(n).ws_ship_customer_sk
            ,nws(n).ws_ship_cdemo_sk
            ,nws(n).ws_ship_hdemo_sk
            ,nws(n).ws_ship_addr_sk
            ,nws(n).ws_web_page_sk
            ,nws(n).ws_web_site_sk
            ,nws(n).ws_ship_mode_sk
            ,nws(n).ws_warehouse_sk
            ,nws(n).ws_promo_sk
            ,nws(n).ws_order_number
            ,nws(n).ws_quantity
            ,nws(n).ws_wholesale_cost
            ,nws(n).ws_list_price
            ,nws(n).ws_sales_price
            ,nws(n).ws_ext_discount_amt
            ,nws(n).ws_ext_sales_price
            ,nws(n).ws_ext_wholesale_cost
            ,nws(n).ws_ext_list_price
            ,nws(n).ws_ext_tax
            ,nws(n).ws_coupon_amt
            ,nws(n).ws_ext_ship_cost
            ,nws(n).ws_net_paid
            ,nws(n).ws_net_paid_inc_tax
            ,nws(n).ws_net_paid_inc_ship
            ,nws(n).ws_net_paid_inc_ship_tax
            ,nws(n).ws_net_profit
        );

    COMMIT;
    RETURN 0;

EXCEPTION
    WHEN OTHERS THEN
        SQLERRNUM := SQLCODE;
        SQLERRMSG := SQLERRM;
        ROLLBACK;
        RETURN SQLERRNUM;

END nwsBulkinsert;
```

```
/*
|| Public Functions and Procedures
*/

PROCEDURE RandomDML (Iteration NUMBER)
/*
|| Procedure:   RandomDML
|| Purpose:     Loads a random number of ...
||
||              into tables TPCDS.INVOICES and TPCDS.INVOICE_ITEMS.
|| Scope:       Public
|| Arguments:   Iteration - Maximum number of Invoices to create
*/
IS
    CstLoopEnd    NUMBER(9) := 0;
    SalesLoopEnd NUMBER(9) := 0;
    SalesPath     NUMBER(1) := 0;
    nCustID       NUMBER(9);

BEGIN
    -----
    -- 1.) Calculate randomized value for Customer ID
    -- 2.) Calculate number of Sales Transactions to create
    -- 3.) COMMIT changes
    -----
    CstLoopEnd := Iteration;

    /*
    || CUSTOMER generation
    */
    FOR idx1 IN 1..CstLoopEnd
        LOOP
            DBMS_APPLICATION_INFO.SET_MODULE(
                 module_name => 'DMLGenerator'
                ,action_name => 'NewCustomer'
            );

        nCustID := seq_customers.NEXTVAL;
            INSERT INTO customer (
                 c_customer_sk
                ,c_customer_id
                ,c_current_cdemo_sk
                ,c_current_hdemo_sk
                ,c_current_addr_sk
                ,c_first_shipto_date_sk
                ,c_first_sales_date_sk
                ,c_salutation
                ,c_first_name
                ,c_last_name
                ,c_preferred_cust_flag
                ,c_birth_day
                ,c_birth_month
                ,c_birth_year
                ,c_birth_country
                ,c_login
                ,c_email_address
                ,c_last_review_date
                )
            VALUES (
                 nCustID
                ,TO_CHAR(nCustID)
                ,ROUND(DBMS_RANDOM.VALUE(MIN_CDEMO_SK, MAX_CDEMO_SK))
                ,ROUND(DBMS_RANDOM.VALUE(MIN_HDEMO_SK, MAX_HDEMO_SK))
                ,ROUND(DBMS_RANDOM.VALUE(MIN_ADDR_SK, MAX_ADDR_SK))
                ,ROUND(DBMS_RANDOM.VALUE(2457755,2459580))
                ,ROUND(DBMS_RANDOM.VALUE(2457755,2459580))
```

```
                    ,DECODE(MOD(nCustID,3), 0, 'Mr.', 1, 'Ms.', '')
                    ,LPAD(' ',DBMS_RANDOM.VALUE(1,20), SUBSTR('abcdefghijklmnopqrstuvwxyz',DBMS_RANDOM
.VALUE(1,26), 1))
                    ,LPAD(' ',DBMS_RANDOM.VALUE(1,30), SUBSTR('abcdefghijklmnopqrstuvwxyz',DBMS_RANDOM
.VALUE(1,26), 1))
                    ,DECODE(MOD(nCustID,25), 0, 'Y', 1, 'P', 'N')
                    ,(1 + MOD(nCustID,27))
                    ,(1 + MOD(nCustID,11))
                    ,(1962 + MOD(nCustID,25))
                    ,'United States'
                    ,'Unassigned'
                    ,'Unassigned'
                    ,TO_CHAR(SYSDATE-30,'yyyy-mm-dd')
                    );

            COMMIT;

        /*
        || Additional Sales Detail Generation
        */

        SalesLoopEnd := Randomizer(nCustID);

        FOR idx2 IN 1..SalesLoopEnd
            LOOP
                SalesPath := MOD(SalesLoopEnd,10);
                IF SalesPath IN (0,1,2,3,7,8) THEN
                        rtnValue := NewWebSale(nCustID, 1, 5);
                END IF;
                IF SalesPath IN (1,4,5,6,7) THEN
                    rtnValue := NewCatalogSale(nCustID, 1, 5);
                END IF;
                IF SalesPath IN (2,3) THEN
                    rtnValue := NewStoreSale(nCustID, 1, 30);
                END IF;
                IF SalesPath = 9 THEN
                    rtnValue := nwsBulkInsert(nCustID, DBMS_RANDOM.VALUE(1,5));
                END IF;
            END LOOP;

        END LOOP;

        COMMIT;

EXCEPTION
    WHEN OTHERS THEN
        SQLERRNUM := SQLCODE;
        SQLERRMSG := SQLERRM;
        ROLLBACK;

END RandomDML;

BEGIN
    -----
    -- Initialization processing:
    -- 1.) Gather minimum and maximum values for dimensions to control
    --        generation of randomized values
    -----
    InitializeAttributeArrays();

END pkg_dml_generator;
```

APPENDIX
C

References

Hopefully it's obvious to even a casual reader of our book that we did our fair share of experimentation to prove out the performance tuning and testing tools we've described. But it also required us to do quite a bit of careful research and peruse reams of documentation as well. We've provided some of the more valuable documentation—including My Oracle Support (MOS) notes, white papers, and other useful reference guides—for your consideration.

Chapter 3: SQL Tuning Sets and Tuning Advisor

MOS Note #	Title
262687.1	Using the DBMS_SQLTUNE Package to Run the SQL Tuning Advisor
276103.1	Performance Tuning Using Advisors and Manageability Features: AWR, ASH, ADDM, and SQL Tuning Advisor
751068.1	How to Move a SQL Tuning Set from One Database to Another
1271343.1	How to Load Queries into a SQL Tuning Set (STS)
1275248.1	Troubleshooting: ORA-16957: "SQL Analyze time limit interrupt" Errors

Chapter 4: SQL Access Advisor

MOS Note #	Title
1567962.1	Oracle12*c*: Using SQL Access Advisor (DBMS_ADVISOR) – Partition Advisor

Chapter 5: SQL Plan Management

MOS Note #	Title
1359841.1	Master Note: Plan Stability Features (Including SQL Plan Management (SPM))
1524658.1	FAQ: SQL Plan Management (SPM) Frequently Asked Questions
1904820.1	Things to Consider Before Upgrading to Avoid Poor Performance, Wrong Results, or SQL Plan Management (SPM) Issues (11.2.0.X and above)
2035897.1	Things to Consider When Upgrading from 12.1.0.1 to Avoid Problems with SQL Plan Management (SPM)

Chapter 6: SQL Monitor

MOS Note #	Title
1380492.1	Monitoring SQL Statements with Real-Time SQL Monitoring
1604469.1	How to Collect SQL Monitor Output for Parallel Query
1613163.1	How to Monitor SQL Statements with Large Plans Using Real-Time SQL Monitoring

Chapter 7: Real-Time Operations Monitoring

MOS Note #	Title
1482811.1	Best Practices: Proactively Avoiding Database and Query Performance Issues

Chapter 8: Real-Time ADDM and Emergency Monitoring

MOS Note #	Title
452358.1	How to Collect Diagnostics for Database Hanging Issues

Chapter 9: ASH Analytics

MOS Note #	Title
1380043.1	Tuning with AWR/ASH
1674086.1	Performance Diagnosis with Automatic Workload Repository (AWR)

Chapter 10: SQL Performance Analyzer

MOS Note #	Title
455889.1	SQL Performance Analyzer Example
562899.1	Using SQL Performance Analyzer to Test SQL Performance Impact of an Upgrade

MOS Note #	Title
1363104.1	Testing Performance Impact of Upgrade from 10g to 11g Using SQL Performance Analyzer
1464274.1	Master Note for Real Application Testing Option
1577290.1	SQL Performance Analyzer Summary
2025019.1	How to Use the DBMS_SQLPA (SQL Performance Analyzer) API to Test Database Upgrades Using CONVERT SQLSET
2082289.1	How Does SQL Performance Analyzer (SPA) Use Binds Sets Stored Within the SQL Tuning Set (STS) During a SPA Trial

Chapter 11: Database Workload Capture and Workload Intelligence

MOS Note #	Title
445116.1	Using Workload Capture and Replay
748895.1	How to Use Database Replay Feature to Help with the Upgrade from 10.2.0.4 to 11g
1083063.1	Real Application Testing (RAT) PL/SQL API Setup and Verification
1287620.1	Comprehensive Database Real Application Testing Diagnostic Information
1600574.1	FAQ: Database Upgrade Using Real Application Testing
1901276.1	Workload Profile Sections of Capture or Replay Report Displays "No data exists for this section of the report"
1920275.1	Real Application Testing: Database Capture FAQ

Chapter 12: Database Workload Replay

MOS Note #	Title
2204090.1	Real Application Testing: Database Replay FAQ

Chapter 13: Database In-Memory Advisor

For the most up-to-date information about all things Database In-Memory, be sure to consult the Oracle Database In-Memory Home Page at www.oracle.com/technetwork/database/in-memory/overview/index.html.

MOS Note #	Title
1987462.1	Using In-Memory Advisor Errors when Running IMADVISOR_ANALYZE_AND_REPORT
2031991.1	Receive "ORA-20001: Statistics capture failed: all candidates with detected activity were too small for In-Memory placement (minimum size=64KB)" when Executing In-Memory Advisor
2121740.1	EM 13c: In-Memory Advisor Not Installed

White Papers

- **Oracle Database Concepts, Memory Architecture (November 2015):**
  http://docs.oracle.com/database/121/CNCPT/memory.htm#CNCPT89659

- **Oracle Database In-Memory White Paper (July 2015):**
  www.oracle.com/technetwork/database/in-memory/overview/twp-oracle-database-in-memory-2245633.html

- **Oracle Database In-Memory Advisor Best Practices White Paper (February 2015):**
  www.oracle.com/technetwork/database/manageability/info/twp-in-memory-advisor-bp-2430474.pdf

Chapter 14: In-Memory Central

MOS Note #	Title
1903683.1	Oracle Database In-Memory Option (DBIM) Basics and Interaction with Data Warehousing Features
1329441.1	Oracle Database In-Memory: In-Memory Aggregation (White Paper)

Index

References to figures are in italics.

A

Active Data Guard, 335
Active Session History Analytics. *See* ASH
    Analytics
ADDM, 141–142
    See also Real-Time ADDM
advisors. *See* In-Memory Advisor (IMADV);
    Optimizer Statistics Advisor (OSA);
    Segment Advisor; SQL Access Advisor;
    SQL Tuning Advisor
ASH Analytics
    in action, 159–163
    configuration parameters, 156
    data collection scheme, *158*
    data cube analytic operations, *160*
    data warehouse design, 157–158
    dimensions, *159*
    direct path reads, 160
    home screen, 159, *161*
    load map, 160, *162*
    in OEM Express, 163
    overview, 156

    time metrics, 156–157
    wait classes, 159, *161*
    wait events, 159–160, *162*
Automated Maintenance Tasks.
    See AUTOTASK maintenance tasks
Automatic Data Optimization (ADO)
    policies, 333–334
Automatic Database Diagnostic
    Monitoring. *See* ADDM
Automatic Tuning Optimizer, 39–42, 169
    evaluation mode, 61
Automatic Workload Repository (AWR),
    40, 356
    capturing SQL statements from AWR
        baselines, 33–34
    capturing SQL statements from AWR
        snapshots, 33
    exporting DWC AWR data, 229–230
    and SPA, 172
AUTOTASK maintenance tasks, 42
    Optimizer Statistics Advisor (OSA),
        356–357
    Segment Advisor, 357
AWR. *See* Automatic Workload
    Repository (AWR)

397

I

idle wait time, 157
IMCO. *See* In-Memory Coordinator
   (IMCO)
IMCS. *See* In-Memory Column
   Store (IMCS)
IMCUs. *See* In-Memory Column Units
   (IMCUs); In-Memory Compression
   Units (IMCUs)
IMEs. *See* In-Memory Expressions (IMEs)
IMEUs. *See* In-Memory Expression
   Units (IMEUs)
indexes, 60
   redundant indexes, 61
Information Lifecycle Management
   (ILM), Automatic Data Optimization
   (ADO) policies, 333–334
In-Memory Advisor (IMADV), 302
   all recommended objects,
     324–325
   all SQL statements, 324
   capturing an application
     workload for analysis,
     313–315
   database details, 323
   deinstallation, 312–313
   generating IMADV advice,
     315–316
   history of, 308–310
   implementation of
     recommendations, 327
   in-memory sizes, 319–321
   installation, 311–312
   interpreting the IMADV HTML
     report, 319–327
   licensing, 308
   metadata views, 310
   overview, 307–308
   performance factors, 317–318

   recommended rationales,
     325–326
   reviewing IMADV
     recommendations, 318
   and security, 313
   top 10 objects, 322–323
   top 10 SQL statements, 321–322
   version 2.0 features, 309–310
   workload database usage, 319
in-memory aggregation, 307
In-Memory Central, 330
   activating Database In-Memory,
     336–338
   adding objects to IMCS, 339–340
   Configuration section, 341–342
   example, 346–351
   heat mapping, 346
   In-Memory Objects Distribution
     Chart, 343
   In-Memory Objects Search
     section, 344–345
   In-Memory Objects Size Map, 346
   Objects Summary section,
     342–343
   overview, 335–336
In-Memory Column Store (IMCS),
   303–306
   adding objects to, 339–340
   architecture enhancements, 330
   FastStart tablespace, 334–335
   resizing dynamically, 334,
     337–338
In-Memory Column Units (IMCUs),
   303, 306
In-Memory Compression Units
   (IMCUs), 330
   join groups, 331–333
In-Memory Coordinator (IMCO), 306
In-Memory Expression Units (IMEUs),
   330–331

Beta Test Oracle Software

Get a first look at our newest products—and help perfect them. You must meet the following criteria:

- ✔ **Licensed Oracle customer or Oracle PartnerNetwork member**

- ✔ **Oracle software expert**

- ✔ **Early adopter of Oracle products**

Please apply at: pdpm.oracle.com/BPO/userprofile

If your interests match upcoming activities, we'll contact you. Profiles are kept on file for 12 months.

Push a Button
Move Your Java Apps to the Oracle Cloud

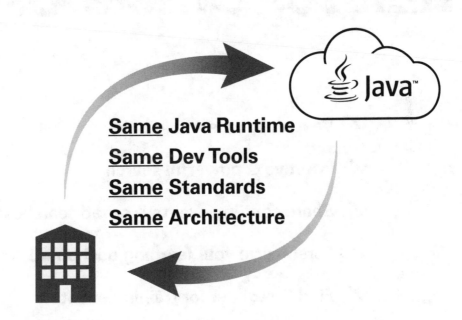

Same Java Runtime
Same Dev Tools
Same Standards
Same Architecture

... or Back to Your Data Center

cloud.oracle.com/java

Oracle Learning Library

Created by Oracle Experts
FREE for Oracle Users

✓ Vast array of learning aids

✓ Intuitive & powerful search

✓ Share content, events & saved searches

✓ Personalize your learning dashboard

✓ Find & register for training events

oracle.com/oll

Reach More than 640,000 Oracle Customers with Oracle Publishing Group

Connect with the Audience that Matters Most to Your Business

Oracle Magazine
The Largest IT Publication in the World
Circulation: 325,000
Audience: IT Managers, DBAs, Programmers, and Developers

Profit
Business Insight for Enterprise-Class Business Leaders to Help Them Build
a Better Business Using Oracle Technology
Circulation: 90,000
Audience: Top Executives and Line of Business Managers

Java Magazine
The Essential Source on Java Technology, the Java Programming Language,
and Java-Based Applications
Circulation: 225,00 and Growing Steady
Audience: Corporate and Independent Java Developers, Programmers,
and Architects

For more information
or to sign up for a FREE
subscription: Scan the
QR code to visit Oracle
Publishing online.